Transforming School Mental Health Services

TRANSFORMING SCHOOL MENTAL HEALTH SERVICES

POPULATION-BASED APPROACHES TO PROMOTING THE COMPETENCY AND WELLNESS OF CHILDREN

BETH DOLL

JACK A. CUMMINGS

A JOINT PUBLICATION

NATIONAL
ASSOCIATION OF
SCHOOL
PSYCHOLOGISTS

CORWIN PRESS
A SAGE Publications Company
Thousand Oaks, CA 91320

For information:

Corwin Press
A Sage Publications Company
2455 Teller Road
Thousand Oaks, California 91320
www.corwinpress.com

Sage Publications India Pvt. Ltd.
B 1/I 1 Mohan Cooperative
  Industrial Area
Mathura Road
New Delhi 110 044
India

Sage Publications Ltd.
1 Oliver's Yard
55 City Road
London EC1Y 1SP
United Kingdom

Sage Publications Asia-Pacific
  Pte. Ltd.
33 Pekin Street #02-01
Far East Square
Singapore 048763

Printed in the United States of America.

Library of Congress Cataloging-in-Publication Data

Transforming school mental health services: population-based approaches to promoting the competency and wellness of children/[edited by] Beth Doll, Jack A. Cummings.
    p. cm.
Includes bibliographical references and index.
ISBN 978-1-4129-5328-3 (cloth: alk. paper)
ISBN 978-1-4129-5329-0 (pbk. : alk. paper)
    1. School children—Mental health services—United States. 2. School health services—United States. 3. Child psychology—United States. I. Doll, Beth, 1952- II. Cummings, Jack A. (Jack Alan), 1953- III. Title.

LB3430.T72 2008
371.7'13—dc22   2007014772

This book is printed on acid-free paper.

07 08 09 10 11 10 9 8 7 6 5 4 3 2 1

Acquisitions Editor:	Jessica Allan
Editorial Assistant:	Joanna Coelho
Production Editor:	Sarah K. Quesenberry
Copy Editor:	Dorothy Hoffman
Typesetter:	C&M Digitals (P) Ltd.
Proofreader:	Carole Quandt
Indexer:	Julie Grayson
Cover Designer:	Michael Dubowe
Graphic Designer:	Karine Hovsepian

Contents

Preface

In November 2002, 740 school psychologists worked together to describe school psychology's hoped-for future, with the ultimate goal of crafting ways to use the profession's limited resources to maximize benefits to children, families, and schools (2002 Multisite Conference on the Future of School Psychology; see Harrison, Cummings, Dawson, Short, Gorin, & Palomares, 2004). This book is a direct outgrowth of the energy generated within the fifth panel of the Future's conference participants. This panel had the particular charge of identifying ways to increase school services that promote the health and mental health of all children and their families. Over the course of a day-and-a-half of deliberation, the fifth panel became convinced that a strikingly different framework for services was needed in order to promote psychological wellness and diminish mental disturbances in the nation's school children. The panel strongly endorsed population-based services as a promising strategy that could extend the scope of psychological services to all enrolled children in a school. It invoked the policies and practices of the nation's public health system as an example of the ways in which school mental health services could be reorganized to enhance all students' mental health and discourage dysfunction. Importantly, the remaining four Futures Conference panels also emphasized serving all students in a school.

The work of the fifth panel has continued in the interim since the Futures Conference adjourned. In the spring of 2004, four major journals in School Psychology coordinated special issues that described the conference, examined its recommendations, and prompted the profession to take actions in response (Cummings, Harrison, Dawson, Short, Gorin, & Palomares, 2004; D'Amato, Sheridan, Phelps, & Lopez, 2004). Task forces have been appointed to follow up with each of the five conference goals. Innumerable journal articles and conference presentations have been provided that address its implementation. This book represents a small part of this continuing effort, describing and refining of the vision of population-based school mental health services that was articulated by the fifth panel.

Within the fifth panel's discussion, key terms were used very thoughtfully so that they accurately represented the inter-relationships underlying schooling and mental health. For example, the term "mental health" referred specifically to psychological wellness and adjustment. This is consistent with psychology's recent attention to positive psychology, which addresses individual characteristics and traits that make it possible for people to flourish (Peterson & Seligman, 2004). The discussion avoided use of the non sequitor, "mental health disorder." Instead, mental health was contrasted with "psychological disturbance" or "psychological disorder"—terms that refer to pathological conditions that threaten the ultimate developmental competence of students. Some, but not all, of these disturbances are recognized within the *Diagnostic and Statistical Manual of Mental Disorders—Fourth Edition* (Text Revision; American Psychiatric Association, 2000). In other cases, developmental research has identified disturbances such as social withdrawal or social victimization that have not been acknowledged as *DSM-IV-TR* diagnoses but are still legitimate objects of attention from school mental health providers. The ultimate goal of school mental health services, and of schools themselves, was recognized to be the promotion of students' competence—their ability to successfully meet the major developmental demands of society. Similarly, the term "interventions" was used broadly to represent traditional therapies as well as effective caretaking practices and institutional policies and practices that promote developmental competence. School mental health providers included a number of distinct professions: school psychologists, school counselors, school social workers, teachers of children with behavior disorders, and in many cases, school nurses. Still, responsibility for supporting the developmental competence of a school's students did not rest solely with school mental health providers, but also engaged the participation of families, community members and the students themselves. Throughout this book, we have worked to respect the work of the fifth panel and its very careful use of terminology.

While work on the book unfolded, our opportunity to read and carefully reflect on the work of our colleagues who are pushing the forefront of population-based services was invigorating. As each chapter arrived, we were excited to learn new insights about mental health services that could be fostered to meet the collective mental health needs of *all* children in a community, not just those children whose problems were obvious to adults or striking enough to warrant referrals. We sent the initial draft of each chapter to two members of our advisory board to solicit their comments. At least one of the reviewers for each chapter was an experienced practitioner with years of experience providing services in the schools, and all of the reviewers were thoughtful and innovative school mental health professionals. Their reviews prompted an engaging dialogue between the chapter authors and their audience and, once again, we learned from the interchange. As our work nears completion, we extend our heartfelt thanks to all of the authors, reviewers, editors and publishers whose contributions strengthened this collective examination of children, their mental health and developmental success, and how school mental health services can maximize their achievements.

Beth Doll
Jack A. Cummings

References

American Psychiatric Association. (2000). *The Diagnostic and Statistical Manual of Mental Disorders—Fourth Edition* (Text Revised). Washington, DC: Author.

Cummings, J. A., Harrison, P. L., Dawson, M., Short, R. J., Gorin, S., & Palomares, R. S. (2004). Follow-up to the 2002 Futures Conference: Collaborating to serve all children, families and schools. *Journal of Educational and Psychological Consultation, 15,* 335–344.

D'Amato, R. C., Sheridan, S. M., Phelps, L., & Lopez, E. (2004). Psychology in the Schools, School Psychology Review, School Psychology Quarterly, and Journal of Education and Psychological Consultation editors collaborate to chart school psychology's past, present, and "futures." *School Psychology Review, 33,* 3–6.

Harrison, P. L., Cummings, J. A., Dawson, M., Short, R. J., Gorin, S., & Palomares, R. (2004). Responding to the Needs of Children, Families, and Schools: The 2002 Multisite Conference on the Future of School Psychology. *School Psychology Review, 33,* 12–33.

Peterson, C., & Seligman, M. E. P. (2004). *Character strengths and virtues: A handbook and classification.* Washington, DC: American Psychological Association.

Acknowledgments

We thank Denise Ferrenz, Kathy Cowan, and Linda Morgan of the National Association of School Psychologists for their assistance, patience, and insight. Their careful attention moved us from an idea to a book.

Finally, we appreciate the detailed and insightful comments of our advisory board. They read drafts of chapters and posed challenging questions, found omissions and made recommendations on how to improve the utility of the chapters. Their input was critical to achieving a balance of science and practice. They kept our feet planted in the realities of contemporary schools.

Dr. Michael W. Bahr, University of Missouri–St. Louis

Dr. John Desrochers, Southport, Connecticut

Dr. David Estell, Indiana University

Dr. Paul Fernandez, Norwalk-La Mirada School District, California; University of California at Los Angeles

Dr. Douglas Fuchs, Peabody College of Vanderbilt University, Tennessee

Dr. Robyn Hess, University of Northern Colorado

Dr. Thomas J. Huberty, Indiana University

Dr. Lisa Kelly-Vance, University of Nebraska–Omaha

Mr. John Lestino, Edgewater Park Schools, New Jersey

Dr. Antoinette Miranda, Ohio State University

Dr. Brett Nelson, California State University–San Bernardino

Dr. Stephen Peverly, Columbia University, New York

Dr. Russ Skiba, Indiana University

Dr. Samuel Song, University of North Carolina

Dr. Barbara Williams, Rowan University, New Jersey

Dr. Chris Willis, Newport County Regional Special Education, Rhode Island

Dr. Georgette Yetter, Oklahoma State University

1

Why Population-Based Services Are Essential for School Mental Health, and How to Make Them Happen in Your School

Beth Doll

Jack A. Cummings

The national discussion of school mental health that emerged during the 2002 Multisite Conference on the Future of School Psychology (Harrison et al., 2004) was both remarkable and exciting, in part because of the very rich conceptual framework that was used to describe mental health and its relevance to schooling. Within this framework, every school is a community, composed of students, their teachers, staff in the building, and the parents who send their children to the school. The principle mission of the school is to provide students with the knowledge and skills necessary to lead productive and successful lives. This mission is not the sole responsibility of schools; it is shared with other important societal entities such as families, churches, the legal system, and social services. Moreover, this mission cannot be narrowly defined as an "instructional" mission. Life success is a product of social and emotional competence and personal ambition as much as academic achievement and literacy. Most important, the attempts of schools to promote instructional success are always constrained by their students' developmental competence. Simply stated, students do not grow into literate adults without also developing social, emotional, and personal competence. Ergo, school mental health goals of promoting psychological wellness are not ancillary to students' academic success, but integral to it.

There was ample evidence prior to the Futures Conference that mental health is critical to academic success (Hoagwood & Johnson, 2003; Meyers, Parsons, & Martin, 1979). In their influential book, Adelman and Taylor (2006) have pointed out that schools cannot provide high-quality instruction without attending to their students' participation in learning. Leading developmental psychologists, including Ann Masten (Masten et al., 2005) and Kathryn Wentzel (Wentzel, 2002; Wentzel & Watkins, 2002), have repeatedly demonstrated that children's school success is integral to and not independent of other facets of developmental competence. The U.S. Department of Education has sponsored a high-powered effort to promote positive behavior supports in schools because these are essential to students' academic achievement (National Technical Assistance Center on Positive Behavioral Interventions and Supports, 2006). More recently, the National Association of School Psychologists' Blueprint III (Ysseldyke et al., 2006) underscores the critical contributions of school psychologists to the mental health of learners, and the central importance of mental health for learners' success.

This book extends the thesis that mental health is essential to schooling by arguing that when school mental health services are framed around population-based strategies, they can be more fully integrated into the core activities of schools. This introductory chapter first describes population-based services and contrasts them with traditional service delivery models. Next, the chapter describes existing knowledge bases that can inform efforts to implement a population-based service model. Finally, it describes the remaining chapters within the framework presented here.

What Are Population-Based School Mental Health Services?

Population-based school mental health services are services that have been carefully designed to meet the mental health needs of all students enrolled in a school. Their premise is that psychological wellness is a precondition for students' success in school and that, as teachers are responsible for teaching all children to read, school mental health providers are responsible for insuring that all students have the psychological competence needed for learning. Within the population-based model, decisions about which mental health interventions to provide and which students will receive interventions are intentional decisions based on carefully collected information about the mental health status of all students in the school. Students can still be referred to the school mental health team within population-based models, but traditional interventions for these individual students are embedded within a larger plan that recognizes and plans for the mental health of referred and nonreferred students alike. Population-based models do not presuppose that all interventions will be delivered school-wide. Instead, the mental health interventions that are implemented may be individual, classwide, school-wide, or district-wide, depending on the needs of the school's students. Similarly, within a population-based model, mental health interventions may be preventive or remedial, depending on evidence of the risk and disorder present within the school's students. Decisions about the kinds of interventions to provide will depend on the urgency of student needs and the importance of anticipated outcomes.

Ideally, population-based mental health services have at least four goals: (a) to promote the psychological well-being of all students so that they can achieve developmental competence; (b) to promote caretaking environments that nurture students and allow them to overcome minor risks and challenges; (c) to provide protective support to students at high risk for developmental failures; and (d) to remediate social, emotional, or behavioral disturbances so that students can develop competence.

The difference between population-based services and traditional referral-based models of school mental health is analogous to the difference between nurturing a single tree showing signs of failing health and maintaining the vitality of a forest. In both cases, the trees require adequate light, space, water, nutrients, and temperature. Either a single tree or a forest can be threatened by disease or maladies, especially if stressed by an absence of necessary nutrients. To care for a single tree, a gifted gardener can inject fertilizer in its roots, soak the surrounding soil with ample water, prune it, and control for any infections that emerge. However, groundskeepers who are caring for a forest must use different and more efficient strategies for assessing the condition of their trees, providing the proper nourishment and conditions for growth, and treating diseases. Of course, the tree analogy falls apart once we consider the value of the individual. While a few trees might be sacrificed for the health of the forest, the same is not true for children. Every student in a school is a valued member of the community, and school mental health interventions must be planned so that no child is sacrificed for the good of the whole. This is the special challenge of population-based services—to balance the needs of individual students with those of the school's community of students.

The intentionality of mental health service planning is central to the provision of population-based services, and so this book uses the following problem-solving cycle to frame their description:

Assess → Identify Resources → Plan → Intervene → Assess

Planning begins with an understanding of the nature of developmental competence and threats to that competence, as derived from the rich developmental research describing children's social, emotional, cognitive, and personal growth. Given what is known about children's developmental competence in general, information is gathered to describe the mental health needs of all students enrolled in a particular school. Based on that data-based portrait, resources with the potential to address these needs are identified within and outside of the school setting. Collaborative partnerships that extend throughout the community and school can create infrastructures that integrate related interventions into comprehensive systems of care and that dismantle programmatic silos—narrowly construed interventions that address a single risk factor or disturbance without regard for students' other risks or needs. Given the identified mental health needs and resources, a plan is constructed that prioritizes the needs of the school's students and allocates mental health resources to interventions that are frequently needed and those that will have high impact on the students' psychological wellness. Periodic reassessment of students' mental health needs allows school mental health providers to evaluate the school's progress and update its mental health plan. Interventions that emerge out of this problem-solving cycle do not need to focus solely on students. They can also focus on the forests, or schools. Indeed, when population-based assessments suggest that large numbers of children are faltering, an immediate possibility is that something is wrong with the school as an environment for learning or development.

Clearly, this cycle will require that school mental health providers have a description of their building's mental health needs that is both accurate and thorough. Consequently, population-based services must be predicated on data-based portraits of the students' mental health needs (Baker, chapter 3; Short & Strein, chapter 2, this volume). Data can include deliberately collected information about students' mental health and psychological disturbance, as might be acquired through a school-wide administration of a risky behavior survey. Alternatively, existing school data might be used to support a plan's development, including data about student attendance, work completion, or behavior problems. Finally, population-based assessment strategies can be used to screen the full student population of a school and identify those children with a demonstrable need for socioemotional support (Doll & Haack, 2005). Data used to support a school's mental health plan might be variously aggregated across all students in a school, aggregated across subgroups of students (e.g., by grade, gender, or risk factors), or used to identify specific children at high risk. Patterns and trends in that data can be used to suggest particular sources of risk, describe the nature of mental health interventions that are required, or make the case for additional interventions from within or outside the educational system.

One of the dilemmas that school mental health providers face is the very profound discrepancy between the number of youth with significant needs for mental health interventions and the very limited resources available for child and adolescent mental health. It is clear that neither school nor community mental health resources are adequate to meet the needs of the one-in-five school-aged children who meet the criteria for at least one psychiatric diagnosis (Doll, 1996; Nastasi, 2004; Strein, Hoagwood, & Cohn, 2003; U.S. Department of Health and Human Services, 1999). Even more children without diagnoses are at risk for significant developmental failure. Needs of this magnitude demand that a school's mental health plan include interventions provided through public or private agencies or through multi-agency agreements, in addition to interventions provided by school-employed mental health providers. Moreover, needs this diverse require a continuum of mental health services extending from individual interventions for children with special needs, much like traditional clinical interventions, to community-wide interventions that address prevalent problems and promote developmental competence (Nastasi, 2004; Nastasi, Moore, & Varjas, 2004).

Population-based services do not discard the traditional clinical model that focuses on the needs of an individual, but require that schools move beyond it. A similar case has been made within

Blueprint III (Ysseldyke et al., 2006), which argues that school psychologists' focus should not remain at the individual level despite their history of collecting individual assessments of student learning. There is no assurance that drafting a population-wide plan for a continuum of mental health interventions will stretch existing resources to meet the needs of a school's students. However, planning for the full school's enrollment can assure that those decisions made about the allocation of mental health interventions will be deliberate and informed.

This continuum of school mental health interventions is likely to look very much like the three-tiered model of service described by Osher, Dwyer, and Jackson (2004). The continuum must address the *universal* mental health needs of students with system-wide or building-wide interventions to promote psychological wellness and to prevent disturbance. The Center for Mental Health in Schools refers to these universal interventions as "systems for positive youth development" and "systems of prevention" (Center for Mental Health in Schools, 2001). For example, all students could benefit from instruction in social problem-solving strategies (Shure & Spivack, 1982) or from a school-wide bullying prevention plan (Olweus, 1993). Universal interventions are similar to services that were historically called "Primary Prevention," but the updated term recognizes that the purpose of these interventions is not simply to prevent problems but also to promote wellness. Planning for universal interventions can draw on the very rich research in developmental competence that has begun to define factors that predict school learners' social, academic, and behavioral success (Masten et al., 2005, Wentzel, 2002; Wentzel & Watkins, 2002).

The second-tier interventions are *selected* mental health interventions (also called systems of early intervention by the Center for Mental Health in Schools, 2001) that are provided to students with demographic risk (i.e., evidence of poverty, family violence, or other characteristics that predict poor outcomes) or functional risk (i.e., evidence of early or emerging symptoms of disturbances). Selected interventions are more concentrated and more intense than universal interventions, and address needs that are not broadly held by all students in a school. They are similar to secondary prevention interventions, but have the purpose of strengthening competence as well as ameliorating risk. Examples of selected interventions are programs to involve parents more fully in their children's schooling (e.g., Check & Connect) (Sinclair, Christenson, Hurley, & Evelo, 1998) or interventions to prevent substance abuse in high-risk families (e.g., Preparing for the Drug-Free Years) (Kosterman, Hawkins, Spoth, Haggerty, & Zhu, 1997). In the prototypic school, 15 to 20% of the school enrollment will benefit from selected mental health interventions. However, particular schools may differ strikingly in the prevalence as well as the nature of selected interventions they need. Demographic risk is not evenly distributed across all school communities, but instead tends to concentrate in niches of very high risk such as those characterizing certain inner-city urban schools or very isolated rural communities (Pianta & Walsh, 1996). One function of population-based mental health planning is to identify the nature and extent of a school's need for selected interventions, drawing on the wealth of research on developmental risk and resilience to develop and evaluate selected interventions.

In every school, a subset of students will require more intensive selected interventions. This third tier of *selected* interventions is necessary for students who show evidence of adjustment disturbances so pronounced that they are not able to benefit from schooling without accommodations. In typical schools, these students represent between 1 and 5% of the enrollment, but, once again, the nature and extent of need can differ markedly from one school to the next. Traditionally, indicated interventions have been referred to as "tertiary prevention," "therapy," or "intervention." Examples include "level" programs for students with severe behavior disorders or desensitization procedures for students with major anxiety disorders. Within a population-based model, interventions to support students with significant disturbances could still occur at the classroom or school level, and students identified for these interventions may be served individually or in groups.

This three-tier pyramid emphasizes a structure for children's mental health services that is profoundly different from current services. In deference to this change, Adelman and Taylor (2006) suggest that the pyramid must be firmly grounded in one more level of services—that of infrastructure-building interventions. The purpose of these interventions is to promote the systemic reforms that are necessary for communities' comprehensive system of mental health services to be planned, funded, implemented, and evaluated on a routine basis.

What Do We Already Know?

Public Health Literature

A roadmap for the design and development of population-based perspectives on school mental health can be found in the annals of the public health professions. Public health professionals in the United States have traditionally focused their interventions on populations, and have emphasized society's shared responsibility for the health of the population. One of the most concise definitions is, "Public health is what we, as a society, do collectively to assure the conditions in which people can be healthy" (Institute of Medicine, 1988, p. 1). Within medicine, the emphasis on public health first emerged in the 1800s, as communities were threatened by high rates of disease and the proliferation of environmental hazards (Nastasi, 2004; Strein et al., 2003). Early public health efforts focused principally on disease prevention through widespread vaccinations and environmental improvements. In the 1970s, public health systems increasingly emphasized carefully conducted research describing the collective health of populations. More recently, in the 1990s, the attention of public health systems has shifted to include health promotion as well as disease prevention. Policies, practices, and empirical research strategies developed within the public health systems can be adapted to understand the mental health of community populations, and particularly the prevention of psychological disturbance and well-being within a school's student body. For example, Table 1.1 describes how the Institute of Medicine's (1988) 10 essential public health services could be applied to school mental health services.

The compelling relevance of public health perspectives to the practice of school psychology has been recognized repeatedly by key leaders in mental health and school psychology (Institute of Medicine, 1994). Hoagwood and Johnson (2003) guest-edited a special issue of the *Journal of School Psychology* that called for this shift in school psychological roles. Nastasi (2004) similarly called for the integration of public health and public education, an essential step toward the national promotion of children's mental health. Power (2003) emphasized the necessary partnerships between mental health and education that must underlie a public health perspective. Even earlier, Eddy, Reid, and Curry (2002) described a public health perspective on the prevention of antisocial behavior and violence in youth.

Research on Developmental Psychopathology

Ample data in the developmental psychopathology research describes the kinds of mental health interventions that will be needed in many schools. For example, epidemiologic studies have shown that the most prevalent psychosocial disorders in both elementary and secondary schools are anxiety disorders (Doll, 1996). The National Cormobidity Study (Kessler, Berglund, Demler, Jin, & Walters, 2005) has shown that the average age of onset for anxiety disorders is 11 years, or approximately during the sixth grade. Anxiety has not

Table 1.1   Application of the 10 Essential Public Health Services to School Mental Health

10 Essential Public Health Services*	Equivalent School Mental Health Services
1. Monitor health status to identify community health problems	Monitor students' mental health status including their academic, social-emotional, and relational competence
2. Diagnose and investigate health problems and health hazards in the community	Diagnose and investigate psychological disturbance in students
3. Inform, educate, and empower people about health issues	Inform, educate, and empower students and their families about mental health issues
4. Mobilize community partnerships to identify and solve health problems	Mobilize school-family-community partnerships to identify and solve psychological disturbances
5. Develop policies and plans that support individual and community health efforts	Develop policies and plans that support student, family, school, and community mental health efforts
6. Enforce laws and regulations that protect health and ensure safety	Implement policies and practices that protect students' mental health and ensure developmental competence
7. Link people to needed personal health services and assure the provision of health care when otherwise unavailable	Link students and their families to universal, selected, and intensive interventions as needed
8. Assure a competent public health and personal health care workforce	Provide appropriate staff training and monitor throughout intervention
9. Evaluate effectiveness, accessibility, and quality of personal and population-based health services	Evaluate effectiveness, accessibility, and quality of school mental health services
10. Research new insights and innovative solutions to health problems	Research new insights and innovative approaches to promoting mental health

*Source: Institute of Medicine (1988).

traditionally received a significant proportion of the focus of school mental health providers, despite the evidence that anxiety disorders significantly interfere with learning and personal adjustment. The ubiquity of anxiety disturbances, and their prevalence throughout the lifespan, suggests that strategies to identify and manage maladaptive anxiety ought to be infused into the curriculum of most schools, regardless of level.

Impulse control disorders have a similarly early average age of onset, and are equally prevalent in elementary and secondary schools. However, the nature of the impulse control disorders shifts as students move into the middle school. In the elementary grades, the incidence of attention deficit disorder with and without hyper-activity (ADD and ADHD) is slightly higher than the incidence of simple conduct disorders and oppositional defiant disorders. Moreover, a significant portion of elementary-aged students struggle with both disorders simultaneously. By the secondary grades, the incidence of ADHD has declined somewhat, although some researchers argue that it is the expression of the disorder that has shifted and not its actual prevalence. However, the incidence of conduct disorders in secondary schools is at least twice that of elementary schools. Impulse control disorders are eminently contextual in origin, and are often moderated by careful manipulation of contingencies and setting events in the school environment.

Impulse control disorders are not only disturbing for the students who evidence them, but also contribute to a climate of interpersonal aggression that can make schools very frightening environments for all students. In particular, Swearer (Swearer, Espelage, Love, & Kingsbury, chapter 8, this volume; Swearer & Cary, 2003) describes patterns of physical, verbal, and relational aggression among students that is frequent, disturbing, and may occur outside the immediate notice of supervising adults in the building. Sugai, Horner, and Gresham's (2002) review of school data suggests that, in many schools, a small proportion of students account for the majority of aggressive and rule-breaking incidents in a building. Thus, information on disruptive disorders suggests that all schools need systematic management plans to address behavioral conduct in positive ways, conflict mediation strategies to help students repair relationships in the face of interpersonal conflicts, and more intense intervention strategies to address the severe behavioral transgressions of the school's few, very disruptive students.

In contrast to anxiety disorders and disruptive disorders, mood disorders are three to four times as prevalent in secondary schools as in elementary schools (Doll, 1996), with as many as 6% of high school students meeting the *Diagnostic and Statistical Manual of Mental Disorders–Fourth Edition, Text Revision* (DSM-IV-TR, American Psychiatric Association, 2000) criteria for a clinical depression. Moreover, the

National Comorbidity Study (Kessler et al., 2005) suggests that these adolescent cases are just the beginning of an increase in mood disorders, whose average age of onset is approximately 30 years of age. Even in adults, delays in seeking treatment for mood disorders tended to stretch across six or eight years. In addition to the unrecognized pain of students with mood disorders, even moderate mood disorders contribute to substance dependence and impairments of school work or life tasks. Consequently, secondary school mental health plans ought to prepare students to recognize mood disorders, know when to seek treatment, and understand how to cope with a predisposition for significant mood disorders.

Neither the National Comorbidity Study (Kessler et al., 2005) nor the *DSM-IV-TR* formally recognizes disturbances in social relationships including severe social withdrawal, social rejection, social neglect, and social isolation. However, developmental research has clearly established that children with significant social difficulties are much more likely to struggle with adult disturbances, including mental illness, unemployment, financial dependence, and educational failure. School bullying research has shown that children without friends are more likely to be victimized by peer bullying (Song, 2006). In contrast, children with friends and ample social support networks will like school more, and are more likely to finish school, succeed in work, and form healthy adult families. Consequently, all school mental health plans should incorporate strategies for promoting friendships and social interactions among students in the building.

Research on Developmental Risk and Resilience

It is not just the onset of disorders but also the predictors of disorders that inform schools' mental health service plans. Developmental data on psychological risk establish that demographic characteristics of students' families and communities can be as important as their individual characteristics in predicting subsequent development of adult disturbances (Coie et al., 1993; Consortium on the School-Based Promotion of Social Competence, 1994; Doll & Lyon, 1998; Masten & Coatsworth, 1998). In particular, students' exposure to poverty, family violence, parental mental illness, or community violence significantly increases their chances of developing debilitating mental illnesses. Moreover, these risk factors tend to concentrate in high-risk communities. Thus, schools serving students from high-risk communities must plan to address a far greater need for school mental health interventions than schools serving more affluent or less violent communities.

Developmental resilience research offers important insights into the kinds of interventions that will be effective in ameliorating these demographic risks. Specifically, students are more likely to be successful despite the odds when they have access to close peer friendships, high self-efficacy, high levels of engagement in productive activities, access to warm relationships and guidance from adults, or access to responsive schools. Thus, the developmental resilience research provides a roadmap for planning school mental health services that address the academic and social problems of a school's students.

Prevention and Intervention Policy and Research

As the place where children routinely congregate, schools are natural sites for early intervention efforts. In addition, schools as community institutions frequently benefit from successful prevention efforts that lower students' risk and foster their developmental competence. Moreover, some of the strongest conceptual frameworks for population-wide interventions are included within the prevention literature.

Nation et al. (2003) conducted a systematic analysis of the most effective preventive interventions from which they distilled a cogent description of key program characteristics. First, effective programs are comprehensive in that they incorporate multiple interventions and are implemented across school, home, community, and peer settings. Second, the most effective programs use varied and interactive teaching methods that actively engage participants in developing specific skills. Third, "dosage" of the best programs was matched to the severity of the problem. More severe problems require interventions that are more intense and of longer duration. Too often interventions are based on past experience and what appears logical. However, the fourth characteristic the researchers found was that programs are most effective when they are theory driven, taking into account the etiology of the problem and drawing from an empirical evidence base. Theory-driven programs "focus on the best methods for changing the etiological risks" (Nation et al., 2003, p. 453). Finally, all effective programs promote strong, positive relationships between parents and children, teachers and children, and children and peers.

Skilled selection and implementation of preventive interventions is critical to their effectiveness (Nation et al., 2003). Interventions may miss the mark if they are delivered too early or too late. Traditional special education referral is a good example of waiting to intervene until failure is evident, when earlier and systematic steps might have avoided the failure altogether. As another example of the power of timing, HIV/AIDS programs have proved to be effective for adolescents before they become sexually active, but ineffective for those who are already sexually active. Skilled intervention planning will also select interventions that are consistent with local sociocultural norms as well as cultural beliefs and attitudes. When implementing population-based interventions, one size does not necessarily fit all communities. Skilled prevention programs also embed evaluation into the intervention planning from the start. Useful evaluation is formative or ongoing and informs continuous improvement in the intervention during implementation. The most effective evaluation is systematic, with methodologically rigorous designs, and not antidotal or limited to a single case study. Finally, a well-trained staff is essential to effective interventions. Skilled interventionists will deliver a program with greater fidelity. Table 1.2 refines the Nation et al. (2003) analysis into 10 critical questions that guide the development and implementation of preventive interventions.

Table 1.2   Questions to Consider When Planning and Implementing Prevention Programs

Is the intervention comprehensive? Does it include multiple interventions and settings?
Are varied teaching methods used that promote specific skills? Are participants actively learning as opposed to passively listening?
Does the dosage of the intervention match the severity of the need or problem? Are booster sessions needed to increase the longevity of the intervention effects?
Does the intervention address the etiological basis of the problem? Does the intervention have an evidence base indicating its effectiveness?
Does the intervention promote positive relationships across teachers, parents, and students?
Is the intervention appropriately timed relative to the developmental status of the targeted population?
Is the intervention socioculturally relevant in terms of community norms as well as cultural attitudes and practices?
Is the evaluation an integral part of the implementation plan and designed to provide formative feedback at various stages of the intervention?
Is the staff well prepared and monitored to promote intervention fidelity during the implementation?

Source: Adapted from Nation et al. (2003).

Evidence-Based Practice

An important recent trend in applied psychology has been to focus on the evidence underlying interventions (Chambless & Hollon, 1998; Chambless et al., 1996; Kratochwill & Stoiber, 2002; U.S. Department of Health and Human Services, 1999). The standards governing demonstrations of empirical support for treatments have been described at length by Chambless et al. (1996), Hayes, Barlow, and Nelson-Gray (1999), Lonigan, Elbert, and Bennett-Johnson (1998), Hughes (2000), and most recently, Kratochwill and Stoiber (2002). The work of these and other groups in documenting a range of efficacious psychological treatments was acknowledged in the Surgeon General's report on mental health (U.S. Department of Health and Human Services, 1999). Some of the most rigorous standards assert that, to be proven effective, a treatment must have been subjected to at least two well-designed group studies conducted by unrelated research teams or by a series of well-conducted single-subject studies. Participants in the studies should be randomly assigned to different treatment groups and comparisons should be made between groups of subjects, one of which is provided with no treatment, others with competing treatments, and one with the treatment of interest. Finally, results should indicate that improvements in symptoms occur, are not due to chance, are due to the treatment of interest, represent an improvement over no treatment at all, and are at least as strong as those produced by existing treatments.

These standards, as articulated, are clearly aspirational rather than absolute. Few mental health interventions meet these criteria, and those that do have typically been examined within the context of a single cultural or socioeconomic group. Still, educational leaders clearly and firmly support the principles underlying evidence-based intervention, and school mental health plans will need to incorporate those interventions with the strongest empirical evidence of effectiveness.

How This Book Will Help

The purpose of this book is to provide a roadmap to the provision of population-based school mental health interventions. Its emphasis is on strategies that are available now, can be put into practice immediately, and have evidence supporting their utility. In the book's first section, school-wide assessment, screening, and monitoring are described as strategies to identify and prioritize the mental health needs of a school's enrollment and use in service planning. In particular, Short and Strein provide an invaluable description of epidemiologic assessment as it applies to the identification of population-wide psychological disorders in schools. Then, Baker explains how an array of formal and informal assessment strategies can be used to detect and describe risk and protective factors in a school's student body.

The second section of the book explains what schools can do to promote the healthy and competent psychological development of all students and to prevent mental illness. The chapters in this section explain how intervention strategies lend themselves to population-based services and the characteristics of these practices that strengthen their impact on students' lives. First, Christenson, Whitehouse, and VanGetson describe the critical role that families play in schools' mental health services, and the school practices that foster highly effective partnerships with families. Because behavioral competence is an important developmental task for all students, Bear explains the school-wide strategies that promote behavioral discipline and prevention behavior problems. Academic success is an equally important developmental task, and Martínez and Nellis describe response-to-intervention strategies that apply data-based problem-solving strategies to academic monitoring and intervention. In deference to the similarly important place of social and emotional competence for students' psychological well-being, Merrell, Gueldner, and Tran explain how school practices can promote students' friendships and social development. School bullying, intimidation, and violence are particularly recognized as common and very destructive aspects of students' peer interactions, and the chapter by Swearer, Espelage, Love, and Kingsbury explains how bullying prevention activities can be integrated into school routines. Finally, as an example of how a traditional mental disorder can be addressed through population-based strategies, Mazza and Reynolds describe school-wide approaches for addressing depression and suicidal behaviors in schools.

It is clear that reframing school mental health services around a population-based perspective is an instance of systemic change. The new perspective articulates a purpose and organization for school mental health services that is more connected to a school's core responsibilities, but it is also quite distinct from the traditional roles that school mental health providers have played within schools. Consequently, the third section of the book describes the fit between population-based services and school and district policies, procedures, practices, and resources. In particular, Nastasi and Hitchcock describe the essential purpose of program evaluation in guiding and propelling the shift from traditional to population-based models of school mental health. Next, Adelman and Taylor discuss ways to enhance the interface between school improvement efforts and new directions for addressing mental health and psychosocial concerns in schools. In this context, they outline ways to reframe student support interventions so that all students have an equal opportunity to succeed at school. They also illustrate how the school's infrastructure can be reworked to facilitate the development of a comprehensive, multifaceted, and cohesive system of learning supports at every school.

The concluding chapter integrates these authors' very comprehensive descriptions of population-based services with the role and mission of school psychology, as defined by the 2002 Multisite Conference on the Future of School Psychology and the National Association of School Psychologists. The transition to a population-based perspective is both necessary and inevitable for school mental health professionals, and this chapter explains how it can happen in your school and your time.

Discussion Questions

1. Given what you already know about children's social and emotional development, what are likely to be the most urgent mental health needs in your community?

2. How are population-based school mental health services similar to the services familiar to your community? How are they different?

3. What is the fit between population-based services and your school district's policies, procedures, practices, and resources?

4. If a school decided to implement a population-based service model in your community, what are some likely barriers to the transformation? What might facilitate the transformation in your community?

5. What ethical dilemmas might arise in your community if school mental health services were reframed around the collective needs of children?

References

Adelman, H. S., & Taylor, L. (2006). *The school leader's guide to student learning supports: New directions for addressing barriers to learning.* Thousand Oaks, CA: Corwin Press.

American Psychiatric Association. (2000). *The Diagnostic and Statistical Manual of Mental Disorders—Fourth Edition, Text Revised.* Washington, DC: Author.

Center for Mental Health in Schools, UCLA. (2001). *Framing new directions for school counselors, psychologists and social workers.* Los Angeles: Author. Retrieved June 15, 2006, from http://smhp.psych.ucla.edu/pdfdocs/Report/framingnewdir.pdf

Chambless, D. L., & Hollon, D. S. (1998). Defining empirically supported therapies. *Journal of Consulting and Clinical Psychology, 66,* 7–18.

Chambless, D. L., Sanderson, W. C., Shoham, V., Bennett-Johnson, S., Pope, K. S., Crits-Christoph, P., et al. (1996). An update on empirically validated therapies. *Clinical Psychologist, 49,* 5–18.

Coie, J. D., Watt, N. F., West, S. G., Hawkins, J. D., Asarnow, J. R., Markan, H. J., et al. (1993). The science of prevention: A conceptual framework and some directions for a national research program. *American Psychologist, 48,* 1013–1022.

Consortium on the School-Based Promotion of Social Competence. (1994). The school-based promotion of social competence: Theory, research, practice, and policy. In R. J. Haggerty, L. R. Sherrod, N. Germezy, & M. Rutter (Eds.), *Stress, risk, and resilience in children and adolescents* (pp. 268–316). New York: Cambridge University Press.

Doll, B. (1996). Prevalence of psychiatric disorders in children and youth: An agenda for advocacy by school psychology. *School Psychology Quarterly, 11,* 20–46.

Doll, B., & Haack, M. K. (2005). Population-based strategies for identifying schoolwide problems. In R. Brown-Chidsey (Ed.), *Assessment for intervention: A problem-solving approach* (pp. 82–102). New York: Guilford Press.

Doll, B., & Lyon, M. (1998). Risk and resilience: Implications for the practice of school psychology. *School Psychology Review, 27,* 348–363.

Eddy, J. M., Reid, J. B., & Curry, V. (2002). The etiology of youth antisocial behavior and delinquency and violence and a public health approach to prevention. In M. A. Shinn, H. M. Walker, & G. Stoner (Eds.), *Interventions for academic and behavior problems II: Preventive and remedial approaches* (pp. 27–51). Bethesda, MD: National Association of School Psychologists.

Harrison, P. L., Cummings, J. A., Dawson, M, Short, R. J., Gorin, S., & Palomares, R. (2004). Responding to the needs of children, families, and schools: The 2002 Multisite Conference on the Future of School Psychology. *School Psychology Review, 33,* 12–33.

Hayes, S. C., Barlow, D. H., & Nelson-Gray, R. O. (1999). *The scientist practitioners: Research and accountability in the age of managed care* (2nd ed.). Boston: Allyn & Bacon.

Hoagwood, K., & Johnson, J. (2003). School psychology: A public health framework. *Journal of School Psychology, 41,* 3–21.

Hughes, J. N. (2000). The essential role of theory in the science of treating children: Beyond empirically supported treatments. *Journal of School Psychology, 38,* 301–330.

Institute of Medicine. (1988). *The future of public health.* Washington, DC: National Academy Press.

Institute of Medicine. (1994). *Reducing risks for mental disorders: Frontiers for preventive intervention research.* Washington, DC: National Academy Press.

Kessler, R. C., Berglund, P., Demler, O., Jin, R., & Walters, E. E. (2005). Lifetime prevalence and age-of-onset distributions of DSM-IV disorders in the national comorbidity survey replication. *Archives of General Psychiatry, 62,* 617–627.

Kosterman, R., Hawkins, J. D., Spoth, R., Haggerty, K., & Zhu, K. (1997). Effects of a preventive parent training intervention on observed family interactions: Proximal outcomes from preparing for the drug free years. *Journal of Community Psychology, 25,* 277–292.

Kratochwill, T. R., & Stoiber, K. C. (2002). Special issue: Evidence-based interventions in school psychology: The state of the art and future directions. *School Psychology Quarterly, 17,* 341–389.

Lonigan, C. J., Elbert, J. C., & Bennett-Johnson, S. (1998). Empirically supported psychosocial interventions for children: An overview. *Journal of Clinical Child Psychology, 27,* 138–145.

Masten, A. S., & Coatsworth, J. D. (1998). The development of competence in favorable and unfavorable environments: Lessons from research on successful children. *American Psychologist, 53,* 205–220.

Masten, A .S., Roisman, G. I., Long, J. D., Burt, K. B., Obradovic, J., Riley, J. R., et al. (2005). Developmental cascades: Linking academic achievement and externalizing and internalizing symptoms over 20 years. *Developmental Psychology, 41,* 733–746.

Meyers, J., Parsons, R. D., & Martin, R. (1979). *Mental health consultation in the schools.* San Francisco: Jossey-Bass.

Nastasi, B. K. (2004). Meeting the challenges of the future: Integrating public health and public education for mental health promotion. *Journal of Educational and Psychological Consultation, 15,* 295–312.

Nastasi, B. K., Moore, R. B., & Varjas, K. M. (2004). *School based mental health services: Creating comprehensive and culturally specific programs.* Washington, DC: American Psychological Association.

Nation, M., Crusto, C., Wandersman, A., Kumpfer, K. L., Seybolt, D., Morrissey-Kane, E., & Davino, K. (2003). What works in prevention: Principles of effective prevention programs. *American Psychologist, 58,* 449–456.

National Technical Assistance Center on Positive Behavioral Interventions and Supports (PBIS). (2006). Retrieved April 3, 2006, from http://www.pbis.org/main.htm

Olweus, D. (1993). *Bullying at school: What we know and what we can do.* Cambridge: Blackwell.

Osher, D., Dwyer, K., & Jackson, S. (2004). *Safe, supportive, and successful schools: Step by step.* Longmont, CO: Sopris Press.

Pianta, R. C., & Walsh, D. J. (1996). *High risk children in schools: Constructing sustaining relationships.* New York: Routledge.

Power, T. J. (2003). Promoting children's mental health: Reform through interdisciplinary and community partnerships. *School Psychology Review, 32,* 3–16.

Shure, M. B., & Spivack, G. (1982). Interpersonal problem solving in young children: A cognitive approach to prevention. *American Journal of Community Psychology, 10,* 341–355.

Sinclair, M. F., Christenson, S. L., Hurley, C., & Evelo, D. (1998). Dropout prevention for high-risk youth with disabilities: Efficacy of a sustained school engagement procedure. *Exceptional Children, 65*, 7–21.

Song, S. (2006). *The role of protective peers and positive peer relationships: How can peers help?* Unpublished dissertation. University of Nebraska, Lincoln.

Strein, W., Hoagwood, K., & Cohn, A. (2003). School psychology: A public health perspective. I. Prevention, populations, and systems change. *Journal of School Psychology, 41*, 23–38.

Sugai, G., Horner, R. H., & Gresham, F. M. (2002). Behaviorally effective school environments. In M. R. Shinn, H. M. Walker, & G. Stoner (Eds.), *Interventions for academic and behavior problems II: Preventive and remedial approaches* (pp. 315–350). Bethesda, MD: National Association of School Psychologists.

Swearer, S. M., & Cary, P. T. (2003). Perceptions and attitudes toward bullying in middle school youth: A developmental examination across the bully/victim continuum. *Journal of Applied School Psychology, 19*, 63–79.

U.S. Department of Health and Human Services. (1999) *Mental health: A report of the surgeon general.* Rockville, MD: U.S. Dept. of Health and Human Services. Available at http://www.surgeongeneral.gov/library/mental health

Wentzel, K. R. (2002). Are effective teachers like good parents? Teaching styles and student adjustment in early adolescence. *Child Development, 73*, 287–301.

Wentzel, K. R., & Watkins, D. E. (2002). Peer relationships and collaborative learning as contexts for academic enablers. *School Psychology Review, 31*, 366–377.

Ysseldyke, J., Burns, M., Dawson, M., Kelly, B., Morrison, D., Ortiz, S., et al. (2006). *School psychology: A blueprint for training and practice III.* Bethesda, MD: National Association of School Psychologists.

About the Authors

Beth Doll is a Professor of Educational Psychology at the University of Nebraska–Lincoln. Her research interests include school mental health service delivery systems, with a special emphasis on the classwide and school-wide factors that enhance children's mental health and academic success.

 **Jack A. Cummings** is a Professor of Educational Psychology at Indiana University in Bloomington. He was co-chair of the 2002 Multisite Conference on the Future of School Psychology and continues to write on the topic of applications of technology to address needs in education.

PART I

Population-Based Assessment

2

Behavioral and Social Epidemiology

Population-Based Problem Identification and Monitoring

Rick Jay Short

William Strein

M any of the problems that plague American schools are systemic and population-based. In the 2003/04 academic year, states identified more than 11,000 schools (~12%) as "low-performing," based on assessments of student achievement (U.S. Department of Education NCES, 2005a). In the United States, eighth-graders in 2003 ranked, *at best,* 10th in math and 8th in science internationally (Gonzales et al., 2004), and an estimated one in eight students in American schools drop out before completing high school (Christenson & Thurlow, 2004). Over half of all high school seniors in 2004 reported that they had used an illicit drug sometime in their lifetime, with nearly a quarter of eighth-graders so responding. Similarly, 39% of high school seniors and 15% of eighth-graders reported illicit drug use within the past year (Johnston et al., 2005). Although lethal violence in schools is extremely rare and serious violence involving weapons is infrequent and has remained steady or declined in the past 10 to 15 years (Greene, 2005), the prevalence of verbal aggression, bullying, and harassment is more common and their prevalence has held steady in recent years (DeVoe et al., 2004). In a recent national survey of school-based mental health professionals (Evans & Andrews, 2005), 68% of respondents indicated that mental health problems, especially adolescent depression, are a "great" or "moderate" problem, rating these problems as more severe than school violence.

Such issues represent critical, and typical, concerns of school administrators and school boards across the nation, from the smallest rural district to the largest urban center. Indeed, millions of dollars, continued employment, and results of elections often depend on how such questions are answered. However, most school districts and communities have relatively few means to get systematic, evidence-based data for addressing and monitoring such issues. As a result, policy decisions often are made based on guesswork or political pressures, with little real data to support them. Additionally, these problems cannot be understood or addressed primarily at the level of the individual student; they are statements regarding populations and, thus, are best understood from a public health perspective (Short, 2003).

School mental health, and specifically school psychology, historically has focused on the individual student and, at best, has been engaged minimally in finding population-wide solutions to such problems (Strein, Hoagwood, & Cohn, 2003). At the individual-student level, some form of a problem-solving model has become a prominent feature in the delivery of psychological services and the training of school psychologists (Reschly & Ysseldyke, 2002). The general problem-solving model typically has four phases similar to the following: (a) problem identification, (b) problem analysis, (c) plan implementation, and (d) evaluation of the implementation (Tilly, 2002). Application of the model in school mental health typically uses indicators *for a single student* to identify a problem or select a target, develop interventions, and evaluate intervention outcomes. For example, Curriculum-Based Assessment (CBA) and Curriculum-Based Measurement (CBM) are frequently used to document a single student's need for an academic intervention, design the specifics of that intervention, then evaluate the results or modify the intervention.

For population-wide interventions, the appropriate units of analysis are population indicators rather than individual student data. Accordingly, the problem-identification, problem-analysis, implementation, and evaluation phases of the problem-solving model are best addressed using techniques from epidemiology. An epidemiologic approach to problem identification would focus on population-wide indicators (e.g., CBM for an entire class, grade, or school) to identify *who* within the population (i.e., which subpopulations) has a problem, *when* such problems exist (time of year), *where* they exist (which grades, which teachers), and *why* they exist (what causes) (Webb, Bain, & Pirozzo, 2005). The current national focus on the "achievement gap" between African-American and European-American students is a quintessential example of an epidemiologic approach to problem identification, because it (a) measures the problem by examining population-wide data on achievement test scores and graduation rates; (b) defines the problem in terms of student populations, without identifying individual schools or students; (c) mandates that changes in the same population-based achievement test scores and graduation rates be regarded as the measure of progress (i.e., "closing the gap"); and (d) infers that interventions broader than those at the individual student level are necessary to address the problem.

A comparison of traditional comprehensive case assessments conducted by school mental health professionals with the practice of public health may be helpful in understanding epidemiology. First, where school practitioners collect data on individual students in psychoeducational assessments, epidemiologists collect data on populations through surveillance systems or descriptive epidemiological studies. School mental health professionals use their data to provide input on special education placement or to develop educational and behavioral interventions. Epidemiologists use data to generate hypotheses about relationships among risk factors, protective factors, and outcomes. Optimally, some form of intervention results from both forms of data collection, but school practitioners' interventions focus on individual children, whereas epidemiologists seek to devise some form of community intervention to influence outcomes for the entire population.

Epidemiology: History and Characteristics

Although the clinical model has remained the dominant way to conceptualize and deal with problems for centuries, a population-based approach has been around for quite a long time as well. As early as 400 BC, Hippocrates proposed that the environment, perhaps combined with host factors, sometimes causes disease. The first modern use of epidemiology occurred in London in 1854. In that year, a cholera epidemic struck the city so severely that 500 people died in 10 days. Treatment fell well behind the need, and nobody knew what caused the problem or how to slow its course. John Snow, considered the father of epidemiology, plotted new cases of cholera on a map of the city, and noted that these cases seemed to be localized around one of the water pumps serving the population. He also noticed, however, that no new cases were reported two blocks east of the suspect pump. If something in the water from the pump caused the cholera outbreak, then such exceptions wouldn't make sense. On investigation, Snow found that citizens east of the offending pump worked at a brewery that had its own source of water. Because they used the brewery's water, they avoided contact with the contaminated pump. Snow used epidemiologic principles to move beyond simply treating the problem to ascertaining and controlling its source.

Since Snow's time, epidemiology has evolved and expanded from disease-specific outcomes to health, social, and behavioral dimensions of functioning. Epidemiology has been defined as "the study of the distribution and determinants of health-related states in specified populations, and the application of this study to control health problems" (Last, 1988, p. 16). Originally it was defined as the study of disease, literally the study of epidemics; more modern definitions encompass "health" broadly defined. Behavioral epidemiology is the study of the distribution of health-related (or education- or mental health–related) behaviors in a population in order to identify population-wide problems and develop effective population-wide interventions. Behavioral and social epidemiology is differentiated from the original 19th-century model by "its insistence on explicitly investigating social determinants of population distributions of health, disease, and wellbeing, rather than treating such determinants as mere background to biomedical phenomena" (Krieger, 2001, p. 693). In school practice, this approach de-emphasizes learning disabilities, conduct disorders, or similar clinical diagnoses with etiologies within the person, and increases focus on sociocultural, family, and environmental determinants of these problems. Further, a behavioral/social epidemiologic approach in school practice would examine learning disabilities or conduct disorders in the population with the intention of preventing them or lowering their incidence and prevalence, rather than addressing them in individual children—often following years of failure or misbehavior.

The tools of epidemiology fall into two broad categories, both of which are covered in most psychological statistics courses: frequency analyses and inferential statistics. Frequency analyses typically are used to provide information within the framework of *descriptive* epidemiology, whereas inferential statistics are the major implements of *analytic* epidemiology.

Descriptive Epidemiology

As its label suggests, descriptive epidemiology is intended to provide objective information about a condition. School mental health professionals are very familiar with practices that describe conditions as reliably and validly as possible. Indeed, much school-based practice involves just this type of activity, albeit at the level of the individual student instead of the population. In the same vein, descriptive epidemiology endeavors to define clearly the condition (*what*), the time frame for its occurrence (*when*), the setting or location of the condition (*where*), and the characteristics of individuals experiencing the condition (*who*). Whereas these dimensions historically have been applied to public health problems (e.g., AIDS, rubella, obesity), they apply just as readily to educational and mental health conditions (e.g., school completion, violence, learning disabilities).

For example, descriptive epidemiology applied to school completion might define and count the number of students (*what*) in a school or community who finish high school. These data might be gathered and reported over a period of several years (*when*) to provide information about trends in graduation. Particularly in large communities with multiple high schools, graduation rates may differ significantly from one school to another. Accordingly, differential data can be gathered by high school (*where*) to provide information concerning where strengths and weaknesses exist in the system. Finally, we can achieve even more specificity by examining characteristics of students who complete or fail to complete school (*who*), including such things as gender, socioeconomic status (SES), race and ethnicity, popularity, and so on. Taken together, these descriptive data provide a picture of the system in relation to some issue of concern, similar to the representation of an individual student you might derive from psychological and educational test information.

Typically, many of the measures in descriptive epidemiology are frequencies and describe two alternatives: alive or dead, case or control, exposed or unexposed, and so forth. Applying this frame to education and psychology, for example, an epidemiologist might count completers versus noncompleters or LD versus non-LD. Using frequency measures allows you to calculate several important statistics for epidemiologic use, including ratios, proportions, and rates. Ratios refer to the relationship between two quantities, where the quantities are independent of each other and expressed as a fraction or a decimal. For example, a pool with 360 females and 120 males yields a 360/120, or 3/1 female-to-male ratio. Proportions are ratios in which the numerator is included in the denominator. Using the preceding example, 360 females in a total pool of 480 individuals (360 females + 120 males) yields a proportion of females in the pool of 360/480, or 3/4. Ratios and proportions are used in several ways in epidemiology, including calculation of risk ratios, odds ratios, proportionate mortality, and point prevalence.

Rates, as special instances of proportions, are important enough to deserve a separate discussion. Rates deal with the occurrence of an event in a population over time. They represent the number of cases or events in a given time period divided by the population at risk during that period. Using the previous school completion example, if 1,917 of 2,500 students completed high school in the 5-year time frame, then the completion rate is 1,917/2,500, or .7668—typically multiplied by 100 to yield a completion rate of almost 77%.

Although several types of rates are calculated in descriptive epidemiology, perhaps the most important rate for applying the public health model to school mental health is morbidity. Morbidity is a frequency measure that describes the presence of a characteristic (typically, a disease in the health domain), or the probability of its occurrence. In addition to overall measures of morbidity, specific measures of the characteristic can be calculated by race, gender, SES, or other important dimensions. In this way, differential risk rates can be determined for significant subgroups of the population. Morbidity measures also can be calculated to yield two common statistics in epidemiology: incidence and prevalence.

Incidence rate is a measure of risk, and is the most commonly used measure for determining and comparing population characteristics. Incidence rate is defined as the probability of occurrence of any characteristic in a population in a given period of time. By using frequency rates rather than raw numbers of cases, assessors can control for differences in group size across populations and allow for cross-population comparisons. A group that exhibits a higher incidence rate than another group is at higher risk of developing the characteristic than the second group. Using a formula, incidence rate is

$$\text{Incidence rate} = \frac{\text{New cases in a time period}}{\text{Population in the same time period}} \times 10^n$$

Incidence rates include only new cases that appear during the time period relative to all persons susceptible to the condition. Generally, this number can represent the average population during the time period. Also, the time period must be specified to allow for comparison of incidence rates across populations or periods. Finally, the power of 10 used in the formula can be varied to make incidence statistics more meaningful [e.g., 472 new cases per 100,000 (10^5) or 4.7 new cases per 1000 (10^3)].

Prevalence rate is similar to incidence rate but deals with *all* cases instead of only *new* cases evident in a population during a specified time interval. Accordingly, the numerator in the prevalence rate formula includes both new and existing cases of the condition, whereas the denominator remains the population within a designated time period:

$$\text{Prevalence rate} = \frac{\text{New and existing cases in a time period}}{\text{Population in the same time period}} \times 10^n$$

Whereas incidence provides information about the rate of change in the population of a disease or attribute, prevalence provides an index of severity or extensiveness of the disease or attribute in the population. Both measures can provide information about who needs services, where they are, and the time frame within which the problem or attribute occurs. However, incidence and prevalence rates are less useful for identifying causal paths and potential intervention targets—the why and how of the condition. These important activities require an analytic epidemiology approach.

Analytic Epidemiology

Analytic epidemiology builds on findings from descriptive epidemiology to investigate possible causes of and influences on the problem or condition in the population. Using the descriptive results, the analytic epidemiologist develops hypotheses to explain the condition, then tests these hypotheses to yield empirical support for surmised correlates and influences. Because the inferential statistics used to develop and test these hypotheses essentially are the same as those included in all school psychology programs and many programs training other school mental health professionals, school practitioners should be quite familiar with much of the language and process of analytic epidemiology. With some modification, the application of these procedures to real-life problems may provide a valuable use for skills that school mental health professionals typically use little as practitioners.

Three domains of investigation comprise the general framework for analytic epidemiology. These dimensions, called the Epidemiologic Triad (presented graphically in Figure 2.1), are Host, Agent, and Environment. A basic assumption of analytic epidemiology is that disease can be explained by factors associated with one or more of these three dimensions. Analytic epidemiological studies often organize results along the lines of the triad.

Figure 2.1   Epidemiologic Triad

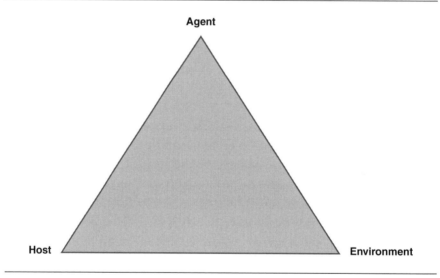

Host factors are intrinsic characteristics of an individual that cause him or her to be more susceptible to the condition. These factors can occur along social, physical, and psychological dimensions. For example, social characteristics, including SES and geographical location, may make students more susceptible to obesity. Physical attributes, including genetic makeup and anatomic structure also may contribute to vulnerability to obesity. And psychological and behavioral factors, such as exercise and eating patterns, may explain even more of the variance associated with being overweight. All of these are characteristics of individual students. It is interesting to note that whereas individual host characteristics traditionally have been the primary domain of psychological assessment, the epidemiological approach broadens assessment to acknowledge a more ecological perspective.

Agent factors originally referred to infectious microorganisms that had to be present for disease to occur. These agents included bacteria, viruses, and parasites and were seen as necessary but not sufficient causes of the disease. In the case of behavioral and social epidemiology, agent factors are less clear and often indistinguishable from environmental factors. Nonetheless, it is productive to examine causal factors as agents when clear and specific links can be demonstrated between such factors and the condition. For example, although not infectious and not actually a disease agent, maternal alcohol use is a causal agent for fetal alcohol syndrome.

Environmental factors represent external determinants of a condition. Environmental factors are important in epidemiology in that they can affect the host, the agent, or the interaction between the host and agent. Additionally, they may serve as mediators among these factors. Examples of environmental factors in public health epidemiology might include crowding, sanitation, and other characteristics that serve to limit or spread disease. Environmental factors are similarly important in behavioral and social epidemiology, as they represent the primary targets of intervention to influence the incidence or prevalence of the problem or condition in the population. For example, school failure may be partly explained by environmental factors such as school climate, teacher quality, parent behaviors, and availability of educational resources. In this example, understanding school failure in the population would require knowledge of the relative contributions of these and other environmental factors to the problem in order to plan interventions to influence its morbidity.

In behavioral and social epidemiology, host and environmental factors are often organized by their primary locus. Accordingly, school environmental factors might include classroom climate, instructional quality, or engaged time. Parent factors might include parenting style and parent education. Peer factors might deal with peer acceptance, number of peers, and peer behaviors. In this way, epidemiological researchers can develop understandable frameworks to guide for monitoring, assessment, intervention, and evaluation. Short and his colleagues (Short & Brokaw, 1994; Short & Shapiro, 1993) have presented a simple example of such a framework for conduct disorders, in which organization of dimensions of correlates of population problems and attributes can provide a useful heuristic for prevention practice and epidemiology. Additionally, such heuristics yield hypotheses concerning risk and protective factors associated with the problem or attribute that can guide intervention and evaluation.

Practicing school mental health professionals can use descriptive epidemiology techniques combined with an analytic epidemiology approach to develop and evaluate empirically derived prevention programs. As a first step, incidence and prevalence of the population problem or attribute can be investigated by generating frequency rates of new cases and all cases within a time frame. Second, school practitioners can identify potential positive and negative correlates (risk and protective factors) from the literature and/or information at the site. Third, these relationships can be evaluated by gathering data on potential risk and protective factors and testing their association with incidence and prevalence of the problem or attribute in the population of interest. Fourth, interventions to influence significant risk and protective factors can be devised and implemented. And finally, changes in morbidity in relation to interventions can be evaluated. In this way, practitioners can make valuable, data-based contributions to remedying problems and promoting solutions to very difficult issues in schools and communities.

Applied Models of Social and Behavioral Epidemiology

Several writers have proposed comprehensive, evidence-based models for conducting analytical epidemiology research in social and behavioral domains. One of the earliest was a framework presented by Coie and others (1993). These frameworks show considerable congruence and may provide school practitioners and trainers with significant guidance to address prevention and wellness promotion in schools and communities. For example, Sallis, Owen, and Fotheringham (2000) suggested that behavioral epidemiology progresses through five phases: (a) conceptualizing links between behavior and outcomes, (b) developing and implementing measures of behaviors, (c) identifying and developing ways to influence behaviors, (d) evaluating these interventions, and (e) using results of this process to guide practice.

Even more relevant to school practitioners are Simeonsson's (1994a) methodological steps for implementing primary prevention for children and youth. These include the following:

1. Operationalize target conditions and risk and protective factors. To be useful to practitioners, researchers, and policy makers, variables of interest must be conceptualized in such a way

that they can be measured and stakeholders can agree on their definition.

2. Generate risk models. A model that hypothesizes the relationship of risk and protective factors to the target outcome, and among risk and protective factors, provides an essential structure for developing, implementing, and evaluating interventions. It is crucial that this model be broad enough to include at least personal, peer, family, school, and community dimensions. A common weakness of school-based prevention programs is focusing almost exclusively on personal factors in risk and resiliency domains, neglecting factors outside of the child in planning and implementing prevention programs.

3. Define risk in terms of child-environment transactions. Because paths in some of the risk models generated in Step 2 are either more relevant to particular settings or easier to address, school practitioner epidemiologists may need to consider carefully characteristics of their particular setting in relation to the population they seek to influence. These considerations should yield reasonable conclusions concerning efficiency and effectiveness of potential interventions.

4. Differentiate the characteristics of universal, selected, and indicated prevention. Although all three levels comprise prevention, different interventions with different samples accrue to different levels of prevention. Epidemiologists should carefully conceptualize and consider these levels in the setting to clarify populations, interventions, and outcomes. Universal-level epidemiology probably will focus on investigating the incidence and prevalence of the outcome of concern in the general population. In this case, identification of individual students or groups of students would not be useful or appropriate. In selected-level epidemiology, identification of subpopulations that exhibit significant risk factors or absence of protective factors is appropriate to target specific groups and to allow for more efficient use of resources. For example, low-SES students likely are at more risk of school failure than higher-SES students. Accordingly, the low-SES student group would be identified for selected prevention programs. Still, individual students would not be identified or targeted for intervention. At the indicated level, the epidemiologic concern lies in identifying

the subpopulation (again, without necessarily identifying individual students) that has begun to exhibit conduct problems.

5. Propose temporal frames. Depending on the outcome to be addressed and the level of prevention, the timing of interventions likely will vary. For example, universal primary prevention for dropping out should be conceptualized to begin no later than the early primary grades, but selected prevention interventions may be most efficacious in late primary or middle grades.

6. Specify and prioritize primary prevention efforts. Prevention activities should be specified and ordered in terms of their major purpose (e.g., reducing risk, enhancing resiliency, managing interactions). Further, because primary prevention occurs at the population level and often becomes diffuse and more difficult to administer than treatment, it is important to define interventions clearly and carefully.

7. Monitor and evaluate prevention outcomes. Because primary prevention deals with populations and not individuals, evaluation often is difficult to implement. Explicit plans to monitor and evaluate risk factors, protective factors, outcomes, and their interaction are crucial to determining the effect on interventions.

Behavioral and Social Epidemiology and School Mental Health: A Natural Congruence

Behavioral and social epidemiology is well-matched to schools and school mental health for several reasons. First, schools increasingly are being held accountable by policy makers and the public for population-wide outcomes such as substance abuse, school violence and bullying, or achievement and school completion. It is increasingly difficult to blame individual students for problems of violence or underachievement, particularly when these phenomena are seen as widespread or generalized. Second, collecting population-wide behavioral and outcome data may be easier in schools than in other community settings; almost all children in the United States attend schools. Third, schools primarily are public, rather than clinical, institutions. In the main, schools provide services to groups of children (i.e., classrooms), rather than to individuals, and tend to make changes school-wide (e.g., choosing a reading curriculum, adopting a character education program)—accordingly, the appropriate unit of analysis is the population. Fourth, a myriad of problems exist for which the major determinants may be demographic. Examples include (a) the black/white achievement gap, (b) the overrepresentation of minorities in special education, and (c) the overrepresentation of minorities receiving disciplinary sanctions. Finally, collection of such data allows for development of much-needed prevention programs and research (Coie et al., 1993). Both practitioners and researchers have identified the need for such research as the highest priority (Strein, Cramer, & Lawser, 2003).

The basic statistical and measurement tools of epidemiology will be familiar to most school practitioners. In fact, the research skills of school mental health professionals likely apply much better to public health activities and epidemiology than to typical school mental health practice because these skills focus on groups rather than individuals. In particular, school psychologists' training at both the specialist and doctoral levels is presumed to include some training in data-based decision making and empirical research methodology. However, school-based psychologists spend far less time in research than any other potential major role, averaging approximately one hour per week, but would prefer a substantial increase in research activity (Hosp & Reschly, 2002). Local epidemiological studies may represent an opportunity for school practitioners to apply their research competencies to practice.

Behavioral and Social Epidemiology in School Practice: An Example

The school mental health literature includes a few examples of the application of epidemiology in schools. Several of these studies focus on medical issues in the school-age populations. For example, Delamater, Bubb, Warren-Boulton, and Fisher (1984) reported on diabetes management and the role of the school psychologist. In their work, they describe incidence and prevalence of diabetes. Horan and Sherman (1988) and Landau, Pryor, and Haefli (1995) address epidemiologic issues associated with HIV and AIDS. Other studies have focused on social and behavioral epidemiology associated with the schools. Doll (1996) and Sullivan and Engin (1986) have addressed the prevalence of psychiatric disorders and implications for school mental health practice. Although these articles provide interesting and helpful examples of the use of epidemiology in school practice, the lack of reports on the integration of such data with interventions remains a significant deficit in our field.

A constructed example of an epidemiologic initiative in school practice is presented below. In this example, we employ the Simeonsson (1994b) epidemiology/prevention framework and the Short and Shapiro (1993) conceptual model for conduct disorders to develop and evaluate a prevention program for conduct disorders. Although the example is fictional, its components are derived from prevention programs developed and implemented by the first author.

The Setting

Hawkins Middle School and its surrounding community were experiencing heightened levels of maladaptive behaviors. Vandalism seemed to increase with every new day, and bullying was a perennial problem in the lunchroom, the halls between classes, and before and after school. Gang activity was evident in graffiti and wearing of colors whenever school officials didn't pay close attention to classrooms and clothing. Parents were beginning to complain about the unsafe environment and tension in the school. After multiple attempts to "crack down" and apprehend perpetrators, school administrators decided to develop a prevention program to address the problem. The superintendent and school board supported the initiative, and the school psychologist volunteered to work on the project.

1. *Operationalize target conditions and risk and protective factors.* Using her skills in research and behavior analysis, the school psychologist interviewed teachers, students, and parents to construct a measurable set of concerns that represented the targets of the program. These included aggressive behaviors (hitting, pushing, tripping, threats, and name-calling), property damage (graffiti and breaking furniture, windows, and equipment), and defiance/disrespect (noncompliance, refusal, and name-calling). Taken together, these dimensions roughly comprise the clinical category of conduct disorder; however, the use of clinical diagnoses is not essential and often not desirable in school settings. Rather, the emphasis should be on identification of clear and measurable targets for intervention. Using the preceding descriptions in collaboration with parents, teachers, and administrators, the school psychologist settled on a criterion of four or more behaviors for inclusion in the conduct problem category. After developing a standard list of the these problem behaviors, the school psychologist asked each teacher to report the number of students in his or her class that exhibited four or more of the behaviors in the last month. In the school population of 560 students, teachers reported a total of 39 students with a behavior score of 4 or

more. Employing the formula presented earlier, the school psychologist determined that the school prevalence rate for conduct problems (as defined by the stakeholders) was about 7% ($39/560 \times 100$). It should be noted here that, at this point, no student had been identified in any way by the school psychologist or the program.

Through a literature search and her own expertise, the school psychologist identified a number of potential risk factors and protective factors associated with conduct problems similar to those reported in Hawkins Middle School. Although a number of these risk and protective factors were associated with characteristics of the students themselves (e.g., impulsivity, alienation), many were peer-related (e.g., pressure to conform, deviant peers), school-based (e.g., perceived unfairness, oppressive rules), family-related (e.g., lack of parent involvement, hostility toward school), and community-based (e.g., lack of social supports, neighborhood disintegration). The school psychologist developed from these factors a list of operationalizations of potential risk and protective factors that likely were associated with conduct problems in Hawkins Middle School, along with ways to measure each factor. These measurements included surveys of students, parents, and school personnel, aggregated data from cumulative records, parent and student attendance records, and systematic analysis of school and community characteristics. Working with the school administration and interested teachers, parents, and community members, the school psychologist coordinated data gathering on these dimensions to determine to what extent they were present in Hawkins Middle School and its catchment area.

2. *Generate risk models.* From her operationalized list of conduct problems and associated measures of risk and protective factors, our school psychologist collaborated with parents, students, administrators, teachers, and support personnel to develop a tentative causal model for conduct problems in Hawkins Middle School. This model comprised a network of risk and protective variables that indicated the site's best guess about how these factors sequenced and interacted to culminate in the conduct problems observed in Hawkins Middle School. From the data gathered in the previous step, the school psychologist and her group developed a risk/protection model based on findings that school rules, student engagement, peer influence, and parent involvement and discipline were clearly associated with levels of conduct problems in Hawkins Middle School. The model integrated existing research and theory on social and behavioral development of conduct problems with stakeholders' expertise about specific characteristics of their setting. Further, the model was comprehensive;

it included both risk and resiliency variables at personal, peer, family, school, and community levels.

3. *Define risk in terms of child/environment transactions.* On careful consideration of all factors in the risk model, the stakeholders decided that school and peer factors, interacting with personal characteristics of disruptive students, represented the most powerful and efficacious explanation for the outcome. Based on the stakeholders' decision, school personnel began to develop a prevention program to decrease risk factors and strengthen protective factors associated with the school, peers, and students exhibiting conduct problems. We note here that selection of personal, peer, or school factors should not be reached solely for political or economic reasons to the exclusion of parent and community variables; that is, stakeholders should consider carefully the etiology of the outcome of concern and select the best possibility for addressing it.

4. *Differentiate the characteristics of universal, selected, and indicated prevention.* As noted earlier, epidemiological strategies differ depending on the level of prevention desired in the program. Accordingly, at the universal level the school psychologist would collect her data to determine what percentage of the population exhibited conduct problems, or what percentage of the population began to exhibit conduct problems, within a particular time frame. At the selected level, our school psychologist would carefully investigate risk and protective factors in the population and identify the subgroup that showed significant risk for developing conduct problems. At the indicated level, the school psychologist might again use the conduct problem list she had developed to determine incidence and prevalence, but she would request that teachers identify students exhibiting four or more of the characteristics on the list. She then would investigate risk and resilience characteristics of the resulting group, making sure to include factors at the personal, peer, school, family, and community levels. Given the nature of the setting, the stakeholders chose to implement an indicated prevention program, which identified the subpopulation of Hawkins Middle School students who exhibited conduct problems. Following identification of the subgroup, the school worked to identify and measure its characteristics that, in interaction with environmental factors (peer, school, family, and community), contributed to the group's problems.

5. *Propose temporal frames.* The stakeholders at Hawkins Middle School, perhaps led by the school psychologist, should determine the most useful and effective point in their students' development to institute prevention programming. This decision will likely be

predicated on the nature of risk and protective factors in the Hawkins Middle School community, the particular risk model chosen for intervention, and the level of prevention selected by the group. Depending on these factors, the school psychologist might suggest a universal primary prevention program focusing on families to begin in kindergarten years; at the indicated prevention level, she might pursue an early middle school program dealing with school and peer concerns. As noted previously, decision makers for the program selected an indicated prevention focus and commissioned the school psychologist and her colleagues to develop a middle school program to deal with peer pressure, perceptions of school unfairness, student alienation, and family discipline.

6. *Specify and prioritize primary prevention efforts.* Primary prevention, being essentially population-based, often suffers from lack of clarity and direction. This is particularly true in light of the fact that most primary prevention activities are implemented by nonprofessionals or professionals not trained in prevention and clinical work. The school psychologist can provide a significant service to the site by working to define carefully interventions and their goals, along with priorities for implementation. Accordingly, the school psychologist surveyed the research literature and selected several preexisting programs to address risk and protective factors associated with the target group. Because demonstrated programs were not available for several of these factors, the school psychologist developed interventions and measures derived from theory and research. Finally, she developed manuals and timelines for all interventions to ensure treatment fidelity.

7. *Monitor and evaluate prevention outcomes.* Although decision makers seemed less interested in measuring compliance and outcomes than in getting a program in place, the school psychologist insisted that evaluation was necessary to determine the success and effectiveness of the program. She argued that many prevention programs have not been shown to be effective, resulting in lost time, effort, and resources for schools and communities. She developed a comprehensive, yet practical, evaluation and monitoring plan that was approved and implemented by the system. The plan involved periodic ongoing measures of the risk and protective factors reported previously, along with monitoring of levels of conduct problems in Hawkins Middle School. Additionally, formative evaluations of intervention implementation and integrity were conducted to facilitate interpretation of any changes in risk/protective factors and conduct problems. Using these data, the school psychologist was able to explore relationships among risk/protective factors, interventions, and conduct problems to provide

information about whether changes occurred in levels of identified risk/protective factors and conduct problems, whether interventions were implemented effectively, and whether interventions were related to changes in risk/protective factors and conduct problems. Also, she was able to determine which risk and protective factors were most relevant to changes in levels of conduct problems.

Social and behavioral epidemiology represents a logical and perhaps necessary extension of school mental health professionals' assessment and research functions. Epidemiology may provide a unique niche for school mental health as schools move toward addressing significant problems in the population. At the least, epidemiology skills provide a mechanism for school practitioners to accomplish the goal to serve all children, departing from the historical emphasis on clinical work with individual children. Used effectively, epidemiology may increase the relevance of school mental health in schools and communities while improving the education, health, and mental health of our children.

Discussion Questions

1. What assessment tools and strategies do you already use that would be useful indicators of when a social or emotional problem was prevalent in your community? What tools and strategies might be useful indicators of which students struggled with a social or emotional problem?

2. What kinds of data do your school already collect that might be useful for an epidemiologic analysis of the social and emotional competence of its students?

3. What is the difference between epidemiologic rates, ratios, and proportions? When might these be important pieces of information to have when planning children's school mental health services?

4. If you were responsible for an epidemiologic assessment in your school, what would be the most challenging and unfamiliar part of this assessment? How would you get the assistance that you needed?

5. Imagine that you were attending a school board meeting to present results of a descriptive epidemiologic study of the mental health of students in your school. What information would be most interesting to the board? How might it shift decisions made by the board?

References

Christensen, S. L., & Thurlow, M. L. (2004). School dropouts: Prevention considerations, interventions, and challenges. *Current Directions in Psychological Science, 13,* 36–39.

Coie, J. D., Watt, N. F., West, S. G., Hawkins, J. D., Asarnow, J. R., Markman, H. J., et al. (1993). The science of prevention: A conceptual framework and some directions for a national research program. *American Psychologist, 48,* 1013–1022.

Delamater, A. M., Bubb, J., Warren-Boulton, E., & Fisher, E. (1984). Diabetes management in the school setting: The role of the school psychologist. *School Psychology Review, 13,* 192–203.

DeVoe, J. F., Peter, K., Kaufman, P., Miller, A., Noonan, M., Snyder, T. D., & Baum, K. (2004). *Indicators of school crime and safety: 2004* (NCES 2005-002/NCJ 205290). U.S. Departments of Education and Justice. Washington, DC: U.S. Government Printing Office.

Doll, B. (1996). Prevalence of psychiatric disorders in children and youth: An agenda for advocacy by school psychology. *School Psychology Quarterly, 11,* 20–46.

Evans, D. L., & Andrews, L. W. (2005). *If your adolescent has depression or bipolar disorder.* New York: Oxford University Press.

Gonzales, P., Guzmán, J. C., Partelow, L., Pahlke, E., Jocelyn, L., Kastberg, D., & Williams, T. (2004). *Highlights from the Trends in International Mathematics and Science Study (TIMSS) 2003* (NCES 2005-005). U.S. Department of Education, National Center for Education Statistics. Washington, DC: U.S. Government Printing Office.

Greene, M. B. (2005). Reducing violence and aggression in schools. *Trauma, Violence, & Abuse, 6,* 236–253.

Horan, P. F., & Sherman, R. A. (1988). School psychologists and the AIDS epidemic. *Professional School Psychology, 3,* 33–49.

Hosp, J. L., & Reschly, D. J. (2002). Regional differences in school psychology practice. *School Psychology Review, 31,* 11–29.

Johnston, L. D., O'Malley, P. M., Bachman, J. G., & Schulenberg, J. E. (2005). *Monitoring the future national results on adolescent drug use: Overview of key findings, 2004.* (NIH Publication No. 05-5726). Bethesda, MD: National Institute on Drug Abuse.

Krieger, N. (2001). A glossary for social epidemiology. *Journal of Epidemiology and Community Health, 55,* 693–700.

Landau, S., Pryor, J. B., & Haefli, K. (1995). Pediatric HIV: School-based sequelae and curricular interventions for infection prevention and social acceptance. *School Psychology Review, 24,* 213–229.

Last, J. M. (1988). *A dictionary of epidemiology* (2nd ed.). New York: Oxford University Press.

Reschly, D. J. & Ysseldyke, J. E. (2002). Paradigm shift: The past is not the future. In A. Thomas & J. Grimes (Eds.), *Best practices in school psychology IV* (pp. 3–20). Bethesda, MD: National Association of School Psychologists.

Sallis, J. F., Owen, N., & Fotheringham, M. J. (2000). Behavioral epidemiology: A systematic framework to classify phases of research on health promotion and disease prevention. *Annals of Behavioral Medicine, 4,* 294–298.

Short, R. J. (2003). School psychology, context, and population-based practice. *School Psychology Review, 32,* 181–184.

Short, R. J., & Brokaw, R. (1994). Externalizing behavior disorders. In R. J. Simeonsson (Ed.), *Risk, resilience, and prevention: Promoting the well-being of all children.* Baltimore: Paul H. Brookes.

Short, R. J., & Shapiro, S. K. (1993). Conduct disorders: A framework for understanding and intervention in schools and communities. *School Psychology Review, 22,* 362–375.

Simeonsson, R. J. (1994a). *Risk, resilience, and prevention: Promoting the well-being of all children.* Baltimore: Paul H. Brookes.

Simeonsson, R. J. (1994b). Toward an epidemiology of developmental, educational, and social problems of childhood. In R. J. Simeonsson (Ed.), *Risk, resilience, and prevention: Promoting the well-being of all children.* Baltimore: Paul H. Brookes.

Strein, W., Cramer, K., & Lawser, M. (2003). School psychology research and scholarship: USA status, international explorations. *School Psychology International, 24,* 421–436.

Strein, W., Hoagwood, K., & Cohn, A. (2003). School psychology: A public health perspective I. Prevention, populations, and systems change. *Journal of School Psychology, 41,* 23–38.

Sullivan, W. O., & Engin, A. W. (1986). Adolescent depression: Its prevalence in high school students. *Journal of School Psychology, 24*(2), 103–109.

Tilley, W. D. III. (2002). Best practices in school psychology as a problem-solving enterprise. In A. Thomas and J. Grimes (Eds.), *Best practices in school psychology IV* (pp. 21–36). Bethesda, MD: National Association of School Psychologists.

U.S. Department of Education, National Center for Education Statistics. [NCES]. (2005a) *State education reform: Standards, assessment, and accountability.* Retrieved September 30, 2005, from http://nces.ed.gov/programs/statereform/saa.asp/

U.S. Department of Education, National Center for Education Statistics [NCES]. (2005b). *The condition of education 2005* (NCES 2005-094). Washington, DC: U.S. Government Printing Office.

Webb, P., Bain, C., & Pirozzo, S. (2005). *Essential epidemiology.* Cambridge, UK: Cambridge University Press.

About the Authors

Rick Jay Short is Associate Dean in the College of Education and Behavioral Sciences, Middle Tennessee State University. His research relates to topics of professional issues in psychology, public health, engagement, and conduct disorders.

William Strein is Associate Professor and Director of the School Psychology program, University of Maryland, College Park. His research is related to prevention and social-emotional learning in K–12 students.

3

Assessing School Risk and Protective Factors

Jean A. Baker

Emelia is a nine-year-old, native Spanish-speaking, Hispanic third-grader who recently transferred into Cedar River Elementary School. She has come to the attention of the school psychologist because of frequent somatic complaints (stomachaches, headaches) occurring late in the morning. Emelia's mother speaks very little English, but the school psychologist discovered that the family has recently become homeless and has temporarily moved in with an aunt following the incarceration of Emelia's stepfather.

Emelia's academic performance is below the class average in all subjects except math, art, and music, for which she has a passion and considerable talent as a vocalist. Her teacher believes that Emelia's English language skills are spotty, and that she could benefit from services for English-language learners. However, those services were reduced in the latest round of budget cuts and it doesn't look promising for Emelia being added to the caseload during this school year.

Emelia has some facial scarring from an accident that occurred when she was a preschooler, and often comes to school appearing dirty and unkempt. When talking with the school psychologist, Emelia revealed that she feels sad "a lot" and that she is teased in the lunchroom and on the playground because of her appearance and her lack of English-language proficiency.

What is "the problem" in Emelia's case—a mental health issue such as depression, academic deficits, or homelessness? Where does the problem reside—within the child, within her recently unstable family system, within the school system that lacks sufficient resources and has a social climate that tolerates bullying on the playground, or within the larger social system that permits families to experience the potentially crushing effects of poverty? Or is it some combination of all of these factors? Further, how many children like Emelia, and with comparable levels of need, exist within this school? How can the school allocate resources to fully understand the mental health needs of all of its students, not just serve them on a case-by-case basis? Furthermore, how can this school or classroom environment be shaped to better support the adaptation and well-being of all of its students? Population-based assessment provides a framework for revealing the multiple, complex, and intersecting factors that influence children's development and can provide a foundation for developing valuable interventions in schools. This chapter highlights some key issues in the assessment of risk and resilience from a population-based perspective, and reviews specific assessment strategies and tools for school-based practice.

Key Issues in Assessing Risk and Resiliency in Populations

Previous chapters have already articulated a rationale for population-based services in schools. In relation to assessment, it is important to note the considerable expertise and experience that school mental health professionals, particularly school psychologists, bring to this new arena. Best practices in school-based assessment highlight the need for sensitivity to measurement issues, issues of bias and culturally appropriate assessments, the ethics governing assessment, and issues of social and ecological validity. These issues are also central to assessment of risk and resilience within school populations.

Population-based assessment of mental health in schools can be conceptualized from a framework of ecological-systems theory (Bronfenbrenner, 1979; Bronfenbrenner & Ceci, 1994). This perspective posits that children are embedded within multiple, mutually influencing systems with which they interact to affect their development.

As children move through time, they become better or less well adapted to the various environmental contexts in which their development unfolds. The developmental competencies and capacities of children, the adequacy of the environmental context and its resources, and the interaction of these dynamic systems together shape adaptation. Assessment within a population-based perspective has three foci: children, the contexts they are in, and the children-within-contexts interactions. In our case example of Emelia, population-based assessments might identify the degree or scope of a social or emotional problem, such as depression-like symptoms or bullying, in the whole school or classroom so that interventions could be targeted effectively. They might include systematic assessments of teachers to identify gaps in services to limited English-language learners or of the community to identify services for homeless or poor families. Within population-based approaches, the traditional focus on individuals broadens to include the contexts within which problems are occurring and to permit interventions at those levels.

In the scope of assessment, population-based approaches may go beyond assessing the need for service so that appropriate interventions can be developed. Whereas the estimated size of the population that will require services defines need, demand is defined by the subset of individuals likely to actually use the services developed (MacMahon & Trichopoulus, 1996). The need for parent training in a school's population may therefore be high, yet the actual number of parents who enroll in school-based parent education classes quite small. Thus, need/demand analysis is the first step in population-based assessments that are linked to service-delivery efforts. Further strategic planning includes assessing the market within which new services will be offered (e.g., does our proposed parent training class replicate services already available in the community), how the school operations would need to change to produce such services (e.g., would the school psychologist's or counselor's work schedule need to be adjusted to accommodate evening programming at the school), and financial analyses (e.g., how can financial resources be shifted to accommodate this new program) (Deprez, 2001). Probes into these areas may thus be included in a comprehensive, data-driven, population-based assessment as part of a program planning initiative.

Models of Population-Based Assessment

Population-based assessments use numerous approaches. Which specific model you select depends on the purposes of the assessment, the size of the population(s) of interest, the available resources, and ethi-cal determinants, such as the cost/benefit ratio, that are discussed in a later section. It is important to note that schools are familiar with some models of population-based assessments. For example, schools are using large-scale, school-wide evaluations of children's reading or mathematical skills with increasing frequency. A population-based perspective on promoting children's thriving within the mental health arena involves expanding this commitment to assessing other domains of children's functioning.

The model school personnel are most likely to be familiar with is large-scale surveying of variables of child behavior, although this is limited to children's academic competencies. Although about 1 in 10 adolescents experiences a social or emotional problem significant enough to impair functioning (USDHHS, 1999), only 2% of American high schools screen all their students, and only 7% screen most of their students for mental health issues (Romer & McIntosh, 2005). Consequently, many children who need services are not involved in systematic processes to identify their needs and refer them to appro-priate services. Furthermore, relatively few teachers are trained to recognize social or emotional problems in children. In the recent nationally stratified Annenberg survey of school-based practices, only 9% of schools reported training all of their teachers, and 12% reported training most of their teachers to recognize such problems (Romer & McIntosh, 2005). Most schools practice the "wait to fail" model of mental health referral, identifying students for mental health services only when problems become significantly impairing. Of course, systematic identification of students evidencing social and emotional problems is only the first step in a clearly defined and coordinated school-based prevention and intervention program. However, school-wide screening is a direct, straightforward method of identifying students at-risk of or already experiencing social and emotional problems.

Within small populations, such as a classroom or a single school, it is possible to survey or screen each individual. For example, children can report on the extent to which bullying is occurring in their school, or teachers can complete behavioral ratings on each child in their class. Reliable, valid paper-and-pencil measures are available commercially and from sources in the public domain. Computerized scoring is available from some publishers or through school-based Scantron-type technology. Surveying can also be done person-to-person, via interviews, with very small populations. Web-based survey software permits delivery and summative scoring of surveys online at no or relatively low cost. Multiple foci are also appropriate for population-based screening. In addition to individual mental health variables, assessment of environmental factors such as the school's social climate or available resources, can also be conducted.

Survey approaches for mental health assessments are often multigated or multistaged procedures, in which the initial screening of the entire population is followed with more in-depth evaluation of individuals or groups selected by their scores according to some criterion. (See Mazza & Reynolds, this volume, for an example of a multigated screening for depression and suicidal behavior among adolescents.) Results from the population-based assessment are used to develop supportive or preventive programming at the universal level, whereas the next stages of assessment data funnel children into selected or targeted services. This multistaged procedure affords efficiencies when the goals of assessment include identifying children or groups of children manifesting specific types or levels of behavior.

For larger populations, such as a school district, survey methods often require sampling. Stratified random sampling, a procedure familiar to most school mental health practitioners, involves identifying pertinent characteristics within the population (e.g., grade level, gender, race) and sampling at random within those strata until the sample approximates the characteristics of the population. For a school system of 50,000 students, a stratified sampling procedure could identify 1% or 5% of students who mirror the larger population and could be affordably screened by individual measures. Decisions regarding population-based services could then be developed based on these population estimates. Other epidemiologic survey methods can be used in large populations. One example is two-stage cluster surveying, in which subgroups of interest are identified (e.g., third-grade classrooms), at least 30 are selected using probability proportionate to size sampling, and then a constant number within each cluster (e.g., children within classrooms) are selected at random (see MacMahon, & Trichopoulus, 1996). Software to design such data collection is available (e.g., Centers for Disease Control, 2002; UCLA, 2005). However, statistical and epidemiologic consultation is warranted for such large-scale projects. Representational sampling approaches are used for purposes of program development, for example, to understand the need for bully prevention programs or food assistance programs within the population, not to identify individual children in need of targeted services. Additionally, the results of representational sampling can be the springboard for further direct assessment of subgroups. For example, high levels of self-reported bullying among the representative sample of middle school students in the population may provide sufficient rationale to survey each student at the middle school level.

In contrast to survey assessment models that collect ratings directly from individuals within the population, community collaboration assessment models involve key stakeholders or representatives of the population as participants (Berkowitz, 2000). Frequently, focus group methods (Krueger & Casey, 2000) are used to identify perceived needs, available resources, and preferences for services within the population. Focus groups involve key stakeholders in structured discussions about the topic of interest—in this case, the mental health characteristics or needs of the population. For example, selected school personnel, parents, and students could be invited to separate focus groups to identify the extent of a bullying problem at a school and brainstorm potential solutions to that problem. Decision makers at the school can then synthesize the results of these focus group discussions and plan programs accordingly. This process can enhance trust and activate the commitment of key stakeholders to mutual problem solving or new programs developed by school personnel (Thompson & Kinne, 1990). Key stakeholders are also likely to be aware of local resources and assets that can be used in program development efforts. These stakeholders can serve as members of a planning or implementation team, thus ensuring that programs are reviewed for acceptability by members of the communities for which they are intended.

On the other hand, focus group methods use indirect data in the form of perceptions of the issue by key stakeholders, and so may misrepresent the nature or extent of the identified concern. Furthermore, key stakeholders may be sufficiently different from the population at large to not adequately reflect its needs or desires. Focus group methods are often used in the initial stages of an assessment process, and their data are combined with other sources to inform program development.

An additional strategy is to assess indicators or markers of the variable of interest within the population. Markers include permanent products, such as disciplinary records in the assessment of bullying in a school, and known demographic or base-rate data, such as the proportion of students participating in the free or reduced-cost lunch program as an indicator of poverty in a school. Analysis of the patterns and variability in these existing data can inform the appropriate distribution of further assessment or program development resources. For example, high levels of disciplinary referrals from particular classrooms may indicate the need for individual surveying of bullying from students in those classrooms and the implementation of more intensive classroom-level programming. Further, such data should encourage the school to examine the ecological context of the problem at that level. For example, spikes in levels of bullying in ninth grade may suggest problems of social integration as children enter high school. This kind of ecological analysis may suggest the need to reform the ninth-grade experience to promote social cohesion (Felner et al., 1993) or implement school-wide programming to prevent bullying.

Each of these methods has strengths and weaknesses. Survey methods provide the most direct assessments, yet require significant commitments of time, personnel, and financial resources. Focus group methods rely on informant perceptions, and thus may not accurately represent the needs or assets in the larger population. Examining existing data is convenient but provides only distal, static information about the dynamic processes of risk and adaptation at work in the population. In actual practice, many methods are needed to form a comprehensive assessment of a population. Appraisal of base-rate data may lead to initial problem formulation or elaboration within the context of a focus group, which then could result in targeted direct assessment via survey methods. Multi-method, multi-rater assessments across methods and informants and triangulation of data are valuable in population-based approaches.

Assessing Risk, Resilience, and Protective Factors Within Populations

An important focus for population-based mental health assessment in schools is the degree to which children are thriving in the school environment. Thriving results when individual hardiness and adaptability variables (e.g., psychological characteristics and competencies), combined with protective factors embedded in socializing institutions (e.g., the availability of social supports or creative opportunities in the school environment), are sufficient to overcome the potential harm derived from risk factors in the child's environment (Bonnano, 2004; Luthar, Cicchetti, & Becker, 2000). Comprehensive population-based assessment is the process of understanding how these three vectors of personal resilience, environmental protection, and risk exposure intersect within the school setting. Assessment often includes the level and type of risk that students experience, the individual capacities and competencies they bring to the adaptation process, and the amount and type of resources available in their environment to support adaptation. The latter two factors are sometimes grouped together in the literature as internal and external components of resilience, and sometimes both are termed protective factors. Here, they will be discussed separately as resilience and protective factors to distinguish between inner resources and external assets, respectively.

This commitment to understanding the ecology within which problems emerge is especially important for school-based service provision efforts. Many schools cannot directly reduce the risk factors to which their students are exposed (e.g., parental psychopathology, poverty). However, they can devote resources to interventions that increase children's adaptive competencies and maximize children's exposure to protective factors.

It is also important to note that risk, resilience, and environmental protection are dynamic processes affecting development. Individual or external assets buffer the effects of risk if they are present in sufficient quantity and are readily accessible when needed. They are also idiosyncratic; assets that may be sufficient to protect one child from the deleterious effects of stress may be inadequate to protect another. Thus, the interplay between the assets and capacities of the child, and the opportunities and constraints of the environment, must be understood as dynamic and contextually sensitive (Bronfenbrenner & Ceci, 1994; Masten & Coatsworth, 1998). Population-based appraisal can give an overall estimate of the strengths, resources, and needs in an extant group, but considerable individual variability exists regarding how those factors interact within the population.

Assessing Risk Factors

Risk factors are the internal and environmental characteristics that place children at risk for poor developmental outcomes (Doll & Lyon, 1998; Rutter, 1979). Numerous factors have been identified in the research literature, and often include factors at the child level, such as a difficult temperament or early antisocial behavior; at the family level, including poor parental bonding, inconsistent discipline, or parental pathology; at the school level, including academic failure, poor bonding to school, or multiple school transitions; and at the community level, such as low socioeconomic status (SES) or high population density. Various risk factors are associated with specific deleterious outcomes. For example, although low SES is associated with poor outcomes for many children, adding easy access to weapons, witnessing of acts of violence, affiliation with antisocial peers, and community poverty is differentially predictive of increased violence in youth (Cohen & Swift, 1993). Children are placed at risk of poor developmental outcomes when these environmental stressors overwhelm their capacity to cope effectively or the capacity of caretakers to protect them from the effects of these stressors.

One example of population-based risk assessment is a recent survey of students in elementary schools serving children living in poverty (Baker, Kamphaus, Horne, & Winsor, 2006). We conducted a wide-scale behavioral needs assessment by asking teachers to complete a broadband behavior rating scale for each child in their classroom. Children with early behavior problems are at tremendous differential risk for poor school adjustment. They transition poorly to school, and perform less well on academic, social, and interpersonal indicators of school adjustment than peers without behavioral difficulties (Ladd, 1996). Without appropriately targeted and early intervention efforts, these children's poor adjustment to schooling becomes compounded. Therefore, we were interested in screening the behavioral adjustment of all students in the participating schools.

Because we were screening young children, who tend to be unreliable reporters of behavioral problems, we used teacher ratings to assess the behavioral adjustment of this population. Teachers are known to be reliable raters of observable behavior associated with mental health problems and educational maladjustment (Verhulst, Koot, & Van der Ende, 1994). Teachers received release-time from teaching and were compensated for their participation in this project; they reported completing the assessments for the students in their classrooms in the equivalent of up to one work day (approximately 6 to 8 hours). Profiles of the behavioral adjustment within each classroom, including the proportion of students displaying typical, mild, moderate, and severe behavioral problems, were shared with the teachers and school staff. These profiles were then used to design professional development programs for teachers, to redeploy resources toward classrooms with higher levels of need, and to tailor classroom-based interventions according to the type of behavioral needs manifest in specific classrooms. For example, one first-grade classroom teacher with a high percentage of very active, impulsive students adapted a number of cognitive-behavioral intervention strategies into her classroom management system to teach self-control, including the "Turtle Technique" (Robin, Schneider, & Dolnick, 1976). Within several weeks of introducing this strategy into general classroom use, all students, including the typically developing children, were "turtling" to give themselves time to calm down and think through a problem situation as an alternative to impulsive responding. Students displaying high degrees of behavioral risk were also referred for further assessment to the school's psychologist.

This example illustrates several important points regarding population-based risk assessment and subsequent service delivery. First, "risk" was defined in reference to research-validated factors associated with poor school adaptation. Second, a method (screening using reliable and valid survey measures) and the appropriate informants (teachers) were chosen in light of the characteristics of the population. Third, the cost/benefit ratio was carefully considered, and resources were redirected so that personnel could complete the behavioral screening. Fourth, local data were used as the basis for intervention planning. In this high-risk population, the screening data suggested that 56% of students needed either selected or indicated prevention services. Generic three-tier service models often suggest a much lower need for such services. Our use of local data permitted more sensitive interventions than would be possible from more generic models. Fifth, interventions designed to promote adaptive functioning of all children, such as increased knowledge of cognitive-behavioral coping techniques, were made available to all children by being delivered at the classroom level. Finally, the assessment was linked to an intervention process so that the local data generated within each school led to appropriately tailored interventions.

The previous example used a commercially available behavior rating scale. Assessment tools are available commercially or in the public domain for a variety of individual risk factors, such as drug/alcohol use, specific forms of social or emotional problems such as aggression or depression, or deficient social processes such as poor bonding to the school environment. The latter example, poor school bonding, is associated with deleterious outcomes for students including delinquency, drug and alcohol use, and poor school adjustment. An eight-item self-report measure of school attachment and commitment for children, developed for use in the Seattle Social Development Project, has adequate psychometric characteristics for elementary and secondary students, and good predictive validity (Hawkins, Guo, Hill, & Battin-Pearson, 2001). Such brief measures can be incorporated into school-wide screenings of students' adjustment. (See Wolfe, 2006, for a variety of publicly available measures.)

Risk not only resides within children, but may also be a characteristic of the social environment. Comprehensive screening should include aspects of the social or physical environment that place children at risk.

These include characteristics of relationships such as poor social support, the lack of caring or mentoring relationships with adults, negative peer relationships, hostile school or family climate, and exposure to violence at school or in the community. One such example is screening for bullying and victimization at school. For example, the *Bully Buster's* program (Horne, Bartolomucci, & Newman-Carlson, 2000) provides self-report inventories for children to report their exposure to or participation in bullying behavior in schools. These assessment measures are linked to a classroom-level intervention in the form of teacher-directed lessons for elementary and middle school students regarding the nature of bullying, alternatives to aggression, victimization response strategies, and strategies for observers of peer-directed violence within schools. This program is a research-based example of survey assessment of a specific environmental risk (e.g., exposure to violence in the school setting) and a targeted, population-based prevention program delivered at the classroom level. The program targets the social climate because it includes strategies for *all* students in the school: those bullying others, those who are the targets of such aggression, and the majority of students who witness such events.

Lack of access to physical resources such as food, clothing, or safety may also be included in comprehensive assessments of environmental risk. For example, many urban schools uncover subpopulations of homeless children when screenings include questions regarding housing and predictable access to food. Knowledge of this population-based need may lead to better coordination between schools and community-based providers of services for homeless families, school-linked shelters, and food distribution programs.

Risk factors are often presented as static variables, such as poverty or homelessness in Emilia's case example. Therefore, it is tempting to use summary statistics such as the number of children living in poverty within a school as a measure of risk within the building. Children's responses to risk are highly individualistic, however, and are negotiated in reference to their own strengths and the supports available to them within the environment. In Emelia's case, the disruption of her social network or effective parenting processes, or the lack of adequate basic resources such as shelter and food, rather than the homelessness per se, place her at increased risk of dysfunction. Further, the effects of exposure to risk differ depending on in what developmental stage they occur and in which social context they are manifest. Consequently, although summary or base-rate statistics can be used as a proxy for risk, the actual response to risk within a population should be assessed directly.

Assessing Resilience Factors

Resilience refers to the process of positive adaptation in the face of significant stress or adversity (Luthar et al., 2000). Resilience research focuses on predictable and alterable characteristics, mechanisms, and interactive processes that enable some high-risk students to succeed despite unfavorable circumstances (Doll & Lyon, 1998). In the literature, a distinction is often made between internal competencies of the child and supports in the external environment. For this discussion, these are termed resilience and environmental protection, respectively. Both factors buffer children from the adverse effects of risk or stress in the environment if they are of sufficient magnitude and duration or timed appropriately so that children can access them when needed (Masten & Coatsworth, 1998).

Numerous dispositional characteristics and skills have been associated with resilience. These include intelligence, psychological hardiness, an easy temperament, and skills that predispose children toward adaptive coping, such as good social and problem-solving skills (Bernard, 1991; Luthar et al., 2000; Masten, Best, & Garmezy, 1990). Several taxonomies have been developed to characterize these resilience factors (Table 3.1). However, none of them has widespread acceptance or empirical justification as the definitive classification of human assets. Within the positive psychology literature, a classification of human strengths and virtues has been developed to parallel the diagnostic taxonomies of mental health problems so well known to psychologists (Seligman, 2002). This work clusters 24 internal assets that promote positive adaptation under 6 main virtues. The Collaborative for Academic, Social, and Emotional Learning (CASEL, 2006) has defined a set of 6 overarching competencies, consisting of 14 adaptive skills that contribute to positive school adjustment and well-being. This taxonomy has strengths in that it is research based and has been developed specifically for child- and school-based applications (Zins, Weissberg, Wang, & Walberg, 2004). The Character Education movement identifies core ethical values and further defines specific character traits associated with each virtue. Although diversity exists within this educational initiative, the Aspen Declaration on Character Education attempted to achieve consensus on 6 core values common to democratic societies (Josephson Institute on Ethics, 2006). However, these lists are derived from ethics as a branch of philosophy rather than from the scientific research literature. Finally, the Search Institute's Developmental Assets model (Scales & Leffert, 1999) defines 20 internal and 20 external assets associated with positive child adaptation. This model is discussed more

Table 3.1   Taxonomies of Resilience Factors

Source	Resilience Dimension	Sample Characteristics
Seligman (2002)	6 main virtues	24 internal assets
	Wisdom/knowledge	Curiosity, love of learning, critical thinking
	Courage	Bravery, perseverance, integrity
	Humanity/love	Kindness, generosity
	Justice	Citizenship, fairness, leadership
	Temperance	Self-control, discretion, humility
	Transcendence	Appreciation of beauty, hope, spirituality
CASEL (2006)	6 composite skills	14 skill clusters
	Self-awareness	Identifying emotions, recognizing strengths
	Social awareness	Perspective-taking, appreciating diversity
	Self-management	Managing emotions, goal setting,
	Responsible decision making	Analyzing situations, assuming personal responsibility, respecting others, problem solving
	Relationship skills	Communication, relationship building, negotiation, refusal
Character Education (Josephson Institute, 2006)	6 core ethical values	Example values
	Responsibility	Perseverance, self-control, accountability
	Trustworthiness	Honesty, reliability, loyalty
	Justice and fairness	Open-mindedness, equity
	Caring	Kindness, compassion
	Civic virtue and citizenship	Cooperation, civic involvement, environmental protection
Developmental Assets (Scales & Leffert, 1999; Search Institute, 2005a)	4 overarching themes: internal assets	20 internal assets
	Commitment to learning	Achievement motivation, bonding to adults at school
	Positive values	Caring, equality, integrity
	Social competencies	Planning and decision making, cultural competence
	Positive identity	Self-esteem, positive view of the future
	4 overarching themes: external assets	20 external assets
	Support	Positive family communication, caring neighborhood
	Empowerment	Safety, community values children
	Clear boundaries and expectations	Adult role models, family boundaries, positive peer influence
	Constructive use of time	Creative activities, community programs

fully in a later section. In sum, several research or educational traditions provide guidance regarding aspects of resilience that could be assessed as part of a population-based evaluation (see Baker, Dilly, Aupperlee, & Patil, 2003, for further discussion).

Many tools are readily available to assess the assets and strengths of a population. Both broadband measures, such as behavior rating scales that include positive markers of development, and narrowband measures, such as inventories for social skills or self-esteem, are familiar to and readily available to school mental health professionals. These tools are available from commercial publishers or Web-based sources (see Wolfe, 2006) or are available within the public domain (see Lopez & Snyder, 2003). Three approaches are described in more detail in this section.

The school-wide screening example discussed in the previous section included assessment of students' competencies, since aspects of positive behavior were included on the broadband behavior rating scale completed by teachers (see Baker et al., 2006). Measures of student's social skills, leadership skills, adaptability, and study skills were included on the measure we used. Again, this model is most appropriate for small populations, because it required extensive time commitments from teachers. However, data were available at the individual level and could be used to tailor individual in addition to class- or school-wide programs.

The most popular large-scale screening of strengths and competencies is the developmental assets approach. Scales & Leffert (1999) describe developmental assets as "positive relationships, opportunities, competencies, values and self-perceptions that children need to succeed" (p. vii). This model identifies 40 assets that fall into the two broad categories of internal and external resources (see Table 3.1). Scales and Leffert's concept of internal resources is consistent with the resiliency framework. These lists are tailored for various age groups. Self-report surveys are available for children across the entire age range of schooling. Additionally, there is a school climate survey for both students and staff. Computerized scoring of the surveys permits rapid turnaround of the data that can be used for school-wide planning because it's aggregated at the school level. Training material to introduce the survey model and its content, and to help parents and teachers understand the findings, are also available to download from the publisher's website (see Search Institute, 2005b). Despite the popularity of this model, there is little research to substantiate the importance of each of the 40 assets, or to help schools prioritize which assets to emphasize in school-based programming.

Doll and her colleagues (2004) have developed a classwide screening model of three individual assets critical to resilience within academic settings. Their ClassMaps survey assesses academic efficacy, behavioral self-control, and academic self-determination among elementary and middle school children. Children complete reliable, short self-report surveys of these constructs associated with successful school functioning. The data are aggregated at the class level. Their model includes an intervention component in which the data are reported back to students within the context of a class meeting. Students and teachers then collaborate to effect change within the classroom to promote resilience. Although this model also requires considerable investment of resources, its reliance on local data, its focus on the classroom as the unit of change, and its empowerment of students to learn about and contribute to effecting change provide a good practical example of linkages between assessment and intervention at the population level. The ClassMaps model also includes three protective factors in the classroom environment that are discussed in the next section.

Assessing Protective Factors

Protective factors are the aspects of social and physical environment that promote children's positive development. Many such factors have been identified, including caring relationships with others, family support, family engagement with schooling, the availability of prosocial role models, safe neighborhoods, clear and high expectations within the community, and school environments characterized by coherence, warmth, instructional excellence, and academic rigor (Luthar et al., 2000). Children's well-being is promoted when these protective factors become embedded in socializing institutions such as schools, making them readily available resources with which children can interact (Baker et al., 2003; Bonnano, 2004; Park & Peterson, 2003).

The potentially protective effects of positive school environments are illustrated by several examples. Structural aspects such as school or class size have direct effects on children's achievement outcomes. Reducing elementary class size to 15 to 20 students is directly related to academic gains, especially for younger students and those in urban schools (Slavin, 1989). In all probability, this effect occurs because of the increased opportunities in smaller classes for personalized instruction, monitoring of student progress, and time on task. Related to attitudinal outcomes of schooling, significant gains in children's intrinsic motivation, prosocial attitudes, and altruistic behavior are associated with the development of an intentional classroom community characterized by warmth and cooperation, developmentally appropriate student autonomy, instructional approaches that emphasize authentic and active learning, and an explicit focus on prosocial values (Battistich, Schaps, Watson, & Solomon, 1996). The degree to which the environment is tailored to support the development of children's competencies is a critical variable in population-based service provision and should be routinely measured in comprehensive assessments.

The World Health Organization (WHO, 2003) defined a healthy school environment as one that emphasizes active learning in a climate characterized by interpersonal warmth, equity, cooperation, and open communication. Healthy school environments permit creativity among learners and are free of violence at all levels. They bridge to students' home communities by involving parents and permitting authentic participation in democratic or decision-making processes by stakeholders. The WHO's (2003) *Psycho-Social Profile (PSE) Profile Questionnaire* assesses these areas of effective school environments. The measure consists of 114 Likert-type items drawn from an international review of the literature on components of health-promoting schools. It was piloted in 20 countries, and is intended to provide a descriptive starting point for school improvement initiatives. It is completed by adults (staff, parents) and scored by calculating the average scores for each of the seven quality areas. The measure was developed as part of the WHO's global school health initiative and can be used in concert with other assessments and advocacy tools available from their website (2006).

Adelman and Taylor (2006; and see chapter 11, this volume) have conceptualized a set of six interacting characteristics of a school environment that enable students to benefit maximally from good quality instruction. Termed "learning supports," these include classroom and curricular adaptations and modifications, a prevention orientation that promotes healthy development and early intervention in crisis situations, a welcoming and caring school community that provides continuity and support for students and families across school transitions, family involvement, community outreach and engagement, and systems to provide specific interventions to students and families. Associated with each of these learning supports is an assessment tool that can be used as part of a school self-study or improvement process. For example, the Classroom-Based Approaches Survey covers six areas of classroom functioning, with items ranging from instructional strategies (e.g., "Is instruction personalized?") to teacher professional development (e.g., "Are teachers clustered for support and staff development?") to classroom climate (e.g., "Are there classroom approaches for supporting high standards of positive behavior?"). A 4-point Likert-type response format permits staff members to rate the degree to which each item is occurring or is desired for the school. In addition to the six learning supports surveys, self-study tools are available to assess how resource staff, including the school psychologist, are deployed and the administrative structures needed to promote and sustain the enabling factors. Adelman and Taylor (2006) provide strategies for mapping, analyzing, and enhancing school resources, and additional strategies are available online at the Center for Mental Health in Schools website (UCLA School Mental Health Project, 2006).

The *ClassMaps* surveys (Doll et al., 2004) described in a previous section include three scales that permit children to rate the relational characteristics of their school environments. Social support and caring relationships are consistently associated with positive outcomes for children in resiliency studies. Children rate the quality of their relationships with their teachers and with their peers, and the degree to which parents support and are involved with their child's schooling on brief (7 or 8 items), self-report surveys. Doll and her colleagues report adequate internal consistency reliabilities for the three scales in an elementary sample (all Cronbach's alpha reliabilities above .70) and for two of the subscales in a middle school sample. In that study, the internal consistency reliability for the peer relationships scale was .56 (Doll et al., 2004). As mentioned previously, the *ClassMaps* strategy involves an intervention component in which data aggregated at the classroom level is shared with students within the context of a class meeting. The classroom community then sets goals to improve aspects of the classroom environment that receive low ratings. Thus, these assessment results can be used to reinforce children's sense of personal agency and autonomy as they take responsibility for shaping their learning environment.

School-wide screening of protective factors is included with the Search Institute's Developmental Assets surveys (Scales & Leffert, 1999; Search Institute, 2005b). Twenty of the 40 resources identified as important to positive development are categorized as protective factors or "external assets" (see Table 3.1). As discussed in the previous section, these surveys are designed for large-scale administrations, are available commercially, and are computer scored by the publisher.

Ethical Issues in Population-Based Assessment

All of the familiar ethical issues related to individual appraisals apply to population-based assessments. Assessment practices must be fair, culturally appropriate, of clear benefit to the population, and conducted with appropriate protections for the confidentiality of individual respondents (Jacob & Hartshorne, 2002). This is especially pertinent in population-based screening in the arena of mental health, because of the stigma associated with psychiatric problems (Penn et al., 2005; Sudhir, Fabienne, & Amartya, 2004). Similarly, ethical issues pertaining to assessment methods, including the dependence on reliable, valid, and culturally appropriate measures, are familiar to school psychologists.

Population-based assessment and services foreground several ethical challenges for schools moving toward prevention models of practice (Anand, Peter, & Sen, 2004). First, there are moral aspects to decisions regarding how to allocate finite resources within institutions. Deciding whom to help, or whom to assess, involves careful consideration of cost/benefit and cost/effectiveness analyses. These decisions are always value-laden. For example, school-wide screening redirects the time of counselors, school psychologists, and social workers engaged in school-based counseling from individuals to the whole group of students, many of whom may not need services. Given psychology's historical allegiance to the individual (Prilleltensky, 1994), personnel may be uncomfortable with this shift because it requires some reappraisal of the value of these two activities.

Furthermore, population-based practices pull at our notions of distributive justice. If we truly value each child equally, and treat all equitably, then each child deserves resources appropriate to his or her needs. And, if we believe that schools are the only equitable and accessible site for all children to receive mental health attention, then prevention-oriented, population-based approaches should be welcomed as consistent with the mission of schooling. However, our "wait-to-fail, refer, test, place" paradigm in schools suggests another prevailing notion—serving the most needy children with high-intensity services. In an era of shrinking resources, this model may be insufficient. For example, in the urban study previously mentioned (Baker et al., 2006), 17% of the children in the first through fifth grades had pervasive, severe externalizing behavior problems, coupled with significant learning problems and poor prosocial competencies. Yet, only a third of these children were being served through the special education system. Another 10% of the students showed at-risk profiles for significant academic problems, but only 35% of them were receiving individualized educational services. This degree of behavioral and academic variability and demand far exceeds the capacity of refer-test-place practice models.

Population-based approaches seem a viable alternative to this individually oriented model. However, shifting our model of practice requires careful attention to the values and ethical underpinnings of the work. Making these subtle moral, value-laden, and ethical aspects of practice explicit is likely to assist staff as they transform their school cultures to support new population-based models of practice (Sarason, 1996).

Summary

In an era of increasing complexity in society, how do we appropriately respond to the Emelias who walk through our schoolhouse doors? One strategy is to recognize that schools have a fundamental role to play in promoting the adaptation and well-being of all children. They may be the only societal institution in which mental health services can be equitably distributed. Systematic, population-based assessment of those children's mental health needs, assets, and resources is an integral aspect of schooling to promote children's mental health. When these assessments are linked to appropriate services delivered at the classroom or school level, schools help all children, including those like Emelia, to thrive.

Discussion Questions

1. What assessment tools and strategies do you already know that would be useful for the assessment of students' risk and protective factors? What information does your school district already collect that could be useful in a population-based assessment?

2. If you were placed in charge of a population-based assessment in your school, what aspect of this task would be most challenging and unfamiliar for you?

3. How would the current roles of school psychologists in your district change if they were to assess risk and protective factors in the district's students?

4. What benefit might accrue to your school if population-based data were available when key decisions were being made about the school's services? Are there any disadvantages to your school having this kind of data about its students?

5. How could a school balance the allocation of finite resources between the population-based assessments described in this chapter and the conventional assessments that are already conducted in the district?

References

Adelman, H. S., & Taylor, L. (2006). *Student learning supports: New directions for addressing barriers to learning.* Thousand Oaks, CA: Corwin Press.

Anand, S., Peter, F., & Sen, A. (2004). *Public health, ethics, and equity.* Oxford, UK: Oxford University Press.

Baker, J. A., Dilly, L., Aupperlee, J., & Patil, S. (2003). The developmental context of school satisfaction: Schools as psychologically healthy environments. *School Psychology Quarterly, 18,* 206–222.

Baker, J. A., Kamphaus, R. W., Horne, A. M., & Winsor, A. (2006). Evidence for population-based perspectives on children's behavioral adjustment and needs for service delivery in schools. *School Psychology Review, 35,* 31–46.

Battistich, V., Schaps, E., Watson, M., & Solomon, D. (1996). Prevention effects of the Child Development Project: Early findings from an ongoing multisite demonstration trial. *Journal of Adolescent Research, 11,* 12–35.

Berkowitz, B. (2000). Collaboration for health improvement: Models for state, community, and academic partnerships. *Journal of Public Health Management Practice, 6,* 67–72.

Bernard, B. (1991). *Fostering resiliency in kids: Protective factors in the family, school and community.* San Francisco: Far West Laboratory.

Bonnano, G. A. (2004). Loss, trauma, and human resilience: Have we underestimated the human capacity to thrive after extremely aversive events? *American Psychologist, 59,* 20–28.

Bronfenbrenner, U. (1979). *The ecology of human development: Experiments by nature and design.* Cambridge, MA: Harvard University Press.

Bronfenbrenner, U., & Ceci, S. J. (1994). Nature-nurture reconceptualized: A bio-ecological model. *Psychological Review, 101,* 568–586.

Centers for Disease Control. (2002). *Epidemiology Program Office: Software.* Retrieved March 6, 2006, from http://www.cdc.gov/epo/pub_sw.htm

Cohen, L., & Swift, S. (1993). A public health approach to the violence epidemic in the United States. *Environment and Urbanization, 5,* 50–66.

Collaborative for Academic, Social, and Emotional Learning (CASEL). (2006). *Introduction to SEL: SEL competencies.* Retrieved March 6, 2006, from http://www.casel.org/about_sel/SELskills.php

Deprez, R. (2001). *Population-based assessment as the backbone of healthcare services planning.* Portland, ME: Public Health Resources Group. Retrieved February 2, 2006, from http://www.phrg.com/planning_article.php

Doll, B., & Lyon, M. A. (1998). Risk and resilience: Implications for the delivery of educational and mental health services in schools. *School Psychology Review, 27*, 348–363.

Doll, B., Zucker, S., & Brehm, K. (2004). *Resilient classrooms: Creating healthy environments for learning.* New York: Guilford.

Felner, R. D., Brand, S., Adan, A. M., Mulhall, P. F., Flowers, N., Sartain, B., et al. (1993). Restructuring the ecology of the school as an approach to prevention during school transitions: Longitudinal follow-ups and extensions of the School Transition Environment Project (STEP). *Prevention in Human Services, 10*, 103–136.

Hawkins, J. D., Guo, J., Hill, K. G., & Battin-Pearson, S. (2001). Long term effects of the Seattle Social Development Intervention on school bonding trajectories. *Applied Developmental Science, 5*, 225–236.

Horne, A. M., Bartolomucci, C. L., & Newman-Carlson, D. (2000). *Bully busters: A teacher's manual for helping bullies, victims, and bystanders.* Champaign, IL: Research Press.

Jacob, S., & Hartshorne, T. S. (2002). *Ethics and law for school psychologists* (4th ed.). New York: John Wiley & Sons.

Josephson Institute on Ethics. (2006). The Aspen Declaration on Character Education. Retrieved March 3, 2006, from http://www.charactercounts .org/aspen.htm

Krueger, R. A., & Casey, M. A. (2000). *Focus groups: A practical guide for applied research* (3rd ed.) Thousand Oaks, CA: Sage.

Ladd, G. W. (1996). Shifting ecologies during the 5 to 7 year period: Children's adjustment during the transition to grade school. In A. J. Sameroff & M. M. Haith (Eds.), *The five to seven year shift* (pp. 363–386). Chicago: University of Chicago Press.

Lopez, S. J., & Snyder, C. R. (2003). *Positive psychological assessment: A handbook of models and measures.* Washington, DC: American Psychological Association.

Luthar, S. S., Cicchetti, D., & Becker, B. (2000). The construct of resilience: A critical evaluation and guidelines for future work. *Child Development, 71*, 543–562.

MacMahon, B., & Trichopoulos, D. (1996). *Epidemiology: Principles and methods.* Boston: Little, Brown.

Masten, A. S., Best, K. M., & Garmezy, N. (1990). Resilience and development: Contributions for the study of children who overcome adversity. *Development and Psychopathology, 2*, 425–444.

Masten, A. S., & Coatsworth, J. D. (1998). The development of competence in favorable and unfavorable environments: Lessons from research on successful children. *American Psychologist, 53*, 205–220.

Park, N., & Peterson, C. (2003). Virtues and organizations. In K. S. Cameron, J. E. Dutton, & R. E. Quinn (Eds.), *Positive organizational scholarship: Foundations of a new discipline* (pp. 33–47). San Francisco: Berrett-Koehler.

Penn, D. L., Judge, A., Jamieson, P., Garczynski, J., Hennessy, M., & Romer, D. (2005). Stigma. In D. L. Evans, E. B. Foa, R. E. Gur, H. Hendin, C. P. O'Brien, M. E. P. Seligman, et al. (Eds.), *Treating and preventing adolescent mental health disorders: What we know and what we don't know, A research agenda for improving the mental health of our youth* (pp. 532–543). Oxford, UK: Oxford University Press.

Prilleltensky, I. (1994). *The morals and politics of psychology: Psychological discourse and the status quo.* Albany: State University of New York Press.

Robin, A., Schneider, M., & Dolnick, M. (1976). The turtle technique: An extended case study of self-control in the classroom. *Psychology in the Schools, 13,* 449–453.

Romer, D., & McIntosh, M. (2005). The roles and perspectives of school mental health professionals in promoting adolescent mental health. In D. L. Evans, E. B. Foa, R. E. Gur, H. Hendin, C. P. O'Brien, M. E. P. Seligman, & B. T. Walsh (Eds.), *Treating and preventing adolescent mental health disorders: What we know and what we don't know, A research agenda for improving the mental health of our youth* (pp. 597–616). Oxford: Oxford University Press.

Rutter, M. (1979). Protective factors in children's responses to stress and disadvantage. In M. W. Kent & J. E. Rolf (Eds.), *Primary prevention of psychopathology. Social competence in children* (Vol. 3, pp. 49–74). Hanover, NH: University Press of New England.

Sarason, S. B. (1996). *Revisiting "The culture of the school and the problem of change."* New York: Teachers College Press.

Scales, P. C., & Leffert, N. (1999). *Developmental assets.* Minneapolis: Search Institute.

Search Institute. (2005a). *40 developmental assets for middle childhood.* Retrieved March 3, 2006, from http://www.search-institute.org/assets/Middle Childhood.html

Search Institute. (2005b). *Search Institute survey services.* Retrieved March 3, 2006, from http://www.search-institute.org/surveys/

Seligman, M. E. P. (2002). *Authentic happiness.* New York: Free Press.

Slavin, R. E. (Ed.). (1989). *School and classroom organization.* Hillside, NJ: Lawrence Erlbaum Associates.

Sudhir, A., Fabienne, P., & Amartya, S. (2004). *Public health, ethics, and equity.* Oxford, UK: Oxford University Press.

Thompson, B., & Kinne, S. (1990). Social change theory: Applications to community health. In N. B. Bracht (Ed.), *Health promotion at the community level* (pp. 45–65). Newbury Park, CA: Sage.

UCLA. (2005). Epidemiology software. Department of Epidemiology, School of Public Health. Retrieved March 6, 2006, from http://www.ph.ucla.edu/epi/software.html

UCLA School Mental Health Project. (2006). *Center for Mental Health in the Schools.* Retrieved September 6, 2006, from http://smhp.psych.ucla.edu/

U.S. Department of Health and Human Services. (1999). *Mental health: A report of the Surgeon General—Executive summary.* Rockville, MD: U.S. Department of Health and Human Services, Substance Abuse and Mental Health Services Administration, Center for Mental Health Services, National Institutes of Health, National Institute of Mental Health. Retrieved September 15, 2003, from http://www.surgeon-general.gov/library/mentalhealth/summary.html

Verhulst, F. C., Koot, H. M., & Van der Ende, J. (1994). Differential predictive value of parents' and teachers' reports of children's problem behaviors: A longitudinal study. *Journal of Abnormal Child Psychology, 22,* 531–546.

Wolfe, C. (2006). *Finding psychological measures.* Retrieved March 3, 2006, from http://www.muhlenberg.edu/depts/psychology/Measures.html

World Health Organization. (2003). *Creating an environment for emotional and social well-being: An important responsibility of a health promoting and child-friendly school. Information Series on School Health, Document 10.* Geneva, Switzerland: Author. Retrieved September 6, 2006, from http://www.who.int/school_youth_health/media/en/sch_childfriendly_03_v2.pdf

World Health Organization. (2006). *Resources and tools for advocacy.* Retrieved September 6, 2006, from http://www.who.int/school_youth_health/resources/en/

Zins, J. E., Weissberg, R. P., Wang, M. C., & Walberg, H. J. (Eds.). (2004). *Building academic success on social and emotional learning: What does the research say?* New York: Teachers College Press.

About the Author

Jean A. Baker is Associate Professor of Counseling, Educational Psychology and Special Education and Co-Director of the School Psychology program at Michigan State University. Her research focuses on the social-ecological context of schooling and its effects on children's mental health outcomes and on community and relational aspects of schooling, with an emphasis on student-teacher relationships and classrooms as caring communities.

PART II

Population-Based Intervention

4

Partnering With Families to Enhance Students' Mental Health

Sandra L. Christenson

Elizabeth M. Whitehouse

Gretchen R. VanGetson

Including families is a key element in population-based approaches to enhance mental health outcomes for youth. Indeed, inclusion that provides universal access to mental health services should be integral to connecting families with services provided for their children in schools. Universal access to mental health service delivery in schools allows for intervention- and prevention-oriented assessment versus assessment for classification, thereby working with all students and teachers versus only referred students and referring teachers. It provides an increased emphasis on proactive practices versus reactive practices, an increased emphasis on early intervention versus waiting for student failure, and an expanded range of intervention/prevention strategies and agents rather than working only with teachers (Christenson, 2001; Stoner, 2006). Thus, it is responsive to parents' need for information and resources to address their concerns and allows for a systemic orientation to enhancing student competence. Also, importantly, it offers the opportunity to build trust with families long before major issues arise or mutual blaming of home and school for the students' behavior—far too common when students have mental health concerns—become the norm. There are advantages to heeding Davies (1991) notion that trust among stakeholders is the essential lubrication for more serious intervention (or the essential ingredient when more individualized and intensive interventions are needed).

Mentally healthy children can learn, relate to others, and regulate their emotions (U.S. Department of Health and Human Services, 1999). They believe that they can meet the demands of the school environment and are willing to make a personal investment in learning—critical components for success in school (Maehr & Midgley, 1996). School-based mental health professionals working collaboratively are in an ideal position to foster a culture of success or to interrupt cycles of failure (Pianta & Walsh, 1996) for students. Doing so requires that we adopt a systems-ecological orientation that views student outcomes as a result of the *child/family system* interacting with the *school/schooling system* (Rimm-Kaufman & Pianta, 2000) and attend to the strong association between students' social and emotional competence and academic outcomes (Durlak & Weissberg, 2005). Christenson and Sheridan (2001) have defined this orientation as partnering. It is a "*student-focused philosophy* wherein educators and families cooperate, coordinate, and collaborate to enhance learning opportunities, educational progress and school success for students in four domains: academic, social, emotional, and behavioral" (p. 37). Partnering with families, variously described in the literature as school-family partnerships, home-school collaboration, and parent-school engagement, is differentiated from parent involvement (Christenson, 2004) in its focus on the relationship between families and educators (Bronfenbrenner, 1992). Partnering with families to foster mental health outcomes is a similar process to fostering academic achievement outcomes: both imply school personnel reaching out to families by inviting them into the partnership and supporting them in ways that enhance their children's development and learning progress.

When working as partners, the emphasis is on the quality of the interface and sustained connection between families and schools. The ability to create a constructive *relationship* (i.e., families and educators working together in meaningful ways) to promote the academic, social, and emotional development of children and youth hinges on a belief in shared responsibility for educating and socializing children—both families and educators are essential and provide resources for children's learning—and a preventive, solution-oriented focus wherein families and educators strive to create conditions that facilitate student learning, engagement, and development (Christenson & Sheridan, 2001). In sum, the "families and schools as partners" approach forms home-school connections that develop an intentional and ongoing relationship between educators and families designed to directly or indirectly enhance children's learning, development, and mental health, and/or to address the obstacles that impede it (Wynn, Meyer, & Richards-Schuster, 1999). Furthermore, because partnering with families occurs over time in grades K–12, ensuring effective service delivery requires attention to how children's development affects services as well as the role of the student.

It is worth noting that the fifth goal of the 2002 Multisite Conference on the Future of School Psychology (Short et al., 2006) underscores the view of families as essential. Specifically, this goal calls for "increased child and family services in schools that promote health and mental health and are integrated with community services" (p. 36). It is the integration with community services that is particularly unique to fostering mental health for youth. Other fields have noted that parents are critical partners in their children's learning as well, and add that a focus on family strengths is critical (Amatea, Smith-Adcock, & Villares, 2006; Woolley & Grogan-Kaylor, 2006).

Substantial evidence supports the effect of family and home influences on children's academic, social, and behavioral competence and level of school performance; thus, support exists for families as intervention agents and as partners in fostering children's mental health. Based on a comprehensive review of the literature, Buerkle, Whitehouse, and Christenson (in press) concluded that (a) family involvement is a moderate, positive, and significant correlate of desired student outcomes (e.g., academic perseverance, positive attitude toward schoolwork, better behavior, avoidance of high risk behavior, achievement motivation, interpersonal skills, problem solving, relating to others); (b) academic and motivational home support for learning has a stronger impact on students' development and school success than demographic characteristics such as income level; (c) what happens during out-of-school time differentiates high and low achievers in urban schools; (d) the involvement of parents in early/intervention programs is beneficial (Shepard & Carlson, 2003); (e) a school-wide philosophy for the critical nature of school-family partnerships has resulted in positive gains in a variety of school performance indicators; and (f) evidence-based parent and family interventions emphasize dialogue about educational programming, two-way communication, and monitoring of children's school performance.

Two findings from the empirical research base for partnering with families illustrate that shared goals, dialogue, and two-way communication with monitoring are partnership variables worthy of attention for future intervention efforts. First, after examining the scientific base of over 100 intervention studies that support the use of parent and family interventions implemented in schools or coordinated with school settings and demonstrate a change in the school-related behaviors and learning problems of children and youth, Christenson and Carlson (2005) concluded that the most effective program components were home-school collaborative interventions that emphasized dialogue about educational programming and two-way communication/monitoring of children's school performance, parent education programs that targeted specific behaviors to be learned, parent involvement strategies that underscored the role of parents as tutors and focused on a single academic area, and parent consultation about child-specific concerns. It is noteworthy that the effective components illustrate a systems-ecological orientation, viewing parents/families and educators as both essential and in a dynamic relationship for improving child outcomes in school.

Second, continuity across home and school about children's academic, social, and emotional learning is an important protective factor in that families are active partners, supportive, and involved and educators invite families, inform and are informed by families, and include families in decisions. Educators support families when they need information about how schools function or how to assist in their children's learning progress or development. For a significant number of students, however, discontinuity between home and school is a risk factor, particularly with respect to expectations, value placed on learning, and communication patterns (Pianta & Walsh, 1996). Consistency across environments significantly influences educational or developmental outcomes, yet is often minimized in interventions. Population-based services provide an opportunity to address discontinuity before a contentious family-school relationship develops. When parents, teachers, and school personnel communicate and plan together, fewer behavioral problems and improved school experiences result (Webster-Stratton, 1993).

In this chapter, we contend that including families in fostering children's mental health requires meeting two needs: the need to

Figure 4.1   Levels of Mental Health Service Delivery

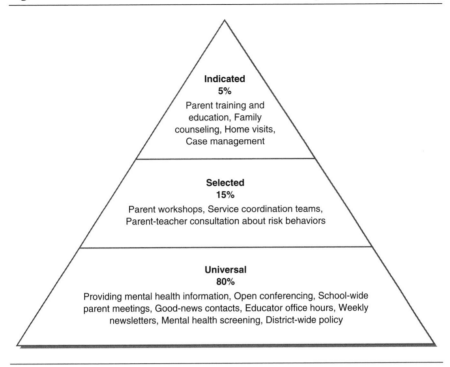

attend to the parent-educator engagement process for developing quality relationships with all families, and the need to organize opportunities for the family-school connection across the three-tiered level of services: universal, selected, and indicated (see Figure 4.1). This organization, when based on quality relationships, is a means to being responsive both to the child/family system and to the school/schooling system. In addition, we posit that addressing children's mental health works best when services are provided by a mental health support team (e.g., school psychologists, nurses, counselors, social workers) and the school is perceived by parents as a resource for their questions and concerns.

Basic Considerations for Partnering With Families

Before discussing the specific needs and strategies for including families in fostering the mental health of students, we must consider the definition of mental health, the parental perspective on this topic, and some of the barriers to partnering with families.

School-Based Mental Health Services

Mental health is not just the absence of mental illness—it is the presence of skills for youth to cope with life's challenges while learning and relating to peers and adults, especially teachers and parents. It involves regulating one's emotions in a developmentally appropriate fashion. It is considered the springboard of thinking and communication skills, learning, emotional growth, resilience, and self-esteem (U.S. Department of Health and Human Services, 1999). Another way to illustrate that mental health is much more than the absence of mental disorders is represented by the work of the Collaborative for Academic, Social, and Emotional Learning (CASEL, 2006), which has identified five core social and emotional competencies in children that are necessary for successful academic and life outcomes. These are self-awareness (i.e., recognizing one's emotions and values as well as one's strengths and limitations), social awareness (i.e., showing empathy and understanding for others), self-management (i.e., managing one's emotions and behaviors to achieve one's goals), relationship skills (i.e., forming positive relationships, working in teams, dealing effectively with conflict), and responsible decision making (i.e., making ethical, constructive choices about personal and social behavior). When children gain skills in these areas, such as problem solving, negotiation, and goal setting, they increase their capacity for learning and adapting to and meeting the demands of the environment. Further, these skills can be taught, focusing efforts on all students, not solely those at risk (CASEL, 2006). CASEL emphasizes that the core competencies should be enhanced through supportive relationships, particularly family involvement, in all stages of intervention (i.e., planning, implementation, evaluation).

Schools have a vital role to play across the continuum of mental health services from prevention to risk reduction to early identification to treatment (Nastasi, 1998). Table 4.1 notes example activities for delivering mental health services school-wide. Prevention and risk reduction activities align with universal services, early identification represents targeted services, and treatment aligns with intensive services (see Figure 4.1). Conceptualizing the delivery of mental health services along a continuum with the levels of services illustrates the role of context, particularly the seminal nature of learning environments in schools and homes and integrating services with community professionals to develop seamless systems of care.

Parental Perspectives

Research on the parental perspective in the area of mental health is sparse. We found few studies that sought the perspectives of

Table 4.1   Sample Activities for Delivering Population-Based Mental Health Services

---

Prevention: Health promotion for all students through system-wide efforts

- Use action research to bring together key stakeholders to identify critical health issues
- Gather information about student needs and sociocultural factors
- Design system-wide programs and prepare staff and parents
- Support and consult teachers and parents implementing programs
- Prepare a program evaluation plan and disseminate information about students' health
- Foster partnerships: meetings with teachers, parents, community agency staff

Risk Reduction: Targets students at high risk for health or mental health difficulties caused by individual or environmental factors by providing more intensive health-promotion activities

- Develop procedures for identifying and referring students
- Select and design intervention programs
- Make referrals to appropriate school/community-based services
- Evaluate the impact of services
- Educate others about indicators of risk
- Implement after-school risk reduction programs
- Disseminate findings about effectiveness of such programs

Early Intervention: Directed toward individuals experiencing mild health or mental health problems; goal is to treat and reduce the risk for more severe problems

- Develop early intervention teams
- Consult with teachers and parents to develop classroom- and home-based behavioral intervention programs (i.e., conjoint behavioral consultation; see Sheridan & Kratochwill, 1992)
- Assist administrators in evaluating effectiveness of programs
- Work with community agencies to bring in additional services
- Develop a system-wide screening process for depressed and anxious students

Treatment: Addresses the needs of students diagnosed with specific health or mental health disorders and requires intensive treatment by medical or mental health professionals

- Conduct assessments leading to diagnoses
- Provide direct services (e.g., cognitive-behavioral interventions)
- Evaluate effectiveness of pharmacologic interventions
- Work with community professionals to ensure coordinated services

---

Source: Drawn from Nastasi (1998).

parents with children who had mental health needs. In one study, several themes emerged that paint a dismal picture about the state of school-family partnerships in the context of mental health service delivery (Tarico, Low, Trupin, & Forsyth-Stephens, 1989). Participants were 35 parents of children who were identified as emotionally and behaviorally disturbed in a large city in a northwestern state. Many parents felt that special education services did not meet the individual mental health needs of their children, and on average could name more than three needs that had not been met. Families also described dealing with mental health service delivery systems as an "exhaustive battle," and only 45% of providers had invited families to participate in service delivery teams.

Perhaps the most informative finding from this study was that parents most wanted information. They desired services for the whole family instead of just the child, and also desired more open communication with mental health service providers, including educators. This theme emerged in another small study of families of individuals with schizophrenia (Gantt, Goldstein, & Pinsky, 1989). The majority of these families were uninformed about the causes of the illness and reported that nothing had been explained to them about medication and therapy. Again, an overwhelming 87% of these families said that they would like to receive more information about the disorder. Although these studies were completed 15 years ago, there is no reason to believe that parents at the beginning of the 21st century are better informed about their children's mental health— either the course of development or particular needs. In fact, parents have identified consulting with school psychologists about their children's social and emotional development and behavioral and academic needs in classrooms as one of the top ways they could be involved in their children's learning (Christenson, Hurley, Sheridan, & Fenstermacher, 1997). Although this study only examined services from school psychologists, most likely parents would respond very similarly to other mental health professionals in our schools.

A more recent study confirms that these issues are still relevant today. In a report regarding family perspectives on their needs in relation to children's mental health services, access to information emerged as one of the top three areas that parents identified as needing improvement (Wrobel, 2004). Over 200 parents from a Midwestern state were somewhat familiar with mental health services, as they had contacted a large agency regarding their children's behavioral and mental health needs. Sixty-seven percent of families thought that finding mental health services for children was difficult or very difficult, and only 37% were satisfied or very satisfied that their ideas regarding their child's services were heard. Another telling finding was that parents overwhelmingly reported that they were the first to notice concerns with their child.

Barriers to Involvement and Collaboration

Myriad factors discourage families from becoming involved in their children's education and interfere with the process of collaboration. Moving beyond the typical logistical factors that prohibit families from being involved at school (e.g., transportation, time, daycare, meetings during school hours that interfere with work schedules), Lowie, Lever, Ambrose, Tager, and Hill (2003) described barriers that involve feelings of the partners. The stigma surrounding mental health issues, the tendency of schools to blame parents, families feeling unwelcome at school, and an imbalance of power were noted. Lack of parental knowledge about available services also contributes to educators' perceived lack of interest or involvement on the part of families. Finally, issues with educators are relevant as well; main concerns include staff not being trained to work with families as partners and minimal administrative support to do so. Of utmost importance in fostering children's mental health is for school personnel to be sensitive to the level of parental self-efficacy, role construction, and need for parental self-care (Cavell, 2000; Hoover-Dempsey & Sandler, 1997).

In addition to factors that obstruct family involvement, there are issues that often surround the collaborative effort. Osher (2002) described factors in eight categories: organizational interests, organizational features, experiential and training factors, communications, focus, time, definitions, and data. The most salient challenges for partnering with families in these areas seem to be lack of structures to bring systems together, the need for decision-making rules, poor communication, lack of time, and disagreement about goals and responsibilities. All of these barriers can contribute to unsuccessful partnerships, which ultimately result in a failure to optimize outcomes for students. The next sections describe the two needs for partnering with families; to meet these needs we address ways to prevent and reduce barriers.

Parent-Educator Engagement Process

Several ideas in the home-school literature convey that connecting and building relationships with families is an intentional process. We believe that these suggestions are particularly useful when applied to the process of including families in mental health service delivery for children. One such framework, the four A's (i.e., Approach, Attitudes, Atmosphere, Actions), embodies a useful process for emphasizing the conditions needed for a quality relationship between families and practitioners (Christenson & Sheridan, 2001). The first three A's are prerequisite conditions and must be in place for actions to be effective.

Approach encompasses the framework for interacting with families, or the philosophy that mental health professionals embrace. We believe that principles of shared responsibility and systems-ecological theory are helpful here. As Seeley (1985) noted, from a shared responsibility viewpoint, learning is achieved by students with the assistance of various support systems, including parents and educators. Optimal outcomes are more likely to be achieved when these stakeholders develop shared goals and congruence across home and school for achievement and behavior; thus, the student's performance is conceptualized as a function of learning supports from school, home, and the family-school relationship. Partnering with parents is viewed as a priority school-wide and it is understood to require a concerted, planned effort (Patrikakou & Weissberg, 1999) with assessment of the school context, namely, the range of students' academic, social, and emotional needs; an understanding of the desires of families and their role; identification of current practices for reaching out to families; and systematic identification of families for whom interaction is minimal or nonexistent.

Schools effective in adopting a school-family partnership to enhance students' mental health do many things in a methodical way; they develop a mission statement or policy about working with families as partners, provide school personnel with training in how to work as partners, provide resources for reaching out to families, recognize the accomplishments of parents and educators for improving educational outcomes, select the types of programs that are important for their school context, clarify the roles parents can play in promoting their children's social and emotional learning and development, and set priorities for school practices that target partnering with parents. School personnel, often through a family-school team or a mental health support team (Comer, Haynes, Joyner, & Ben-Avie, 1996), conduct a school-level demographic profile (Edwards, 2004) to address with whom and how they are going to partner, guide the planning and program monitoring process, and examine and strive to systematically remove barriers for parents, teachers, and the family-school relationship. Because parents are viewed as essential to their children's optimal school success and overall development, they are co-assessors and co-interventionists (Christenson, 2004; Harry, 1993).

Attitudes involve parents' and educators' perceptions of the value of the partnership. Several characteristics of collaborative processes are important for developing a valued perception, such as respecting the other's ideas and opinions, viewing divergence in opinion as a strength and opportunity for change, employing a non-blaming communication style, and genuinely listening to and incorporating all perspectives (Christenson & Sheridan, 2001). Successful attitudes encourage a belief in (a) co-constructing the bigger picture about the child's performance by including parents to address concerns, (b) the value of problem solving across home and school, and (c) the value of a positive, asset-based orientation for all educational planning and programming. Schools that are successful at *engaging with families* to foster children's mental health ensure parents have access (i.e., parental right to inclusion in decision-making processes), voice (i.e., parents feel they were heard and listened to at all points in the process), and ownership (i.e., parents agree with and are contributing to any action plan affecting them and their child; Comer et al., 1996; Osher, 1997). These attitudes, beliefs, and values set the stage for a productive atmosphere.

Atmosphere, or the climate in which family-school interactions occur, is the final prerequisite condition that must be met before actions are implemented. A productive atmosphere is welcoming; of particular importance is the degree to which the school environment includes parents' input on school policies and practices as well as suggestions for their children (Comer et al., 1996), fosters mutual support between educators and families through problem solving when concerns arise (Swap, 1993), and uses solution-oriented communication strategies (see Table 4.2; Carlson, Hickman, & Horton, 1992; deShazer, 1988). The power of solution-oriented communication is that it helps parents view their children as learners, enhances personal beliefs that parents can influence their child's behavior, and enhances parents' comfort level at school and with issues related to education.

Also, a positive atmosphere that promotes school-family partnerships around social and emotional learning for students is built on a foundation of trust. Recent data have shown that trust positively predicts the variance in student achievement in reading and mathematics (Goddard, Tschannen-Moran, & Hoy, 2001). These authors also found that teachers trusted low-income students and parents less. On the whole, other studies revealed that parents trust teachers more than teachers trust parents (Adams & Christenson, 1998; 2000). However, the literature still asserts that schools are responsible for reaching out to parents to build positive partnerships. Fortunately,

Table 4.2   Guidelines for Effective Communication With Families

1. Maintain a positive, honest orientation to all communication.
   - Involve parents by calling at the first sign of concern and keeping them informed.
   - Use non-blaming language.
   - Emphasize student progress and improvement toward goals, and solutions not problems:
     o Focus on solutions by identifying what is working already.
     o Reframe a school-based concern as a learning goal.
     o Use different language: Concerns, goals, and possible solutions, not problems (de Shazer, 1988).
   - Maintain an optimistic perspective:
     o Keep the focus on encouraging development of student competence.
     o Persistence, ongoing sharing of information and resources, and solution-oriented problem solving are necessary to engage some students in learning.

2. Develop a regular, reliable home-school communication system that increases the potential for two-way communication.
   - Listen to parents, and understand their educational goals and aspirations for their children.
   - Create opportunities for exchange of information.
   - Encourage perspective taking and two-way communication by asking:
     o What is the issue/concern?
     o What do I need to say about the issue (specific, observable language)?
     o What do I need to understand from the parent about the issue?
     o How can we develop a better plan/practice to address the concern?

3. Focus communication and dialogue on children's engagement with schooling and learning.
   - Keep the focus on what the student needs for the best school experience this year.
   - Find solutions through mutual problem solving. A good plan satisfies all team members.
   - Strive to have a doable plan by (a) constructing solutions that fit the personal constraints of the situation, and (b) breaking student behavior into parts and tackling it one step at a time.

4. Ensure that parents have the information they need to support their children's schooling and learning.
   - Invite parent assistance and explain why parents are essential to children's engagement with learning.
   - Guide and show parents different ways to support their child's engagement with schooling and learning; avoid simply telling parents what to do.
   - Explain school policies and practices and encourage parents to gather information from school personnel and question school procedures.
   - Engage in structured problem solving with school personnel to create a better action plan for the student. SOLVE may be helpful here:

     S Share thoughts, feelings needs.
     O Obtain a list of possible solutions.
     L Locate the best solution (one that satisfies mutual needs).
     V Validate the solution by implementing the plan.
     E Evaluate the plan and modify as needed (Lombana, 1983).

- Help parents see there are many ways they can foster their children's engagement at school and with learning.

5. Recognize that trusting relationships take time.
   - Trust is built in stages. According to Holmes and Rempel (1989), trust is built in three stages: *predictability* refers to the stage at which the individual is watching for specific behaviors to occur, *dependability* refers to the stage at which the individual looks for follow through on specific behaviors and is beginning to think of trust as an attribute of the other person, and *faith* refers to the stage at which the individual knows the other person is trustworthy, regardless of the specific behavior; there is confidence that the person will meet their expectations.
   - Trust depends on getting to know each other, ongoing communication and positive interaction, and being instructive to one another.
   - Trust is fostered when educators engage in specific actions such as accepting parents as they are; sharing information and resources; focusing on parents' aspirations, concerns, and needs; following through on plans at school; and discussing objectives openly (Margolis & Brannigan, 1990).
   - Act in ways that preserve the relationship with parents. Listen to parents and understand the importance of building a relationship by being responsive to parents' needs.

6. Underscore the importance of both in-school time and out-of-school time (i.e., shared responsibility) for children's engagement at school and with learning.
   - Share information with families about the curriculum of the home (Christenson & Buerkle, 1999; Walberg, 1984). Strive for continuity in the messages given to the student.
   - Differentiate blame and conflict for parents and educators:
     o Conflict is natural and can be managed; differences of opinions are okay.
     o Conflict can be viewed as an opportunity for change.
     o Blame occurs when the misunderstandings are left unresolved.
     o Use negotiation skills to develop a win-win perspective (we vs. the concern) for the student: (a) view the person separately from the concern/issue—understand the position of each person and strive to co-construct the big picture; (b) focus the communication on mutual interests (e.g., What is best for the student?) and (c) generate many options before making a one-sided decision about the action plan.

Source: Adapted from Christenson & Hirsch (1998).

schools can provide many opportunities for this trust building to occur, from traditional activities such as conferences and volunteering in the classroom to more in-depth efforts at partnership development, like holding workshops for parents at the school and forming school-family partnership committees. An important point to note here is that the quality of parent-teacher relationships is more strongly associated with child outcomes than amount of contact (Adams & Christenson, 2000; Patrikakou & Weissberg, 2000). Perhaps it is through this emphasis on quality relationships that schools can begin to build trust with all families, particularly minority families and those living in poverty.

Many families who are reluctant to participate in school activities or communicate with school personnel may have a history of negative interactions with school, whether because of a specific personal experience or a long-held familial belief. School personnel must work through mistrust by persistent efforts to contact families, frequent efforts to invite all families to school functions and activities, and a welcoming school climate. Persistent efforts such as frequent letters home and good news phone calls convey the message that the school personnel wish to work with the family and share the successes of the child. School personnel may need to visit families in a comfortable or neutral environment (e.g., the family's home, a fast-food restaurant) before families feel welcome at school. Practices such as making sure the child is well known by at least one staff member help to create a positive atmosphere that is conducive to partnership. Physical factors such as bulletin boards with current social and emotional learning activities and information parents can take with them as they walk through the hallways indicate the school values social and emotional learning and encourages parents to partner with them around this issue.

Persistent efforts on the part of educators are essential, communicating the message that parents' opinions and efforts are valued, and in fact integral to the success of students. When parents feel they are welcomed and wanted at school, they more readily take ownership of their role in the partnership. Thus, a climate for school-family interactions *invites* parents into the partnership, *informs* parents about their child's school performance and *is informed* by the parents' observations, and *includes* parents in decisions about how to help the child reach a school-based goal (Sinclair, Christenson, Lehr, & Anderson, 2003).

Finally, Christenson and Sheridan (2001) recommend the following seven actions: garner administrative support for partnering with families, act as a systems advocate, implement family-school teams, increase problem solving across home and school, identify and manage conflict, support families to increase learning at home, and consult with teachers to improve communication and relationships with families. Grounded in the systems-ecological perspective, these actions are distinguished from activities, in that they involve shared responsibility, an interface of socializing systems for youth, and collaboration rather than disparate duties assigned to one system. As a result, the separate systems together achieve more than either one can alone. A shift in thinking is necessary from the traditional to more contemporary roles that parents and educators play. Related to this point are several benefits of partnering with families, which include enhanced coordination between parents and educators; continuity in programs and approaches across family and school contexts; shared ownership and commitment to educational goals; increased understanding of the complexities of the child and his or her situation; and pooling of resources to increase the range and quality of solutions, diversity in expertise, and integrity of educational programs (Christenson & Sheridan, 2001).

The parent-school engagement process illustrated by the four A's is consistent with the posture of cultural reciprocity, which ties in awareness of cultural differences as well as self-awareness of one's own culture when partnering with families (Kalyanpur & Harry, 1997). Cultural differences represent another potential barrier to successful partnering with families. In developing a posture of cultural reciprocity, key stakeholders listen to the others' points of view as they agree to a compromise that leads to the best outcomes for students. Guidelines for the posture of cultural reciprocity include four steps:

Step 1: Identify the cultural values imbedded in the professional interpretation of a student's difficulties or in the recommendation for service.

Step 2: Find out whether the family being served recognizes and values these assumptions and, if not, how their view differs from that of the professional.

Step 3: Acknowledge and give explicit respect to any cultural differences identified, and fully explain the cultural basis of the professional assumptions.

Step 4: Through discussion and collaboration, set about determining the most effective way of adapting professional interpretations or recommendations to the value system of the family. (Kalyanpur & Harry, 1997, p. 498)

Five primary features of this approach make it particularly useful for partnering with families about their children's mental health needs (Kalyanpur & Harry, 1997). The posture of cultural reciprocity accounts for *self-awareness* in addition to *awareness of others* and emphasizes that practitioners look for subtle levels of differences, increasing understanding of the reasoning for educational decisions. Further, this concept can and should be *applied universally* with all families rather than solely in those situations in which differences are expected. As such, this model *avoids stereotyping*, as educators see each family as unique and seek to understand their viewpoint. Finally, the culture of reciprocity *empowers all systems.*

Osher and Osher's (2002) description of the paradigm shift in mental health services from practitioner-focused to family-focused to family-driven is particularly salient and supports the aforementioned suggestions for partnering with families. They argue that family-driven services are the most effective because families that genuinely participate in goal-setting and other tasks related to their child's needs take ownership and are more effective participants in the process of helping their child achieve his or her goals. A key to this shift in thinking is that families are knowledgeable members of the team, and thus they must have the same information as everyone else. Further, families bring in their vast experience and expertise about students. It is worth noting that the parent-educator engagement process corroborates family-driven services; again, educators reach out to partner or team with parents to address their concerns. Thus, the child/family system is the client.

In the same study, Osher and Osher (2002) efficiently describe family-driven services in a number of areas, including source of solutions, relationship, and orientation, which are factors that affect the interaction between systems. In family-driven services, all systems generate solutions, share in the decision making, and take an ecological approach to helping the student achieve goals. The next tasks of service delivery are assessment and expectations, which use an assets-based approach and have high expectations for success. The final areas are planning, access to services, and evaluation. In the family-driven model, services are based on the needs of the family and resources available, and the authors encourage teams to be creative when identifying support systems. For more information on family-driven services, interested readers will want to contact the Research and Training Center on Family Support and Children's Mental Health at http://www.rtc.pdx.edu/pgFeaturedDiscussions19.php.

Organizing Mental Health Service Delivery for the Child/Family System

True collaborative partnerships between families and schools prepare for action to be taken with respect to fostering children's mental health. Reorganizing mental health service delivery from universal to indicated services allows for an assessment-to-intervention link that provides appropriate supports to address the child referral, is responsive to family needs and desires, and provides for the wise use of finite resources available (see Figure 4.1). It offers less costly but extremely important health promotion and prevention services to all families while focusing more costly, in-depth intervention services on families with the greatest level of need. The three levels of services for including families can be globally conceptualized as (a) disseminating information, (b) attending to a unique child/family need, and (c) addressing the familial need for ongoing support. For example, most families desire and need only general information on how to best promote CASEL's five social and emotional competencies or reduce risks for health or mental health difficulties within their family, while a smaller percentage of families also require attention to some unique aspect of the family's circumstances (e.g., maternal depression, substance abuse, excessive work demands, economic stress). Further, an even smaller percentage of families (i.e., at the top of the triangle) require all three—information, attention to a unique need, and ongoing support—to be engaged in fostering their children's mental health.

System-wide mental health promotion and prevention strategies are considered universal strategies; they are useful for disseminating information relevant to all families, but likely will assist approximately 80% of the school-community population. In Adelman and Taylor's (2003) model, these universal efforts, labeled "system to promote healthy development and systems of prevention," target all students and families, including those with low need, and incur very little cost. Selected and indicated strategies supplement universal efforts. Selected strategies attend to particular issues or needs of families and generally involve working with families of a child who has been identified as needing early intervention (e.g., anger management for aggressive behavior). Typically, this involves 15% of the school population. Adelman and Taylor's label for selected efforts is "systems of early intervention"; these efforts target students and their families with a moderate need soon after onset of difficulties, and incur only a moderate cost. Indicated strategies build on the previous two levels but offer extensive ongoing support, typically needed by approximately 5% of families. This level is labeled by Adelman and Taylor as "systems of care," and offers treatment for ongoing or severe difficulties for those with high need, and it often incurs the greatest cost. Population-based services rest on mental health professionals identifying the student population across these three levels of service delivery.

We contend that school mental health professionals have a role to play across the three levels of mental health service delivery; however, their primary efforts will be at the universal and selected levels. For example, the National Association of School Psychologists (NASP) supports school psychologists as mental health service providers in these prevention and early intervention roles, as well as in constructing collaborative interagency partnerships with relevant community mental health service providers; together with families, these partners may address students' mental health at a universal level (e.g., public policy) along with the more focused selected and indicated levels, thereby improving the mental health of all students (NASP, 2002).

A caveat is warranted. We are aware of evidence that information alone does not always alter behavior (Larson, 1994). It is our contention that the levels of services must be embedded within a quality family-school relationship that allows for open, honest, and clear communication and the flexibility to add supplemental services when information alone is not working to enhance the functioning of youth.

Adelman and Taylor (2003) have recommended that school personnel conduct an analysis of mental health services and needs through a procedure referred to as resource mapping. Briefly, resource mapping begins with conducting a needs assessment of current mental health resources available to students and their families at school and in the community. The results of this assessment are analyzed to better coordinate existing resources and develop new school-based resources to fill in any gaps in service; this process leads to improved organization and tailored services for each school and community. We concur; delivering well-matched population-based services is contingent on organizing services for each school context across the universal, selected, and indicated levels. Examples of activities (see Table 4.1 and Figure 4.1) across the three levels are summarized briefly in the following sections.

Universal Service Delivery

Universal service delivery consists mostly of educational activities; of particular importance are identifying critical mental health issues and disseminating information about health-promoting environments and indicators of risk to key stakeholders. Both parents and teachers need information, although most apparent in the literature is the effect of providing information to families. For example, Osher and Osher (2002) describe true collaboration as relying on "families having accurate, understandable, and complete information necessary to make choices for improved planning for individual children" (p. 22). Indeed, families need information to "recognize and understand mental health problems or to locate appropriate, effective services" (Huang et al., 2005, p. 619). With respect to the five core social and emotional learning competencies articulated by CASEL (www.casel.org), resource materials exist for both parents and teachers. Similarly, the Minnesota Association for Children's Mental Health provides mental health fact sheets with information on how to access various resources in consumer-friendly formats available to schools and families (MACMH, 2003). For example, the fact sheet on depression includes symptoms and behaviors associated with the disorder, information about the disorder, the impact the disorder may have on education, instructional strategies and classroom accommodations that are effective for students with depression, and contact information of resource organizations. Disseminating such information as these fact sheets to families could be the beginning of bidirectional information flow about students' mental health.

At the universal level, school personnel employ varied means, including print and personal contact, to connect with families. The critical dimension links to a learning component and the degree to which the school is viewed as a resource by families. School-wide parent meetings are an effective universal approach to connecting with all families (Duckworth et al., 2001). Not only do these meetings offer an opportunity to disseminate valued information to families, they also promote family-school communication, provide an opportunity for families to voice their issues and find support in other families with similar challenges, and allow families to network together and collectively organize in a way that promotes systems change (Osher & Osher, 2002). Christenson and Sheridan (2001) advocated that meetings should address topics of interest to families and teachers and be offered at multiple times. They should also include a systematic approach to reach parents not in attendance (i.e., follow-up phone calls, home visits, mailings).

Other universal-level prevention strategies include good-news contacts, in which educators contact families, via the phone, notes, or home visits, about the students' successes within social and emotional competencies (Christenson & Sheridan, 2001; MACMH, 2003). Schools can incorporate mental health information in weekly newsletters sent to families, provide flexible educator office hours (e.g., early morning, evening), and offer open conferencing for families to discuss school or home issues in their child's life. Also, it is possible to increase the presence of the school's mental health staff at family events, such as back-to-school nights and Parent-Teacher Association (PTA) meetings (Christenson & Sheridan, 2001; Lowie et al., 2003). Parents may assist school staff in informal student mental health screening procedures, collaboratively assessing students for indicators of risk (Vanderbleek, 2004) or levels of social and emotional competence (CASEL, 2006).

Beyond the school level, school districts may want to create a district-wide policy of student mental health prevention that incorporates many of these universal strategies (Vanderbleek, 2004). Also, school personnel delivering population-based services will want to be knowledgeable about the numerous school-wide programs targeting students' social and emotional health that require family-school and community partnerships for their success (Elias et al., 1997; Rones & Hoagwood, 2000). One example is Project Northland, which aims to prevent adolescent alcohol use by employing a multicomponent program with intensive parent involvement during sixth, seventh, and eighth grades (Rones & Hoagwood, 2000). As a sample program component, sixth-grade students are instructed on how to speak with their parents about alcohol. Project Northland outcomes included a self-reported decrease in alcohol use in adolescents.

Selected Service Delivery

With a universal focus on promoting the mental health of students and their families, the infrastructure is in place for supporting more concentrated individualized interventions. Services at the selected level focus on both prevention for selected children at risk for mental health problems and early intervention for children identified as experiencing mental health problems. One example of selected prevention is periodic scheduling by school mental health professionals of brief check-in meetings with students who frequently experience low academic performance, increased disciplinary actions, or other characteristics or behaviors that indicate risk of poor mental health. These check-ins act as a means of monitoring the student's mental health and provide an opportunity for family input by inviting family members to take part in these meetings. As an additional component, these meetings include consulting with teachers about these students to provide opportunities to implement academic or behavioral interventions before their school-based difficulties translate into mental health problems. Another example extends the universal service delivery strategy of educating students and families about risk indicators of poor mental health by providing explicit instructions on how to refer students displaying risk signs of mental health problems to a school mental health professional.

Once identified as experiencing poor mental health, students are identified for early intervention. One of the best ways for school professionals to attend to the needs and issues of these students and their families is to create service coordination teams (Anderson & Mohr, 2003; Ho, 2001; Taylor & Adelman, 2000). Team members are carefully selected and consist of both school professionals and home support individuals such as family members, friends, after-school program counselors, and religious group leaders (Anderson & Mohr, 2003; Eber, Sugai, Smith, & Scott, 2002). The service coordination team progresses in a stepwise manner, beginning with engaging in initial conversations that focus on the strengths within the child's life. Next the team develops goals for improving the mental health of the child and family, identifies and prioritizes the child's and family's needs, develops actions or specific strategies for reaching goals based on natural supports, assigns and commits to those actions, and, finally, monitors, evaluates, and refines the plan (Anderson & Mohr, 2003; Christenson & Sheridan, 2001; Eber et al., 2002). All team members work collaboratively as equal partners throughout this entire process (Anderson & Mohr, 2003; Ho, 2001; Osher & Osher, 2002).

Other selected actions include workshops for parents on specific mental health topics, such as childhood anxiety, anger management, and relational aggression to educate parents on issues directly affecting their child (Christenson & Sheridan, 2001). Schools may want to create family-school communication systems, such as daily e-mails or a home-school notebook, with selected families to maintain constant, positive contact with families whose children are at risk for mental health problems (Christenson & Sheridan, 2001). Further, a direct collaborative relationship between parents and teachers known as parent-teacher consultation—in which these partners systematically identify difficult student behaviors, brainstorm and select appropriate interventions, and monitor intervention effectiveness—may prove helpful in targeting mentally unhealthy behaviors (Sheridan & Kratochwill, 1992). A more involved approach is the Family Check-Up (FCU), a brief school-based family prevention/intervention that is the first step in the intervention process (Stormshak & Dishion, 2002). In one prevention trial, the FCU was successful in decreasing the growth of substance use by middle school students (Stormshak & Dishion, 2002). The FCU includes a therapist who works with the family in three sessions: an initial interview, a careful and detailed assessment session, and a feedback session; families in need of more support following the FCU are provided intensive interventions from a menu of change options that are tailored to them and planned with the therapist.

Indicated Service Delivery

The most rigorous interventions, reserved for the approximately 5% of children and families who were not fully assisted by universal prevention or selected interventions, are at the indicated level. Indicated-level interventions involve treatment of children diagnosed with a mental health disorder and/or special education classifications and their families. These interventions often involve connections with community-based services, and school mental health professionals are in an ideal position to serve as liaisons to create coordinated programming for children and their families. Examples of indicated interventions include family counseling, parent training, case management, and home visits (Duckworth et al., 2001). These intervention modalities target family issues, a focus that Stormshak and Dishion (2002) describe as arguably "the single most important point of therapeutic intervention for children and adolescents" (p. 201). Many examples of intensive interventions come from family-focused interventions aimed at reducing childhood aggression and include parent management training, expanded parent management training, family therapy, and multisystemic approaches; please consult Christenson, Anderson, and Hirsch (2004) for a complete review of these interventions, and Cavell (2000) for in-depth descriptions of specific approaches, such as behavior-management parent training (BMPT), child relationship enhancement family therapy (CREFT), and responsive parent therapy (RPT). Some school-based programs exist. For example, the Vanderbilt School-Based Counseling program provides need-based tailored services, including family therapy and parent training and education, to students with identified emotional or behavioral problems, thereby increasing service accessibility for these families (Rones & Hoagwood, 2000).

Specific ways to connect with families change as the child/family system moves from the universal to the indicated level, and as a result, school-based mental health professionals (e.g., school psychologists, counselors, social workers) spend more time with some families. Consistent with recommendations by others (Adelman & Taylor, 2003; Graczyk, Domitrovich, & Zins, 2003), we believe a mental health support team composed of varied support personnel provides the best services to children and their families. Finally, the team will want to be knowledgeable about resources and evidence-based interventions. In this regard, CASEL's (2006) review of social and emotional learning programs to identify quality programs at various levels of mental health service delivery is particularly helpful. The programs are categorized in terms of availability of evidence for positive outcomes as well as a school-family partnership rating. In addition, CASEL has published a toolkit for fostering students' social and emotional learning competencies across the levels of service delivery, partnering with families at each level (Devaney, O'Brien, Resnik, Keister, & Weissberg, 2006). Although it is necessary to be aware of these various strategies and programs, awareness is not sufficient for delivering population-based mental health services. Communicating effectively with families is essential.

The Role of Communication in Partnering With Families

Dialogue and two-way communication are undisputed components of effective school-family partnerships that enhance student outcomes (Christenson & Carlson, 2005; Graczyk et al., 2003; Osher & Osher, 2002). Six communication guidelines for interacting with families that were identified from a literature review (Christenson & Hirsch, 1998) and applied in the Check & Connect intervention appear in Table 4.2. Check & Connect is a model designed to promote student engagement with school through relationship building, problem solving, and persistence. It consists of three main components: (a) a mentor working with students and families over an extended period of time (years), (b) regularly checking on the educational progress of the student, and (c) intervening in a timely manner to reestablish and maintain students' connection to school and learning (Lehr, Sinclair, & Christenson, 2004; Sinclair, Christenson, & Thurlow, 2005). The mentor attended to these guidelines as they designed interventions to enhance school completion for students at high risk of dropping out of school. The guidelines were used to create collaborative connections between schools and families and to integrate services to support disengaged students, most of whom had mental health needs best served at the targeted or intensive levels.

The guidelines in Table 4.2 primarily represent the "what" of effective interaction with families. Equally critical is "the how"—or the manner in which these guidelines were implemented in Check & Connect. The work of McWilliam, Tocci, and Harbin (1998) was influential to address this need. They contend that the process of communication is influenced by dimensions of family-centered practice, which is defined as "a friendly, respectful partnership with families that provides (a) emotional and educational supports, (b) opportunities to participate in service delivery and to make decisions, and (c) activities to enhance family members' capacities to carry out their self-determined roles" (p. 209). The dimensions include the following:

- A family orientation (*Opening the Door*): This is a willingness to orient services to the whole family, rather than just to the child. Providers must establish enough trust with parents to be able to ask them about their own concerns.
- Positiveness (*Thinking the Best of Families*): Positiveness is a philosophy of thinking the best about parents without passing judgment. It is characterized by a belief in parents' abilities, a nonjudgmental mind-set, an optimistic view of children's development, and an enthusiasm for working with families.
- Sensitivity (*In the Parents' Shoes*): Being sensitive refers to an ability to recognize and understand families' concerns, needs, and priorities. It is the idea of putting oneself in the parent's position in order to anticipate how families might feel as opposed to prejudging families or thinking for them.
- Responsiveness (*Doing Whatever Needs to Be Done*): Two forms of responsiveness include paying attention and taking action when parents express a need (e.g., for information, for support) or a complaint. This incorporates an individualized and flexible approach to service provision.
- Friendliness (*Treating Parents as Friends*): Being a "professional friend" entails developing a reciprocal relationship, building trust, taking time to talk to parents about their concerns, listening to parents, encouraging them, offering practical help, and conveying caring for both parents and the child.
- Child and community skills (*Being a Resource*): This dimension includes child-level skills (e.g., having knowledge about helping children become engaged with school and learning) and community-level skills (awareness of economic/cultural climate, familiarity with community resources, and a willingness to collaborate).

It cannot be stressed enough that parents desire information, and in most instances, educators have the capacity to provide it. The "what" and "how" of communication and interaction with families corroborates the four A's illustrated in the parent-school engagement process to develop a quality relationship to promote children's mental health (i.e., positive academic, social, and emotional outcomes), and to do so for all students. Thus, these guidelines are relevant to population-based services or addressing the needs of students across universal, targeted, or intensive levels of mental health service delivery.

Considerations for Implementation

Moving from a traditional to a partnership focus for working with families to deliver population-based mental health services, albeit challenging, is precisely what is called for in *The Blueprint for Training and Practices* (Ysseldyke et al., 2006). Fortunately, well-trained school psychologists have the foundational competencies (e.g., interpersonal and collaborative skills, cultural sensitivity and responsiveness) and functional competencies (e.g., data-based decision making, systems-based service delivery, and intervention knowledge in cognitive, academic, social skills, and mental health) to draw on to build the capacity of systems to achieve improved competence for each child and all children.

In addition to individual competencies, we offer four broad considerations when discussing how to infuse partnering with families to enhance the mental health of youth; namely, awareness of goals, use of problem-solving structures, attention to seminal principles for systems change, and the availability of resources. With respect to goals, we suggest that the concept of quality family-school partnerships is not new; what we are adding is a systemic focus and an organizational framework for thinking of efficient and effective service delivery with the child/family system. The model for systematic and structured planning and problem solving that attends to the uniqueness of each school (e.g., type and percentage of students with mental health concerns) described by Curtis, Castillo, and Cohen (in press) is a valuable resource. Finally, although structured planning and problem solving is seminal for systems change, mental health providers will find principles of educational change, such as systems advocates committed to "the long haul" (p. 470), creation of a purpose focus, investment in building the knowledge and skill base of school personnel to support the change, and promotion of the innovation through communication and responsiveness to the needs of the context to be equally informative (Grimes & Tilley, 1996). Both principles and procedures for systems change should be considered by individuals wanting to move from a traditional to a partnership focus in working with families. Finally, the availability of resources has increased immeasurably with easy access to websites. We offer the following:

- Center for School Mental Health Analysis and Action, http:// csmha.umaryland.edu/

The CSMHA website provides links to helpful articles and resource packets related to mental health services in schools. It lists upcoming conferences on this topic and details the organization's major research projects as well.

- The Collaborative for Academic, Social, and Emotional Learning, http://www.casel.org

The CASEL website provides essential definitions and information about social and emotional learning at school and home. Many helpful tools for families and educators are available for download or purchase, such as newsletters, publications, books, videos, and assessment tools.

- The National Mental Health Association, http://www.nmha .org/children/index.cfm

This page on the NMHA website focuses specifically on children and families, providing strategies for working with children experiencing issues such as loss, school transitions, and homelessness. The broader website also addresses general mental health and current news.

- Public Health Service Report—Mental Health: A Report of the Surgeon General, http://www.surgeongeneral.gov/library/ mentalhealth/home.html

This report challenges those working with and for children to take action in the area of mental health. Information is given about fundamentals of mental health, children and mental health, and financing and organizing services. Suggestions are made for the future of mental health research and service delivery.

- Research and Training Center on Family Support and Children's Mental Health, http://www.rtc.pdx.edu/pgFeaturedDiscussions 19.php

This featured discussion focuses on the importance of promoting family-driven care and gives definitions, characteristics, and guiding principles. Other related discussions are available to view and comments can be posted as well. This site contains a youth resources page, including links for online and print resources.

- School Mental Health Project, UCLA, http://smhp.psych.ucla.edu/

This site offers information about mental health in the schools, resources on topics of interest in mental health and policy issues, and a connection to the Center for Mental Health in Schools. The website also offers opportunities for interacting and networking with other professionals.

- Screening for Mental Health, http://www.mentalhealthscreening.org/

This website offers information on large-scale mental health screenings for various issues, such as depression, anxiety, and eating disorders. Descriptions of youth programs and community organizations, as well as contact information, are also available.

- The Substance Abuse and Mental Health Service Administration's National Mental Health Information Center—Center for Mental Health Services, http://www.mentalhealth.samhsa.gov/cmhs/

This website gives information concerning programs and activities offered by CMHS for people with mental health needs, their families, and their communities. Publications on a variety of topics are available to read and frequently asked questions about mental health and mental health services are answered, and the site contains a kid's page as well.

Concluding Remarks

While the benefits of involving families in efforts to enhance social, emotional, and academic outcomes for students are well established, the actual process of partnering with families is often ignored. School mental health professionals are uniquely trained in both the fields of education and mental health, qualifying them to reach out to families and take the time to form these key relationships. Partnerships require trust and are essential for promoting shared responsibility. Further, making sure families have key information is crucial. The three-tiered model of mental health service delivery provides the structure to include all students and their families in mental health promotion. This model is prevention oriented and offers an efficient way to provide effective services along a continuum of care. Finally, mental health does not consist solely of the absence of mental illness—it involves building skills that help students adapt to and experience success in the various and challenging environments in which they live.

Discussion Questions

1. What are universal practices in your school that promote parent-educator engagement? What universal practices do not yet exist in your school, but should?

2. How does your own practice already accommodate the barriers that parents report to parental involvement in school mental health services?

3. If you were to assess the perspectives of parents in your school, what barriers might they describe to securing mental health services for students? How might the barriers be viewed as opportunities and challenges that lead to potential solutions?

4. Choose one of the practices that this chapter describes for promoting family-educator partnerships when children are at risk for developing social or emotional problems. What might result if this practice were implemented in your school?

5. If limited resources meant that you had to choose between implementing check-in meetings for parents of students at risk of behavior disorders, or behavioral parent management training for students already demonstrating severe behavior disorders, which would you choose and why?

References

Adams, K. S., & Christenson, S. L. (1998). Differences in parent and teacher trust levels: Implications for creating collaborative family-school relationships. *Special Services in the Schools, 14*, 1–22.

Adams, K. S., & Christenson, S. L. (2000). Trust and the family-school relationship: Examination of parent-teacher differences in elementary and secondary grades. *Journal of School Psychology, 38*, 477–497.

Adelman, H. S., & Taylor, L. (2003). Toward a comprehensive policy vision for mental health in schools. In M. D. Weist, S. W. Evans, & N. A. Lever (Eds.), *Handbook of school mental health: Advancing practice and research* (pp. 23–43). New York: Kluwer Academic/Plenum Publishers.

Amatea, E. S., Smith-Adcock, S., & Villares, E. (2006). From family deficit to family strength: Viewing families' contributions to children's learning from a family resilience perspective. *Professional School Counseling, 9*, 177–189.

Anderson, J. A., & Mohr, W. K. (2003). A developmental ecological perspective in systems of care for children with emotional disturbances and their families. *Education and Treatment of Children, 26*, 52–74.

Bronfenbrenner, U. (1992). Ecological systems theory. In R. Vasta (Ed.), *Annals of child development. Six theories of child development: Revised formulations and current issues* (pp. 187–249). London: Jessica Kingsley.

Buerkle, K., Whitehouse, E. M., & Christenson, S. L. (in press). Partnering with families for educational success. In T. Gutkin (Ed.), *The handbook of school psychology IV.*

Carlson, C. I., Hickman, J., & Horton, C. B. (1992). From blame to solutions: Solution-oriented family-school consultation. In S. L. Christenson & J. C. Conoley (Eds.), *Home-school collaboration: Enhancing children's academic and social competence* (pp. 193–213). Silver Spring, MD: National Association of School Psychologists.

Cavell, T. A. (2000). *Working with parents of aggressive children: A practitioner's guide.* Washington, DC: American Psychological Association.

Christenson, S. L. (2001). School psychologists as health care providers: A means to success for all. *School Psychology Review, 29*, 555–556.

Christenson, S. L. (2004). The family-school partnership: An opportunity to promote the learning competence of *all* students. *School Psychology Review, 33*, 83–104.

Christenson, S. L., Anderson, A. R., & Hirsch, J. A. (2004). Families with aggressive children and adolescents. In J. C. Conoley & A. P. Goldstein (Eds.), *School violence intervention: A practical handbook* (2nd ed., pp. 359–399). New York: Guilford Press.

Christenson, S. L., & Buerkle, K. (1999). Families as educational partners for children's school success: Suggestions for school psychologists. In C. R. Reynolds & T. B. Gutkin (Eds.), *Handbook of school psychology* (pp. 709–744). New York: Wiley & Sons.

Christenson, S. L., & Carlson, C. (2005). Evidence-based parent and family intervention in school psychology: State of scientifically-based practice. *School Psychology Quarterly, 20*, 525–527.

Christenson, S. L., & Hirsch, J. (1998). Facilitating partnerships and conflict resolution between families and schools. In K. C. Stoiber & T. Kratochwill (Eds.), *Handbook of group interventions for children and families* (pp. 307–344). Boston: Allyn & Bacon.

Christenson, S. L., Hurley, C. M., Sheridan, S. M., & Fenstermacher, K. (1997). Parents' and school psychologists' perspectives on parent involvement activities. *School Psychology Review, 26*, 111–130.

Christenson, S. L., & Sheridan, S. M. (2001). *Schools and families: Creating essential connections for learning.* New York: Guilford Press.

Collaborative for Academic, Social, and Emotional Learning (CASEL). (2006). *Safe and sound: An education leader's guide to evidence-based social and emotional learning (SEL) programs.* Retrieved February 28, 2006, from http://www.casel.org/projects_products/safeandsound.php

Comer, J.P., Haynes, N.M., Joyner, E.T., & Ben-Avie, M. (1996). *Rallying the whole village: The Comer process for reforming education.* New York: Teachers College Press.

Curtis, M. J., Castillo, J. M., & Cohen, R. M. (in press). Best practices in systems level change. In A. Thomas & J. Grimes (Eds.), *Best practices in school psychology V.* Washington, DC: National Association of School Psychologists.

Davies, D. (1991). Schools reaching out: Family, school, and community partnerships for student success. *Phi Delta Kappan, 72,* 376–382.

deShazer, S. (1988). *Clues: Investigating solutions in brief therapy.* New York: Norton.

Devaney, E., O'Brien, M. U., Resnik, H., Keister, S., & Weissberg, R. P. (2006). *Sustainable schoolwide SEL: Implementation guide and toolkit.* Chicago: University of Illinois at Chicago, Collaborative for Academic, Social, and Emotional Learning (CASEL).

Duckworth, S., Smith-Rex, S., Okey, S., Brookshire, M. A., Rawlinson, D., Rawlinson, R., et al. (2001). Wraparound services for young school children with emotional and behavioral disorders. *Teaching Exceptional Children, 33*(4), 54–60.

Durlak, J. A., & Weissberg, R. P. (2005, August). *A major meta-analysis of positive youth development programs.* Invited presentation at the Annual Meeting of the American Psychological Association, Washington, DC.

Eber, L., Sugai, G., Smith, C. R., & Scott, T. M. (2002). Wraparound and positive behavioral interventions and supports in the schools. *Journal of Emotional and Behavioral Disorders, 10,* 171–181.

Edwards, P. A. (2004). *Children's literacy development: Making it happen through school, family, and community involvement.* Boston: Pearson Education.

Elias, M. L., Zins, J. E., Weissberg, R. P., Frey, K. S., Greenberg, M. T., Haynes, N. M., et al. (1997). *Promoting social and emotional learning: Guidelines for educators.* Alexandria, VA: Association for Supervision and Curriculum Development.

Gantt, A. B., Goldstein, G., & Pinsky, S. (1989). Family understanding of psychiatric illness. *Community Mental Health Journal, 25,* 101–108.

Goddard, R. D., Tschannen-Moran, M., & Hoy, W. K. (2001). A multilevel examination of the distribution and effects of teacher trust in students and parents in urban elementary schools. *The Elementary School Journal, 102,* 3–17.

Graczyk, P. A., Domitrovich, C. E., & Zins, J. E. (2003). Facilitating the implementation of evidence-based prevention and mental health promotion efforts in schools. In M. D. Weist, S. W. Evans, & N. A. Lever (Eds.), *Handbook of school mental health: Advancing practice and research* (pp. 301–318). New York: Kluwer Academic/Plenum Publishers.

Grimes, J., & Tilly, W. D., III. (1996). Policy and process: Means to lasting educational change. *School Psychology Review, 25,* 465–476.

Harry, B. (1993). *Cultural diversity, families, and the special education system: Communication and empowerment.* New York: Teachers College Press.

Ho, B. S. (2001). Family-centered, integrated services: Opportunities for school counselors. *Professional School Counseling, 4,* 357–362.

Holmes, J. G., & Rempel, J. K. (1989). Trust in close relationships. In C. Hendrick (Ed.), *Close relationships* (pp. 187–220). Newbury Park, CA: Sage.

Hoover-Dempsey, K. V., & Sandler, H. M. (1997). Why do parents become involved in their children's education? *Review of Educational Research, 67,* 3–42.

Huang, L., Stroul, B., Friedman, R., Mrazek, P., Friesen, B., Pires, S., & Mayberg, S. (2005). Transforming mental health care for children and their families. *American Psychologist, 60,* 615–627.

Kalyanpur, M., & Harry, B. (1997). A posture of reciprocity: A practical approach to collaboration between professionals and parents of culturally diverse backgrounds. *Journal of Child and Family Studies, 6,* 487–509.

Larson, J. (1994). Violence prevention in the schools: A review of selected programs and procedures. *School Psychology Review, 23,* 151–164.

Lehr, C. A., Sinclair, M. F., & Christenson, S. L. (2004). Addressing student engagement and truancy prevention during the elementary years: A replication study of the Check & Connect model. *Journal of Education for Students Placed At-Risk, 9,* 279–301.

Lombana, J. H. (1983). *Home-school partnerships: Guidelines and strategies for educators.* New York: Grune & Stratton.

Lowie, J. A., Lever, N. A., Ambrose, M. G., Tager, S. B., & Hill, S. (2003). Partnering with families in expanded school mental health programs. In M. D. Weist, S. W. Evans, & N. A. Lever (Eds.), *Handbook of School Mental Health: Advancing Practice and Research* (pp. 135–148). New York: Kluwer Academic/Plenum Publishers.

Maehr, M. L., & Midgley, C. (1996). *Transforming school cultures.* Boulder, CO: Westview Press.

Margolis, H., & Brannigan, G. G. (1990). Strategies for resolving parent-school conflict. *Reading, Writing, and Learning Disabilities, 6,* 1–23.

McWilliam, R. A., Tocci, L., & Harbin, G. L. (1998). Family-centered services: Service providers' discourse and behavior. *Topics in Early Childhood Special Education, 18,* 206–221.

Minnesota Association for Children's Mental Health (MACMH). (2003). *A teacher's guide to children's mental health.* St. Paul, MN: Author.

Nastasi, B. (1998). A model for mental health programming in schools and communities: Introduction to the mini-series. *School Psychology Review, 27,* 165–174.

National Association of School Psychologists (NASP). (2002). *Position statement on interagency collaboration to support the mental health needs of children and families.* Retrieved April 2, 2007, from http://www.nasp online.org/about_nasp/pospaper_iac.aspx

Osher, D. M. (2002). Creating comprehensive and collaborative systems. *Journal of Child and Family Studies, 11,* 91–99.

Osher, T. (1997, July). IDEA Reauthorized—role for families enhanced. *Claiming Children,* 1–8.

Osher, T. W., & Osher, D. M. (2002). The paradigm shift to true collaboration with families. *Journal of Child and Family Studies, 11,* 47–60.

Patrikakou, E. N., & Weissberg, R. P. (1999, February 3). Seven P's to promote school-family partnership efforts. *Education Week, 34,* 36.

Patrikakou, E. N., & Weissberg, R. P. (2000). Parents' perceptions of teacher outreach and parent involvement in children's education. *Journal of Prevention & Intervention in the Community, 20,* 103–119.

Pianta, R., & Walsh, D. B. (1996). *High-risk children in schools: Constructing sustaining relationships.* New York: Routledge.

Rimm-Kaufman, S. E., & Pianta, R. C. (2000). An ecological perspective on the transition to kindergarten: A theoretical framework to guide empirical research. *Journal of Applied Developmental Psychology, 21,* 491–511.

Rones, M., & Hoagwood, K. (2000). School-based mental health services: A research review. *Clinical Child and Family Psychology Review, 3,* 223–241.

Seeley, D. S. (1985). *Education through partnership.* Washington, DC: American Enterprise Institute for Public Policy Research.

Shepard, J., & Carlson, J. S. (2003). An empirical evaluation of school-based prevention programs that involve parents. *Psychology in the Schools, 40,* 641–656.

Sheridan, S. M, & Kratochwill, T. R. (1992). Behavioral parent-teacher consultation: Conceptual and research considerations. *Journal of School Psychology, 30,* 117–139.

Short, R., Kaufman, J., Desrochers, J., Fournier, C., Hazel, C., Hess, R., et al. (2006, Winter). Public health and school psychology: The future of school psychology goal 5 working group. *The School Psychologist, 60*(1), 36.

Sinclair, M. F., Christenson, S. L., Lehr, C. A., & Anderson, A. R. (2003). Facilitating student engagement: Lessons learned from Check & Connect Longitudinal studies. *The California School Psychologist, 8*(1), 29–42.

Sinclair, M. F., Christenson, S. L., & Thurlow, M. L. (2005). Promoting school completion of urban secondary youth with emotional or behavioral disabilities. *Exceptional Children, 71,* 465–482.

Stoner, G. (2006, April). *Prevention- and intervention-oriented school psychology: Issues and challenges for research, training, and practice.* Paper presented at the meeting of the University of Minnesota School Psychology Program, Minneapolis, MN.

Stormshak, E. A., & Dishion, T. J. (2002). An ecological approach to child and family clinical and counseling psychology. *Clinical Child and Family Psychology Review, 5,* 197–215.

Swap, S. M. (1993). *Developing home-school partnerships: From concepts to practice.* New York: Teachers College Press.

Tarico, V. S., Low, B. P., Trupin, E., & Forsyth-Stephens, A. (1989). Children's mental health services: A parent perspective. *Community Mental Health Journal, 25,* 313–326.

Taylor, L., & Adelman, H. S. (2000). Connecting schools, families, and communities. *Professional School Counseling, 3,* 298–308.

U.S. Department of Health and Human Services. (1999). *Mental health: A report of the surgeon general executive summary.* Rockville, MD: Substance

Abuse and Mental Health Services Administration, Center for Mental Health Services, National Institute of Health, National Institute of Mental Health.

Vanderbleek, L. M. (2004). Engaging families in school-based mental health treatment. *Journal of Mental Health Counseling, 26,* 211–224.

Walberg, H. J. (1984). Families as partners in educational productivity. *Phi Delta Kappan, 65,* 397–400.

Webster-Stratton, C. (1993). Strategies for helping early school-aged children with oppositional defiant and conduct disorders: The importance of home-school partnerships. *School Psychology Review, 22,* 437–457.

Woolley, M. E., & Grogan-Kaylor, A. (2006). Protective family factors in the context of neighborhood: Promoting positive school outcomes. *Family Relations, 55,* 93–104.

Wrobel, G. (2004). *Family needs research report: Emotional, behavioral and mental health services for children in Minnesota.* Minneapolis, MN: PACER Center, Inc.

Wynn, J., Meyer, S., & Richards-Schuster, K. (1999, September). Furthering education: The relationship of schools and other organizations. *The CEIC Review, 8(2),* 8–9, 17–19.

Ysseldyke, J., Burns, M., Dawson, P., Kelley, B., Morrison, D., Ortiz, S., et al. (2006). *School psychology: A blueprint for training and practice III.* Bethesda, MD: National Association of School Psychologists.

About the Authors

Sandra L. Christenson is the Birkmaier Professorship of Educational Leadership, a Professor of Educational and Child Psychology, and a faculty member in the School Psychology Program at the University of Minnesota. Her research interests include interventions that enhance student engagement at school and with learning, identification of contextual factors that facilitate student engagement and increase the probability for student success in school, and the development of family-school relationships to enhance students' academic, social, and emotional learning.

Elizabeth M. Whitehouse is in her final year of the doctoral program in School Psychology at the University of Minnesota. Her current research interests include early intervention and prevention, and the role of trust in family-school partnerships.

Gretchen R. VanGetson is a doctoral student in School Psychology at the University of Minnesota. Her current research interests include family-school partnerships and data-driven decision making in education.

5

School-Wide Approaches to Behavior Problems

George G. Bear

Consistent with a population-based mental health framework, and particularly with an emphasis on prevention and promotion of social and emotional competencies, a foremost aim of American education has always been to prepare students to function as responsible citizens in a democratic society. In the context of school discipline, this refers to developing *self-discipline*—social, cognitive, and emotional competencies that guide responsible behavior with minimal external monitoring and regulation. Over the years, this aim has always coexisted with another important educational aim: To establish and maintain a safe and orderly school climate that promotes academic achievement. This includes the *use* of discipline, when necessary, to correct behavior problems. What has changed and been debated the most over the years, including recent ones, is the relative emphasis placed on these two traditional educational aims and the various strategies and techniques used to achieve them (Bear, 1998; 2005).

Prior to the 19th century, it was believed that schools could achieve both aims by focusing primarily on "governing"—by shaping, managing, and correcting student behavior (Finkelstein, 1989).

Typically, this translated into the direct teaching of rules combined with the use of harsh forms of punishment, particularly corporal punishment or removal from school. Beginning in the first half of the 20th century, schools began to shift their emphasis to use of more "positive" techniques for governing student behavior. In the first half of the 20th century, and particularly in schools concerned primarily about governing students, these techniques were based largely on James Watson's (1913) *behaviorism* and Edward Thorndike's (1920) behavioral *laws of learning* (which emphasized that behavior was primarily the function of reinforcement or punishment). In the second half of the 20th century, B. F. Skinner's (1953) principles of operant learning guided behavior management in many classrooms.

Indeed, behavior modification (i.e., the systematic application of behavioral principles of learning to change behavior) and, to a lesser extent, applied behavior analysis (derived from behavioral modification, but with greater emphasis on frequent measurement of observed behaviors, increasing appropriate behaviors, and establishing a functional relationship between a target behavior and the environment) were popular in schools in the 1970s and 1980s, and continue to be used in many schools today (Landrum & Kauffman, 2006). Unfortunately, as in previous centuries, many schools during that period adopted an authoritarian take charge approach to school-wide discipline. This was largely in response to public and teacher perceptions that student disobedience and violence were increasing rapidly. Indeed, *Assertive Discipline: A Take Charge Approach for Today's Educator* (Canter, 1976) was read by over a million educators and its techniques of behavior modification were widely used in the schools. To be sure schools, for decades, if not centuries, have used highly structured reward and punishment systems, including the use of tokens (e.g., tickets and points) to reinforce appropriate behavior (Kazdin, 1977; 1981). However, Assertive Discipline was the first formalized and systematic application of behavior modification techniques (e.g., systematic use of rewards, including tokens; response cost, small number of clearly defined rules) to classroom management used across the nation (Canter, 1989).[1]

By the 1980s, research had shown that positive reinforcement techniques were effective alternatives to punishment in the prevention and correction of misbehavior, not only for increasing appropriate behavior but also for decreasing inappropriate behavior (Kazdin, 1981). Likewise, before the 1980s it was well established that behavioral techniques could be used effectively to modify thoughts related to self-control, or self-discipline (McLaughlin, 1976). Nevertheless, as reflected in the popularity of Assertive Discipline, with its take charge philosophy, most schools in the late 20th century chose to use behavioral techniques to shape, manage, and govern student behavior. Compared to previous centuries, the techniques were certainly less harsh and positive reinforcement was used more often, but the primary aim was one and the same—to shape, manage, and govern students.

To a great extent, this continues to be true today. That is, many schools have chosen to respond to behavior problems with a take charge approach of external control, especially with the use of punishment. Punishment is emphasized in the continued use of corporal punishment in 22 states (primarily in the South; Center for Effective Discipline, 2006). It is particularly evident in the strict and harsh *zero tolerance approach* to school discipline, characterized by the frequent removal of students from school (i.e., suspension, expulsion, and placement in alternative programs), "criminalization" of behaviors (i.e., students being arrested by police for behaviors that schools typically dealt with in the past), use of surveillance cameras and security guards to closely monitor behavior, and elaborate codes of conduct that detail specific rules and consequences for violating them (Skiba & Noam, 2002; Wald & Losen, 2003). Unlike more reasonable zero tolerance *policies* for serious behavior problems that might harm others (e.g., possession of weapons and drugs, bodily injury), a pervasive zero tolerance *approach* is applied to relatively minor rule violations that seldom resulted in removal from school in previous decades (Bear, 2005). There is little support for the effectiveness of the zero tolerance *approach*; research shows that the common use of suspension and expulsion fails to improve student behavior, fosters a negative school climate, and often is racially discriminatory (resulting in a disproportionate number of school removals of African American males; see Skiba & Rausch, 2006).

In contrast to a take charge zero tolerance approach to school-wide discipline with its emphasis on correcting behavior problems primarily with punishment, other schools have adopted a more *positive* approach. The primary goals of a positive approach are preventing behavior problems (instead of correcting them); developing social, emotional, and behavioral competencies; and promoting a positive school-wide climate characterized by safety, caring, and student engagement in learning. These three goals are closely interrelated, in that each influences the other. It should be noted that emphasis on these three goals, largely in response to the overuse of punishment in the schools, is not new in American education. Indeed, these goals were a major focus of progressive educators who espoused character education in the early 20th century (e.g., see Germane & Germane, 1929; McKown, 1935). Unfortunately, this movement did not last for more than a few decades (Hampel, 1986; Lickona, 1991).

A Positive Approach to School-Wide Discipline: Two Contrasting School Reform Programs

Today, the positive approach can be seen in nearly all popular models of classroom management (e.g., Positive Discipline [Nelsen, Lott, & Glenn, 2000]; Assertive Discipline [Canter & Canter, 2001]), popular curriculum programs designed more specifically for preventing school violence and promoting social and emotional competencies or social skills (e.g., *Second Step: A violence prevention curriculum* [Committee for Children, 2003]; *Skillstreaming* [Goldstein & McGinnis, 1997; McGinnis & Goldstein, 1997]), and more comprehensive school-wide reform programs that focus primarily on issues of discipline and social and emotional development. Such classroom management models, curriculum packages, and reform programs share many of the same positive, and empirically supported, techniques, including the strategic use of positive reinforcement and modeling. However, they often differ greatly in the extent to which behaviorally oriented and teacher-centered techniques are used versus more cognitively and emotionally oriented student-centered techniques. The relative emphasis on these techniques often reflects an important underlying difference in the primary aim of the respective programs—to either shape, manage, and govern student behavior or help students develop social, emotional, and behavioral competencies for self-discipline.

This important difference in the primary aim of school-wide discipline, and the methods and techniques used to achieve it, is perhaps best seen in two school-wide reform movements in the United States: (a) Caring School Community (CSC) programs (see Battistich, Schaps, Watson, Solomon, & Lewis, 2000; Watson, & Battistich, 2006; also see www.devstu.org) and closely related Responsive Classroom programs (Charney, 2002; Rimm-Kaufman & Sawyer, 2004; also see www.responsiveclassroom.org), and (b) school-wide positive behavior supports (PBS) programs (see Horner, Sugai, Todd, & Lewis-Palmer, 2005; Lewis, Newcomer, Trussell, & Richter, 2006; Sprague & Horner, 2006; also see www.pbis.org). CSC and Responsive Classroom programs use a variety of *student-centered* techniques for developing social and emotional competence and qualities of character associated with self-discipline, and also for preventing and correcting behavior problems. In contrast, PBS programs emphasize the use of a variety of *teacher-centered* behavioral techniques, grounded in the basic behavioral principles of learning proposed by Watson, Thorndike, and Skinner, for preventing and correcting behavior problems. PBS programs also place much greater emphasis on addressing the needs of students with serious and chronic behavior problems.

CSC and PBS programs are reviewed briefly in the following sections. (Note that because of space limitations, the Responsive Classroom program is not reviewed, but it is very similar in philosophy and techniques to CSC programs.) Following these brief reviews, I draw recommendations for school-wide discipline from both programs as well as additional research. These recommendations are grouped into four general components of comprehensive school-wide discipline (Bear, 2005): (a) developing self-discipline, (b) preventing behavior problems, (c) correcting behavior problems, and (d) providing supports, resources, and services to address the needs of students who have serious or chronic behavior problems or are at-risk for such.

Caring School Community

Key Features

CSC programs are grounded in research and theory in developmental psychology, especially in the areas of prosocial development, attachment, and motivation. Previously referred to as the Child Development Project, CSC programs were first implemented in three elementary schools in 1982 as part of a seven-year longitudinal study of school-wide reform to help children "become caring, principled, and self-disciplined" (Schaps, Battistich, & Solomon, 1997, p. 127). The project quickly expanded to other schools across the nation and added the goal of enhancing children's intellectual/academic development. CSC programs emphasize developing self-discipline, preventing behavior problems, and increasing academic motivation and achievement through creating a strong sense of belonging, or connectedness, to school (Battistich, Schaps, Watson, Solomon, & Lewis, 2000; Watson & Battistich, 2006). The aim of CSC programs is to "help build children's capacity to think clearly and critically, while simultaneously deepening their commitment to the values of kindness, helpfulness, personal responsibility, and respect for others" (retrieved June 4, 2006, from http://www.devstu.org). CSC programs are guided by four key principles: (a) *respectful, supportive relationships,*

(b) *opportunities for autonomy and influence,* (c) *opportunities for collaboration,* and (d) *emphasis on common purpose and ideals.* These four principles, which are closely interrelated (e.g., respectful, supportive relationships help develop self-discipline), are embedded throughout all school practices, policies, instruction, and curriculum materials.

Foremost among those principles are respectful, supportive relationships. These include teacher-student, student-student, and school-home relationships. Emphasized throughout all aspects of CSC programs, respectful and supportive relationships are viewed as critical to establishing and maintaining shared norms centered on caring, and a commitment to them. It is within the context of respectful, supportive relationships that all other program elements are implemented. This includes instruction and curriculum lessons that target various social and emotional competencies, such as social problem solving and decision making, that are commonly the focus of social and emotional learning (SEL) programs (Collaborative for Academic, Social, and Emotional Learning [CASEL], 2003; also see www.casel .org) and character education programs (Berkowitz & Schwartz, 2006; also see www.character.org). As in other school-wide SEL and character education programs, in CSC programs there is no one scheduled time or period for developing social and emotional competencies or character. This occurs throughout the day, as lessons are infused throughout the curriculum. Research shows those programs to be effective in enhancing not only social-emotional adjustment, but also academic achievement (Berkowitz & Bier, 2004; Greenberg, et al., 2003; Zins, Weissberg, Wang, & Walberg, 2004).

Supported by research on peer-assisted learning (see Ginsburg-Block, Rohrbeck, Fantuzzo, & Lavigne, 2006), another component of CSC is *Buddies,* in which older students in one class are paired with younger "buddies" in another class to assist, tutor, and practice general caring toward others. This includes completion of structured learning activities in language arts, math, science, social studies, art, music, and physical education. Further infusion of social and emotional learning activities for promoting caring is seen in the CSC reading comprehension program for Grades K–8, *Making Meaning* (Developmental Studies Center, 2003). While they learn reading comprehension skills, students also are taught SEL competencies, such as basic classroom procedures, appreciating and respecting one another's ideas, giving reasons to support thoughts and opinions, asking clarifying questions, reaching agreement, discussing opinions respectfully, and confirming the understanding of another person. These skills also are taught and, more important, practiced in class meetings (Developmental Studies Center, 2000). Class meetings are routinely held, preferably daily, to develop a true sense of involvement, responsibility, and caring in the school community and to highlight prosocial values. During class meetings, as well as in many curriculum lessons, teachers facilitate discussion, group decision making, and social problem solving, while strongly encouraging moral reasoning based on empathy, caring, perspective taking, fairness, and justice. Class rules are developed collaboratively among all members of the school community, with an emphasis on understanding and appreciating the reasons for the rules.

Another important component of CSC programs, especially with respect to school-wide discipline, is the method used to correct disciplinary problems, referred to as *developmental discipline* (Battistich, Solomon, Watson, & Schaps, 1997; Watson, 2003). It is understood that students make mistakes, and with appropriate support and guidance they can learn from them. Thus, behavior problems are not viewed as occasions for teachers and administrators to simply punish inappropriate behavior and rule violations, but as opportunities to help students develop social-emotional and behavioral competencies associated with self-discipline and promote a strong commitment to the school community. External control, including removal to another classroom, is used for the purpose of correction. However, the primary technique of correction is *induction,* which emphasizes the impact of one's behavior on others, as opposed to the consequences to oneself (e.g., avoiding punishment or earning future tangible rewards). This fosters empathy, empathy-based guilt (not to be confused with shame), assumption of responsibility for one's behavior, and pride in one's good behavior (Hoffman, 2000). An additional focus during disciplinary encounters is teaching prosocial alternative behaviors, repairing any harm that has been done, and avoiding similar behavior problems in the future. A scaffolding approach guides the teaching of prosocial behaviors by individualizing the amount of guidance and support based on each child's social and emotional competencies. Guidance and support are systematically reduced, and ultimately removed, as students demonstrate social and emotional competencies, including responsibility for their behavior.

In addition to an emphasis on induction, CSC programs also emphasize the active involvement of students in establishing and maintaining norms that foster student motivation and learning, safety, a sense of community, and self-discipline. Such student involvement is not limited to issues of discipline, but applies to all components of the program. This is consistent with the program's guiding student-centered philosophy that

"When children genuinely have a say in the life of the classroom—class norms, study topics, conflict resolution, field-trip logistics, and so on—then they are committed to the decisions they have been trusted to make and feel responsible for the community they have helped shaped" (Schaps, Battistich, & Solomon, 1997, p. 129).

Other components of CSC programs are an after-school program and a home component. Both are designed to foster generalization and maintenance of academic and social-emotional competencies learned throughout all elements of the program.

Supporting Research

Few school-wide programs for promoting social and emotional development have been researched as extensively as those of the CSC. Studies, including those with longitudinal designs and control groups, show that participating students display greater empathy for others, prosocial motivation, and conflict resolution skills (Battistich, Solomon, Watson, Solomon, & Schaps, 1989; Solomon, Battistich, Watson, Schaps, & Lewis, 2000; Solomon, Watson, Battistich, Schaps, & Delucchi, 1996); more prosocial behavior (Solomon, Watson, Delucchi, Schaps, & Battistich, 1988), and reduced substance abuse and delinquent behaviors (Battistich & Hom, 1997; Battistich, Schaps, Watson, Solomon, & Lewis, 2000; Solomon et al. 2000). Recent research also shows CSC programs to be among the most cost-effective programs for youth development: With an average cost of only $16 per student, CSC programs yield $28.42 in benefits for every dollar spent (Aos, Lieb, Mayfield, Miller, & Pennucci, 2004). A wealth of additional research (reviewed in the following sections on Developing Self-Discipline and Preventing Behavior Problems) supports each component of the program, including its focus on promoting teacher-student relations, student-student relations, and home-school relations; developing social cognitive and emotional processes associated with self-discipline; using peer-assisted learning activities; and generally creating a positive school climate.

Despite extensive research demonstrating increased prosocial behavior, concern for others, conflict resolution skills, and democratic values, there is little evidence that students in CSC schools actually exhibit fewer behavior problems. This is likely related to two of its shortcomings with respect to school-wide discipline. First, whereas the methods and techniques of developmental discipline may help promote the previously mentioned positive outcomes and prevent misbehavior among many students, they may not be sufficient for *decreasing* behavior problems that students already exhibit. Indeed, as recently noted by Watson and Battistich (2006), two developers and researchers of CSC programs, teachers in several CSC schools have rejected the developmental discipline's student-centered approach to correcting misbehavior in which the use of rewards and punishment is strongly discouraged. As a result, developmental discipline is now less emphasized in CSC programs (Watson & Battistich, 2006). A second limitation, particularly with respect to providing comprehensive school-wide discipline, is that CSC programs fail to address the needs of students with serious and chronic behavior problems. As seen in the next section, these two limitations of CSC programs are relative strengths of PBS programs.

School-Wide Positive Behavior Supports

Key Features

The rapidly growing interest in school-wide PBS programs can be attributed largely to inclusion of the term "positive behavioral interventions and supports" in the 1997 and 2004 versions of the Individuals with Disabilities Education Act. The term "school-wide PBS" does not appear in the act, but is commonly used in the literature in the context of schools implementing early intervening services to prevent problem behaviors and to address any discrepancies in the rates of long-term suspensions and expulsions of children when compared to the rates for children without disabilities (as required in the act). States may use federal funds to implement school-wide prevention-oriented programs, including school-wide PBS programs. Common definitions of school-wide PBS vary considerably along a continuum from a rather limited focus on the strict, systematic use of applied behavioral analytic techniques to directly teach compliance with behavioral expectations (which typically means posting rules and the systematic use of tangible rewards) to a more general perspective that values the integration of a broad range of strategies and techniques for improving school climate and developing student social-emotional and behavioral competencies. However, it is the former perspective that appears most often in the literature (e.g., Horner et al., 2005).

At the core of the school-wide PBS approach is the three-tier model for prevention and intervention, adapted from the public mental health model of prevention (Adelman & Taylor, 2006), consisting of (a) *universal* intervention, with an emphasis on school-wide positive interventions for *all* children to prevent behavior problems, (b) *selected* intervention (generally consisting of intensive social skills training) for children who are at-risk for serious behavior problems and/or experiencing negative outcomes resulting from the presence of risk factors, and (c) *indicated* or *intensive* intervention for individual students who exhibit serious behavior problems and need intensive, comprehensive, and individualized interventions and services (i.e., often referred to as *wraparound* services, as discussed later). Across each tier, four key elements, or defining features apply (Horner et al., 2005): (a) *student outcomes,* (b) *research-validated procedures,* (c) *supportive systems,* and (d) *ongoing collection and use of data for decision making.*

1. *Student outcomes.* In addition to academic achievement, the most important school-wide outcome of PBS programs is observable social skills. PBS schools determine the social skills to be targeted and define them as measurable standards for social behavior and safety. Typically, this translates into a small number of school-wide expectations, or rules that students are to learn, as evidenced in their compliance, such as: "Follow directions." "Be respectful." "Be responsible." "Be kind." "Do your best." For example, Horner et al. provide the following sample for teaching the school-wide behavioral expectation of responsibility:

- Be responsible:

  In the classroom: Bring books and pencil to class. Do homework.

  In gym: Participate. Wear appropriate shoes.

  In the hallway: Keep books, belongings, litter off floor.

  On the playground: Stay within the recess area.

  In the bus area: Keep your books and belongings with you.

2. *Research-validated practices.* As noted by Horner et al. (2005), "These include the curriculum, classroom management, instructional procedures, rewards, and contingencies that are used on a daily basis to build and sustain student competence" (p. 365). The most common practice in the PBS research literature for teaching social behavior is a combination of direct instruction methods, consisting primarily of social skills instruction, the posting of rules throughout the building, reinforcement of rule-following behavior, and punishment for noncompliance. For example, at all grade levels PBS schools are advised to follow "5 guiding practices" (Horner et al., 2005):

- Clearly define 3–5 behavioral expectations in positive terms (see samples above), post them throughout the school ("in at least 80% of public spaces in the school"), and review them every day.
- Directly teach behavioral expectations using the basic principles of social skills training: Teachers are to tell students behavioral expectations (or rules), give them concrete behavioral examples of behavior that is compliant with the expectations, and have students rehearse and reinforce examples of those behaviors.
- Monitor and encourage expected behavior throughout the building, and throughout the day, using "tangible rewards or simple verbal statements" (p. 370).
- Prevent and discourage problem behaviors by providing a continuum of clear and fair consequences that are consistently enforced when problem behaviors are observed. All problem behaviors, both minor and major, are to be distinct and operationally defined.
- Collect and use data for decision making.

Those practices are consistent with a primary goal of PBS being to teach "basic social skills" (Sugai, Horner, & Gresham, 2002, p. 320). As Horner et al. (2005) note, "every child entering school should receive clear instruction on what is acceptable, and ongoing recognition when he or she engages in appropriate behavior" (p. 362).

3. *Supportive systems.* Emphasis is placed on the following "systems" to support and sustain effective practices: (a) team-based implementation, (b) administrative leadership, (c) documented commitment (i.e., at least 80% of the staff agrees to actively participate and support the program), (d) adequate personnel and time, (e) budgeted support, and (f) an information system. Team-based implementation assumes that the team will develop and implement an action plan based on the team's completion of a needs assessment.

4. *Ongoing collection and use of data for decision making.* Consistent with an applied behavior analysis approach, PBS schools are expected to engage in the ongoing collection of data and apply such data to guide decision making. Several data-based instruments have been developed for the purposes of planning and monitoring the fidelity of program implementation (see www.pbssurveys.org). In examining outcomes, by far the most common measure has been to

count disciplinary referrals (e.g., Lohrman-O'Rourke et al., 2000; Luiselli, Putnam, & Sunderland, 2002; Sadler, 2000; Taylor-Greene & Kartub, 2000). PBS schools are to organize, and analyze, disciplinary data "(1) per day and per month, (2) per type of problem behavior, (3) per location in the school, (4) per time of day, and (5) per child" (Horner et al., 2005, p. 374). Consistent with the applied behavior analysis and PBS frameworks, the recommended method for analyzing data is the same as that used in conducting an individual functional behavioral assessment (FBA).

Supporting Research

As reviewed later, research shows that the basic techniques of reinforcement and punishment are quite effective in bringing about changes in the behavior of individual students and small groups of students, especially short-term changes. Likewise, as cited later, longitudinal research demonstrates the school-wide effectiveness of the Good Behavior Game, an interdependent group contingency system used in some PBS programs. Although certainly not unique to PBS, emphasis on creating a positive school climate also is supported by research, as noted previously in the review of CSC programs. Likewise, there is much support in the mental health literature for the three-tier framework of services and an emphasis on team planning, school commitment, and data-based decision making (Adelman & Taylor, 2006).

Although research supports several components of PBS programs, very little empirical research has been published on their *school-wide* effectiveness. Such studies are underway, however (Sprague & Horner, 2006). Particularly lacking are comparative studies in which students or schools are assigned to treatment and control conditions and longitudinal studies demonstrating generalization and maintenance of positive behaviors. And, as Landrum and Kauffman (2006) note with respect to behavioral interventions in general: "The failure of researchers to produce treatment effects that routinely generalize to other settings, times, and responses has been a sharp and essentially legitimate criticism of behavioral programming since its early application to classroom settings" (p. 59). Studies that do exist tend to be within-school studies demonstrating reductions in office referrals (an outcome measure widely recommended in the PBS literature). Unfortunately, office discipline referrals can be a very poor measure of program effectiveness because of their often questionable reliability and validity (Morrison, Redding, Fisher, & Peterson, 2006; Sugai, Sprague, Horner, & Walker, 2000).

Several key features of PBS programs also lack research support, especially social skills training and the use of FBA. With respect to the effectiveness of social skills training, effect sizes are typically of small magnitude, and there is very little evidence supporting the generalization and maintenance of skills taught (Bullis, Walker, & Sprague, 2001; DuPaul & Eckert, 1994). Likewise, there is little support for using FBAs in guiding PBS interventions and school-wide supports (as frequently recommended by PBS advocates, e.g., Bambara, 2005; Crone & Horner, 2003; Lewis et al., 2006). This is especially true for students without disabilities or beyond the early grades, or for common discipline problems in which antecedents and consequences are not easy to observe and manipulate (e.g., substance use, many acts of violence, stealing, cheating, lying). Research has raised serious questions about whether FBAs can be conducted in a reliable manner, if they lead to more effective interventions, and if they are practical in the schools (Gresham, McIntyre, Olson-Tinker, Dolstra, McLaughlin, & Van, 2004; Landrum & Kauffman, 2006; Sasso, Conroy, Stichter, & Fox, 2001; Scott, Bucalos et al., 2004; Scott, McIntyre et al., 2005).

Comprehensive School-Wide Discipline

Obviously, it is much better that schools adopt a positive approach to discipline, as seen in CSC, SEL, character education, and PBS programs, instead of a punitive zero tolerance approach. However, it is unfortunate that many schools adopt one *or* the other of the two types of positive approaches seen above. In so doing, they often ignore weaknesses of the program adopted and the strengths of other programs. As a result, few schools are sufficiently comprehensive in their school-wide discipline program to achieve the two traditional aims of school discipline with *all* students—to develop self-discipline and to establish and maintain an orderly, safe, and positive environment conducive to learning. Neither are schools' discipline programs sufficiently comprehensive to achieve the four goals of population-based mental health services:

(a) to promote the psychological well-being of all students so that they can achieve developmental competence, (b) to promote caretaking environments that nurture students and allow them to overcome minor risks and challenges, (c) to provide protective support to students at high risk for developmental failures, and (d) to remediate social, emotional or behavioral disturbances so that students can develop competence. (Doll & Cummings, this volume, chapter 1).

With respect to school-wide discipline, Goal 1 must include the development of social and emotional competencies related to self-discipline. This is the primary aim of CSC programs, but an aim that is rarely mentioned in the PBS literature or adequately addressed in PBS programs. Goal 2, focusing on prevention and establishing a positive school climate, is a goal of both programs, but the programs differ greatly in the preventive strategies and techniques emphasized. Whereas CSC programs highlight the social and emotional aspects of teacher-student, student-student, and school-home relations (e.g., caring, trust, flexibility), PBS programs tend to focus on observable communications and behavioral expectations, and the systematic use of reinforcement (e.g., posting rules or behavioral expectations throughout the school building, communicating the expectations to parents, and rewarding students for good behavior). With a foundation largely in special education, as reviewed later, PBS programs address Goals 3 and 4 to a greater extent than do CSC programs. This includes not only providing specific techniques of behavior change, especially for addressing behavior problems of students with serious or chronic behavior problems and for those deemed at-risk, but also offering guidelines for a more comprehensive system of support, resources, and services.

The four goals of population-based mental health services fit nicely with four goals and components of comprehensive school-wide discipline (Bear, 2005): (a) to develop self-discipline, (b) to prevent behavior problems, (c) to correct behavior problems, and (d) to remediate behavior problems. I discuss each of these components in the following sections, while emphasizing that to be truly comprehensive, a school-wide discipline program needs to include key features of both CSC and PBS programs. It is important to note that, although these four components of school-wide discipline are interrelated and use many of the same strategies and techniques, they are not one and the same. Achieving one does not necessarily achieve the other. For example, it is not uncommon for schools to be effective in preventing and correcting behavior problems, but ineffective in developing self-discipline (a limitation of PBS programs) and addressing the needs of students with serious and chronic behavior problems (a limitation of CSC programs). Thus, all four components are important, and none should be neglected.

Component 1: Developing Self-Discipline

In CSC programs, this component is referred to as developing autonomy. An advantage of the term *self-discipline* is that it highlights that school-wide *discipline* should not focus on adults governing students and managing their behavior, but on helping students develop social cognitive and emotional competencies associated with socially and morally responsible behavior (Bear & Watkins, 2006). In this context, self-discipline refers to socially and morally responsible behavior that is guided by the internalization of the values, standards, and beliefs important in one's society (Grusec & Goodnow, 1994). Internalization is not the same as simply *knowing* rules or standards of behavior and the consequences of disobeying, or obeying, them. Content knowledge is a poor predictor of behavior (e.g., nearly all students know they are not supposed to steal, hit others, cheat, use drugs, fight, and so forth). Programs that focus on teacher-centered, direct instructional methods for teaching such knowledge have consistently been found to have little effectiveness in preventing behavior problems (Gottfredson, 1997; Hartshorne & May, 1928). To be internalized, values, standards, and beliefs must be accepted as one's own. This promotes *willing* or *committed* compliance with rules and directives, as opposed to *grudging* or *situational* compliance (Brophy, 1996; Kochanska, 2002). It also promotes responsible citizenship when monitoring by adults, the promise of rewards, and the likelihood of punishment are not salient—the ultimate aim of school discipline.

In addition to being associated with increased compliance in school, and responsible citizenship in society, there are three other reasons why self-discipline should be a primary aim of school-wide discipline (Bear, Manning, & Izard, 2003). First, self-discipline promotes positive relations with peers (Wentzel, 1996) and teachers (Birch & Ladd, 1998; Hughes, Cavell, & Willson, 2001). This is seen in an overall positive school climate characterized by greater empathy and caring about others and fewer discipline problems (Battistich, Schaps, Watson, Solomon, & Lewis, 2000; Osterman, 2000). Second, self-discipline has a positive impact on academic achievement (Berkowitz & Bier, 2004; Caprara, Barbaranelli, Pastorelli, Bandura, & Zimbardo, 2000; Malecki & Elliott, 2002; Zins et al., 2004). Third, self-discipline, but particularly self-perceptions thereof, promotes feelings of overall positive self-worth, which in turn foster general emotional well-being and motivate further good behavior (Harter, 1999; Kochanska, 2002).

Undoubtedly, behavioral techniques (e.g., positive reinforcement, modeling, response cost) can, and should, be used to help promote self-discipline. However, behavioral techniques should not be limited to teaching observable motor behaviors as seen in many PBS programs. Instead, they should be used, in combination with other techniques discussed later, to teach social cognitive and emotional processes (observed in verbalizations as well as reflected in motoric behaviors) that research has linked to prosocial behavior (Eisenberg, Fabes, & Spinrad, 2006), resilience (Doll & Lyon, 1998), and inhibition of antisocial behavior (Dodge, Coie, & Lynam, 2006). For example, such research shows that compared to children without behavior problems, and especially to those who exhibit frequent prosocial behavior, aggressive and antisocial children exhibit a variety of social cognitive and emotional deficits and deficiencies (see Dodge et al, 2006; Dodge & Pettit, 2003, for reviews). These include (a) having difficulty reading social cues (Hubbard, Dodge, Cillessen, Coie, & Schwartz, 2001), including a strong tendency to overly interpret hostile intentions in others (see Orobio de Castro, Veerman, Koops, Bosch, & Monshouwer, 2002, for review); (b) responding impulsively, failing to inhibit aggressive responses (Barkley et al., 2002); (c) having difficulty regulating anger, especially with respect to reactive (or opposed to proactive) aggression (Hubbard et al., 2002); (d) generating lower quality solutions to interpersonal problems (e.g., Dodge & Pettit, 2003), believing these aggressive or self-centered solutions are justified and lead to positive outcomes (Boldizar, Perry, & Perry, 1989; Burks, Laird, Dodge, Pettit, & Bates, 1999; Crick & Ladd, 1990; Erdley & Asher, 1998); (e) being motivated by the goal of getting what they want, irrespective of the impact of their behavior on others, rather than by the values and goals of social acceptance, respect from others, and a sense of integrity (Covington, 2000; Erdley & Asher, 1999); and (f) believing that aggression is easier and more effective in getting them what they desire than more prosocial alternatives (Erdley & Asher, 1998; Quiggle, Garber, Panak, & Dodge, 1992). These deficits and deficiencies are reflected in well-established and rehearsed *cognitive scripts* stored in memory and impulsively drawn on to guide the students' behavior (Burks et al., 1999; Huesmann, 1988; Zelli, Dodge, Lochman, & Laird, 1999).

Integral to social information processing is moral reasoning. Research shows that the moral reasoning of aggressive and antisocial children tends to be hedonistic, or self-centered, focusing on consequences of getting caught and seeking rewards, rather than the impact of one's behavior on others or anticipating and experiencing feelings of guilt (Hoffman, 2000; Kuther, 2000; Manning & Bear, 2002; Palmer & Hollin, 2001). Bullies share this self-centered perspective (Menesini, Sanchez, Fonzi, Ortega, Costabile, & Lo Feudo, 2003). Research also shows that, whereas the pathway to serious conduct problems for many children is poor parenting, low intelligence, high emotional reactivity, and poor self-regulation, the pathway for others is a self-centered perspective. This self-centeredness is characterized by a failure to experience and anticipate empathy-based guilt, a lack of sensitivity to cues of danger and punishment, and a strong desire to gain rewards (Frick, Cornell, Barry, Bodin, & Dane, 2003; Pardini, Lochman, & Frick, 2003).

Bandura and colleagues (1997, 2001; Bandura, Caprara, Barbaranelli, & Regalia, 2001) have identified specific mechanisms of moral disengagement or cognitive distortions that are directly linked to moral reasoning. Individuals use them to justify their decisions to act (or not to act) in a certain way to others and to themselves, and to avoid feelings of responsibility or guilt. Such cognitive distortions are often seen in the excuses that students give for violating school rules or their own standards. Mechanisms of moral disengagement that are most relevant to violations of classroom and school rules are (a) moral or social justification ("He deserved it."), (b) euphemisms and convoluted language ("I was just joking."), (c) exonerative or advantageous comparison ("Others did it too."), (d) displacement and diffusion of responsibility ("He made me do it."), and (e) blame-shifting ("He started it.").

In order to develop self-discipline and to promote a positive school climate, it makes sense that schools target social cognitions and emotions—especially those that promote prosocial behavior and resilience and those that inhibit antisocial behavior. Strategies and techniques for helping to achieve this important aim include the following:

1. *Implement curriculum activities that teach social, emotional, and behavioral competencies.* A wealth of guidance, lessons, and activities for achieving this objective are provided in recent research and literature in social and emotional learning (see CASEL, 2003, for a review). Among packaged programs that have been shown to improve behavior, two were the focus of several control-group studies: *Second Step: A Violence Prevention Curriculum* (Committee for Children, 2003; Fitzgerald & Van Schoiack-Edstrom, 2006) and the *Promoting Alternative Thinking Strategies* curriculum (PATHS; Greenberg & Kusché, 2006; Kusché & Greeenberg, 1994). Instead of, or in addition to, adopting a packaged curriculum, one should give serious consideration to *infusing* instruction and activities for promoting self-discipline throughout the general curriculum, as CSC programs do. Many schools are likely to find this strategy to be less disruptive to the existing curriculum because it requires no "add-on" or additional expense.

2. *Provide multiple models of social and moral problem solving, moral and regulated emotions, and responsible behavior.* The learning and motivational

advantages of modeling are well known (Bandura, 1986). Multiple models of targeted social cognitions, emotions, and behaviors should be included in the school's curriculum (literature, videos), and more important, in the real life of the classroom and school. As CSC programs do, models of targeted cognitions, emotions, and behaviors should routinely be integrated into the curriculum and the life of the school, exhibited by teachers and staff, and reinforced and highlighted when displayed by students.

3. Provide multiple opportunities for students to apply skills of social and moral problem solving and responsible behavior. As in CSC programs, ample opportunities should be provided for students to apply the processes and skills taught and modeled. Such opportunities would include class meetings (Developmental Studies Center, 2000), student government, and school-wide activities in which students actively participate in conflict resolution, peer mediation, and peacemaking (Johnson & Johnson, 2006).

4. De-center self-centered thinking, especially during disciplinary encounters. Corrective techniques, including techniques for reducing inappropriate behavior and increasing replacement behavior, are necessary and critical components of school-wide discipline. Induction can be used during disciplinary encounters with individual students, and in class meetings when social and moral issues are discussed. Where appropriate, induction should be combined with tactful confrontation of cognitive distortions, excuses, and mechanisms of disengagement, as used in the empirically supported *Aggression Replacement Training* program (Goldstein, Glick, & Gibbs, 1998) and the *EQUIP* program (Gibbs, Potter, & Goldstein, 1995) for aggressive youth. These programs combine strategies for confronting self-centered moral reasoning with social skills and anger control training. Both induction and confrontation should be used in the context of a respectful and supportive teacher-student relationship, and scaffolded so that the level of support through verbal guidance, supporting questions, and modeling depends on the individual competencies of the student. They should also be used in a reflective, non-interrogative manner that promotes social cognitive and emotional processes instead of simple repetition of rules and consequences. Additional opportunities for teaching, modeling, reinforcement, and practice of social cognitive and emotional processes and skills linked to self-discipline include peer-assisted and cooperative learning opportunities, sports and extracurricular activities, and service learning opportunities.

Component 2: Preventing Behavior Problems

As one can see in both CSC and PBS programs, prevention is a critical component of school-wide discipline. In addition to developing self-discipline, the best method of preventing behavior problems is establishing a school climate in which caring, respect, fairness, and safety are the norm and clear sanctions against antisocial behavior are communicated. Important elements of such a positive climate are (a) respectful, supportive relationships, (b) clear behavioral expectations, (c) a physical environment conducive to learning and safety, (d) academic instruction that engages and motivates learning, (e) the strategic use of praise and rewards, and (f) immediate response to early signs of behavior problems.

Respectful, Supportive Relationships

Teacher-Student Relationships

As emphasized in CSC programs, students feel more comfortable and supported in schools in which teachers are caring, respectful, and emotionally supportive (e.g., Battistich, Solomon, Watson, & Schaps, 1997; Birch & Ladd, 1998; Hamre & Pianta, 2006; Pianta, 1999). They are more likely to internalize the school's values (Wentzel, 1997, 2004), as reflected in greater prosocial behavior and fewer antisocial behaviors. For example, students in schools with positive teacher-student relations report less cheating (Murdock, Hale, & Weber, 2001), greater peer acceptance (Hughes et al., 2001), and greater motivation to act responsibly and prosocially (Wentzel, 1996). They also experience higher rates of school completion (Reschly & Christenson, 2006), greater academic achievement (Gregory & Weinstein, 2004; Hamre & Pianta, 2001), and less oppositional and antisocial behavior (Bru, Murberg, & Stephens, 2001; Bru, Stephens, & Torsheim, 2002; Meehan, Hughes, & Cavell, 2003; Murdock, 1999). Although important to all children, teacher support is likely to be most critical to those children who lack support from parents, peers, and close friends (Harter, 1999; Pianta, 1999).

In light of research highlighting the critical importance of teacher-student relations, Hughes et al. (2001) suggest that schools should focus intervention efforts on building personal relationships instead of, or in addition to, interventions that focus on social skills training. This should include increased quality time in which teachers are able to demonstrate sincere interest in every student; show respect and understanding of student interests, opinions, and suggestions; and provide social, emotional, and academic support in times of difficulty. Additional recommendations for enhancing teacher-student relationships include reducing teacher-student ratios (e.g., creating small teacher-student teams in middle school and high school) and *Banking Time* (teachers arranging for brief, regular interactions with individual students to build student-teacher relationships; Hamre & Pianta, 2006).

Student-Student Relationships

The influence of peers on student behavior is well established, as reflected in the vast amount of research on peer relations and friendships (see Rubin, Bukowski, & Parker, 2006). Thus, it is understandable that many published curriculum packages for promoting social and emotional learning and preventing school violence, including Second Step and PATHS, emphasize enhancing peer relationships and developing skills of empathy, conflict resolution, peer pressure resistance, and social problem solving. Likewise, enhancing peer relationships is the primary focus of school-wide anti-bullying programs designed to change a school's norms and culture (see Swearer et al., this volume, chapter 8).

Home-School Relationships

In recognition of the profound impact families have on the academic, social, and emotional development of their children (Parke & Buriel, 2006), CSC programs emphasize home-school relationships, as do more comprehensive school reform efforts (e.g., Comer, Haynes, Joyner, & Ben-Avie, 1996). This includes informing parents about school discipline policies, procedures, and rules, as well as their children's behavior (both good and bad), and inviting them to play an active, collaborative, and supportive role in their development (Christenson & Sheridan, 2001). Trusting home-school communication and collaboration is particularly critical when intensive interventions are needed and when behavior problems are first observed to be resistant to common classroom interventions.

Clear Behavioral Expectations for All Students

Clear behavioral expectations is a common element of nearly all evidence-based models of classroom management (e.g., Evertson, Emmer, & Worsham, 2006; Weinstein & Mignano, 2007), as well as both CSC and PBS programs. It is widely recognized that schools should convey the attitude that *all* children can behave appropriately, while also being responsive to individual and developmental differences. Expectations should be communicated clearly, in policies and practices (including rules, procedures, and routines), with the understanding that meeting such expectations is a responsibility shared by students, teachers, school staff, and the home. This includes the expectation that students will act in a manner that is consistent with the lessons taught to develop self-discipline (e.g., respecting and caring about others). It also includes following school rules, which should remind students that, although self-discipline is expected, it is necessary to use externally imposed behavior management in the absence of self-discipline. As discussed later under Component 4, a continuum of academic and behavioral supports should also be provided. These offer varying degrees of remedial instruction and practice, and are most effective if they begin when problems requiring remediation are first recognized.

Physical Environment That Is Conducive to Learning and Safety

Research shows that behavior problems are more likely to occur in certain social contexts than in others, such as when students are in very close physical proximity to other students, such as during transitional periods, recess, lunch, and in hallways and on the bus, and especially when they are not supervised by adults (Astor, Benbenishty, Marachi, & Meyer, 2006). Many behavior problems that occur under these conditions can be prevented by providing close supervision and monitoring; imposing clear expectations, routines, procedures, and rules specific to those situations; and providing a supportive physical environment that is conducive to learning. This includes classrooms that are physically attractive and in which furniture, seating arrangements, materials, and supplies are organized to foster student attention to instruction and teacher monitoring of behavior. It also includes buildings and grounds with appropriate lighting, alarm systems, fences, locks, and class schedules and traffic flow to minimize behavior problems. Surveillance cameras, metal detectors, locker inspections, and other more intrusive techniques should be used only where appropriate and necessary.

Academic Instruction That Engages and Motivates Learning

Behavior problems are much less likely to occur when students are actively engaged in academic learning. Thus, many behavior problems are prevented when teachers engage in highly effective instruction (Brophy, 2004; Morrone & Pintrich, 2006). Such teachers exhibit the following: interest and enthusiasm toward the subject matter taught; momentum and smoothness in instruction; high rates of success, especially when new concepts are introduced; high, clear, and reasonable expectations, standards, and requirements; accountability for meeting standards; use of peer-assisted learning activities; participation of students in instructional decisions as appropriate; and adaptation of instruction and curriculum materials to meet the individual needs, goals, interests, and abilities of *all* students.

Strategic Use of Praise and Rewards

Praise and tangible rewards, but particularly the latter, should be used in a manner that is responsive to the ongoing debate about their impact on intrinsic motivation and behavior (see Akin-Little, Eckert, Lovett, & Little, 2004; Cameron, 2001; Deci, Koestner, & Ryan 1999, 2001; Reeve, 2006). It is beyond the scope of this chapter to adequately address this debate. It should be stated, however, that research shows praise and rewards, as generally used in classrooms, are powerful techniques for preventing (and correcting) behavior problems and for teaching and motivating prosocial behavior (see Bear, 2005, for a review of this literature and recommended strategies). Generally, reviews of the literature conclude that most schools need not worry about harmful effects on student motivation and behavior. Nevertheless, educators are advised to use praise and rewards strategically, rather than in a nonreflective and haphazard manner. In particular, teachers should use praise much more often than tangible rewards, with the latter used only occasionally and primarily when students show little motivation. Students should be discouraged from perceiving praise and rewards as manipulating or controlling, because such perceptions increase the likelihood that praise and rewards will stifle intrinsic motivation and a sense of autonomy. To prevent such perceptions, research suggests that teachers should emphasize the informational aspect (i.e., convey "you are competent"), instead of the controlling aspect (i.e., conveying "you did it to earn a reward") of rewards (Tang & Hall, 1995). To this end, placing greater emphasis on *why* rewards are given than on *which* rewards are given is recommended (Reeve, 2006).

Immediate Response to Early Signs of Behavior Problems

Although grouped here under the component of prevention, this recommendation certainly applies also to the component of correction.

Responding quickly to the first indication of a behavior problem (e.g., a student rises from his seat to tease or bully a classmate), and thus intervening at the earliest point possible in the progression of a problem, helps to ensure the minor behavior problems do not become disciplinary problems. As a result, mild corrective techniques (e.g., physical proximity, redirection, verbal warning) often are sufficient, precluding the need for harsher ones (e.g., verbal reprimand, in-school suspension). This principle applies at the classroom and school-wide levels in addition to the level of the individual student. In the absence of early responses to teasing and bullying, problem behavior may become "contagious," spreading among others in the class and school building.

Component 3: Correcting Behavior Problems

The primary purpose of correction should be to reduce the likelihood that the problem behavior recurs in the future and increase the likelihood that more appropriate behavior occurs in its place. Although punitive techniques might occasionally be necessary and effective, disciplinary encounters should be viewed primarily as opportunities to *teach* replacement behaviors, including social cognitive and emotional processes associated with developing self-discipline. Correction would include the use of specific techniques of applied behavior analysis shown to be effective in managing and correcting student behavior (see Alberto & Troutman, 2006; Gresham, 2004; Stage & Quiroz, 1997; Walker, Ramsey, & Gresham, 2003), but also those having clear applications for developing self-discipline (e.g., reinforcing, ignoring, or challenging verbalizations of targeted social cognitive processes). Behavioral techniques are of two general types: *behavioral replacement techniques*, which focus on teaching or strengthening appropriate behaviors that should replace the problem behavior, and *behavior reduction techniques*, which focus on decreasing or eliminating the behavior problem.

Behavior Replacement Techniques

It is well established that various types of positive reinforcement are effective in managing, teaching, and strengthening behavior. These include the general use of praise, privileges, tangible rewards, and tokens (Alberto & Troutman, 2006). Likewise, a large body of literature supports the use of various forms of modeling, especially when combined with positive reinforcement (Bandura, 1986). Other behavior replacement techniques of demonstrated effectiveness are:

contingency contracts (Anderson, 2002), especially those in which students are involved in the contract's design (Lassman, Jolivette, & Wehby, 1999); *school-home report cards* of behavior (Kelley & McCain, 1995); *behavioral momentum* (Mace et al., 1988); and *self-management of behavior* (Polsgrove & Smith, 2004; Shapiro & Cole, 1994). With behavioral momentum, the likelihood of a student responding favorably to a request or directive is increased by first requesting a behavior that the teacher has strong reason to believe the student will comply with, then requesting a behavior that is more likely to be met with noncompliance (if the first request had not been made). Self-management techniques include self-observations, self-recording, self-evaluation, self-monitoring, and self-reinforcement. Not only have these techniques been found to be effective in changing behavior, but they also have the advantage of focusing less on external control than other behavioral techniques.

The preceding techniques are most commonly used at the individual level, and often in individual behavior plans for students with behavior problems. Such plans are required under the Individuals with Disabilities Act for children with disabilities whose behavior impedes the learning of others. Additional behavior replacement techniques commonly used with groups of students are dependent, independent, and interdependent group contingency systems (Litow & Pumroy, 1975). Indeed, the one school-wide behavior replacement technique with the strongest evidence of effectiveness in improving behavior is an interdependent group contingency program, the Good Behavior Game (Barrish, Saunders, & Wolf, 1969; Embry, 2002; Van Lier, Vuijk, & Crijnen, 2005).

Behavior Reduction Techniques

Educators are often offered a hierarchy of behavior reductive techniques. Although these techniques include punishment, their recommended use is responsive to the many limitations of punishment (see Bear, 2005, for discussion) as well as to the general expectation that "punishment should fit the crime" (Bear, 2005; Martella, Nelson, & Marchand-Martella, 2003). At the bottom of the hierarchy are techniques for mild behavior problems or for very early response in the progression toward more serious problem behaviors. These techniques are intended to *avoid* the use of punishment. They include the various types of differential reinforcement (i.e., differential reinforcement of incompatible behavior, the omission of behavior, and low rates of behavior), extinction, redirection, proximity control, verbal warnings, and reprimands. Moving up in the hierarchy are behavioral techniques for targeting behavior problems that are either more serious (e.g., harming others) or found to be resistant to milder interventions. These include response cost, various forms of time-out (including being sent to the office), detention, in-school suspension, unconditioned aversive strategies, physical restraint, out-of-school suspension, and expulsion. Aversive strategies include corporal punishment; although its use is not recommended by most professional organizations and researchers, including the author, it is used in 22 states. Because long-term suspension and expulsion often result in the denial of academic instruction and school-based mental health services, over half of the states require that schools provide alternative programs for suspended and expelled students (Advancement Project/Civil Rights Project, 2000).

Component 4: Addressing Serious and Chronic Behavior Problems

Whereas the first three components of school-wide discipline provide a system of support for *all* students, Component 4 is specific to students who need a level of supports, services, and resources that cannot reasonably be provided in the regular classroom. What differentiates those students from others are (a) the continuation of behavior problems that adversely impact the learning of the student or others, despite the use of interventions, or (b) a serious behavior problem, regardless of its frequency, for which the school's code of conduct requires a student's removal from school for an extended period of time. Remedial strategies are used for students in the first category only after less intensive and evidence-based interventions have already been implemented with fidelity in the student's classroom. Students in this group are generally described in the mental health literature as requiring supports and services at the tertiary, or indicated, level of prevention. With respect to issues of school discipline, this includes many students already diagnosed with conduct disorders and oppositional defiant disorder. However, it also includes some at-risk students typically described in the mental health literature as needing supports and services at the secondary, or targeted, level of prevention. The needs of most at-risk students can be met with supports and interventions under Components 1, 2, and 3, with no need to remove these students from the classroom. Clearly, such supports and interventions should be more intense and systematic than those provided to students deemed not at-risk, but nevertheless the point of delivery should be the student's classroom (with collaborative consultative assistance to the teachers from other members of a school-wide intervention support team). The second category of students needing supports and services under Component 4 are those students, primarily adolescents, who commit serious violations of a school's codes of conduct (e.g., drug possession, fighting) for which they are suspended or expelled and often arrested, regardless of their history of behavior problems or risk factors (Moffitt, 1993). Indeed, although often not the result of a serious violation, 15% of students in regular education and 17% in special education are suspended and/or placed in alternative educational settings (U.S. General Accounting Office, 2001). Without the provision of additional supports during an extended school removal, there is an increased risk of continued behavior problems.

With respect to school-wide discipline, the need for Component 4 is typically indicated by (a) a special education diagnosis and an Individual Education Program indicating the need for intensive interventions to address behavior problems (e.g., many students diagnosed with emotional disturbance, and a much smaller number diagnosed with attention deficit hyperactivity disorder or specific learning disability); (b) a psychiatric diagnosis of conduct disorder or oppositional defiant disorder; (c) office referrals, suspensions, and expulsion; and (d) comprehensive screening systems that rely primarily on teacher ratings, especially when problem behaviors are first noticed and resistant to early interventions (e.g., *First Step to Success*; Walker, Stiller, Severson, Feil, & Golly, 1998). As recommended by Doll and Haack (2005), screening data, including data from the preceding sources, should be aggregated across various subgroups of students not only to identify individual students who need additional supports and resources, but also for the purpose of a school-wide needs assessment.

It is important to note that the same strategies and techniques presented under Components 1, 2, and 3 certainly apply to students with serious and chronic behavior problems, but are needed at a greater level of intensity. Students with serious behavior problems certainly benefit from opportunities to learn and practice social and emotional competencies; caring teachers, peers, and families; high expectations, clear rules, and fair consequences; adapted instruction and curriculum; close monitoring and supervision; home-school collaboration; and ongoing, systematic application of behavioral techniques for reducing problem behavior and strengthening replacement behaviors. Although many of the same strategies and techniques are clearly needed, albeit more frequently and intensely, so too are additional supports and resources that cannot reasonably be provided by classroom teachers. These include the following evidence-based programs for addressing serious behavior problems (or the risk thereof): parent management training (Kazdin, 2003), anger control training (Lochman, Powell, Clanton, & McElroy, 2006), Aggression Replacement Training (Gibbs et al., 1995), multisystemic therapy (Henggeler, Schoenwald, Bourduin, Rowland, & Cunningham, 1998), medication (but particularly stimulant medication for attention deficits; Dodge et al., 2006), mentoring from someone other than the classroom teacher, such as provided in Big Brothers/Big Sisters (Gottfredson, 1997; Jekielek, Kristin, Moore, & Hair, 2002), and after-school programs, especially those for older students, which place great emphasis on developing competencies associated with self-discipline (Gottfredson, Gerstenblith, Soulé, Womer, & Shaoli, 2004).

A useful and popular framework for providing intensive supports, interventions, and services is the *wraparound* framework, as used in school-wide PBS programs (Eber, Osuch, & Redditt, 1996; Epstein et al., 2005). The wraparound framework entails a case management process in which a team, composed of family members, educators, mental health specialists, and others as needed (e.g., social worker, school nurse, school resource officer), plan for a network of supports and services that extend beyond the school to the home and community. Key elements of the effectiveness of such a network, or system, are that the supports and services include evidenced-based interventions provided by well-qualified individuals, and these supports, services, and interventions are individualized (developmentally and culturally appropriate, based on the student's strengths and needs), family focused, intensive and sustained, comprehensive (targeting a wide range of protective and risk factors), developed collaboratively including parents, and begin early when intensive intervention is first warranted (Bear, Webster-Stratton, Furlong, & Rhee, 2000; Brestan & Eyberg, 1998; Burchard, Burns, & Burchard, 2002; Eber et al., 1996).

Also under Component 4, comprehensive school-wide discipline must be responsive to the most serious acts of antisocial behavior, especially school violence. As the Federal Bureau of Investigation found (Vossekuil, Reddy, & Fein, 2000), the most horrendous acts of school violence, school shootings, are often committed by individuals with no histories of antisocial behavior. Thus, schools cannot prepare adequately for school shootings by focusing only on students in the targeted and intensive tiers of the mental health/PBS triangle. In addition to the full range of prevention and intervention strategies and techniques presented previously in this chapter, a school-wide safety plan would include the careful awareness of early warning signs of school violence (including not only training teachers and staff in early warning signs, but also strongly encouraging students to report any threats of violence) and specific procedures for responding to potential and actual acts of violence (see Jimerson & Furlong, 2006, for a comprehensive review of research and recommended practices on school violence).

Summary

Two types of positive approaches to school-wide discipline have increased in popularity in recent years: (a) those that emphasize strategies and techniques of developing self-discipline, generally referred to as SEL and character education programs, and (b) those that emphasize the school-wide application of behavioral techniques to teach specific social skills. The first type is exemplified in CSC programs and the second type in school-wide PBS programs. Given that each type has different emphases and is supported by research, albeit limited, as to its effectiveness, it behooves schools to integrate strategies and techniques from both types of programs. The intent would be to provide a comprehensive school-wide program that is consistent with the four goals of population-based mental health services. Such a program would include strategies and techniques for developing self-discipline, preventing behavior problems, and correcting behavior problems, and providing the supports, resources, and services to address the needs of students with serious or chronic behavior problems.

Note

1. It should be noted that although Canter (1989) claimed his early model of Assertive Discipline was based on behavior modification research and emphasized positive reinforcement, others have argued that in practice the program relied primarily on the use of punishment and thus was inconsistent with the behavioral approach's tenet that punishment should be used as a last resort (Render, Padilla, & Krank, 1989). It also should be noted that more recent versions of Assertive Discipline are clearly more "positive," as reflected in the program's new title, Assertive Discipline: Positive Behavior Management for Today's Classroom (Canter & Canter, 2001), and its emphasis on positive

reinforcement, teacher-student relations, and social problem solving (Bear, 2005).

Discussion Questions

1. Think about the school-wide discipline practices in your school. Are these teacher-centered practices or student-centered practices, and why? How could these practices be shifted to enhance their effectiveness?

2. In what ways does your school develop students' self-discipline? prevent behavior problems? correct behavior problems? address serious and chronic behavior problems?

3. If you were to implement one new discipline practice in your school, what would it be and why?

4. What kinds of school-wide data could you collect that would be useful in planning school-wide discipline practices?

5. Does your school place more resources in developing students self-discipline or in addressing chronic and serious behavior problems? If you were to reverse these resource allocations, who would benefit and who would not?

6. To what extent are strategies and techniques for developing self-discipline, including social and emotional competencies, infused throughout your school's curriculum, practices, and policies?

References

Adelman, H. S., & Taylor, L. (2006). *The school leader's guide to student learning supports: New directions for addressing barriers to learning.* Thousand Oaks, CA: Corwin Press.

Advancement Project/Civil Rights Project. (2000). *Opportunities suspended: The devastating consequences of zero tolerance and school discipline policies.* Cambridge, MA: Harvard University.

Akin-Little, K. A., Eckert, T. L., Lovett, B. J., & Little, S. G. (2004). Extrinsic reinforcement in the classroom: Bribery or best practice. *School Psychology Review, 33,* 344–362.

Alberto, P. A., & Troutman, A. C. (2006). *Applied behavior analysis for teachers* (7th ed.). Upper Saddle River, NJ: Merrill Prentice-Hall.

Anderson, J. (2002). Individualized behavior contracts. *Intervention in School & Clinic, 37,* 168–175.

Aos, S., Lieb, R., Mayfield, J., Miller, M., & Pennucci, A. (2004). *Benefits and costs of prevention and early intervention programs for youth.* Olympia: Washington State Institute for Public Policy.

Astor, R. A., Benbenishty, R., Marachi, R., & Meyer, H. A. (2006). In S. R. Jimerson & M. J. Furlong (Eds.), *Handbook of school violence and school safety: From research to practice* (pp. 221–233). Mahwah, NJ: Erlbaum.

Bambara, L. M. (2005). Evolution of positive behavior support. In L. M. Bambara & L. Kern (Eds.), *Individualized supports for students with problem behaviors: Designing positive behavior plans* (pp. 1–24). New York: Guilford Press.

Bandura, A. (1986). *Social foundations of thought and action: A social cognitive theory.* Upper Saddle River, NJ: Prentice Hall.

Bandura, A. (1997). *Self-efficacy: The exercise of control.* New York: Freeman.

Bandura, A. (2001). *Social cognitive theory: An agentic perspective.* Annual review of psychology (Vol. 52; pp. 1–26). Palo Alto, CA: Annual Reviews.

Bandura, A., Caprara, G. V., Barbaranelli, C., & Regalia, C. (2001). Sociocognitive self-regulatory mechanisms governing transgressive behavior. *Journal of Personality and Social Psychology, 80,* 125–135.

Barkley, R. A., Shelton, T. L., Crosswait, C., Moorehouse, M., Fletcher, K., Barrett, S., et al. (2002). Preschool children with disruptive behavior: Three-year outcome as a function of adaptive disability. *Development and Psychopathology, 14,* 45–67.

Barrish, H. H., Saunders, M., & Wolf, M. M. (1969). Good behavior game: Effects of individual contingencies for group consequences on disruptive behavior in a classroom. *Journal of Applied Behavior Analysis, 2,* 1969, 119–124.

Battistich, V., & Hom, A. (1997). The relationship between students' sense of their school as a community and their involvement in problem behaviors. *American Journal of Public Health, 87,* 1997–2001.

Battistich, V., Schaps, E., Watson, M., Solomon, D., & Lewis, C. (2000). Effects of the Child Development Project on students' drug use and other problem behaviors. *Journal of Primary Prevention, 21,* 75–99.

Battistich, V., Solomon, D., Watson, M., & Schaps, E. (1997). Caring school communities. *Educational Psychologist, 32,* 137–151.

Battistich, V., Solomon, D., Watson, M., Solomon, J., & Schaps, E. (1989). Effects of an elementary school program to enhance prosocial behavior on children's social problem-solving skills and strategies. *Journal of Applied Developmental Psychology, 10,* 147–169.

Bear, G. G. (1998). School discipline in the United States: Prevention, correction, and long-term social development. *School Psychology Review, 27,* 14–32.

Bear, G. G. (with Cavalier, A., & Manning, M.). (2005). *Developing self-discipline and preventing and correcting misbehavior.* Boston: Allyn & Bacon.

Bear, G. G., Manning, M. A., & Izard, C. (2003). Responsible behavior: The importance of social cognition and emotion. *School Psychology Quarterly, 18,* 140–157.

Bear, G. G., & Watkins, J. M. (2006). Developing self-discipline. In G. G. Bear & K. M. Minke (Eds.), *Children's needs III: Development, prevention, and intervention* (pp. 29–44). Bethesda, MD: National Association of School Psychologists.

Bear, G. G., Webster-Stratton, C., Furlong, M., & Rhee, S. (2000). Preventing aggression and violence. In K. M. Minke & G. G. Bear (Eds.), *Preventing school problems—promoting school success: Strategies and programs that work* (pp. 1–69). Bethesda, MD: National Association of School Psychologists.

Berkowitz, M. W. & Bier, M. C. (2004). Research-based character education. *Annals of the American Academy of Political and Social Science, 591,* 72–85.

Berkowitz, M. W., & Schwartz, M. (2006). Character education. In G. G. Bear & K. M. Minke (Eds.), *Children's needs III: Development, prevention, and intervention* (pp. 15–27). Bethesda, MD: National Association of School Psychologists.

Birch, S. H., & Ladd, G. W. (1998). Children's interpersonal behaviors and the teacher-child relationship. *Developmental Psychology, 34,* 934–946.

Boldizar, J. P., Perry, D. G., Perry, L. C. (1989). Outcome values and aggression. *Child Development, 60,* 571–579.

Brestan, E. V., & Eyberg, S. M. (1998). Effective psychosocial treatments of conduct-disordered children and adolescents: 29 years, 82 studies, and 5,272 kids. *Journal of Clinical Child Psychology, 27,* 180–189.

Brophy, J. E. (1996). *Teaching problem students.* New York: Guilford Press.

Brophy, J. E. (2004). *Motivating students to learn.* Mahwah, NJ: Erlbaum

Bru, E., Murberg, T. A., & Stephens, P. (2001). Social support, negative life events and pupil misbehavior among young Norwegian adolescents. *Journal of Adolescence, 24,* 715–727.

Bru, E., Stephens, P., & Torsheim, T. (2002). Students' perceptions of class management and reports of their own misbehavior. *Journal of School Psychology, 40,* 287–307.

Bullis, M., Walker, H., & Sprague, J. R. (2001). A promise unfulfilled: Social skills training with at-risk and antisocial children and youth. *Exceptionality, 9,* 67–90.

Burchard, J., Burns, E., & Burchard, S. (2002). The wraparound approach. In B. Burns & K. Hoagwood (Eds.), *Community treatment for youth: Evidence-based interventions for severe emotional and behavioral disorders* (pp. 69–90). New York: Oxford University Press.

Burks, V. S., Laird, R. D., Dodge, K. A., Pettit, G. S., & Bates, J. E. (1999). Knowledge structures, social information processing, and children's aggressive behavior. *Social Development, 8,* 220–236.

Cameron, J. (2001). Negative effects of reward on intrinsic motivation—a limited phenomenon: Comment on Deci, Loestner, and Ryan (2001). *Review of Educational Research, 71,* 29–42.

Canter, L. (1976). *Assertive discipline: A take charge approach for today's educator.* Los Angeles: Canter and Associates.

Canter, L. (1989). Assertive discipline: A response. *Teachers College Record, 90,* 631–640.

Canter, L., & Canter, M. (2001). *Assertive discipline: Positive behavior management for today's classroom.* Los Angeles: Canter and Associates.

Caprara, G. V., Barbaranelli, C., Pastorelli, C., Bandura, A., & Zimbardo, P. G. (2000). Prosocial foundations of children's academic achievement. *Psychological Science, 11,* 302–306.

Center for Effective Discipline (2006). *Discipline and the law.* Retrieved October 24, 2006, from http://www.stophitting.com/laws/legalInformation.php

Charney, R. S. (2002). *Teaching children to care: Classroom management for ethical and academic growth, K-8* (Rev. ed.). Greenfield, MA: Northeast Foundation for Children.

Christenson, S. L., & Sheridan, S. M. (2001). *Schools and families: Creating essential connections for learning.* New York: Guilford Press.

Collaborative for Academic, Social, and Emotional Learning (CASEL). (2003). *Safe and sound: An educational leader's guide to evidence-based social and emotional learning (SEL) Programs.* Retrieved July 8, 2003, from http://www.CASEL.org

Comer, J. P., Haynes, N. M., Joyner, E. T., & Ben-Avie, M. (Eds.). (1996). *Rallying the whole village: The Comer process for reforming education.* New York: Teachers College Press.

Committee for Children. (2003). *Second Step: A violence prevention curriculum.* Seattle: Author.

Covington, M. V. (2000). Goal theory, motivation, and school achievement: An integrative review. *Annual Review of Psychology, 51,* 171–200.

Crick, N. R., & Ladd, G. W. (1990). Children's perceptions of the outcomes of aggressive strategies: Do the ends justify being mean? *Developmental Psychology, 26,* 612–620.

Crone, D. A., & Horner, R. H. (2003). *Building positive behavior support systems in schools: Functional behavioral assessment.* New York: Guilford Press.

Deci, E. L., Koestner, R., & Ryan, R. M. (1999). A meta-analytic review of experiments examining the effects of extrinsic rewards on intrinsic motivation. *Psychological Bulletin, 125,* 627–668.

Deci, E. L., Koestner, R., & Ryan, R. M. (2001). Extrinsic rewards and intrinsic motivation in education: Reconsidered once again. *Review of Educational Research, 71,* 1–27.

Developmental Studies Center (2000). *Ways we want our class to be: Class meetings that build commitment to kindness and learning. Ideas from the Child Development Project.* Oakland, CA: Author.

Developmental Studies Center (2003). *Making meaning.* Oakland, CA: Author.

Dodge, K. A., Coie, J. D., & Lynam, D. (2006). Aggression and antisocial behavior in youth. In W. Damon & R. M. Learner (Series Eds.), & N. Eisenberg (Vol. Ed.), *Handbook of child psychology, Vol. 3. Social, emotional, and personality development* (6th ed., pp. 719–788). New York: Wiley.

Dodge, K. A., & Pettit, G. S. (2003). A biopsychosocial model of the development of chronic conduct problems in adolescence. *Developmental Psychology, 39,* 349–371.

Doll, B., & Haack, M. K. (2005). Population-based strategies for identifying schoolwide problems. In R. Brown-Chidsey (Ed.), *Assessment for intervention: A problem-solving approach.* (pp. 82–102). New York: Guilford Press.

Doll, B., & Lyon, M. (1998). Risk and resilience: Implications for the practice of school psychology. *School Psychology Review, 27,* 348–363.

DuPaul, G. J., & Eckert, T. L. (1994). The effects of social skills curricula: Now you see them, now you don't. *School Psychology Quarterly, 9,* 113–132.

Eber, L., Osuch, R., & Redditt, C. A. (1996). School-based applications of the wraparound process: Early results on service provision and student outcomes. *Journal of Child and Family Studies, 5,* 83–89.

Eisenberg, N., Fabes, R. A., & Spinrad, T. L. (2006). Prosocial behavior. In W. Damon & R. M. Learner (Series Eds.), & N. Eisenberg (Vol. Ed.),

Handbook of child psychology, Vol. 3. Social, emotional, and personality development (6th ed.; pp. 646–718). New York: Wiley & Sons.

Embry, D. D. (2002). The Good Behavior Game: A best practice candidate as a universal behavioral vaccine. *Clinical Child and Family Psychology Review, 5,* 273–297.

Epstein, M. H., Nordness, P., Gallagher, K., Nelson, J. R., Lewis, L., & Schrepf, S. (2005). School as the entry point: Assessing adhering to the basic tenets of the wraparound approach. *Behavioral Disorders, 30,* 85–93.

Erdley, C. A., & Asher, S. R. (1998). Linkages between children's beliefs about the legitimacy of aggression and their behavior. *Social Development, 7,* 321–339.

Erdley, C. A., & Asher, S. R. (1999). A social goals perspective on children's social competence. *Journal of Emotional and Behavioral Disorders, 7,* 156–167.

Evertson, C. M., Emmer, E. T., & Worsham, M. E. (2006). *Classroom management for elementary teachers* (7th ed.). Boston: Allyn & Bacon.

Finkelstein, B. (1989). *Governing the young: Teacher behavior in popular primary schools in 19th century United States.* New York: Falmer Press.

Fitzgerald, P. D., & Van Schoiack-Edstrom, L. (2006). Second Step: A violence prevention curriculum. In S. R. Jimerson & M. J. Furlong (Eds.), *Handbook of school violence and school safety: From research to practice* (pp. 383–395). Mahwah, NJ: Erlbaum.

Frick, P. J., Cornell, A. H., Barry, C. T., Bodin, S. D., & Dane, H. E. (2003). Callous-unemotional traits and conduct problems in the prediction of conduct problem severity, aggression, and self-report of delinquency. *Journal of Abnormal Child Psychology, 31,* 457–470.

Germane, C. E., & Germane, E. G. (1929). *Character education: A program for the school and the home.* New York: Silver, Burdett, and Company.

Gibbs, J. C., Potter, G. B., & Goldstein, A. P. (1995). *The EQUIP program: Teaching youth to think and act responsibly through a peer-helping approach.* Champaign, IL: Research Press.

Ginsburg-Block, M., Rohrbeck, C., Fantuzzo, J., & Lavigne, N. (2006). Peer-assisted learning strategies. In G. G. Bear & K. M. Minke (Eds.), *Children's needs III: Development, prevention, and intervention.* Bethesda, MD: National Association of School Psychologists.

Goldstein, A. P., Glick, B., & Gibbs, J. C. (1998). *Aggression Replacement Training: A comprehensive intervention for aggressive youth.* Champaign, IL: Research Press.

Goldstein, A. P., & McGinnis, E. (1997). *Skillstreaming the adolescent.* Champaign, IL: Research Press.

Gottfredson, D. (1997). School-based crime prevention. In L. W. Sherman, D. Gottfredson, D. MacKenzie, J. Eck, P. Reuter, & S. Bushway (Eds.), *Preventing crime: What works, what doesn't, what's promising: A report to the United States Congress.* (pp. 5.1–5.74). Washington, DC: U.S. Department of Justice, Office of Justice Programs.

Gottfredson, D. C., Gerstenblith, S. A., Soulé, D. A., Womer, S. C., & Shaoli, L. (2004). After school programs reduce delinquency? *Prevention Science, 5,* 253–266.

Greenberg, M. T. & Kusché, C. A. (2006). Building social and emotional competence: The PATHS curriculum. In S. R. Jimerson & M. J. Furlong

(Eds.), *Handbook of school violence and school safety: From research to practice* (pp. 395–412). Mahwah, NJ: Erlbaum.

Greenberg, M. T., Weissberg, R. P., O'Brien, M. U., Zins, J. E., Fredericks, L., Resnik, H., et al. (2003). Enhancing school-based prevention and youth development through coordinated social and emotional learning. *American Psychologist, 58,* 466–474.

Gregory, A. & Weinstein, R. S. (2004). Connection and regulation at home and in school: Predicting growth in achievement for adolescents. *Journal of Adolescent Research, 19,* 405–427.

Gresham, F. M. (2004). Current status and future directions of school-based behavioral interventions. *School Psychology Review, 33,* 326–343.

Gresham, F. M., McIntyre, L. L., Olson-Tinker, H., Dolstra, L., McLaughlin, V., & Van, M. (2004). Relevance of functional behavioral assessment research for school-based interventions and positive behavioral support, *Research in Developmental Disabilities, 25,* 19–37.

Grusec, J. E., & Goodnow, J. J. (1994). Impact of parental discipline methods on the child's internalization of values: A reconceptualization of current points of view. *Developmental Psychology, 30,* 4–19.

Hampel, R. L. (1986). *The last little citadel: American high schools since 1940.* Boston: Houghton Mifflin.

Hamre, B., & Pianta, R. (2001). Early teacher-child relationships and the trajectory of children's school outcomes through eighth grade. *Child Development, 72,* 625–638.

Hamre, B. K., & Pianta, R. C. (2006). Student-teacher relationships. In G. G. Bear & K. M. Minke (Eds.), *Children's needs III: Development, prevention, and intervention* (pp. 59–71). Bethesda, MD: National Association of School Psychologists.

Harter, S. (1999). *The construction of the self: A developmental perspective.* New York: Guilford Press.

Hartshorne, H., & May, M. A. (1928). *Studies in the nature of character: Vol. I: Studies in deceit.* New York: Macmillan.

Henggeler, S. W., Schoenwald, S. K., Bourduin, C. M., Rowland, M. D., & Cunningham, P. B. (1998). *Multisystemic treatment of antisocial behavior in children and adolescents.* New York: Guildford Press.

Hoffman, M. L. (2000). *Empathy and moral development: Implications for caring and justice.* Cambridge, UK: Cambridge University Press.

Horner, R. H., Sugai, G., Todd, A. W., & Lewis-Palmer, T. (2005). Schoolwide behavior support. In L. M. Bambara & L. Kern (Eds.), *Individualized supports for students with problem behaviors: Designing positive behavior plans* (pp. 359–390). New York: Guilford Press.

Hubbard, J. A., Dodge, K. A., Cillessen, A. H. N., Coie, J. D., & Schwartz, D. (2001). The dyadic nature of social information processing in boys' reactive and proactive aggression. *Journal of Personality and Social Psychology, 80,* 268–280.

Hubbard, J. A., Smithmyer, C. M., Ramsden, S. R., Parker, E. H., Flanagan, K. D., Dearing, K. F., et al. (2002). Observational, physiological, and self-report measures of children's anger: Relations to reactive versus proactive aggression. *Child Development, 73,* 1101–1118.

Huesmann, L. R. (1988). An information processing model for the development of aggression. *Aggressive Behavior, 14,* 13–24.

Hughes, J. N., Cavell, T. A., & Willson, V. (2001). Further support for the developmental significance of the quality of the teacher-student relationship. *Journal of School Psychology, 39,* 289–301.

Jekielek, S., Kristin, M. A., Moore, A., & Hair, E. C. (2002). *Mentoring programs and youth development: A synthesis.* Washington, DC: Child Trends.

Jimerson, S. R., & Furlong, M. J. (Eds.). (2006). *Handbook of school violence and school safety: From research to practice.* Mahwah, NJ: Erlbaum.

Johnson, D. W., & Johnson, R. T. (2006). Conflict resolution, peer mediation, and peacemaking. In C. M. Evertson & C. S. Weinstein (Eds.), *Handbook of classroom management: Research, practice, and contemporary issues* (pp. 803–832). Mahwah, NJ: Erlbaum.

Kazdin, A. E. (1977). *The token economy: A review and evaluation.* New York: Plenum.

Kazdin, A. E. (1981). Behavior modification in education: Contributions and limitations. *Developmental Review, 1,* 34–57.

Kazdin, A. E. (2003). Problem-solving skills training and parent management training for conduct disorder. In A. E. Kazdin & J. R. Weisz (Eds.), *Evidence-based psychotherapies for children and adolescents* (pp. 242–262). New York: Guilford Press.

Kelley, M. L., & McCain, A. P. (1995). Promoting academic performance in inattentive children: The relative efficacy of school-home notes with and without response cost. *Behavior Modification, 19*(3), 357–375.

Kochanska, G. (2002). Committed compliance, moral self, and internalization: A mediational model. *Developmental Psychology, 38,* 339–351.

Kusché, C. A., & Greenberg, M. T. (1994). The PATHS (Promoting Alternative Thinking Strategies) curriculum. South Deerfield, MA: Channing-Bete.

Kuther, T. L. (2000). Moral reasoning, perceived competence, and adolescent engagement in risky activity. *Journal of Adolescence, 23,* 599–604.

Landrum, T. J., & Kauffman, J. M. (2006). Behavioral approaches to classroom management. In C. M. Evertson & C. S. Weinstein (Eds.), *Handbook of classroom management: Research, practice, and contemporary issues* (pp. 47–71). Mahwah, NJ: Erlbaum.

Lassman, K. A., Jolivette, K., & Wehby, J. H. (1999). Using collaborative behavioral contracting. *Teaching Exceptional Children, 31,* 12–18.

Lewis, T. J., Newcomer, L. L., Trussell, R., & Richter, M. (2006). Schoolwide Positive Behavior Support: Building systems to develop and maintain appropriate social behavior. In C. M. Evertson & C. S. Weinstein (Eds.), *Handbook of classroom management: Research, practice, and contemporary issues* (pp. 833–854). Mahwah, NJ: Erlbaum.

Lickona, T. (1991). *Educating for character: How our schools can teach respect and responsibility.* New York: Bantam.

Litow, L., & Pumroy, D. K. (1975). A brief review of classroom group-oriented contingencies. *Journal of Applied Behavior Analysis, 8,* 341–347.

Lochman, J. E., Powell, N. R., Clanton, N., & McElroy, H. K. (2006). Anger and aggression. In G. G. Bear & K. M. Minke (Eds.), *Children's needs III: Development, prevention, and intervention* (pp. 115–133). Bethesda, MD: National Association of School Psychologists.

Lohrman-O'Rourke, S., Knoster, T., Sabatine, K., Smith, D., Horvath, B., & Llewellyn, G. (2000). School-wide application of PBS in the Bangor Area School District. *Journal of Positive Behavior Interventions, 2,* 238–240.

Luiselli, J. K., Putnam, R. F., & Sunderland, M. (2002). Longitudinal evaluation of behavior support intervention in a public middle school. *Journal of Positive Interventions, 4,* 182–188.

Mace, F. C., Hock, M. L., Lalli, J. S., West, B. J., Belfiore, P., Pinter, E., & Brown, D. K. (1988). Behavioral momentum in the treatment of noncompliance. *Journal of Applied Behavior Analysis, 21,* 123–141.

Malecki, C. K., & Elliott, S. (2002). Children's social behaviors as predictors of academic achievement: A longitudinal analysis. *School Psychology Quarterly, 17,* 1–23.

Manning, M. A., & Bear, G. G. (2002). Are children's concerns about punishment related to their aggression? *Journal of School Psychology, 40,* 523–539.

Martella, R. C., Nelson, J. R., & Marchand-Martella, N. E. (2003). *Managing disruptive behaviors in the schools: A schoolwide, classroom, and individualized social learning approach.* Boston: Allyn & Bacon.

McGinnis, E., & Goldstein, A. P. (1997). *Skillstreaming the elementary school child.* Champaign, IL: Research Press.

McKown, H. C. (1935). *Character education.* New York: McGraw-Hill.

McLaughlin, T. F. (1976). Self-control in the classroom. *Review of Educational Research, 46,* 631–663.

Meehan, B. T., Hughes, J. N., & Cavell, T. A. (2003). Teacher-student relationships as compensatory resources for aggressive children. *Child Development, 74,* 1145–1157.

Menesini, E., Sanchez, V., Fonzi, A., Ortega, R., Costabile, A., & Lo Feudo, G. (2003). Moral emotions and bullying: A cross-national comparison of differences between bullies, victims and outsiders. *Aggressive Behavior, 29,* 515–530.

Moffitt, T. E. (1993). Adolescent-limited and life-course-persistent antisocial behavior: A developmental taxonomy. *Psychological Review, 100,* 674–701.

Morrison, G. M., Redding, G. M., Fisher, E., & Peterson, R. (2006). Assessing school discipline. In S. R. Jimerson & M. J. Furlong (Eds.), *Handbook of school violence and school safety: From research to practice* (pp. 211–220). Mahwah, NJ: Erlbaum.

Morrone, A. S., & Pintrich, P. R. (2006). School completion. Achievement motivation. In G. G. Bear & K. M. Minke (Eds.), *Children's needs III: Development, prevention, and intervention* (pp. 431–442). Bethesda, MD: National Association of School Psychologists.

Murdock, T. B. (1999). The social context of risk: Predictors of alienation in middle school. *Journal of Educational Psychology, 91,* 62–75.

Murdock, T. B., Hale, N. M., & Weber, M. J. (2001). Predictors of cheating among early adolescents: Academic and social motivations. *Contemporary Educational Psychology, 26,* 96-115.

Nelsen, J., Lott, L., & Glenn, H. (2000). *Positive discipline in the classroom.* Rocklin, CA: Prima.

Orobio de Castro, B., Veerman, J. W., Koops, W., Bosch, J., & Monshuwer, J. J. (2002). Hostile attribution of intent and aggressive behavior: A meta-analysis. *Child Development, 73,* 916–934.

Osterman, K. F. (2000). Students' need for belonging in the school community. *Review of Educational Research, 70,* 323–367.

Palmer, E. J., & Hollin, C. R. (2001). Sociomoral reasoning, perceptions of parenting, and self-reported delinquency in adolescents. *Applied Cognitive Psychology, 15,* 85–100.

Pardini, D. A., Lochman, J. E., & Frick, P. J. (2003). Callous/unemotional traits and social cognitive processes in adjudicated youth. *Journal of the American Academy of Child and Adolescent Psychiatry, 42*(3), 364–371.

Parke, R. D., & Buriel, R. (2006). Socialization in the family: Ethnic and ecological perspectives. In W. Damon & R. M. Learner (Series Eds.), & N. Eisenberg (Vol. Ed.), *Handbook of child psychology, Vol. 3. Social, emotional, and personality development* (6th ed., pp. 429–504). New York: Wiley & Sons.

Pianta, R. C. (1999). *Enhancing relationships between children and teachers.* Washington, DC: American Psychological Association.

Polsgrove, L., & Smith, S. W. (2004). Informed practice in teaching self-control to children with emotional and behavioral disorders. In R. B. Rutherford, M. M. Quinn, & S. R. Mathur (Eds.), *Handbook of research in emotional and behavioral disorders* (pp. 399–425). New York: Guilford Press.

Quiggle, N. L., Garber, J., Panak, W. F., & Dodge, K. A. (1992). Social information processing in aggressive and depressed children. *Child Development, 63,* 1305–1320.

Reeve, J. (2006). Extrinsic rewards and inner motivation. In C. M. Evertson & C. S. Weinstein (Eds.), *Handbook of classroom management: Research, practice, and contemporary issues* (pp. 645–664). Mahwah, NJ: Erlbaum.

Render, G. F., Padilla, J. N., & Krank, M. (1989). Assertive discipline: A critical review and analysis. *Teachers College Record, 90,* 607–630.

Reschly, A., & Christenson, S. L. (2006). School completion. In G. G. Bear & K. M. Minke (Eds.), *Children's needs III: Development, prevention, and intervention* (pp. 103–113). Bethesda, MD: National Association of School Psychologists.

Rimm-Kaufman, S. E., & Sawyer, B. E. (2004). Primary-grade teachers' self-efficacy beliefs, attitudes toward teaching, and discipline and teaching practice priorities in relation to the Responsive Classroom approach. *Elementary School Journal, 104,* 322–341.

Rubin, K. H., Bukowski, W. M., & Parker, J. G. (2006). Peer interactions, relationships, and groups. In W. Damon & R. M. Lerner (Series Eds.), & N. Eisenberg (Vol. Ed.), *Handbook of child psychology, Vol. 3. Social, emotional, and personality development* (6th ed., pp. 571–645). New York: Wiley & Sons.

Sadler, C. (2000). Effective behavior support implementation at the district level: Tigard-Tualatin School District. *Journal of Positive Behavior Interventions, 2,* 241–243.

Sasso, G. M., Conroy, M. A., Stichter, J. P., & Fox, J. J. (2001). Slowing down the bandwagon: The misapplication of functional assessment for students with emotional and behavioral disorders. *Behavioral Disorders, 26,* 282–296.

Schaps, E., Battistich, V., & Solomon, D. (1997). School as a caring community: A key to character eduction. In A. Molnar (Ed.), *The construction of children's character, part II: 96th yearbook of the National Society for the Study of Education* (pp. 127–139). Chicago: University of Chicago Press.

Scott, T. M., Bucalos, A., Nelson, C. M., Liaupsin, C., Jolivette, K., & Deshea, L. (2004). Using functional assessment in general education settings: Making a case for effectiveness and efficiency. *Behavioral Disorders, 29*(2), 190–203.

Scott, T. M., McIntyre, J., Liaupsin, C., Nelson, C. M., Conroy, M., & Payne, L. D. (2005). An examination of the relation between functional behavior assessment and selected intervention strategies with school-based teams. *Journal of Positive Behavior Interventions, 7,* 205–215.

Shapiro, E. S., & Cole, C. L. (1994). *Behavior change in the classroom: Self-management interventions.* New York: Guilford Press.

Skiba, R. J., & Noam, G. G. (2002). *Zero tolerance: Can suspension and expulsion keep schools safe?: New directions for youth development.* San Francisco: Jossey-Bass.

Skiba, R. J., & Rausch, M. K. (2006). School disciplinary systems: Alternatives to suspension and expulsion. In G. G. Bear & K. M. Minke (Eds.), *Children's needs: Development, prevention, and intervention* (pp. 87–102). Bethesda, MD: National Association of School Psychologists.

Skinner, B. F. (1953). *Science and human behavior.* New York: Macmillan.

Solomon, D., Battistich, V., Watson, M., Schaps, E., & Lewis, C. (2000). A six-district study of educational change: Direct and mediated effects of the Child Development Project. *Social Psychology of Education, 4,* 3–51.

Solomon, D., Watson, M., Battistich, V., Schaps, E., & Delucchi, K. (1996). Creating classrooms that students experience as communities. *American Journal of Community Psychology, 24,* 719–748.

Solomon, D., Watson, M. S., Delucchi, K. L., Schaps, E., & Battistich, V. (1988). Enhancing children's prosocial behavior in the classroom. *American Educational Research Journal, 25,* 527–554.

Sprague, J. R., & Horner, R. H. (2006). Schoolwide positive behavioral supports. In S. R. Jimerson & M. J. Furlong (Eds.), *Handbook of school violence and school safety: From research to practice* (pp. 413–427). Mahwah, NJ: Erlbaum.

Stage, S. A., & Quiroz, D. R. (1997). A meta-analysis of interventions to decrease disruptive classroom behavior in public education settings. *School Psychology Review, 26,* 333–368.

Sugai, G., Horner, R. H., & Gresham, F. M. (2002). Behaviorally effective school environments. In M. R. Shinn, H. M. Walker, & G. Stoner (Eds.), *Interventions for academic and behavior problems II: Preventive and remedial approaches* (pp. 315–350). Bethesda, MD: National Association of School Psychologists.

Sugai, G., Sprague, J. R., Horner, R. H., & Walker, H. M. (2000). Preventing school violence: The use of office discipline referrals to assess and monitor school-wide discipline interventions. *Journal of Emotional and Behavioral Disorders, 8,* 94–101.

Taylor-Greene, S. J., & Kartub, D. T. (2000). Durable implementation of school-wide behavior support: The High Five Program. *Journal of Positive Behavior Interventions, 2,* 233–235.

Thorndike, E. L. (1920). *Educational psychology, Volume 1: The original nature of man.* New York: Teachers College Press.

U.S. General Accounting Office. (2001). *Student discipline: Individuals with Disabilities Education Act.* Report to the Committees on Appropriations, U.S. Senate and House of Representatives. Washington, DC: Author. Available at http://www.gao.gov

Van Lier, P. A. C., Vuijk, P. & Crijnen, A. M. (2005). Understanding mechanisms of change in the development of antisocial behavior: The impact of a universal intervention. *Journal of Abnormal Child Psychology, 33,* 521–535.

Vossekuil, B., Reddy, M., & Fein, R. (2000). *An interim report on the prevention of targeted violence in schools.* Washington, DC. U.S. Secret Service

National Threat Assessment Center. Available at http://www.treas.gov/usss/ntac

Wald, J., & Losen, D. J. (2003). Defining and redirecting a school-to-prison pipeline. In J. Wald & D. J. Losen (Eds.), *New directions for youth development* (no. 99; Deconstructing the school-to-prison pipeline, pp. 9–15). San Francisco: Jossey-Bass.

Walker, H. M., Ramsey, E., & Gresham, F. M. (2003). *Antisocial behavior in schools: Evidence-based practices* (2nd ed.). Belmont, CA: Wadsworth/Thomson Learning.

Walker, H., Stiller, B., Severson, H. H., Feil, E. G., & Golly, A. (1998). First step to success: Intervening at the point of school entry to prevent antisocial behavior patterns. *Psychology in the Schools, 35,* 259–269.

Watson, J. B. (1913). *Psychology from the standpoint of a behaviorist.* Philadelphia: Lippincott.

Watson, M. (with L. Ecken). (2003). *Learning to trust: Transforming difficult elementary classrooms through developmental discipline.* San Francisco: Jossey-Bass.

Watson, M., & Battistich, V. (2006). Building and sustaining caring communities. In C. M. Evertson & C. S. Weinstein (Eds.), *Handbook of classroom management: Research, practice, and contemporary issues* (pp. 253–279). Mahwah, NJ: Erlbaum.

Weinstein, C. S., & Mignano, A. J. (2007). *Elementary classroom management: Lessons from research and practice* (4th ed.). Boston: McGraw-Hill.

Wentzel, K. R. (1996). Social and academic motivation in middle school: Concurrent and long-term relations to academic effort. *Journal of Early Adolescence, 16,* 390–406.

Wentzel, K. R. (1997). Student motivation in middle school: The role of perceived pedagogical caring. *Journal of Educational Psychology, 89,* 411–419.

Wentzel, K. R. (2004). Understanding classroom competence: The role of social-motivational and self-processes. In R. V. Kail (Ed.), *Advances in child development and behavior, Vol. 32* (pp. 213–241). San Diego: Elsevier Academic Press.

Zelli, A., Dodge, K. A., Lochman, J. E., & Laird, R. D. (1999). The distinction between beliefs legitimizing aggression and deviant processing of social cues: Testing measurement validity and the hypothesis that biased processing mediates the effects of beliefs on aggression. *Journal of Personality and Social Psychology, 77,* 150–166.

Zins, J. E., Weissberg, R. P., Wang, M. C., & Walberg, H. J. (Eds.). (2004). *Building academic success on social and emotional learning: What does the research say?* New York: Teachers College Press.

About the Author

George G. Bear is Professor of School Psychology at the University of Delaware. His primary research interests are in the areas of school discipline; children's moral reasoning, emotions, and classroom behavior, and children's self-perception.

6

Response to Intervention

A School-Wide Approach for Promoting Academic Wellness for All Students

*Rebecca S. Martínez**

Leah M. Nellis

Response to intervention (RTI) is a data-driven systematic method for identifying and responding to the needs of students who demonstrate academic and behavioral difficulties (Brown-Chidsey & Steege, 2005). At its core, RTI is a set of school-wide procedures intended to promote successful school outcomes for all students. When implemented with fidelity, RTI is a program in which school

*The first author would like to acknowledge Mr. James A. Rubush, former Assistant Superintendent of the Richland-Bean Blossom Community School Corporation (RBBCSC). Mr. Rubush passed away in July 2006 after a long battle with cancer. He was a great supporter of Response to Intervention and helped make possible the partnership between RBBCSC and Indiana University's Academic Well-Check Program.

personnel apply a twofold system of reliable high-quality instruction and frequent formative assessment of student progress (Mellard, Byrd, Johnson, Tollefson, & Boesche, 2004). Decisions in RTI are anchored within a multitier system of options that correspond to student need. Decision makers in RTI include teachers across general and special education as well as other key stakeholders including paraprofessionals, school psychologists, administrators, parents, and other related services personnel. Decision making in RTI underscores the prevention of problems, including learning disabilities, and timely interventions at the first sign of risk.

Despite abundant evidence that most students can attain basic academic skills in reading, writing, and mathematics, too many students fail to master fundamental academic skills. Although schools and school districts are held accountable for ensuring that all students attain fundamental academic skills, especially in reading (e.g., No Child Left Behind Act [NCLB] of 2001), only 31% of fourth-graders are proficient readers and only 36% of fourth-graders perform at a proficient level in mathematics (National Center for Education Statistics, 2005a, 2005b).

The far-reaching implications of low levels of educational attainment on students' lifelong personal wellness are unmistakable (Brown-Chidsey, 2005), and staggering statistics highlight numerous crises threatening students' psychosocial and academic wellness (Crockett, 2004). While a causal link between chronic school failure and poor psychosocial functioning has yet to be made (Chapman, 1988), chronic academic failure is related to loneliness (Margalit, 1998), depression (Bender, Rosenkrans, & Crane, 1999), and school maladjustment (Martínez & Semrud-Clikeman, 2004). Further, comorbidity has been demonstrated between chronic school failure and risky behaviors in adolescence such as underage drinking (Crosnoe, 2006) and delinquency (Center on Crime, Communities, and Culture, 1997). Moreover, students who fail to master basic academic skills are frequently retained at grade level, a practice that is highly predictive that a student will drop out of high school (Jimerson, 1999). By acting early to prevent more pervasive academic and psychosocial problems from developing, reform efforts such as RTI strive to rapidly and systematically decrease the skill gap between students who are experiencing school success and students who are at risk for school failure (Lyon et al., 2001).

The purpose of this chapter is to provide a broad overview of RTI as a population-based model of prevention and remediation of academic difficulties. First, we discuss the importance of helping all students attain basic academic skills, especially in reading. The discussion focuses on the need for schools to improve their screening and early intervention programs and segues to an explanation of the conceptual foundations of RTI. Next, we provide an historical perspective that has led to the widespread interest in RTI. Then we cover the core components of RTI by describing how assessment and intervention activities are generally implemented. Finally, we discuss one school-university partnership that exemplifies effective RTI practice.

School-Wide Efforts for Decreasing Academic Risk

Arguably, one of the central missions of the early elementary school years is to teach all children how to read. A substantial corpus of empirically sound research illustrates how children learn to read and what we can do to ensure reading success. In the best-case scenario, students are learning to read through the third grade. At about the fourth grade, a decisive pedagogical switch happens: Students must *read to learn.* Beyond the fourth grade, the curriculum in all subjects depends on students possessing a basic level of reading proficiency. For many children, learning to read comes naturally as a result of adequate instruction during the first few years of elementary school. Some young children even learn to read without any systematic instruction (Anbar, 1986).

However, learning to read can be a formidable task, and for as many as 20% of all young children it will be the most difficult challenge of their lives (Torgesen, 2003), which means that approximately 10 million American children struggle to read (Fletcher & Lyon, 1998). Reading disability is well understood and preventable for many children, if identified and addressed early (Snow, Burns, & Griffen, 1998). The primary deficit underlying reading disability is at the word recognition level (Share, 1995), and is rooted in impaired phonological processing skills (Stanovich & Siegel, 1994). A phonological deficit characterizes virtually all poor readers and is considered the primary symptom of reading problems (Pennington, 1989).

The U.S. Department of Education (2004) reports that there were approximately 2.9 million students with learning disabilities during the 2001–2002 school year, representing an increase from 1.2 million in 1970–1980. In the last 25 years, schools in the United States have experienced a 283% increase in the number of students identified with learning disabilities and receiving special education services

(Gresham, 2002). Vaughn, Linan-Thompson, and Hickman (2003) explain that the increased number of students with learning disabilities in special education may be attributable to the *overidentification* of students who do not have learning disabilities, *misidentification* of students with disabilities other than learning disability, and *underidentification* of students with true learning disabilities. Similarly, Lyon (2002) has argued that many of these children do not have genuine learning disabilities, but are *instructional casualties* who were simply never taught how to read (Lyon, 2002). Population-based models, such as RTI, that emphasize universal prevention and swift intervention of basic academic problems may reduce the overrepresentation of learning disability in special education.

Waiting to serve children who demonstrate academic risk (e.g., students who are in the bottom 30% on a critical prereading skill such as phonemic awareness) until they are farther along in school increases their odds of being identified with a learning disability by 450% (Gresham, VanDerHeyden, & Witt, 2005). Children who struggle early on, but do not receive the academic help they need, may "learn to be learning disabled" (Clay, 1987, cited in Gresham, VanDerHeyden, & Witt, 2005).

By the fourth grade, 2 hours of specialized daily instruction is required to make the same gains that would have resulted from only 30 minutes of daily instruction if begun when the child was in kindergarten (National Reading Panel, 1999). Current research shows that a combination of effective classroom instruction and targeted small-group instruction can remediate up to 98% of students performing below the 30th percentile in early reading skills (Denton & Mathes, 2003; Torgesen, 2004). Similarly, King and Torgesen (2000) reported a reduction in reading failure from 31.8% to 3.7% at one elementary school. Mounting empirical research indicates that appropriate classroom instruction, together with intensive intervention, can result in up to 95% of the classroom population performing in at least the average range in reading (Fletcher & Lyon, 1998).

RTI holds significant promise as a method for preventing many learning difficulties, especially reading problems. Underlying RTI is a framework and a set of activities that emphasize prevention and swift, data-driven intervention as soon as student difficulties are detected. Unlike traditional educational approaches that address learning problems after students have experienced academic failure (e.g., the wait-to-fail discrepancy model), RTI emphasizes global prevention and is focused on positive academic outcomes for all students.

Conceptual Foundations of RTI

Response to intervention is a multitiered model of intervention and assessment activities offered along a continuum to all students district-wide or school-wide. The type and intensity of the instruction and assessment services that are provided across the tiers depend on the severity of the academic difficulty the students are experiencing. In RTI, as student needs increase, school resources increase proportionally (Grimes, 2002). A fundamental component of all RTI models is universal screenings that identify struggling students as early as kindergarten and target their skill deficits through proven instructional methods. Decisions regarding services for struggling individuals or groups of students are made objectively and systematically through the application of a problem-solving process (National Association of State Directors of Special Education [NASDSE], 2005).

Generally, RTI models underscore three objectives. First, RTI ensures that all students receive scientifically supported instruction in general, remedial, and special education. The emphasis on selecting and implementing only sound, research-backed core curricula and interventions increases the likelihood that most students will make some positive individual progress (NASDSE, 2005). Second, RTI programs screen populations of students frequently and monitor their progress to determine who is lagging. Finally, through RTI, students receive appropriate, research-based interventions at the appropriate frequency and intensity, specifically targeting their academic areas of difficulty.

Data gathered through RTI may also be used to determine if a learning disability is present and whether a student is eligible for special education. While RTI is based on a conceptual framework that emphasizes a continuum of services in general and special education, much of the recent conversation has discussed the suitability of RTI as an alternate procedure for identifying learning disabilities.

Historical Perspective on the Diagnosis of Learning Disabilities

Traditionally, the identification of learning disabilities has been based on unexpected underachievement relative to intellectual potential. However, there has been fierce backlash against discrepancy-based models from scientists and practitioners. Reschly (2003) succinctly noted that discrepancy-based models to identify children with learning disabilities (a) are unreliable and unstable, (b) are invalid because poor readers with high IQs are not much different from poor readers with commensurate IQs, (c) undermine best practices in that examiners often administer multiple tests to obtain the desired discrepancy or overlook exclusionary criteria (e.g., mental retardation and cultural impoverishment) in order to serve students in need, and (d) are harmful because the models represent a "wait-to-fail" paradigm that delays intervention until children are in the middle elementary grades. Perhaps the most serious flaw in the discrepancy-based definition, however, is that traditional standardized testing procedures are minimally related to designing, implementing, or evaluating classroom instruction (Gresham, 2002).

Widespread interest in RTI is rooted in the need for significant improvements in general and special education. Historically, educators have had long-standing concerns about (a) the insufficient emphasis on prevention and early intervention, (b) the unreliable special education eligibility processes for specific learning disabilities, and (c) the limited use of research-based instructional practices (NASDSE, 2005). Critical educational elements, articulated in a National Research Council report on the validity of special education classifications (Heller, Holtzman, & Messick, 1982), constitute what many regard as the first time RTI was delineated in print. Heller and colleagues proposed that the validity of special education classification procedures be measured using the following criteria: (a) the quality of the system's general education program, (b) the benefit of special education services for students' educational outcomes, and (c) the validity of the assessment processes in identifying students with disabilities. Fuchs and Fuchs (1998) operationalized the criteria by proposing that Curriculum-Based Measurement (CBM; Deno, 1985) procedures ought to be used to determine students' response to instruction delivered in general education.

RTI has received support in numerous national reports and meetings convened by experts in the field. In 2001, the U.S. Department of Education, Office of Special Education Programs, brought together a national panel of experts to discuss the identification of students with learning disabilities. The summit report, *The Learning Disabilities Summit: Building a Foundation for the Future* marked a national response to mounting concerns about overidentification rates and limitations inherent in learning disability identification practices. Subsequently, the panel produced a series of nine white papers germane to the topic of learning disabilities including Gresham's (2002), *Responsiveness to Intervention: An alternative approach to the identification of learning disabilities,* which specifically discussed RTI.

RTI was further supported in the President's Commission on Excellence in Special Education report, *A New Era: Revitalizing Special Education for Children and Their Families*. In this report, the Commission emphasized three focal points for special education reform: (a) focus on process and results; (b) embrace a model of prevention not a model of failure; and (c) consider children with disabilities as general education children first. These three foci support RTI philosophy, including its viability over the discrepancy model for identifying learning disabilities. Finally, the National Research Council Panel on Minority Overrepresentation also supported RTI as a potential strategy to decrease the incidence of overrepresentation of minority students identified for special education services (Donovan & Cross, 2002).

The December 2004 reauthorization of the *Individuals with Disabilities Education Act of 1997* (IDEA) included RTI as an alternative method for identifying a specific learning disability. Final IDEA 2004 regulations were released in August 2006, including language specifying that, in the identification of specific learning disabilities, state educational agencies must not require that local education agencies (LEAs) use a severe discrepancy between intellectual ability and achievement and must permit LEAs to incorporate the use of a process based on the child's response to scientific research-based intervention section (§300.307). To advance RTI research and practice, the Office of Special Education Programs, U.S. Department of Education, recently established national centers such as the National Research Center on Learning Disabilities (http://www.nrcld.org/) and the National Center on Student Progress Monitoring (http://www.studentprogress.org/).

Operationalization of RTI

The system underlying RTI is often operationalized as a three-tier model, although variations may include two tiers (e.g., Fuchs, Fuchs, & Compton, 2004; Vaughn, Linan-Thompson, & Hickman, 2003), three tiers (e.g., Denton & Mathes, 2003; University of Texas System/Texas Education Agency, 2005), or four or more tiers (e.g., Reschly & Ysseldyke, 2002; Tilly, 2002). Resources and personnel flexibility influence the number of tiers in a given RTI model. Researchers believe that fewer tiers (e.g., two) ensure better intervention fidelity and facilitate more effective identification procedures for special education (Fuchs, Mock, Morgan, & Young, 2003). Multidisciplinary, school-wide teams that include general and special education staff review students' formative assessment data to make decisions about students' placement within and movement between tiers. Such teams use a problem-solving process to analyze the students' difficulty. The importance of considering a student's cultural background as part of the problem-solving process has been encouraged as best practice (National Center for Culturally Responsive Educational Systems, 2005). Both intervention and assessment activities increase in intensity as more targeted and individualized services are needed across the tiers.

Generally, researchers suggest that the needs of approximately 80% to 90% of students can be met with universal services at Tier 1, with 5% to 15% needing additional services at Tier 2% and 1% to 5% needing more intense services at Tier 3 (Walker & Shinn, 2002). While all schools should have the full continuum of services available, the degree to which the suggested percentages play out depends on many factors. Schools should offer a continuum of services based on knowledge of local needs and resources and, as recommended by Adelman and Taylor (this volume), integrating both school and community services in a purposeful manner. The following sections describe the intervention activities and assessment procedures that generally take place at each tier of service in a prototypical three-tier model.

Tier 1: School-Wide Instruction and Universal Screening

Tier 1 is best understood as a mechanism for widespread prevention of academic problems. Within the three-tier model of service delivery, Tier 1 is set up to meet the needs of all students within a school system. Because Tier 1 involves a high-quality school and classroom environment, scientifically sound core curriculum and instruction, and intentional instructional practices, all students are given an opportunity to access the general curriculum and make academic gain.

In Tier 1, school personnel must objectively and systematically evaluate whether their core curriculum materials are of sufficiently high quality and backed by research. School staff must also evaluate teachers' instructional methods to make sure that their teaching techniques adhere to sound instructional practice and are delivered as intended by the curriculum or intervention program. Ruling out poor instruction as a factor contributing to students' failure is done systematically throughout the RTI process (Graner, Faggella-Luby, & Fritschmann, 2005), but it is a cornerstone activity at Tier 1.

In early reading, core curricula emphasize the five big ideas of early literacy: phonemic awareness, phonics, fluency, vocabulary, and comprehension (Good, Kame'enui, Simmons, & Chard, 2002). One hallmark of all effective, research-based core reading curricula is that they cover all grade level standards with ample quality, breadth, and depth (Simmons & Kame'enui, 2003). That is, within Tier 1, students receive instruction in the general education classroom in large groups using a core, research-based curriculum that is implemented with fidelity. At least 90 minutes of daily reading instruction is recommended at Tier 1 (McCook, 2006). Effective and strategic instruction in all classrooms for all students in Tier 1 is the responsibility of general education teachers (Fuchs & Fuchs, 2005).

To verify that students are making adequate progress toward basic academic goals, it is imperative to gather data on the population. In Tier I, school-wide screenings are conducted to gauge students' performance in the core academic areas (e.g., reading fluency and mathematics calculations). All students are typically screened three times per year (e.g., fall, winter, and spring). The purpose of conducting school-wide screenings is to gather critical data about all students and identify individuals and groups who are not making satisfactory progress in the core curriculum. Students who are not mastering basic academic skills may require additional or different forms of instruction. General education teachers may or may not conduct the universal screenings, but they are responsible for using the assessment information to modify instructional strategies and other environmental factors over which they have control (Good, Kaminski, Smith, Simmons, Kame'enui, & Wallin, 2002). Systematic reviews of assessment data are often carried out by collaborative instructional support teams (Kovaleski & Glew, 2006).

Curriculum-Based Measurement

For assessment activities at all tiers in the RTI process, including universal screening and progress monitoring, Curriculum-Based Measurement (CBM) is the formative assessment method of choice. CBM is a method of monitoring student progress through direct, frequent assessment of core academic skills (Deno, 1985). In the early grades, K–1, early literacy is assessed using CBM tasks that may include letter naming fluency, letter sound fluency, phoneme segmentation fluency, and nonsense word fluency. CBM of early numeracy skills in K–1 may include the Tests of Early Numeracy (Clarke & Shinn, 2004), which include oral counting, missing number, number identification, and quantity discrimination.

For older students, CBMs of oral reading fluency (i.e., Reading Curriculum-Based Measurement, or R-CBM), comprehension (i.e., Maze task), spelling, written expression, and mathematics computations can be administered to directly assess basic academic skills and monitor student progress over time. CBM tests (or probes) are standardized, time efficient, inexpensive, and quick to administer and score. CBM has other advantages over traditional, norm-referenced assessment of student performance in that students' performance can be compared to their own performance and to same-grade peers (Deno, Lembke, & Anderson, n.d.). CBM data are plotted and displayed graphically to monitor individual and group student growth over time. This visual representation of the data (e.g., by classroom or grade level) assists teams in evaluating whether students are making sufficient progress at each tier and whether the interventions are working.

Several Web-based systems are available for CBM assessment and data management. The National Center on Student Progress Monitoring (http://www.studentprogress.org/) evaluates and disseminates information on the technical adequacy and scientific rigor of commercial progress monitoring systems. One example of a comprehensive CBM data management and reporting application that was favorably reviewed by the Center is AIMSweb® (Edformation, 2006).[1] AIMSweb® (http://www.aimsweb.com/) provides CBM assessment tools/probes for Grades K–8 as well as a sophisticated Web-based information management system that documents student progress.

The Web-based software system also manages, charts, and reports CBM assessment results, facilitating the process of using data to inform instruction for individuals and groups of students. Developers of AIMSweb® recently added the AIMSweb® RTI module, which provides a powerful, effective mechanism for RTI decision-making teams to evaluate individual students' responses to interventions (Shinn, 2006).

Within an RTI model, universal screening data are analogous to "academic thermometers" (Shinn, 1998) that gauge whether basic levels of academic achievement are present or absent. With CBM, students are assessed on academic skills that are core indicators of achievement in broader areas. For example, a good indicator of general reading ability is the number of words on a grade level passage that a student reads correctly during a one-minute period (Deno, Mirkin, & Marston, 1980). Increases in a student's raw "words read correct" scores across time and in direct response to a particular intervention indicate that improvement in overall reading achievement is taking place.

For RTI to be a successful enterprise, it is essential that decision-making teams accurately determine which students are actually at risk and in need of more intensive interventions at Tier 2 (Compton, Fuchs,

Fuchs, & Bryant, 2006). Thus, purposeful, systematic, and informed reviews of data will reduce false positives (inaccurately identifying students who are not at risk) and false negatives (failing to identify students who are at risk). Graphing both group and individual student data allows school personnel to make effective, data-based instructional decisions. Based on estimates in the literature of how much slope or growth typically achieving students make, teachers can compare the slopes of their students to expected rates of progress (based on local or national norms) to identify who is at risk and in need of supplemental interventions (Brown-Chidsey & Steege, 2005).

Tier 2: Supplementary Instruction and Progress Monitoring

Tier 2 includes targeted academic and behavioral services for students considered at risk and for whom research-based universal interventions were not sufficient at Tier 1. Services at Tier 2 are more intense and focused on small groups of students to address specific needs. Tier-2 interventions are provided to students in addition to the core curriculum, and might be delivered for a minimum of 30 minutes a day, 3 to 4 days a week (McCook, 2006). Fuchs and Fuchs (2005) highlight best practice in the delivery of Tier 2, which includes the delivery of research-based, targeted interventions for up to three students at a time, three times per week for 30 minutes. The interventions are given across a 10-week span and delivered only by certified school personnel.

Tier 2 interventions can be applied through one of two methods: (a) standard protocol/researcher approach or (b) problem-solving/school practitioner approach (Fuchs et al., 2003). Optimally, a combination of standard protocol approaches and problem-solving methods can be integrated in RTI (Barnett, Daly, Jones & Lentz, 2004). In standard-protocol approaches, all children whose data indicate difficulty in a certain academic area (e.g., reading fluency) are given the same intervention that has been empirically validated to promote progress in that area. Several examples of standard protocol interventions are provided in the literature (e.g., Torgesen, Alexander, Wagner, Rashotte, Voeller, Conway, & Rose, 2001; Vaughn, Linan-Thompson, & Hickman, 2003).

In the Vaughn et al. (2003) study, a standard intervention addressing fluency, phonemic awareness, instructional level reading, word analysis, and writing was delivered to a group of 45 at-risk second-graders. Student data were reviewed at weeks 10, 20, and 30 and, as students demonstrated progress, they were exited from the treatment accordingly. The authors report that while the groups did not benefit from the supplemental instruction equally, all students profited to some extent from the supplemental instruction, especially in the first 10 weeks.

The second approach to the selection and delivery of appropriate Tier 2 interventions involves the problem-solving model, which was borrowed from behavioral problem-solving and collaborative consultation (Fuchs et al., 2003). The problem-solving model involves building- or grade-level problem-solving teams that systematically review student data (i.e., CBM profiles) to select appropriate intervention strategies and determine (through data-based decision making) if the strategies need to be modified, maintained, or terminated to ensure success. Implicit in the problem-solving approach is the notion that solutions to students' academic and behavioral difficulties are identified through the systematic review of data in a four-stage problem-solving process (Fuchs et al., 2003). The four-step problem-solving archetype answers four questions: (a) What is the problem or issue?; (b) Why is the problem occurring?; (c) What should be done about it?; and (d) Did it work? (Tilly, 2002). Once need is established and interventions are selected, interventions at Tier 2 are delivered by school personnel including, but not limited to, general and special education teachers, paraprofessionals, counselors, and graduate students.

In addition to the implementation of more targeted, systematic interventions at Tier 2, student progress at Tier 2 is monitored more frequently (often weekly) than it is at Tier 1 to determine student responsiveness to the interventions. Typically, students who respond well to Tier 2 interventions and whose data demonstrate that they are progressing at an acceptable rate (e.g., above the 16th percentile) are returned to the general education setting, or Tier 1. These students continue to participate in universal screenings.

Tier 3: Intensive Instruction and Continued Progress Monitoring

Despite best efforts in the activities and assessments given at Tiers 1 and 2, some students will continue to struggle and be unresponsive to the extra assistance. More intensive services may be warranted and may be provided through special education in Tier 3. The intervention-assessment sequence in Tier 3 is markedly more intensive and individualized, and progress is monitored more frequently than it is in Tier 2. Current best practice in the field suggests that students who do not make adequate progress at Tier 2 or 3 be further evaluated to rule out conditions such mental retardation and emotional disturbance (Fuchs & Fuchs, 2005).

Persistent failure to make academic gains at Tier 2 or 3 may substantiate the presence of a learning disability (Fuchs et al., 2003). Fuchs and Fuchs (1998) proposed a treatment validity approach for identifying learning disability From within this "dual discrepancy" model students are considered for special education eligibility only when their CBM scores indicate (a) a discrepancy in performance relative to peers and (b) a discrepancy in their rate of learning (growth or slope) relative to peers. Additionally, teams making decisions about eligibility for special education must document that the learning problems are not due to other disabilities, poor instruction, or limited English proficiency (IDEA, 2004).

One Example: The Academic Well-Check Program

Numerous examples of model RTI sites and descriptions of "lessons learned" can be found in the literature and online. (See Haubner, Staum, & Potter, 2002; Marston, Canter, Lau, & Muyskens, 2002; Sornson, Frost, & Burns, 2005, for descriptions of model programs in Milwaukee, Minneapolis, and Michigan, respectively.) At the same time, in response to changes in the field, RTI is emerging as a focus of personnel preparation at many school psychology training programs around the country.

The Academic Well-Check Program (AWCP; http://profile.educ .indiana.edu/awcp) is one example of a school/university partnership that simultaneously strengthened RTI practices in a school and didactic training in RTI skills within a school psychology training program.

The AWCP is a partnership between the Institute for Child Study (ICS) of Indiana University and four schools (three elementary and one middle school) in a local school district. It is based on an RTI framework and operates within a three-tier model spotlighting universal screening and the delivery of small remedial interventions. The AWCP's core activity is to benchmark or screen the population of students at the four partner schools three times a year. Specifically, graduate students in the AWCP conduct mini-academic "well checks" using curriculum-based measurement technology. Then advanced graduate students plan and implement data-driven, research-based academic interventions. The AWCP is very timely considering the emphasis research, policy, and federal law are placing on the prevention and remediation of learning problems before it is too late.

The participating AWCP schools are located in a lower- to middle-class neighborhood where 27% of the children receive free or reduced-cost lunches (Indiana Department of Education, 2006). During the 2005–2006 school year, the district had 95% White, 2% multiracial, and 1% Asian, Hispanic, and African American students, respectively. The district has three elementary schools, one junior high school, and one high school. The 2005–2006 enrollment was 2,841 students, 19.3% of whom were in special education.

Prior to the fall of 2004, the ICS operated as a conventional university-based clinic staffed by school psychology graduate students under the supervision of school psychology faculty. Then, as part of the faculty planning process during the 2003–2004 academic year, the faculty identified a number of limitations associated with the university-based model. First, the number of clients served through the ICS was strictly limited by the number of experienced graduate students and available faculty time. Second, children were only served *after* evidencing significant academic and behavioral problems, letting them fail before providing service. In response, the faculty revised the scope and focus of the ICS to serve a larger population of students and reflect a problem-solving, interventions-based orientation.

The AWCP was launched and sustained with relatively limited financial resources, holding promise for its replication by other school-university partnerships. Internal university funds were used to support one graduate assistant and a one-course buyout for the faculty member who directs the ICS. Since 2004, the first author of this paper has been in that role. Another resource that has made the AWCP possible is the AIMSweb® Pre-Service Training Package that is available free of charge for university-based preservice trainers. The Pre-Service Training Package includes access to the training manuals for didactic training of students. The package also includes a subscription to AIMSweb® assessments and various Web-based reporting components, including AIMSweb® RTI. Also, the faculty restructured the university program to require student participation in the AWCP.

The success of the AWCP would not be possible without the buy-in and support of school administrators and teachers at the partner schools. A series of initial meetings with district administrators, including the associate superintendent and director of special education facilitated early discussions about the AWCP and how the program would benefit the district. This was "Step 0," the step that precedes implementation of the actual program (Gutkin, 2000, cited in Allen & Graden, 2002) and involves relationship building among stakeholders. Allen and Graden (2002) articulated the goals of Step 0 as "establishing and maintaining rapport among participants, formulating a sense of trust and respect among participants, and clarifying expectations for participation..." (p. 570). Numerous follow-up meetings and e-mail correspondences reassured school principals followed Step 0. In implementing any educational, systemic change, it is imperative that all constituents "communicate, communicate, communicate!" (Grimes & Tilly, 1996), which was done extensively in the spring and summer of 2004. The relational aspect of the collaboration cannot be overemphasized. For months prior to launching the program, rapport and trust were fostered between the university and school personnel. University faculty emphasized the service component of the AWCP, while underscoring the importance of research.

In three short years, school psychology students working in the Indiana University Academic Well Check Program benchmarked thousands of students and served many of them through research-based reading and math interventions. Over 3,800 students have been screened, and approximately 420 students (across almost 73 classrooms) have been served in Tier 2 and Tier 3 interventions (Martínez, 2006). Faculty and students in the AWCP have also begun to make scholarly contributions through presentations at national conferences and peer and non-peer reviewed journals. Students have made presentations about their interventions using peer tutoring (Gibb et al., 2005) and paired reading (Dick, Humphreys, & Martínez, 2005). A non-peer reviewed article on the use of instructional level assessment (ILA) within RTI was recently published (Hopf & Martínez, 2006) and numerous empirical manuscripts and one dissertation are also well under way.

Currently, there are two overarching goals of AWCP. The first is to foster a professional, collaborative relationship with administrators, staff, students, and parents at the four partner schools. The second is to mentor graduate students to be consumers of and contributors to the scholarly literature in education and school psychology. Thus, AWCP activities focus on (a) maintaining a positive relationship with the partner schools (e.g., providing the free benchmarking service and numerous in-services throughout the years) and (b) supporting graduate students' new and ongoing interventions, writing and submitting manuscripts to be considered for publication, and presenting at local, state, and national conferences.

Based on estimates that it takes four to six years to implement RTI (NASDSE, 2005), AWCP's efforts in training new school psychology leaders for RTI and collaborating with local school partners in adopting RTI procedures are a work in progress. So far, the results have been rewarding and very encouraging. Willingness to change (by local partner schools and faculty at Indiana University) indicates an awakening to paradigm shifts in education and the need to do things differently and better than they have been done in the past. An ongoing process of improving and refining the activities in the AWCP will continue in 2008 and beyond. Students and faculty will expand on the work already begun in the AWCP emphasizing the implementation and evaluation of standard treatment protocol research and contributing to the RTI literature.

Conclusion

This chapter reviewed RTI, describing it as a school-wide system of screening and early intervention for students who experience difficulties in school, particularly in reading. We described the core components of RTI and provided a historical foundation leading up to RTI. The chapter concludes with a description of an exemplary university/school partnership that supports high-quality RTI practice and training. Pressure at the national level for education reform based on research-based evidence is pervasive, and fundamental change in the role of school mental health professionals and other educators is the cornerstone of a school system that is ready to embrace an RTI overhaul.

Note

1. The Center on Student Progress Monitoring rated AIMSweb's® reading fluency (R-CBM) and comprehension (MAZE) tools as demonstrating sufficient evidence to meet the seven technical adequacy standards set forth by the Center's Technical Review Committee.

Discussion Questions

1. What academic assessment and intervention skills do you already have that you could use if you implemented a response to intervention program in your school?

2. How could response to intervention shift your school's emphasis toward the prevention of learning problems? How could it increase the reliability of eligibility decisions made by your school's multidisciplinary team?

3. How could you find out the proportion of students in your school who struggle with chronic academic failure?

4. What could you do to marshal the resources to implement an academic well-check program in your school?

5. One criticism of response to intervention, and other tiered intervention systems, is that they sometimes redirect resources away from students with severe academic delays and toward students who are just beginning to lag behind their classmates. Is this shift likely to occur if your school implemented an RTI program? And, if so, is this an ethical shift?

References

Allen, S. J., & Graden, J. L. (2002). Best practices in collaborative problem solving for intervention design. In A. Thomas & J. Grimes (Eds.), *Best practices in school psychology* (4th ed., pp. 565–582). Washington, DC: National Association of School Psychologists.

Anbar, A. (1986). Reading acquisition of preschool children without systematic instruction. *Early Childhood Research Quarterly, 1*, 69–83.

Barnett, D. W., Daly, E. J., Jones, K. M., & Lentz, F. E. (2004). Response to intervention: Empirically-based special service decisions for increasing and decreasing intensity using single case designs. *The Journal of Special Education, 38*, 66–79.

Bender, W. N., Rosenkrans, C. B., & Crane, M. (1999). Stress, depression, and suicide among students with learning disabilities: Assessing the risk. *Learning Disability Quarterly, 22*, 143–156.

Brown-Chidsey, R. (2005). Academic skills are basic (to) children's personal wellness. *Trainer's Forum: Periodical of the Trainers of School Psychologists, 25*(1), 4–10.

Brown-Chidsey, R., & Steege, S. M. (2005). *Response to intervention: Principles and strategies for effective practice.* New York: Guilford Press.

Center on Crime, Communities, and Culture. (1997). Education as crime prevention: Providing education to prisoners. *Research Brief (Occasional Paper Series No. 2).* New York: Author.

Chapman, J. W. (1988). Cognitive-motivational characteristics and academic achievement of learning disabled children: A longitudinal study. *Journal of Educational Psychology, 80*, 357–365.

Clarke, B., & Shinn, M. R. (2004). A preliminary investigation into the identification and development of early mathematics curriculum-based measurement. *School Psychology Review, 33*, 234–248.

Clay, M. (1987). *Writing begins at home.* Portsmouth, NH: Heinemann.

Compton, D. L., Fuchs, D., Fuchs, L. S., & Bryant, J. D. (2006). Selecting at-risk readers in first grade for early intervention: A two-year longitudinal study of decision rules and procedures. *Journal of Educational Psychology, 98*, 394–409.

Crockett, D. (2004). Critical issues children face in the 2000s. *School Psychology Review, 33,* 78–82.

Crosnoe, R. (2006). The connection between academic failure and adolescent drinking in secondary school. *Sociology of Education, 79,* 44–60.

Deno, S. L. (1985). Curriculum-based measurement: The emerging alternative. *Exceptional Children, 52,* 219–232.

Deno, S., Lembke, E., & Anderson, A. R. (n.d.) *Progress monitoring: Study group content module.* Retrieved June 7, 2006, from http://education.umn.edu/EdPsych/Projects/cbmMOD1.pdf

Deno, S. L., Mirkin, P. K., & Marston, D. (1980). *Relationships among simple measures of written expression and performance on standardized achievement tests* (Research Report No. 22). Minneapolis: University of Minnesota, Institute for Research on Learning Disabilities.

Denton, C., & Mathes, P. (2003). Interventions for struggling readers: Possibilities and challenges. In B. Foorman (Ed.), *Preventing and remediating reading difficulties. Bringing science to scale* (pp. 229–251). Baltimore: York Press.

Dick, A. C., Humphreys, L. A., & Martínez, R. S. (2005, August). *Evaluating the effects of paired reading and parent education on first graders' early literacy skills.* Poster presented at the 2005 meeting of the American Psychological Association, Washington, DC.

Donovan, M. S., & Cross, C. T. (Eds.). (2002). *Minority students in special and gifted education.* National Research Council; Committee on Minority Representation in Special Education. Washington, DC: National Academy Press.

Edformation. (2006). *AIMSweb.* Retrieved June 1, 2006, from www.edformation.com/

Fletcher, J. M., & Lyon, G. R. (1998). *Reading: A research-based approach.* Retrieved June 28, 2006, from http://www.nichd.nih.gov/crmc/cdb/approach.pdf

Fuchs, D., & Fuchs, L. (2005, May). *Operationalizing Response-To-Intervention (RTI) as a method of LD identification.* Retrieved April 5, 2007, from http://state.tn.us/education/speced/doc/sefuopertifaq.pdf

Fuchs, D., Fuchs, L., & Compton, D. L. (2004). Identifying reading disabilities by responsiveness-to-instruction: specifying measures and criteria. *Learning Disability Quarterly, 27,* 216–227.

Fuchs, D., Mock, D., Morgan, P. L., & Young, C. L. (2003). Responsiveness-to-intervention: Definitions, evidence, and implications for the learning disabilities construct. *Learning Disabilities Research and Practice, 18,* 157–171.

Fuchs, L. & Fuchs, D. (1998). Treatment validity: A unifying concept for reconceptualizing the identification of learning disabilities. *Learning Disabilities Research and Practice, 13,* 204–219.

Gibb, A. C., Edl, H., Benton, S., Oz, A., & Martínez, R. S. (2005, August). Kindergarten *peer tutoring: Monitoring progress in math achievement and self-efficacy.* Poster presented at the American Psychological Association's 2005 Annual Convention, Washington, DC.

Good, R. H., Kame'enui, E. J., Simmons, D. S., & Chard, D. J. (2002). *Focus and nature of primary, secondary, and tertiary prevention: The CIRCUITS model* (Tech. Rep. No. 1). Eugene: University of Oregon, College of Education, Institute for the Development of Educational Achievement.

Good, R. H., Kaminski, R. A., Smith, S. B., Simmons, D. C., Kame'enui, E. J., & Wallin, J. (2002). Reviewing outcomes: Using DIBELS to evaluated kindergarten curricula and interventions. In S. Vaughn & K. Briggs (Eds.), *Reading in the classroom: Systems for the observation of teaching & learning* (pp. 221–266). Baltimore: Brookes Publishing.

Graner, P. S., Faggella-Luby, M. N., & Fritschmann, N. S. (2005). An overview of responsiveness to intervention: What practitioners ought to know. *Topics in Language Disorders, 25,* 93–105.

Gresham, F. (2002). Responsiveness to intervention: An alternative approach to the identification of learning disabilities. In R. Bradley, L. Danielson, & D. Hallahan (Eds.), *Identification of learning disabilities: Research to practice* (pp. 467–529). Mahwah, NJ: Erlbaum.

Gresham, F. M., VanDerHeyden, A., & Witt, J. C. (2005). Response to intervention in the identification of learning disabilities: Empirical support and future challenges. Unpublished manuscript. Retrieved May 5, 2006, from http://www.joewitt.org/Downloads/Response%20to%20Intervention%20MS%20Gresham%20%20Vanderheyden%20Witt.pdf

Grimes, J. (2002). Responsiveness to intervention: The next step in special education identification, service, and exiting decision-making. In R. Bradley, L. Danielson, & D. Hallham (Eds.), *Identification of learning disabilities: Research to practice* (pp. 467–519). Mahwah, NJ. Erlbaum.

Grimes, J., & Tilly, III, W. D. (1996). Policy and process: Means to lasting educational change. *School Psychology Review, 25,* 465–476.

Haubner, C., Staum, M., Potter, A. (2002). Optimizing success through problem solving: School reform in Milwaukee public schools. *Communiqué, 30.* Retrieved June 22, 2006, from http://www.nasponline.org/publications/cq/cq308index.aspx

Heller, K. A., Holtzman, W. H., & Messick, S. (Eds). (1982). Placing children in special education: A strategy for equity. Washington, DC: National Academy Press.

Hopf, A., & Martínez, R. S. (2006). Implementation of Instructional Level Assessment (ILA) within a Response to Intervention (RTI) model of service delivery. *The School Psychologist, 60* (2), 75–78.

Indiana Department of Education (2006). Corporation snapshot, Richland-Bean Blossom C S C #5705. Retrieved June 29, 2006, from http://mustang.doe.state.in.us/SEARCH/snapcorp.cfm?corp=5705

Jimerson, S. R. (1999). On the failure of failure: Examining the association of early grade retention and late adolescent education and employment outcomes. *Journal of School Psychology, 37,* 243–272.

King, R., & Torgesen, J. K. (2000). *Improving the effectiveness of reading instruction in one elementary school: A description of the process* (Technical Report #3). Florida Center for Reading Research.

Kovaleski, J. F., & Glew, M. C. (2006). Bringing instructional support teams to scale: Implications of the Pennsylvania experience. *Remedial & Special Education, 27,* 16–25.

Lyon, G. R. (2002, June). Testimony of Dr. G. Reid Lyon. *Learning disabilities and early intervention strategies: How to reform the special education referral and identification process.* Hearing before the Subcommittee on Education Reform Committee on Education and the Workforce United States

House of Representatives. Retrieved June 22, 2006, from http://www .house.gov/ed_workforce/hearings/107th/edr/idea6602/lyon.htm

Lyon, G. R., Fletcher, J. M., Shaywitz, S. E., Shaywitz, B. A., Torgesen, J. K., Wood, F. B., et al. (2001). Rethinking learning disabilities. In C. E. Finn, Jr., R. A. J. Rotherham, & C. R. Hokanson, Jr. (Eds.), *Rethinking special education for a new century* (pp. 259–287). Washington, DC: Thomas B. Fordham Foundation and Progressive Policy Institute.

Margalit, M. (1998). Loneliness and coherence among preschool children with learning disabilities. *Journal of Learning Disabilities, 31*(2), 173–181.

Marston, D., Canter, A., Lau, M., & Muyskens, P. (2002, June). Problem solving: Implementation and evaluation in Minneapolis schools. *Communiqué, 30* (8).

Martínez, R. S., & Semrud-Clikeman, M. (2004). Psychosocial functioning of young adolescents with multiple versus single learning disabilities. *Journal of Learning Disabilities, 37*, 411–420.

McCook, J. E. (2006). *The RTI guide: Developing and implementing a model in your schools.* Horsham, PA: LRP Publications.

Mellard, D. F., Byrd, S. E., Johnson, E., Tollefson, J. M., Boesche, L. (2004). Foundations and research on identifying model responsiveness-to-intervention sites. *Learning Disabilities Quarterly, 27*, 243–256.

National Association of State Directors of Special Education. (2005). Response to Intervention: Policy considerations and implementation. Alexandria, VA: Author.

National Center for Culturally Responsive Educational Systems. (2005). Cultural considerations and challenges in response-to-intervention models: An NCCRESt position statement. Retrieved March 21, 2006, from http://www.nccrest.org/

National Center for Education Statistics (NCES). (2005a). *Average math scale scores for the nation at grades 4 and 8.* Retrieved June 24, 2006, from http://nces.ed.gov/nationsreportcard/nrc/reading_math_2005/s0018 .asp?printver=

National Center for Education Statistics (NCES). (2005b). *Average reading scale scores for the nation at grades 4 and 8.* Retrieved June 24, 2006, from http://nces.ed.gov/nationsreportcard/nrc/reading_math_2005/s0003 .asp?printver

National Reading Panel. (1999). *Teaching children to read.* Report, National Institute of Child Health and Human Development, National Institutes of Health.

Pennington, B. F. 1989. Using genetics to understand dyslexia. *Annals of Dyslexia, 39*, 81–93.

Reschly, D. J. (2003, December). *What if LD identification changed to reflect research findings?* Paper presented at the National Research Center on Learning Disabilities Responsiveness-to-Intervention Symposium, Kansas City, MO.

Reschly, D. J., & Ysseldyke, J. E. (2002). Paradigm shift: The past is not the future. In A. Thomas & J. Grimes (Eds.), *Best practices in school psychology IV* (pp. 1–20). National Association of School Psychologists: Washington, DC.

Share, D. L. (1995). Phonological recording and self-teaching: sine qua non of reading acquisition. *Cognition, 55*, 151–218.

Shinn, M. R. (Ed.). (1998). *Advanced applications of curriculum-based measurement*. New York: Guilford Press.

Shinn, M. (2006). *AIMSweb Response-to-Intervention (RTI): A standard protocol-based system for managing and reporting problem-solving outcomes*. Retrieved May 17, 2006, from http://www.edformation.com/

Simmons, D. C., & Kame'enui, E. J. (2003, March). *A consumer's guide to evaluating a core reading program grades K-3: A critical elements analysis*. Eugene, OR: Institute for the Development of Educational Achievement.

Snow, C. E., Burns, M. S., & Griffen, P. (1998). Preventing reading difficulties in young children. Washington, DC: National Academy Press.

Sornson, R., Frost, F., & Burns, M. (2005, February). Instructional support teams in Michigan: Data from the Northville public schools. *Communiqué, 33*(5), 28–29.

Stanovich, K. E., & Siegel, L. S. (1994). Phenotypic performance profile of children with reading disabilities: A regression-based test of the phonological-core variable difference model of reading. *Journal of Educational Psychology, 86*, 24–53.

Tilly, D. W. (2002). Best practices in school psychology as a problem-solving enterprise. In A. Thomas & J. Grimes (Eds.), *Best practices in school psychology-IV* (pp. 21–36). Bethesda, MD: National Association of School Psychologists.

Torgesen, J. K. (2003). *Operationalizing the response to intervention model to identify children with disabilities: Specific issues with older children*. Paper presented at the National Research Center on Learning Disabilities Responsiveness-to-Intervention Symposium. Kansas City, MO.

Torgesen, J. K. (2004). Lessons learned from the last 20 years of research on interventions for students who experience difficulty learning to read. In P. McCardle & V. Chhabra (Eds.) *The voice of evidence in reading research* (pp. 355–382). Baltimore: Brookes Publishing.

Torgesen, J. K., Alexander, A. W., Wagner, R. K., Rashotte, C. A., Voeller, K., Conway, T., & Rose, E. (2001). Intensive remedial instruction for children with severe reading disabilities: Immediate and long-term outcomes from two instructional approaches. *Journal of Learning Disabilities, 34*, 33–58.

University of Texas System/Texas Education Agency. (2005). *3-Tier reading model*. Austin, TX: Author.

U.S. Department of Education. (2004). *Individuals with Disabilities Education Improvement Act of 2004 (IDEA)*. Retrieved June 1, 2006, from http://www.house.gov/ed_workforce/issues/109th/education/idea/ideafaq.pdf

Vaughn, S., Linan-Thompson, S., & Hickman, P. (2003). Response to instruction as a means of identifying students with reading/learning disabilities. *Exceptional Children, 69*, 391–409.

Walker, H. M., & Shinn, M. R. (2002). Structuring school-based interventions to achieve integrated primary, secondary, and tertiary prevention goals for safe and effective schools. In M. R. Shinn, G. Stoner, & H. M. Walker (Eds.), *Interventions for academic and behavior problems: Preventive and remedial approaches*. Silver Spring, MD: National Association of School Psychologists.

About the Authors

Rebecca S. Martínez is Assistant Professor of School Psychology at Indiana University in Bloomington. She is a former elementary school teacher and holds adjunct status in the Department of Latino Studies at Indiana University. Her research agenda focuses on the psychosocial functioning of adolescents with mild and severe learning disabilities, with particular interest in their feelings of depression and anxiety as well as their perceptions of social support.

Leah M. Nellis is Director of the Blumberg Center for Interdisciplinary Studies in Special Education at Indiana State University and serves as project director for the Collaborative Problem Solving Project. She has worked as a school psychologist, special education coordinator, and school psychology trainer. Her research interests include assessment, teaming and problem solving, and the elements of professional development that support implementation, sustainability, and positive student outcomes.

7

Social and Emotional Learning

A School-Wide Approach to Intervention for Socialization, Friendship Problems, and More

Kenneth W. Merrell

Barbara A. Gueldner

Oanh K. Tran

The acquisition of social competence and the development and maintenance of peer friendships are two of the key challenges of social-emotional development in childhood. Acquisition of adequate social competence (self-management, assertion, cooperation, independence, and other social skills), and the development of mutually beneficial and satisfying relationships with peers provide a solid foundation for academic, social, and occupational success and are associated with higher levels of social support, family cohesion, and life satisfaction (Asher & Gottman, 1981; Merrell, 2003; Merrell & Gimpel, 1998). Conversely, failure to acquire adequate levels of socialization and social skill and pervasive problems with peer relationships are associated with many negative outcomes, including higher than average rates of mental illness, incarceration, family strife, and unemployment or underemployment (Asher & Coie, 1990; Merrell & Gimpel, 1998; Rudolph & Asher, 2000).

Many children begin their school careers well equipped to negotiate the adjustments and developmental tasks required for effective socialization and development of positive peer relations within the school environment. Unfortunately, a large—and some would say increasing—percentage of youngsters begin their formal schooling with substantial deficits in these areas. Such deficits can create an insidious risk system where the child may not only "fail to thrive" in both an academic and social sense, but become involved in a cycle of peer rejection, social failures, isolation, and school adjustment problems that lead to a continued spiral of difficulties. Other students may enter the school system with socialization and skills deficits that are less severe, but still constitute a risk factor for the children, and a challenge for the educators who serve them and the other children who are part of the social network of the classroom and school.

There is a vast literature on children's social skills development, assessment, and intervention. For the past quarter century, individual and small-group social skills training has been the primary intervention used to address socialization and friendship problems of children in school settings. Several meta-analyses and reviews of the child social skills training literature have consistently indicated that, although social skills training interventions tend to produce some meaningful effects, these effects are typically modest in size, limited to certain types of social or behavioral outcomes, and usually not very long-lasting (e.g., Beelman, Pfingsten, & Losel, 1994; Forness & Kavale, 1996; Gresham, Sugai, & Horner, 2001). Clearly, social skills training interventions targeted at individuals and small groups of students, although important and necessary, are not sufficient to effectively address the vast problems educators face with respect to teaching socialization and peer friendship skills to the many at-risk children and youth they serve.

This chapter provides a review and discussion of an increasingly important alternative intervention for promoting socialization and positive peer relations within school settings: *social and emotional learning*. Within this discussion, social and emotional learning is detailed from a classwide and school-wide framework. First, the need for classwide and school-wide social and emotional learning efforts in schools is discussed, along with the problems and needs that make this approach so appealing, and some examples of how needs and outcomes might be gauged are provided. Second, the compatibility of the three-tiered model of school interventions in schools (described in chapter 1 , this volume) with classwide and school-wide social and emotional learning efforts is reviewed. Finally, the *Strong Kids* social and emotional learning programs, which have been developed by the authors and our colleagues, are reviewed and discussed in terms of their purpose, applicability to socialization and friendship concerns, and natural compatibility with classwide and school-wide intervention approaches.

School-Wide Intervention Needs for Social and Emotional Learning

Educators concur that social and emotional factors greatly influence learning and academic achievement (Collaborative for Academic, Social, and Emotional Learning [CASEL], 2003). Understandably, children with social-behavioral complications may have difficulties learning (Greenberg et al., 2003). Elias (2001) captured the impact of social and emotional competency on academic performance, emphasizing that "unless students are given strategies to regulate their emotions and direct their energies toward learning, it is unlikely that added instructional hours or days will eventuate in corresponding amounts of academic learning" (p. 131). Outcomes for children who fail to learn and incorporate social and emotional skills into their coping repertoires include not making sufficient academic gains and experiencing significant difficulties obtaining and generalizing skills necessary for independent living. In order to ensure better outcomes, educators, families, and communities must consider reforming the approaches used to instruct and foster these skills in a more effective manner (Greenberg et al., 2003).

Social and Emotional Learning

In response to growing concerns regarding the fragmentation of prevention and early intervention efforts in schools to promote academic success and social and emotional health, researchers, educators, and child advocates met in 1994 to develop an organized plan of action (Greenberg et al., 2003). The result was a conceptual framework for social and emotional learning (SEL) that focuses on the social and emotional competence of school-age children and simultaneously supports academic success (Greenberg et al., 2003). Social and emotional learning was subsequently defined as "the process through which children and adults develop the skills necessary to recognize and manage emotions, develop care and concern for others, make responsible decisions, form positive relationships, and successfully handle the demands of growing up in today's complex society" (CASEL, 2002, p. 1).

Social and emotional learning has been associated with students' success in school, including their social-emotional competence and academic success as well as students' attitudes, behavior, and overall school performance (Zins, Bloodworth, Weissberg, & Walberg, 2004). Examples of these outcomes include student motivation to perform, feelings of attachment to school, engagement, attendance, study habits, and daily grades and test scores (Zins et al., 2004). The SEL framework is intended to guide educational programming with the premise that prevention and intervention instruction should not be limited to academics, but should also include instruction in the area of social and emotional learning (Greenberg et al., 2003). Research has demonstrated that SEL skills can be learned in the classroom (Elias, Arnold, & Steiger Hussey, 2003), and many schools have applied this framework to successfully integrate strategies and programs promoting social and emotional learning into students' typical school days (Greenberg et al., 2003).

Gauging the Problem

How do schools identify students who need social and emotional learning supports? A primary objective of American education is to facilitate social development, safe and healthy behavior, and skills that lead to work habits and abilities to meaningfully contribute to society (Greenberg et al., 2003). Ideally, children will thrive within a system that provides a structured safety-net approach composed of early detection and intervention supports *and* inoculation efforts intended to buffer children from inevitable and unavoidable life stressors.

General School Practices That Promote Socialization and Friendship Among Students

Obtaining and maintaining successful social relationships is elemental for youth to have a sense of belongingness and support while juggling multiple academic demands. Elias (1987, as cited in Romasz, Kantor, & Elias, 2004) asserts that providing positive socialization practices, support, and opportunities for youth to be socially connected substantially contributes to their protection when dealing with life's challenges. The acquisition of these skills is facilitated across multiple primary ecologies including home, community, and school. Although schools cannot and should not be expected to take on most of the responsibility for promoting and expediting opportunities to acquire and practice these skills, the school setting is a natural forum for structured learning and support to occur (Ross, Powell, & Elias, 2002).

Schools support students' social development through the use of school-wide practices such as social-emotional learning curricula chosen to address identified areas of concern, organized and coordinated school-wide behavior management strategies such as positive behavior supports (PBS), and general classroom practices. Many packaged curricula are designed to be used school-wide and in individual classrooms to enhance school climate, promote socialization and problem-solving skills, decrease bullying and school violence, and improve anger management skills and manage emotions. Although choosing curricula with strong theoretical and evidence bases is paramount, additional considerations must be taken into account for schools to not only maximize a goodness-of-fit between the curricula and school setting, but adopt practices that promote a positive and healthy school climate.

An increasing body of research supports a "school reform" approach to social and emotional programming (CASEL, 2002). This approach highlights the importance of moving away from fragmented delivery of individual, topic-specific curricula that target identified problem behaviors, and toward a planned, coordinated, systematic approach to school-wide service delivery that will be monitored over time and improved on regularly. The significant problems that students face are quite often inextricably linked and grow in complexity over time and context. The goal for schools should be to develop a school ecology that is supportive of all students and uses a variety of coordinated efforts. Ideally, programs would span a student's school tenure and be integrated into existing school curriculum. Well-trained staff would implement selected commercial curricula, and continual support would be available to all school personnel before, during, and following implementation. The link between academic learning and necessary intra- and interpersonal skills (e.g., classroom participation, motivation, study skills) would be acknowledged, supported, and communicated to parents and community members by supportive school leaders. Regular evaluation of current practices and outcomes as well as time allocation and resources for staff development would ensure that successful practices will continue to support students in their social and emotional development.

Positive behavior support is an empirically supported approach to promoting student socialization from a systems-level perspective (Sugai & Horner, 2002). PBS is "a broad range of systemic and individualized strategies for achieving important social and learning outcomes while preventing problem behaviors in all students" (Sugai et al., 2000, as cited in Sugai & Horner, 2002, p. 130). The school as a dynamic, ecological entity is considered to be the foundation for promoting prosocial behavior through PBS. To accomplish this, school- and classroom-wide discipline and behavior management instructional practices are used to prevent or decrease the number of problem behaviors and reduce the number of entrenched problem behaviors that have the potential to escalate, placing students at high risk of chronic emotional, behavioral, and social difficulty (Sugai & Horner, 2002). Classroom and school expectations are taught as part of a primary prevention effort and, when indicated, additional interventions are implemented (e.g., function-based behavior plans, special education services).

Schools foster socialization and friendships through social-emotional classroom practices facilitated by classroom teachers. Teachers set the tone of their classrooms through their verbal and nonverbal communications with their students (Knoll & Patti, 2003). Teachers communicate interest in and caring for each individual student, a sense of mutual respect and acceptance is exhibited, and inappropriate verbal and nonverbal behaviors are not accepted (Knoll & Patt). Expectations are high and problem-solving strategies are used regularly, with students' voices being heard and respected along with the teacher's.

Students have positive peer relationships when *all* students have supportive friendships and can engage in mutually satisfying conflict resolution strategies (Doll, Zucker, & Brehm, 2004). Classroom activities can be strategically organized to support this process. When classroom teachers use structured activities having specific intervention goals or even general classroom climate objectives, it is important that the activities be applied in the natural context of the classroom to provide concrete, relevant learning examples and promote generalization of skills. Teachers can provide frequent opportunities for students to have fun together while working and playing, either in prearranged groups that are routinely rearranged or in groups found spontaneously as appropriate opportunities arise (Doll et al., 2004). Tasks should match students' sociodevelopmental level (Pianta, 1999, as cited in Doll et al., 2004), students with complementary skill sets should be grouped together, and explicit instruction should be provided within groups when necessary (Doll et al., 2004). Overall, a theme of cooperative learning serves well to promote positive socialization skills in children as well as a positive classroom climate.

Challenges in Impacting the General School Environment and Culture

Although schools are excellent venues for promoting social and emotional learning, several challenges make many SEL efforts ineffective, unsustainable, and less socially valid. For SEL efforts to be both effective and sustainable, it is critical to consider the school environment and culture and how these impact SEL efforts. Environment and culture in school systems encompass social relationships among administrators, staff, teachers, and students; the expectations within each school; the resources available to students and staff; cultural, gender, religious, and linguistic diversity; the system goals; and how goals are accomplished. Schools are confronted with these challenges, while needing to provide efficacious services. These factors are important to be aware of when promoting intervention and prevention efforts, to achieve the greatest possibilities of SEL success.

Although the challenges in implementing social and emotional learning programs vary, most schools face primary barriers because they are systems of organizations and organisms that are required to work together. Some common challenges that schools may encounter when using SEL are fragmented and uncoordinated efforts, limited training for staff who implement SEL programming, uncoordinated staff efforts to initiate and direct SEL, the need to recruit staff and personnel to be involved, leadership responsibilities, and failure to document the implementation process to ensure its fidelity (Zins, 2001). These issues are critical and can impact the school environment and culture when SEL programming is implemented or promoted. Crone, Horner, and Hawken (2004) have suggested that significant behavioral programming efforts may take three to five years to make a positive impact and changes in schools. The reality and complexity of barriers to implementing new programs or best practices in schools should not be underestimated. An intervention that has been proven effective within a highly controlled research study may have little appeal to teachers or administrators if it lacks a high degree of social validity, usability, and appeal, despite its evidence-based pedigree. The research-to-practice gap and the absence of social validity or ease of usability in some research-based practices provides an argument for considering other factors besides efficacy when selecting an intervention program (Merrell & Buchanan, 2006). Barriers to implementation absolutely must be addressed if SEL programming is to be effective, sustainable, and successful in schools.

For SEL prevention and promotion efforts to be successful, school personnel should have support and training to integrate SEL with academics, account for changing demographics, document implementation efforts, and embrace a strength-based and needs-based approach in the school setting. In addition, the effectiveness of such efforts will be strengthened if there is good communication among school personnel, a coordinator who oversees the implementation process, ongoing formal and informal training, high visibility in schools, and varied and engaging instructional approaches (Elias, Zins, Graczyk, & Weissberg, 2003; Zins, Weissberg, & O'Brien, 2003). These efforts should be conspicuous, conscious, and purposeful. Such a direct process will require energy from all individuals in the school environment to make changes and increase intervention and prevention success.

Another barrier that impacts school culture and climate is diversity within schools. Valuing diversity means accepting and respecting cultural or linguistic differences as well as differences of gender, religion, socioeconomic status, age, and values. Students, teachers, staff, and administrators come from different backgrounds, and their customs, thoughts, ways of communicating, values, traditions, and institutions vary accordingly (Ortiz & Flanagan, 2002). Each individual is further exposed to many cultures and subcultures, through school, television, books, and community opportunities. Cultural experiences influence behaviors, interactions with others, and choices that each individual makes (e.g., activities, subjects of study, beliefs). Moreover, diversity between cultures should be recognized and the diversity within them should be respected. For example, in regard to ethnic diversity, a larger ethnic group may share common geographic and historical experiences; however, individual students may share little beyond similar physical characteristics, language, or spiritual beliefs. Such differences impact ways of thinking, interacting, and accepting. The differences between groups and within groups have a significant impact on overall school outcomes. By valuing what is "different" rather than seeing what is "wrong" in school-based interactions, individuals within schools can foster acceptance of, and respect for, diversity, making service delivery more effective (Ortiz & Flanagan, 2002; Rogers, et al., 1999).

Ortiz and Flanagan (2002) suggested that cultural competency in schools should include communication skills and cultural knowledge, particularly for education professionals (e.g., school psychologists). Such professionals should be aware of their own values and the values of other cultures; it is particularly important to understand the school culture and be aware of how that system operates on and defines particular values of the individual. Professionals should be aware of the learning context and fully understand how the context affects learning and development of each student. It is important to also consider and be aware of the family culture. School professionals do not work only with individual students, but also with family members; thus it is important to be aware of the family system, the dynamics within a particular family, and its cultural values. Awareness of appropriate ways of communicating with individuals and their families can decrease the incidence of miscommunication. Self-awareness of personal values and biases and how these affect interactions within school systems is critical to effecting the expected changes in SEL intervention and promotion efforts.

The barriers that exist in school environments and culture vary among school systems. Although there are differences, there are also some common challenges. Schools should be aware of such barriers and proactively make changes that create environments for success for all individuals. SEL intervention and promotion efforts are effective only when barriers are addressed and outcomes are desirable.

The Three-Tiered Approach to Prevention and Intervention

As is described in chapter 1, *universal* interventions target an entire group (school-wide/classroom-wide) that has not been identified as at risk. This level of intervention supports an environment that encourages prosocial behaviors, predictability, a positive school-classroom climate, and protective factors to prevent minor problems and difficulties from increasing in severity and students from becoming at risk for social and emotional problems. The intervention goals at this level are directed at *all* students in a specific setting and with the same degree of intensity.

More specifically, in the area of social and emotional learning, *Second Step* may be applied as a universal support for preschool through Grade 9. *Second Step* is a violence prevention program developed and published by the Committee for Children (1992). The program includes a research-based, teacher-friendly curriculum, training for educators, and parent-education components. The social and emotional skills taught to all students include (a) empathy, (b) impulse control, (c) problem solving, and (d) anger management/conflict resolution. The lessons are taught in each grade level, taking into account the maturity and cognitive level of children at each grade. The lessons are approximately 30 minutes long and can be taught by the classroom teacher once or twice per week. For Pre–K through Grade 5, skills are taught using lesson photo cards, classroom videos, classroom posters, and puppets and song CDs for the younger ages. Each lesson card includes the lesson objectives, a script, discussion questions, role-plays or other activities, and suggestions for how teachers can model the skills taught in the lesson throughout the week. Research on *Second Step* indicates that students who participated in the program showed an increase in prosocial behaviors, decrease in aggressive behaviors, and appropriate perspective-taking and problem-solving skills over control groups (see Walker & Shinn, 2002). Another universal SEL program to consider is *Strong Kids*, which is discussed in detail later in this chapter. *Strong Kids* is an evidence-based program that has been shown to help students build resiliency skills.

Selected interventions target students with increased risk factors, whose probability of developing social or emotional problems is significantly higher than the average. A selected intervention in social and emotional learning is *First Step to Success*, an intervention designed to provide at-risk young children (K–2) with early school success by assisting them with the school-to-home transition and addressing behavior issues (e.g., antisocial behavior patterns) in the classroom (Walker, Stiller, Severson, Feil, & Golly, 1998). The primary goal of *First Step* is to redirect children at risk from a path that often leads to school failure, antisocial behaviors, delinquency, and other destructive outcomes. *First Step* is a two-month school- and home-based intervention. Services are coordinated by a Coach, who plays a behavioral game in the classroom with the child and classroom peers and works with parents to provide supportive collaboration for early school success. The intervention uses positive reinforcement, behavior cues, practice of appropriate behaviors, group classroom rewards, and communication with parents. The school-based component lasts about two months and the home-based piece includes six one-hour meetings with the Coach and parent(s). "Home-base" enlists parents in teaching their children cooperation, listening, friendship building, accepting limits, problem solving, and sharing as they develop their self-esteem and confidence. *First Step* is considered an exemplary program that produces significant behavior changes as measured through teacher ratings and behavioral observations in playground and classroom settings (see Walker & Shinn, 2002). In addition, longitudinal studies indicate that behavioral gains are maintained into upper elementary grades. The *Strong Kids* curricula, discussed later, is also a useful second-tier intervention.

Indicated interventions are appropriate for students who exhibit clear symptoms related to social, emotional, or behavior problems and require more immediate and intensive interventions (Sugai & Horner, 2002). An example is *Multisystemic Therapy* (MST) for social and emotional problems. MST is an intensive family-based treatment that addresses the known determinants of serious antisocial behavior in adolescents and their families (Schoenwald, Brown, & Henggeler, 2000). MST applies an ecological, wraparound approach to treat those factors in the student's environment that are contributing to his or her behavior or social and emotional problems. Such factors might pertain to individual characteristics of the student (e.g., poor problem-solving skills), family relations (e.g., inept discipline), peer relations (e.g., association with deviant peers), and school performance (e.g., academic difficulties). On a highly individualized basis, treatment goals are developed in collaboration with the family, and family strengths are used as levers for therapeutic change. Specific interventions used in MST are based on the best empirically validated treatment approaches, such as cognitive behavior therapy and the pragmatic family therapies (Kazdin, 1998; Walker & Shinn, 2002). The primary goals of MST are to reduce rates of antisocial behavior in the adolescent, reduce out-of-home placements, and empower families to resolve future difficulties. MST requires substantial personnel time, investment, and effort from all involved (Walker & Shinn).

Social and emotional problems in schools warrant the need for a three-tiered approach to intervention and prevention that targets various needs in students' mental health. For schools to be most effective, using established and promising strategies at different levels of the triangle will allow *all* students, from those not at risk to those at greatest risk for mental health problems, the opportunities to live healthy, productive, successful lives as students and as adults. Specifically, intervention and prevention efforts should focus on multiyear programs for maximum effect rather than short-term programs and risk and resiliency factors rather than categorical factors (Greenberg, Domitrovich, & Bumbarger, 2001). Schools are great venues for using prevention and intervention strategies through the three-tiered model of teaching, educating, and promoting resiliency skills to prevent or decrease social and emotional problems. Evidence-based programs that have strong utility and effectiveness are available for schools to implement; however, prevention and universal supports through classwide and school-wide approaches are optimal to targeting more students and preventing problems from occurring or intensifying. It is critical that schools consider the three-tiered approach so that student supports are provided effectively and efficiently for successful student outcomes, while supportive environments are created for socialization, friendships, and more.

The *Strong Kids* Programs: An Example for Classwide and School-Wide Intervention

As an example of a practical and promising curriculum tool to promote social and emotional learning in schools, this section provides an overview of the *Strong Kids* programs, which have been developed and field tested by the authors and our colleagues (Merrell, Carrizales, Feuerborn, Gueldner, & Tran, 2007a, 2007b, 2007c; Merrell, Parisi, & Whitcomb, 2007). These companion programs are semi-scripted curriculum tools that educators and mental health professionals can use to focus on the prevention of or early intervention for internalizing problems, promotion of social and emotional competence, and teaching students skills to increase their resilience to life stressors. Essentially, the *Strong Kids* programs are SEL interventions aimed at promoting *strengths, assets,* and *personal resources,* including socialization and friendship. The *Strong Kids* programs were developed primarily for use in classwide and school-wide situations as a universal intervention program, and for use in targeted classrooms and pullout groups as a selected intervention. Our experience with these programs has demonstrated that they can also be used as part of an indicated intervention for high-risk students, provided they are only one component of comprehensive intervention plan.

The programs within *Strong Kids* are comprehensive in scope, designed for use with kindergarten through Grade 12 students who are typically developing, are at risk, or are at high risk for developing significant social-emotional problems. Although the differing curriculum components share similar aims and core focus, these programs were developed to be developmentally appropriate for four specific age clusters:

- *Strong Start—Grades K–2* is for kindergarten and primary grade students
- *Strong Kids—Grades 3–5* is for use with intermediate grade students
- *Strong Kids—Grades 6–8* is for use with middle school students
- *Strong Teens—Grades 9–12* is for use with high school students

These curricula are practical and easy to use. They are all relatively brief (10 lessons of 35 to 45 minutes each for *Strong Start*, and 12 lessons of 45 to 50 minutes each for *Strong Kids* and *Strong Teens*). Each lesson manual includes an optional booster lesson for use two to three months following completion of the initial program. The programs are adaptable across a range of students and settings, and designed to be taught in small groups or with entire classrooms by educators or support service professionals. Minimal training is needed to teach these curricula, and the manuals for each program include self-contained instructions for becoming proficient in delivering the curricula.

Strong Start shares the same general aims as *Strong Kids* and *Strong Teens*, but is specifically focused on the unique developmental needs of kindergarten and primary grade students. As such, the lessons are fewer in number and shorter in length, and rely much less on students' reading ability and ability to process abstract cognitive concepts or to apply meta-cognitive strategies. Instead, *Strong Start* promotes social and emotional learning in young children by focusing on familiar routines, activities, and objects. Suggested books from popular children's literature are used to support the main concepts of each lesson. The major lesson concepts and aims are simplified substantially from the *Strong Kids* and *Strong Teens* components. Although the *Strong Start* lessons include optional worksheets and activities that may be used to help support literacy instruction through basic reading and writing tasks, such tasks are modifiable for preliterate children or children who struggle with basic literacy. Each lesson includes direct instruction, examples and non-examples of the new social-emotional concepts, opportunities for modeling and role playing, and reinforcement of the main concepts through the continued use of a "mascot" (a stuffed animal such as a bear) coupled with stories describing how the mascot deals with key social-emotional learning tasks. *Strong Start* is much less cognitively oriented in the lesson presentations than the *Strong Kids/Teens* components, and instead follows a more psychoeducational, affective, and behavioral pattern. The 10 lessons in *Strong Start* are

1. *The Feelings Exercise Group* (introduction of curricula and mascot, confidentiality)

2. *Understanding Your Feelings, Part 1* (basic emotional vocabulary, identification of "good" and "not good" feelings," generalization of feelings across situations)

3. *Understanding Your Feelings, Part 2* ("okay" and "not okay" ways of expressing feelings, review and mastery of six basic emotions)

4. *When You're Angry* (identification and appropriate expression of anger, basic anger management techniques)

5. *When You're Happy* (learned optimism training, ABCs of positive thinking)

6. *Understanding Other People's Feelings* (basic empathy training, focus on physical cues and situational interpretation, emphasis on individual differences)

7. *Being a Good Friend* (basic social skills training, friendship skills)

8. *Solving People Problems* (essentials of interpersonal conflict resolution and problem solving)

9. *When You're Worried* (identifying and managing anxiety, fear, worry)

10. *Finishing UP!* (review of major concepts, reteaching where necessary, closure activities)

The lesson titles and content focus of *Strong Kids* and *Strong Teens* are generally similar, but the examples, language, and difficulty level have been shaped particularly for the targeted age range of the students. The lessons in these programs combine cognitive-behavioral and affective education techniques, with each lesson containing opportunities for review of prior concepts, instruction and practice of new skills, corrective feedback, generalization activities, and student handouts/worksheets. Although the lessons are scripted, they are easily adaptable for specific circumstances, and the manuals include suggestions for adapting the curricula for specific social, cultural, geographic, or other circumstances. The 12 basic lessons in these three curricular components are

1. *About Strong Kids/Teens* (pretesting, curriculum overview, rules, ice-breaker activities)

2. *Understanding Your Emotions, Part 1* (increasing emotional vocabulary, defining emotions)

3. *Understanding Your Emotions, Part 2* (appropriate expression of emotions)

4. *Dealing With Anger* (understanding anger, cognitive-behavioral anger management training)

5. *Understanding Other People's Feelings* (empathy training, taking perspective of others)

6. *Clear Thinking, Part 1* (identifying thinking errors and maladaptive beliefs)

7. *Clear Thinking, Part 2* (actively changing maladaptive beliefs and thinking errors)

8. *The Power of Positive Thinking* (learned optimism training)

9. *Solving People Problems* (interpersonal conflict resolution skills and practice)

10. *Letting Go of Stress* (practice in cognitive and behavioral methods of relaxation)

11. *Achieving Your Goals* (goal-setting, behavior education, behavior-affect connection)

12. *Finishing UP!* (cumulative review of major concepts, planning for future, posttesting)

The various *Strong Kids* programs include, but are not limited to, intervention activities specifically designed to positively impact children's socialization and friendship problems. In the *Strong Start* component, the *Understanding Other People's Feelings*, *Being a Good Friend*, and *Solving People Problems* modules are directly relevant to socialization and friendship concerns. Within the *Strong Kids/Teens* components, the *Understanding Other People's Feelings* and *Solving People Problems* modules are aimed directly at these issues. In addition, the other modules within each component are designed to have a corollary impact on socialization and friendship. For example, the emotional education lessons are aimed to help children learn to express their own emotions in ways that are more likely to be socially appropriate, and the *Clear Thinking* lessons in *Strong Kids/Teens* teach students how to identify distortions and errors in their perceptions and thought processes, which has an obvious connection to peer relationships.

Development, refinement, and pilot testing efforts for the various *Strong Kids* programs have been ongoing since 2001. To date, several studies have been completed that have demonstrated significant gains in student's knowledge of healthy social-emotional functioning, as well as significant reductions in negative social-emotional symptoms following participation in the program (Feuerborn, 2004; Gueldner, 2006; Isava, 2006; Merrell, Juskelis, Tran, & Buchanan, 2006). Some of these studies have investigated treatment fidelity and social validity of the curricula, and have identified very positive findings in both areas. In addition, one study to date (Castro-Olivo, 2006) has shown that the curricula can be adapted with cultural and linguistic enhancements to promote similar effects in Latino immigrant youths. These studies have been conducted at all three levels of the triangle of services (universal, selected, indicated), with positive results across levels, albeit with limited samples. Additional studies are currently underway to investigate specific aspects of intervention implementation, including optimum tempo or pacing of instruction (12 lessons delivered once a week for 12 weeks versus twice a week for 6 weeks), efficacy of *Strong Start* with young children, and impact of the curricula on students who are at the second tier (targeted) level of risk. At this time, we consider the *Strong Kids* social-emotional learning programs to be promising and to have the beginnings of an empirical body of supporting evidence. We are working on continuing our field testing efforts with the goal of collecting enough supporting evidence for *Strong Kids* to be considered an evidence-based intervention.

Summary and Concluding Comments

Children, families, and schools in 21st-century America face many challenges. Socialization and friendship problems of children reflect difficulty with or failure of a primary developmental task, and place children with these deficits at great risk for many negative outcomes. As we have shown, the intense focus on individual and small group social skills training that has been the primary method of treating such concerns has several limitations. One limitation is the intensive time requirements and disruption to the educational process in classrooms needed to conduct "pullout" programs. Another concern is that the research on social skills training effectiveness has demonstrated that this method tends to produce modest gains that are time-limited.

As an alternative approach, we propose that comprehensive systems of social and emotional learning within school systems offer a promising way to deal with socialization and friendship problems. SEL methods are more inclusive, systemic, and broader than any skill training approach, yet still allow educators and mental health professionals to promote specific life skills. Another advantage of SEL approaches is that they tend to be better integrated with academics, and often focus on a variety of related important skills (i.e., specific social skills, empathy training, emotional education) that are more likely to provide students with a broader skill set. Although there are some very real barriers to effectively implementing SEL programs, making SEL an important part of the fabric of American schools is a highly worthwhile endeavor. Recognizing the importance of SEL, Illinois has become the first U.S. state to mandate the use of SEL in all schools and to provide initiatives supporting such efforts. SEL programs are highly compatible with the three-tiered public health or prevention science models that educators are increasingly considered as a way to plan for *all* students. Whether at the universal, selected, or indicated levels of the "triangle of support," the SEL approach has something to offer *all* students. The *Strong Kids* programs, consisting of four developmentally specific curriculum components aimed at the K–12 population, constitute one of the most recent examples of using the integrated SEL approach to teach students important life skills, including socialization and friendship skills. These programs currently have a growing empirical base of support, are brief and easy to use, and are sufficiently flexible to allow for use across levels of student need. We advocate these programs as one way to address students' social-emotional needs within an SEL framework. The next decade will be a critical time in determining whether SEL approaches can begin to fulfill the promise they appear to hold, and how to best implement these approaches across the amazing diversity of needs and assets within America's schools and students.

Discussion Questions

1. What practices does your school already employ to promote social competence and problem solving among all students?

2. Imagine that you are making a presentation at a school faculty meeting on social-emotional learning. What information would be essential to enlist the support of teachers in your building?

3. Social-emotional learning places teachers and other school staff in the role of promoting children's social and emotional competence. What skills do they possess that make them ideal people to assume this responsibility?

4. What resources, skills, and knowledge would you need in order to implement one of the *Strong Kids* programs in your school? How would you secure them?

5. If your school were to implement one of the *Strong Kids* programs immediately and continue the program with fidelity and commitment for at least five years, what difference might be evident in your school five years later?

References

Asher, S. R., & Coie, J. D. (Eds.). (1990). *Peer rejection in childhood.* Cambridge, UK: Cambridge University Press.

Asher, S. R., & Gottman, J. M. (1981). *Children's friendship skills.* Cambridge, UK: Cambridge University Press.

Beelman, A., Pfingsten, U., & Losel, F. (1994). Effects of training social competence in children: A meta-analysis of recent evaluation studies. *Journal of Consulting and Clinical Psychology, 23,* 260–272.

Castro-Olivo, S. M. (2006). *The effects of a culturally-adapted social-emotional learning curriculum on social-emotional and academic outcomes of Latino immigrant high school students.* Unpublished doctoral dissertation, University of Oregon, Eugene.

Collaborative for Academic, Social, and Emotional Learning (CASEL). (2002). *Guidelines for social and emotional learning: High quality programs for school and life success.* Retrieved August 1, 2005, from http://www.casel.org/downloads/GuidelinesAug02.pdf

Collaborative for Academic, Social, and Emotional Learning (CASEL). (2003). *Safe and sound: An educational leader's guide to evidence-based social and emotional learning programs.* Retrieved August 1, 2005, from http://www.casel.org/projects_products/safeandsound.php

Committee for Children. (1992). *Second Step: A violence prevention curriculum.* Seattle, WA: Author.

Crone, D. A., Horner, R. H., & Hawken, L. A. (2004). *Responding to problem behavior in schools: The behavior education program.* New York: Guilford Press.

Doll, B., Zucker, S., & Brehm, K. (2004). *Resilient classrooms: Creating healthy environments for learning.* New York: Guilford Press.

Elias, M. J. (2001). Strategies to infuse social and emotional learning into academics. In J. E. Zins, R. P. Weissberg, M. C. Wang, & H. J. Walberg (Eds.), *Building academic success on social and emotional learning* (pp. 131–134). New York: Teachers College Press.

Elias, M. J., Arnold, H., Steiger Hussey, C. (2003). *EQ + IQ = Best leadership practices for caring and successful schools.* Thousand Oaks, CA: Corwin Press.

Elias, M. J., Zins, J. E., Graczyk, P. A., & Weissberg, R. P. (2003). Implementation, sustainability, and scaling up of social-emotional and academic innovations in public schools. *School Psychology Review, 32,* 303–319.

Feuerborn, L. L. (2004). *Promoting emotional resiliency through instruction: The effects of a classroom-based prevention program.* Unpublished doctoral dissertation, University of Oregon, Eugene.

Forness, S. R., & Kavale, K. A. (1996). Treating social skills deficits in children with learning disabilities: A meta-analysis of the research. *Learning Disabilities Quarterly, 19,* 2–13.

Greenberg, M. T., Domitrovich, C., & Bumbarger, B. (2001, March). The prevention of mental disorders in school-aged children: Current state of the field. *Prevention and Treatment, 4,* n.p.

Greenberg, M. T., Weissberg, R. P., O'Brien, M. U., Zins, J. E., Fredericks, L., Resnik, H., et al. (2003). Enhancing school-based prevention and youth development through coordinated social, emotional, and academic learning. *American Psychologist, 58,* 466–474.

Gresham, F. M., Sugai, G., & Horner, R. H. (2001). Interpreting outcomes of social skills training for students with high incidence disabilities. *Exceptional Children, 67,* 331–344.

Gueldner, B. A. (2006). *An investigation of the impact of a social-emotional learning curriculum with and without teacher consultation support on social and emotional characteristics of middle school students.* Unpublished doctoral dissertation, University of Oregon, Eugene.

Isava, D. M. (2006). *An investigation on the impact of a social emotional learning curriculum on problem symptoms and knowledge gains among adolescents in a residential treatment center.* Unpublished doctoral dissertation, University of Oregon, Eugene.

Kazdin, A. E. (1998). Conduct disorder. In R. J. Morris & T. R. Kratochwill (Eds.), *The practice of child therapy* (pp. 199–230). Needham Heights, MA: Allyn & Bacon.

Knoll, M., & Patti, J. (2003). Social-emotional learning and academic achievement. In M. J. Elias, H. Arnold, & C. Steiger Hussey, (Eds.), *EQ + IQ = Best leadership practices for caring and successful schools.* Thousand Oaks, CA: Corwin Press.

Merrell, K. W. (2003). *Behavioral, social, and emotional assessment of children and adolescents* (2nd ed.). Mahwah, NJ: Erlbaum.

Merrell, K. W., & Buchanan, R. (2006). Intervention selection in school-based practice: Using public health models to enhance systems capacity of schools. *School Psychology Review, 35,* 167–180.

Merrell, K. W., Carrizales, D., Feuerborn, L., Gueldner, B., & Tran, O. (2007a). *Strong Kids—Grades 3–5: A social and emotional learning curriculum for use with elementary-age students.* Baltimore: Paul H. Brookes Publishing.

Merrell, K. W., Carrizales, D., Feuerborn, L., Gueldner, B., & Tran, O. (2007b). *Strong Kids—Grades 6–8: A social and emotional learning curriculum for use with middle school students.* Baltimore: Paul H. Brookes Publishing.

Merrell, K. W., Carrizales, D., Feuerborn, L., Gueldner, B., & Tran, O. (2007c). *Strong Teens: A social and emotional learning curriculum for use with high school students.* Baltimore: Paul H. Brookes Publishing.

Merrell, K. W., & Gimpel, G.A. (1998). *Social skills of children and adolescents: conceptualization, assessment, treatment.* Mahwah, NJ: Erlbaum.

Merrell, K. W., Juskelis, M. P., & Tran, O. K., & Buchanan, R. (in press). Social and emotional learning in the classroom: Impact of Strong Kids and Strong Teens on students' social-emotional knowledge and symptoms. Journal of Applied School Psychology.

Merrell, K. W., Parisi, D., & Whitcomb, S. (2007). *Strong Start: A social-emotional learning curriculum for kindergarten and primary grade students.* Baltimore: Paul H. Brookes Publishing.

Ortiz, S. O., & Flanagan, D. P. (2002). Best practices in working with culturally diverse children and families. In A. Thomas & J. Grimes (Eds.), *Best practices in school psychology* (pp. 337–351). Bethesda, MD: National Association of School Psychologists.

Rogers, M. R., Ingraham, C. L., Bursztyn, A., Cajigas-Segredo, N., Esquivel, G., Hess, R., et al. (1999). Providing psychological services to racially, ethnically, culturally, and linguistically diverse individuals in the schools. *School Psychology International, 20,* 243–264.

Romasz, T. E., Kantor, J. H., & Elias, M. J. (2004). Implementation and evaluation of urban school-wide social-emotional learning programs. *Evaluation and Program Planning, 27,* 89–103.

Ross, M. R., Powell, S. R., & Elias, M. J. (2002). New roles for school psychologists: Addressing the social and emotional learning needs of students. *School Psychology Review, 31,* 43–52.

Rudolph, K. D., & Asher, S. R. (2000). Adaptation and maladaptation in the peer system: Developmental processes and outcomes. In A. J. Sameroff, M. Lewis, & S. M. Miller (Eds.), *Handbook of developmental psychopathology* (pp. 157–175). New York: Kluwer Academic/Plenum Publishers.

Schoenwald, S. K., Brown, T. L., & Henggeler, S. W. (2000). Inside multisystemic therapy: Therapists, supervisory, and program practices. *Journal of Emotional and Behavioral Disorders, 8,* 113–127.

Sugai, G., & Horner, R. H. (2002). Introduction to the special series on positive behavior support in schools. *Journal of Emotional and Behavioral Disorders, 10,* 130–135.

Walker, H. M., & Shinn, M. R. (2002). Structuring school-based interventions to achieve integrated primary, secondary, and tertiary prevention goals for safe and effective schools. In M. R. Shinn, G. Stoner, & H. M. Walker (Eds.), *Interventions for academic and behavior problems: Preventive and remedial approaches* (pp. 1–26). Silver Spring, MD: National Association of School Psychologists.

Walker, H. M., Stiller, B., Severson, H. H., Feil, E. G., & Golly, A. (1998). First step to success: An effective preventive intervention for anti-social behavior in primary grades. *Psychology in the Schools, 35,* 259–269.

Zins, J. E. (2001). Examining opportunities and challenges of school-based prevention and promotion: Social and emotional learning as an exemplar. *Journal of Primary Prevention, 21,* 441–446.

Zins, J. E., Bloodworth, M. R., Weissberg, R. P., & Walberg, H. J. (2004). The scientific base linking social and emotional learning to school success. In J. E. Zins, R. P. Weissberg, M. C. Wang, & H. J. Walberg (Eds.), *Building academic success on social and emotional learning: What does the research say?* New York: Teachers College.

Zins, J. E., Weissberg, R. P., & O'Brien, M. U. (2003, October). *Links Between Safe School Environments and Academic Achievement.* PowerPoint presentation given at the Annual Office of Safe and Drug Free Schools Technical Assistance Meeting. Retrieved April 12, 2006, from http://www.doe .state.in.us/isssa/pdf/newpubsSEL%20Programs.pdf

About the Authors

Kenneth W. Merrell is Professor of School Psychology at the University of Oregon. He has served as director and codirector of the program, as well as head of the Department of Special Education and Clinical Sciences. He coordinates the Oregon Resiliency Project research team. His research interests are focused on social-emotional assessment and intervention for at-risk children and adolescents, and social-emotional learning and mental health promotion in schools.

Barbara A. Gueldner is a visiting Assistant Professor of School Psychology at the University of Oregon, where she received her PhD in School Psychology in 2007. She is completing a clinical internship at The Children's Hospital in Denver, Colorado, and has 10 years' experience as a school psychologist. Her primary interests are in the areas of universal prevention and early intervention of children's mental health concerns, social and emotional learning in the schools, and consultation.

Oanh K. Tran is an Assistant Professor of School Psychology at California State University, East Bay. She received her PhD in School Psychology from the University of Oregon in 2007. She completed her predoctoral internship at a community mental health agency working with children and youths with emotional and behavioral disorders. Her research interests include promoting social and emotional learning through teaching resiliency skills for the prevention and early intervention of mental health problems, behavioral consultation and assessment, and parent-child interactions.

8

School-Wide Approaches to Intervention for School Aggression and Bullying

Susan M. Swearer

Dorothy L. Espelage

Kelly Brey Love

Whitney Kingsbury

B ullying and school aggression are negative social interactions that have plagued students for centuries. However, not until recent violent events such as the high-profile school shootings and other acts of school violence, did these phenomena receive much attention from researchers in the United States. A recent study indicated that an estimated 29.9% of students were involved in bullying as a bully, victim, or a bully-victim (Nansel et al., 2001). Additional studies have found that between 8.4% (Nansel et al., 2001) and 20% (Limber & Small, 2000) of children reported being victimized several times per week. Prevalence rates for those who observe bullying interactions, or witnesses, have been found to be much higher. Salmivalli, Lagerspetz, Bjorkqvist, Osterman, and Kaukiainen (1996) report that 87% of students fulfill the role of "participant" or witness to bullying interactions (Salmivalli, Lagerspetz, Bjorkqvist, Osterman, & Kaukiainen, 1996). Thus, most students will either experience or witness bullying interactions during their school career.

Linkages Between Bullying and School Aggression

Just as constructs of "violence" and "aggression" are often used without distinction, this also occurs with use of the terms "bullying" and "aggression." Many researchers view bullying as a specific form of aggression (Espelage, Bosworth, & Simon, 2000; Pellegrini, 2002; Pellegrini & Long, 2002; Smith et al., 1999, 2002). Dodge and Coie (1987) further identify bullying as a form of proactive aggression, where the bully is unprovoked and perpetrates the bullying behaviors. This intertwined relationship between bullying and aggression is also present in the first component of Olweus's (Olweus & Limber, 1999) definition of bullying, in that bullying is first and foremost characterized as "aggressive behavior." To differentiate bullying from other aggressive acts, the interaction must also possess the components of imbalance of power between the perpetrator and the target, and occurrence over a long period of time (Olweus & Limber, 1999). While they are indeed two distinct constructs, Morrison and Furlong (1994) illustrate the potential interchangeability and similarity of the terms "aggression" and "bullying." For instance, bullying may include one person making physical threats to another person without actually being physically aggressive. Nevertheless, these threats may create psychological distress to the victim. Thus, the imbalance of power, the use of either overt or covert aggression, and the repetitive nature of bullying differentiate bullying behaviors from other aggressive behaviors.

Best Practices in Assessing School Bullying

Best practices in assessing school bullying dictate that multiple methods and multiple informants should be used (Espelage & Swearer, 2003). However, many school districts do not have adequate funding for this approach. Thus, schools should, at minimum, use school-wide surveys and self-report scales to assess the scope and frequency of bullying behaviors. Additionally, assessments of bullying are best conducted in the spring after peer groups have formed, and should be conducted annually in order to examine trends and changes in bullying behaviors. When school administration, school staff, students, and parents embrace thoughtful, ongoing assessment of bullying, a prevention-oriented model and a population-based perspective on bullying can guide the selection of universal, selected, and indicated interventions (Baker, Kamphaus, Horne, & Winsor, 2006).

Social-Ecological Models of School Bullying

A population-based perspective on aggression and bullying is supported by an ecological framework of bullying and aggressive interactions, including ecological theory (Bronfenbrenner, 1977, 1979), ecological transactional theory (Cicchetti & Toth, 1997; Lynch & Cicchetti, 1998, 2002), and social-ecological theory (Cairns & Cairns, 1994; Newman, Horne & Bartolomucci, 2000; Swearer & Doll, 2001; Swearer & Espelage, 2004). The underlying principle of ecological theory is that the different levels of a child's environment continually interact and subsequently influence one another (Lynch & Cicchetti, 1998, 2002; Swearer & Espelage, 2004). Social-ecological theory has been referred to as an integration of ecological perspectives, social interactions, and individual differences (Cairns & Cairns, 1994). Endorsing a model of bullying behaviors that does not account for the many different systemic influences incorrectly focuses on the individual, instead of accounting for the complex interactions between multiple systems.

The components that comprise an individual's ecology, as originally proposed by Bronfenbrenner (1979), are the macrosystem, exosystem, mesosystem, and microsystem. The macrosystem consists of the cultural values and beliefs that influence familial and societal functioning (Bronfenbrenner, 1977). At the macrosystem level, the prevailing societal view may be that bullying is an expected and unavoidable component of a child's educational experience. The exosystem consists of the social structures (e.g., neighborhood, employment opportunities, availability of services) in which families and children reside (Lynch & Cicchetti, 1998). At the exosystem level, the anti-bullying policies enforced by a school district could affect the environment of a school (Swearer & Espelage, 2004).

Within social-ecological theory, the mesosystem is considered at the individual level and depicts the congruence between multiple environments (Swearer & Espelage, 2004). For example, if youth reside in a community where they are continually exposed to or are victims of community aggression, then observing bullying and aggressive interactions or even being victimized at school may have little impact on their psychological functioning. In this scenario, the student has likely developed effective coping mechanisms, or has become desensitized to observing or being victimized by aggressive acts. Another example of environmental impact on bullying or victimization is the amount or level of familial support. If a student is victimized frequently at school, but has a positive, supportive family, impairment may be reduced relative to another student without this level of familial support.

The microsystem is any setting in which the individual spends a substantial amount of time (i.e., home, work, or school: Bronfenbrenner, 1977; Lynch & Cicchetti, 1998), and reflects the child's relationship within one system (Swearer & Espelage, 2004). Those students who are involved along the bully/victim continuum (i.e., bully, bully-victim, victim, or bystander) "interact(s) with others in his or her social environment, and this interaction either exacerbates or mitigates bullying and/or victimization behaviors" (Swearer & Espelage, 2004, p. 4). Bullying at the microsystem level can be illustrated by the reactions of students who witness another student being bullied. Several other students witness a bullying incident, and become visibly upset, crying and yelling for the bully to stop. The bully does not stop. As a result, the anxiety of the bystanders is elevated, along with their feelings of powerlessness. In this situation, the bystanders' participation in aggression may increase if they view the bully's use of aggression as successful. Conversely, the bystanders' level of aggression may also increase as a result of their feelings of powerlessness or helplessness to intervene in the situation. In the microsystem, peer groups also play an instrumental role in modeling bullying behavior and socializing their members over time, especially during early adolescence (Espelage, Holt, & Henkel, 2003).

Another influence on bullying at the microsystem level is the climate of the school. If the school climate is one that does not support bullying or aggression, effective interventions are in place, and there are many people to offer support (i.e., counselors, teachers), students may be less impaired by being victimized than others at a school with a climate that permits bullying or aggression, where support systems are not available, and where bullying and aggression are considered "normative" behavior. The school environment or ethos of the school is vital in either maintaining or discouraging bullying behaviors.

Relationship Between School Climate and Bullying

The relationship between school climate and bullying and aggression is of particular interest to school psychologists. In a recent study (Love et al., 2005), students who were victimized reported significantly more negative perceptions of school climate than bystanders and students not involved in bullying ($F(2, 142) = 3.08, p > .05$). These findings are also supported by a second study by Oliver, Hoover, and Hazler (1994), who found that students who believed their school had a positive school climate reported a lower frequency of bullying than those who believed their school had a negative climate. In yet a third study, youth in schools characterized as high on conflict showed increased involvement in bullying over a two-year period, while students in schools reporting low conflict and high expectations for learning showed less involvement in bullying (Kasen, Berenson, Cohen, & Johnson, 2004). A summation of these studies indicates that students involved in bullying endorse more negative perceptions of school climate than students not involved in bullying.

Taking into account the developing literature on the importance of school climate, prevention efforts aimed at reducing bullying and aggression have begun to focus on more proactive approaches that address the school environment. Zero-tolerance approaches (i.e., suspensions and expulsions), have been endorsed by many administrators and politicians in recent years in the face of highly publicized incidences of aggressive acts in school. However, there is little empirical support that such policies and consequences are effective in reducing serious incidents. In fact, research has demonstrated that punitive interventions for those exhibiting antisocial and violent behavior are often associated with increases in problem behavior (Sprague et al., 2001). Moreover, reactive responses including zero-tolerance policies, adding surveillance cameras and metal detectors, and hiring additional security personnel have been ineffective in fostering positive school climates and, in the long term, these approaches reduce student academic engagement (Sugai & Horner, 2002).

Bullying Prevention and School-Wide Practices

A proactive, universal approach that is gaining empirical support for creating measurable and durable reductions in aggressive behaviors and bullying in schools is *Positive Behavior Supports* (*PBS;* Sprague & Walker, 2005; Sugai & Horner, 2002). School-wide PBS encourages and reinforces natural social supports with a broad range of systemic and individualized strategies applied school-wide to provide efficient reinforcement and training of expected social behaviors. PBS includes four critical elements: attention to outcomes that are uniquely defined and meaningful to the stakeholders (e.g., teachers, students, families); use of research-validated practices and curricula; reliance on data taken across settings and from multiple sources to guide decision making; and implementation of these validated practices across systems, giving consideration to resource supports, administrative leadership, and working structures (e.g., committees) within those systems.

Under the PBS model, school-wide anti-bullying teams composed of principals, selected staff, and representative parents from the community should guide bullying approaches to prevention and intervention (Sugai & Horner, 2002). The team should draft anti-bullying policies and practices, and expectations for students regarding appropriate behaviors should be clearly defined as well as the positive and negative consequences if such expectations are not met. This information should be posted publicly via posters, school newsletters, and other visible means (Bullis, Walker, & Sprague, 2001). Teachers should also be supported with guidance in managing peer interactions and concrete reinforcement of their efforts to facilitate positive interactions among students (Hanish, Kochenderfer-Ladd, Fabes, Martin, & Denning, 2004).

Connection Between School Climate and PBS

Adopting a school-wide PBS approach can positively affect school climate, as indicated by a decrease in behavioral problems (Sugai &

Horner, 2002). Under this model, administrators support bullying intervention efforts by ensuring that physical environments within the school foster a positive climate. Uncomfortable noise, flickering or dim lights, overcrowded spaces, or rooms that are too hot or too cold can make it more difficult for students to regulate their emotional responses and undermine behavioral self-control (Doll, Song, & Siemers, 2004). Most incidences of bullying tend to occur in unsupervised locations including the halls, restrooms, cafeteria, and during recess (Kasen et al., 2004; Olweus, 1993). Therefore, another universal strategy of School-wide PBS is to build systems of support in these specific nonclassroom settings (Lewis, Powers, Kelk, & Newcomer, 2002; Sprague & Walker, 2005).

Recess has been identified as a particularly problematic setting for bullying behaviors at the elementary level. Research has demonstrated that administrators can support school-wide efforts by ensuring that children have multiple, highly attractive games available (Doll et al., 2004a). In one study with a fifth-grade classroom, Doll and colleagues found that the number of suspensions and office visits decreased dramatically when teachers provided simple games that students could take outside at lunch recess. Simple games such as Frisbees, hula-hoops, and bingo can help channel students' behaviors in positive directions. Finally, there should be opportunities for staff training in defining and identifying bullying behaviors, given that teacher training has been shown to increase teachers' level of intervention in bullying episodes as reported by students (Holt & Keyes, 2004; Olweus, 1994).

At the classroom level, teachers can facilitate PBS efforts by using cooperative learning strategies to promote friendships and create opportunities to learn in noncompetitive groups. Moreover, creating multiple roles for students to fill encourages students to have new interactions with each other, for example, assigning classroom chore assignments in pairs. Likewise, teachers should redirect children's solitary activities into appropriate outlets and activities if students appear to be isolating themselves, as research has shown certain solitary play behaviors are associated with high rates of victimization (Hanish et al., 2004). Increasing the degree to which all students in a class are included raises the likelihood that peers will be willing to intervene against bullying in general and allows students who rarely interact with their peers opportunities to develop positive social skills (Hanish et al., 2004).

Students should be given numerous opportunities to practice tolerance in the classroom to enhance social skills, and teachers can use overt praise and even token economies to reinforce appropriate behavior (Doll et al., 2004b). For example, in one study employing a group contingency system, playground monitors gave elastic loops to students complying with targeted social skills and these were collected by the teacher in a can. Once the can was full, the class earned group rewards. This intervention reduced problem behaviors at recess considerably across three grade levels (Lewis et al., 2002).

Bullis, Walker, and Sprague (2001) advocate embedding social skills training programs into the regular school curriculum such that teachers instruct on social skills as subject matter and the techniques of coaching, prompting, precorrections, and debriefing are used to support students in demonstrating and practicing these skills. In the teaching of social skills, educators are often encouraged to consider how they can serve as effective role models, given that negative teacher behaviors (i.e., coercion, laissez-faire classroom management styles) toward students can exacerbate bullying and harassment in schools (Holt & Keyes, 2004).

Likewise, attending to teacher attitudes about equity and diversity is crucial; teachers must be mindful that they are using inclusive activities and not inadvertently creating unhealthy competition through their teaching methods or differential responses to students. Latham (1992) suggests that teachers maintain a ratio of six to eight positive social interactions for every negative engagement in order to encourage instructional success and promote a positive classroom climate.

Beyond teaching social skills, Walker and colleagues (1996) also emphasize the importance of teaching students conflict-resolution or peer negotiation skills. Teachers must adequately respond to emotionality in students, given that bullies and victims have been found to struggle with regulating emotions and often express frequent or intense negative affect in the forms of anxiety, anger, or sadness (Hanish et al., 2004). Teachers can address negative emotions before they spiral into high-conflict interactions among students by being attuned to the emotions in the classroom and teaching skills related to conflict resolution, including problem recognition, situational analysis, and role taking (Bullis et al., 2001). Aggressive youth tend to demonstrate cognitive errors that contribute to their inappropriate behavior, such as interpreting ambiguous interactions as being hostile or aggressive, so conflict-resolution training assists these students in seeing alternate perspectives and generating more alternative responses (Bullis et al., 2001; Doll et al., 2004a).

Another benefit of teaching students general problem-solving strategies is that it addresses goals of PBS at the peer level. Research has demonstrated that students who are taught strategies to identify conflict, consider both sides, generate alternative solutions, and pursue a shared solution are more likely to settle aggressive interactions without adult assistance (Johnson & Johnson, 1994; Peterson, Larson, & Skiba, 2001). By equipping students with such negotiation skills, one increases their willingness to intervene if they witness conflict emerge among peers. Peers can be powerful "defenders" in discouraging victimization in addition to the messages being conveyed by teachers, school staff, and even school policy (Doll et al., 2004a).

For instance, one study found a program that taught students peer negotiation skills was effective in dramatically reducing discipline referrals, and 54% of the students reported a decrease in concerns about bullying (Smith, 1992). Furthermore, victims of bullying who are taught negotiation skills and conflict resolution will be more likely to respond to bullies in ways that do not reinforce such behavior (Colvin, Tobin, Beard, Hagan, & Sprague, 1998). Assertiveness training can also be incorporated into the lesson plans, addressing problem-solving strategies so that bullies learn ways to express negative affect without resorting to aggressive behaviors or intimidation, peers feel more comfortable speaking up if they observe bullying occurring, and victims generate alternate, more positive ways to cope with bullying (Colvin et al., 1998; Holt & Keyes, 2004). All of these efforts, in combination, facilitate more positive interactions among peers and ultimately contribute to an improved classroom and school climate.

Finally, in implementing PBS, it is crucial to incorporate the parents by addressing the family level. Although parents are rarely present when bullying interactions occur, intervention efforts are more effective when parents are aware and engaged in efforts to improve peer interactions and their children's experiences in the classroom. A direct relation has been found between parents being actively involved in their children's schools and students mirroring their parents' supportive and positive attitudes toward school practices and routines (Shumow & Millert, 2001). Higher parent engagement is also positively associated with higher job satisfaction reported by teachers and higher principal ratings of teacher performance (Christenson, 1995). Conversely, an increased incidence of problem behaviors and suspension has been linked with parental disengagement from their children's education (Steinberg, 1996). Thus, while research supports the importance of parent engagement, the reality of increasing parental interactions in schools is often quite difficult.

One way to facilitate home-school collaboration (Cowan, Swearer, & Sheridan, 2004) is to provide multiple opportunities for interactions between school personnel and families. Parents should be provided with materials (i.e., a parents' handbook) describing the positively stated school rules and giving them suggestions on how to implement PBS principles within their own home, modeled on the school rules and expectations (Sprague & Horner, 2006). Such consistency across settings would facilitate students generalizing these appropriate behaviors across various contexts. Even before information regarding PBS efforts implemented in the schools is disseminated, it is advisable to meet with parents to create mutual understanding of local needs and develop collaborative relationships.

Key Ingredients of School-Wide Bullying Prevention and Intervention

Whole-school preventive interventions for bullying have been introduced over the last decade following the introduction in 1993 of the Norway-based Olweus Bullying Prevention Program (OBBP). Although the OBBP successfully reduced bullying by 50% in Norway (Olweus, 1993), these data have yet to be replicated in U.S. samples, and there appears to be no single peer-reviewed article highlighting the effectiveness rates of the OBBP in U.S. schools. However, components of the OBBP have been incorporated into numerous prevention programs under the assumption that its basic tenets are transferable to other school contexts. Based largely on the OBBP, the U.S. Department of Health and Human Services recently launched its *Stop Bullying Now: Take a Stand, Lend a Hand* campaign and provides schools and administrators with 10 best practices in bullying prevention and intervention (*Stop Bullying Now,* n.d.). These best practices are exemplified in some of the most popular and effective school-wide preventive interventions, four of which (i.e., Olweus Bullying Prevention Program, Peaceful Schools Project, Bully-Proofing, and Steps to Respect) are described in detail in the following pages. Three themes emerge from these 10 best practices that incorporate universal, selected, and indicated interventions and are summarized in the following sections.

Theme 1: Focus on School Environment

Emphasis is placed on changing the school climate and the social norms surrounding bullying. In essence, it is important to create a culture where bullying is not tolerated and is not rewarded or seen as "cool" (Rodkin & Hodges, 2003). Before it can be discouraged, however, bullying has to be noticed and addressed by all stakeholders in the school, including teachers, administrators, playground staff, bus drivers, and teacher aides. In addition, it is imperative for each school to assess its unique school climate and bullying environment. Climate cannot be changed if it is not understood. Where is the bullying happening? What are the students' attitudes toward bullying? What is supporting bullying behavior? How do victims perceive their school environment? Why do victims become bullies within the school context?

Theme 2: Widen the Circle of Bully Prevention Stakeholders

School-wide approaches to bullying prevention are somewhat misleading because best practices include the need to secure buy-in from parents, and in many of the programs discussed here, provide training to parents about bullying. It is important to reinforce prosocial, anti-bullying behaviors in multiple contexts, including the school and home. Parents should also be part of a school-based planning committee that oversees the implementation and evaluation of school-wide programming, incorporating universal, selected, and indicated interventions.

Theme 3: Training, Consistency, and Persistence

The last set of best practices highlights the importance of broad training for staff on definitions of bullying and its effects, how to respond to bullying, and how to work with other staff to maintain bullying prevention attitudes and behaviors. Training needs to be followed by clearly articulated school rules and policies related to bullying. Staff are provided with assessment results from their own school to determine where the bullying is occurring. Creative ways should be employed to increase adult supervision in these locations. Effective bullying programs also include a classroom curriculum component, during which students hold frank and safe discussions about bullying, their role, and its effects on victims, bullies, and bystanders.

Widely Distributed School-Wide Bullying Preventative Interventions

While certainly not an exhaustive list of school-wide bullying prevention and intervention programs, four programs are highlighted here. For a more comprehensive list, the reader is encouraged to read *Bullying Prevention: Creating a Positive School Climate and Developing Social Competence* (Orpinas & Horne, 2006).

Steps to Respect: A Bullying Prevention Program

This program was developed and evaluated by the Committee for Children and appears to be the only school-wide program with empirical data published in peer-reviewed journals (Frey et al., 2005; Hirschstein & Frey, 2006). The foundation of the school-wide program includes creating a "safe, caring, and respectful" culture and increasing adult intervention in bullying episodes. The student curriculum is provided for three levels: Level 1 for Grades 3 and 4, Level 2 for Grades 4 and 5, and Level 3 for Grades 5 and 6. The program unfolds in three phases. *Phase 1* includes establishing a school-wide framework before the curriculum is implemented. A program guide provides details on the role of the principal or administrator as supportive, leader of the implementation, and monitor of the program evaluation. To facilitate this process a steering committee should be formed to include teachers and administrators, but also bus drivers, nurses, secretaries, social workers, and other persons who encounter students during the school day. This phase includes four implementation steps with worksheets to guide the steering committee in their planning and increase the efficacy and sustainability of the program. For example, worksheets focus on challenges such as securing buy-in, capturing a school "snapshot," developing an anti-bullying policy and procedures, assessing the school's physical features, planning for staff training, and rolling out the curriculum.

Phase 2 includes training of all staff (e.g., teachers, administrators, playground aides), training of staff who will be coaching children (coaching training), curriculum orientation for classroom teachers, and then booster training for staff and faculty. Coaching teachers learn the 4-A response process: affirming the child's feelings, asking questions, assessing the child's safety, and acting. Coaching teachers are taught to define and recognize bullying, handle bullying reporting, and create and maintain a positive school climate. Formats include large group presentation, small group discussions, video segments, worksheets, and role-plays.

Phase 3 is the curriculum for the classroom. Curriculum kits include a comprehensive teacher's guide and skill lessons, literature units, one copy of each of the books, six posters, and a classroom video. Skill sets that are taught include learning to recognize bullying, learning bullying-refusal skills, learning to seek help and help someone else who is being bullied, practicing friendship-making skills, and developing bullying-reporting skills. Effects were strongest when teachers "coached" students involved in bullying.

Olweus Bullying Prevention Program

The comprehensive Olweus Bullying Prevention Program (OBPP) was designated as a Blueprints program by the Office of Juvenile Justice and Delinquency Prevention (Olweus & Limber, 1999). The Blueprints designation means that this program meets rigorous standards and has been proven effective in reducing adolescent aggression. The OBPP was developed and systematically evaluated in Norway by Daniel Olweus. This comprehensive program aims to reduce bullying among elementary and middle school students by reducing opportunities and rewards for bullying behavior. Consistent with data from the extant literature, teachers are trained to improve peer relations and create a positive school climate for all students. The intervention focuses on increasing awareness among students, teachers, and parents, highlighting the need for clear and consistent guidelines or rules against bullying, and protecting victims. Program ingredients are delivered at school, classroom, and individual levels.

At the *school level,* it is important to first conduct a comprehensive assessment by administering a student questionnaire to determine the extent of the problem. The OBPP program uses the English version of the Olweus Bully/Victim Questionnaire (Solberg & Olweus, 2003). These data can then be presented at a school conference day, which should be attended by teachers, administrators, counselors/psychologists, and parents. After the data collected from the school are presented, attendees should arrive at a long-term plan of action for addressing the bullying problem. While plans vary across schools, research indicates that certain school-level interventions should be included. Attention to the density of supervisors during recess and breaks is vital. Bullying occurs most often during lunchtime, recess, and passing periods. It is therefore necessary to have plenty of adult supervisors on hand who can all intervene quickly and decisively when bullying occurs. All children/adolescents have to receive the message that "bullying is not tolerated." Supervisors should have a way of reporting to each other what they see during these time periods, in case some children are consistently bullies or victims. In addition, schools should consider having separate break times for older and younger students. Olweus also recommends that schools have a "contact telephone" during which counselors, psychologists, or teachers spend several hours a week responding to phone calls from students who are being bullied or parents who have concerns about bullying situations.

A general PTA meeting is also recommended in order to build collaboration between school faculty and parents in the community. In this meeting, members of the school faculty explicitly inform parents that they will be focusing on minimizing bullying and social exclusion in their school. A plan of action should be articulated and circulated to all parents, not only those in attendance. Recognizing that teachers need support to embark on a bullying prevention program, Olweus encourages teachers to create a social milieu group in which 10 to 12 teachers meet on a regular basis to discuss efforts and challenges. The goal is to foster collegial support among small groups of teachers.

In the *classroom*, class rules about bullying are generated collaboratively between the teacher and students. While all classrooms have rules, the Olweus program outlines specific rules related to bullying. Olweus recommends three basic rules to start with: (a) We shall not bully other students; (b) We shall try to help students who are bullied; and (c) We shall make a point to include students who become easily left out. Students and teachers should also generate sanctions for violating the rules. Possible sanctions include a serious individual talk with the student who broke a rule, depriving the student of some privilege, and making the student stand next to the teacher during recess. The rules and sanctions should be reviewed and evaluated in weekly class meetings in which students and teachers sit in a circle and discuss incidents of bullying. What is important in minimizing bullying at the classroom level is to promote a positive climate. Teachers need to praise students when they do not engage in bullying behavior, to foster collaboration among students by designing group activities, and to allow students to attend PTA meetings in which they report on their experiences with the bullying prevention program.

Finally, *individual interventions* are offered for bullies, victims, and their parents. This program encourages serious talks with bullies and victims. These talks have to happen quickly after incidents. Bullies should not be allowed to make excuses for their behavior or to blame others. They should be told that bullying will not be tolerated. Talks with the victim need to guarantee him or her protection against harassment. Parents of victims are encouraged to consider seeking professional help for their children if the victimization has been occurring for a long time. Parents of bullies are encouraged to create family rules at home against bullying as well as sanctions when these rules are broken.

Research by the program developer and colleagues (Olweus & Alsaker, 1991) reveals a substantial correlation in Norway between the reduction of bully/victim problems and more complete implementation of the program. In addition, implementation of this program in the southeastern United States yielded small reductions in bully/victim problems in the intervention schools, while these problems increased in the comparison schools (Olweus & Limber, 1999). The success of this program rests with its assumption that in order to reduce bullying, one must restructure the social environment that supports this behavior. This program is based on the social-ecological approach to bully prevention, incorporates findings from the empirical literature, and has undergone systematic evaluation.

The Peaceful Schools Project

The Peaceful Schools Project (Twemlow, Fonagy, & Sacco, 2001a) was developed in 2000 in response to an attempted rape of a second-grade girl by several second-grade boys. The defining feature of Peaceful Schools Project is that it is a "philosophy, rather than a program" (Twemlow, Fonagy, & Sacco, 2005, p. 296). The foundation of the project is mentalization—a focus on relationships and setting interpersonal priorities. As such, it focuses on developing empathy and valuing relationships over all else. The paramount goal of the Peaceful Schools Project is to alter the school climate in permanent and meaningful ways. In a school or community where a mentalizing approach is espoused, bullying would cease to exist.

The philosophy of the Peaceful Schools Project includes five important components (Twemlow et al., 2005). First, schools embrace a positive climate campaign that includes counselor-led discussions and the creation of posters and other tangibles that help alter the language and the thinking of everyone in the school (i.e., "Back off bullies!" or "Stop bullying now"). In essence, all participants in the school are flooded with an awareness of the bullying dynamic, and understanding bullying from this philosophical orientation requires an understanding of the relationships that foster bullying. Second, teachers are fully supported in classroom management techniques and are taught specific techniques to diffuse disruptive behavior from a relational perspective rather than from a punishment perspective. Parents are also taught how to resolve power dynamics in the home using the same philosophy. Third, peer and adult mentorship are used to help everyone in the school resolve problems collaboratively and without blame. These adult mentors are particularly important on the playground and during times when adult supervision might be minimal. The key is that the mentors have a consistent relationship with the students and trust is developed in these relationships. The fourth component is called the "gentle warrior physical education program." This component combines role playing, relaxation, and defensive martial arts techniques to help students develop strategies to protect themselves and others. These are essentially confidence-building skills that help create a mentalizing environment that enhances positive coping skills. Fifth, reflection time is an important part of creating a peaceful school climate. Teachers and students engage in a conversation for at least 10 minutes at the end of the day about bully, victim, and bystander behaviors. By engaging in this important conversation, "the system through its members becomes more psychologically aware, and eventually the rules, regulations, and policy of the system will embody mentalizing principles" (Twemlow et al., 2005, p. 300). The Peaceful Schools Project reflects a holistic philosophy that attempts to alter the social architecture in schools that supports bullying and aggressive behaviors.

While the majority of publications on the Peaceful Schools Project have focused on its development and philosophy, several empirical articles illustrate positive outcomes of engaging in this unique approach to altering the conditions that support bullying behaviors. In a study of 2,206 elementary school students, those in schools that had adopted the Peaceful Schools Project for two consecutive years showed significant reductions in bullying behaviors compared to matched controls whose schools in the same district did not adopt the Peaceful Schools Project (Fonagy, Twemlow, Vernberg, Sacco, & Little, 2005). In addition, adherence to the Peaceful Schools Project has resulted in significant decreases in discipline referrals and expulsion, and an increase in feelings of safety (Twemlow, Fonagy, & Sacco, 2001b). Thus, some preliminary empirical studies lend support to the efficacy of the Peaceful Schools Project.

Bully-Proofing Your School

The Bully-Proofing Your School (BPYS) program (Garrity, Jens, Porter, Sager, & Short-Camilli, 2004) was developed by several Cherry Creek School District professionals in Colorado who were working with children who reported recurrent victimization and the lack of adult response to student concerns. BPYS was developed in 1994 after several years of consultation between developers and the school district. It was modeled, in fact, after the OBPP and includes two series, one for students in elementary school (kindergarten through the sixth grade) and one for students in middle school (sixth through the eighth grades). During 1999–2000, BPYS was mandated in all K–8 schools in the district.

Similar to *Steps to Respect* and OBPP, BPYS rests on the tenet that every school should have the goal of developing a safe, respectful, inclusive environment where teachers can teach and students can learn. BPYS program objectives include teaching students to recognize bullying behavior, setting class rules, responding consistently, quickly, and effectively to bullying, enhancing empathy, developing effective communication skills, and learning a range of conflict-resolution skills. Components of the program are teacher/staff training, parent education, student- and classroom-level intervention, creating a caring environment, and victim support. The program incorporates three phases of implementation. First, the program begins with defining bullying and discussing its impact and ways to establish classroom rules regarding bullying. Second, skills and techniques for dealing with bullying and increasing resilience to victimization are presented. Third, focus then turns to changing the school culture using activities and worksheets to convert the "silent majority" or "bystanders" into the "caring majority." Review and revision of school policies and procedures for addressing the problem of bullying also occur throughout. The BPYS materials include a parent's guide in both English and Spanish. A preliminary study of the effectiveness of BPYS (Epstein, Plog, & Porter, 2002) found reductions in bullying behavior and increased student perceptions of safety over a four-year period in a suburban elementary school.

A Word of Caution

Although school-wide approaches are intuitively appealing to many practitioners and scholars, there is insufficient empirical support for such approaches. J. D. Smith and colleagues (2004) attempted to answer the question of whether school-wide approaches are efficacious through a meta-analytic investigation of 14 primary and secondary prevention programs from Italy, Canada, Germany, Belgium, England, Switzerland, Norway, and the United States. Eight of these studies were controlled and four included random assignment of classes or schools to intervention and control conditions. Six were uncontrolled studies. Effect size data on changes in self-report levels of bullying and victimization indicated that the majority of effects were small, negligible, and negative, even under highly controlled situations. These authors conclude, "It is clear that the whole school approach has led to important reductions in bullying in a number of cases, but the results are simply too inconsistent to justify adoption of these procedures to the exclusion of others" (Smith, Schneider, Smith, & Ananiadou, 2004). Indeed, this meta-analysis was conducted prior to the recent support for the Steps to Respect program; therefore, it would be important to conduct another meta-analysis incorporating more recent data for school-wide preventive interventions.

Targeted Interventions Can Be Incorporated Into School-Wide Efforts

Bully Busters: A Teacher's Manual for Helping Bullies, Victims, and Bystanders

While many school-wide comprehensive approaches to bully prevention are intuitively appealing, school districts and school personnel frequently do not have the financial resources to implement these programs. Counselors, psychologists, and teachers often ask for a more affordable approach. *Bully Busters* (Newman, Horne, & Bartolomucci, 2000) is a program that school faculty can easily use with individuals, groups, and classrooms, which has demonstrated strong empirical support. While this manual is specifically written for teachers, the materials have been used by clinicians to conduct workshops and work individually with bullies, victims, and bystanders.

The program includes seven modules. The first module is designed to increase awareness of bullying on the part of teachers and students. Teachers are encouraged to develop a definition of bullying collaboratively with students. Exercises are used to facilitate a conversation among students about who the bullies are, what bullying is, and where it happens. Students then participate in several activities to recognize how their words or actions can be hurtful and they role play more constructive ways of interacting. The second module includes a discussion with students about how bullying develops and the variety of forms it can take. Activities in this module include viewing movies in which characters are victims or bullies. Students discuss both aggressive and passive forms of bullying, and differences between male and female bullying. This module ends with a focus on the misconceptions related to bullying.

Recognizing the victim is the topic of the third module. Students discuss the effects of victimization and challenge the myths about victims. It is key that students recognize there are different types of victims, including individuals who are passive, provocative, and bystanders. What differentiates the Bully Busters program from other prevention efforts is the incorporation of the bystander. The majority of students are not actively engaged in bullying episodes, but their reluctance to intervene in a bullying incident promotes this behavior.

Students are encouraged to break the "code of silence" and create a safer climate for all students.

The fourth module includes specific strategies for teachers to create a bully-free classroom. Newman and colleagues (2000) instruct teachers on the four R's of bully control: Recognizing the problem, Removing oneself and stepping back (i.e., assessing the situation), Reviewing the situation, and Responding to the situation. As in the classroom-level interventions proposed by Olweus, teachers are given specific strategies (e.g., setting rules, acting quickly), but are also given some instruction in empathy skills training, social skills training, and anger control training. Module five expands on these skills by giving teachers specific strategies for working with victims. Several activities are used with children/adolescents to help victims become aware of their strengths, to teach students to view themselves in a positive manner, and to build skills and confidence in joining groups. These activities are clearly outlined in each module and include the objectives of the activity, the materials needed to do the activity, and specific directions for completing the activity and suggestions for group discussions after the activity.

Module six includes a discussion of the role of prevention. Activities are designed to educate teachers about the need for prevention as well as provide a basic introduction to prevention theory. Teachers are encouraged to identify how their attitudes and behaviors influence student behavior and how school-level factors relate to bullying. The last module focuses on teaching relaxation and coping skills to teachers. Finally, the manual includes a teacher inventory as well as additional worksheet activities. These activities are appropriate for a wide range of age groups, from early elementary school students through middle school students. These activities are also effective when working with individual students, as the worksheets provide a forum for students to discuss incidents of bullying. As a result, the students become more willing to recognize the serious consequences of bullying and are encouraged to problem solve more appropriate ways of interacting with others. Much of this work is described in detail in a recently published book by Orpinas and Horne (2006).

Recognizing When School-Wide Services Have Not Sufficiently Addressed Bullying Problems

Schools are increasingly faced with a plethora of academic and social pressures that demand time, intervention, and outcomes from a variety of stakeholders (i.e., parents, community activists, school boards, etc.). Previous models have argued that 80% of students need universal prevention techniques (*School-Wide PBS*, n.d.). However, Baker and colleagues have recently argued that 46% of students actually need universal prevention strategies, with 54% of students needing selected prevention and indicated intervention techniques (Baker et al., 2006). Thus, school personnel are faced with the challenge of implementing programming that will effect behavior change among bullies, victims, and bystanders.

Before prevention and intervention strategies are chosen and implemented, school mental health professionals can play an instrumental role in assessing staff burnout, student apathy, and parental apathy. If the school climate is an unhealthy one, characterized by low morale, high levels of bullying, and distrust among adults and students, then any intervention will fall short of the desired behavioral outcomes. First and foremost, the adults in the school system need to be committed to creating a peaceful and healthy school environment. Once the adult level of the system is healthy, bullying prevention and intervention programming can be adopted in order to create lasting and meaningful change.

Case Example

The teachers in a large high school noticed a surge in bullying behaviors among the students. The teachers and the school administration decided that responding effectively to bullying behaviors would be a goal for the following year. A consultant was hired and results of an anonymous school-wide survey indicated that, indeed, bullying was a problem among the students. Results from the survey also showed that the students felt bullying behaviors were rewarded in the school culture. In follow-up focus groups, it was discovered that the popular students were perpetrating the bullying behaviors and there was a culture of acceptance for these behaviors, which were seen as "cool." Furthermore, the consultant was able to discover an underlying issue, which was an intense disconnect between the school administration and the teachers. The culture at the adult level was one of harassment, distrust, and an "us against them" attitude. The clear dynamic was that the bullying behaviors at the student level mirrored the bullying behaviors at the adult level. Since the relationship among the teaching staff and the administration was so poor, this had a clear effect on the students' relationships. The consultant's final recommendation was that the adults needed to interact in a healthy way before they could expect the bullying behaviors among the students to decrease.

This case illustrates that it is imperative for adults in schools to create both healthy work and healthy learning environments. If the adult community is not functioning well, it stands to reason that the student community will not be healthy. As Mahatma Ghandi wisely noted, "Be the change you want to see in the world."

Discussion Questions

1. What skills do you already possess that you could use to conduct a bullying survey of your school's students?

2. What procedures does your school use to assess bullying? to discourage bullying? How could you enhance these practices?

3. What single practice could you implement to strengthen your school's anti-bullying climate?

4. Parents, teachers, and other school staff are vested with much of the responsibility for discouraging bullying in a school or community. What skills and knowledge do they possess that make them ideal candidates for this role?

5. If you were responsible for bully prevention training for your school's staff, what are the five most important principles you would emphasize in your training?

References

Baker, J. A., Kamphaus, R. W., Horne, A. M., & Winsor, A. P. (2006). Evidence for population-based perspectives on children's behavioral adjustment and needs for service delivery in schools. *School Psychology Review, 35,* 31–46.

Bronfenbrenner, U. (1977). Toward an experimental ecology of human development. *American Psychologist, 32,* 513–531.

Bronfenbrenner, U. (1979). Contexts of child rearing: Problems and prospects. *American Psychologist, 34,* 844–850.

Bullis, M., Walker, H. M., & Sprague, J. R. (2001). A promise unfulfilled: Social skills training with at-risk and antisocial children and youth. *Exceptionality, 9,* 67–90.

Cairns, R. B., & Cairns, B. D. (1994). *Lifelines and risks: Pathways of youth in our time.* Cambridge, UK: Cambridge University Press.

Christenson, S. L. (1995). Supporting home-school collaboration. In A. Thomas & J. Grimes (Eds.), *Best practices in school psychology III* (pp. 253–267). Washington, DC: National Association of School Psychologists.

Cicchetti, D., & Toth, S. L. (1997). Transactional ecological systems in developmental psychopathology. In S. S. Luthan & J. A. Burack (Eds.), *Developmental psychopathology: Perspectives on adjustment, risk, and disorder* (pp. 317–349). New York: Cambridge University Press.

Colvin, G., Tobin, T., Beard, K., Hagan, S., & Sprague, J. (1998). The school bully: Assessing the problem, developing interventions, and future research directions. *Journal of Behavioral Education, 8,* 293–319.

Cowan, R., Swearer, S. M., & Sheridan, S. M. (2004). Home-School collaboration. In C. Spielberger (Ed.), *Encyclopedia of Applied Psychology, Volume 2* (pp. 201–208). San Diego, CA: Academic Press.

Dodge, K. A., & Coie, J. D. (1987). Social information processing factors in reactive and proactive aggression in children's peer groups. *Journal of Personality and Social Psychology, 53,* 389–409.

Doll, B., Song, S., & Siemers, E. (2004a). Classroom ecologies that support or discourage bullying. In D. L. Espelage & S. Swearer (Eds.), *Bullying in American schools: A socio-ecological perspective on prevention and intervention* (pp. 161–184). Mahwah, NJ: Lawrence Erlbaum Associates, Inc.

Doll, B., Zucker, S., & Brehm, K. (2004b). *Resilient classrooms: Creating healthy environments for learning.* New York: Guilford Press.

Espelage, D. L., Bosworth, K., & Simon, T. (2000). Examining the social environment of middle school students who bully. *Journal of Counseling and Development, 78,* 326–333.

Espelage, D. L., Holt, M. K., & Henkel, R. R. (2003). Examination of peer group contextual effects on aggression during early adolescence. *Child Development, 74,* 205–220.

Espelage, D. L., & Swearer, S. M. (2003). Research on school bullying and victimization: What have we learned and where do we go from here? *School Psychology Review, 32,* 365–383.

Epstein, L., Plog, A. E., & Porter, W. (2002). "Bully-Proofing Your School: Results of a Four-Year Intervention," *Emotional & Behavioral Disorders in Youth, 2,* 74–78.

Fonagy, P., Twemlow, S. W., Vernberg, E., Sacco, F. C., & Little, T. D. (2005). Creating a peaceful school learning environment: The impact of an anti-bullying program on educational attainment in elementary schools. *Medical Science Monitor, 11,* 317–325.

Frey, K. S., Hirschstein, M. K., Snell, J. L., Van Schoiack Edstrom, L., MacKenzie, E. P., & Broderick, C. J. (2005). Reducing playground bullying and supporting beliefs: An experimental trial of the Steps to Respect Program. *Developmental Psychology, 41,* 479–491.

Garrity, C., Jens, K., Porter, W., Sager, N., & Short-Camilli, C. (2004). *Bully proofing your school: A comprehensive approach for elementary schools.* Longmont, CO: Sopris West.

Hanish, L. D., Kochenderfer-Ladd, B., Fabes, R. A., Martin, C. L., & Denning, D. (2004). Bullying among young children: The influence of peers and teachers. In D. L. Espelage & S. Swearer (Eds.), *Bullying in American schools: A socio-ecological perspective on prevention and intervention* (pp. 141–160). Mahwah, NJ: Lawrence Erlbaum Associates.

Hirschstein, M., & Frey, K. S. (2006). Promoting behavior and beliefs that reduce bullying: The Steps to Respect Program. In S. R. Jimerson & M. Furlong

(Eds.), *Handbook of school violence and school safety: From research to practice* (pp. 309–323). Mahwah, NJ: Lawrence Erlbaum Associates.

Holt, M. K., & Keyes, M. A. (2004). Teachers' attitudes toward bullying. In D. L. Espelage & S. Swearer (Eds.), *Bullying in American schools: A socio-ecological perspective on prevention and intervention* (pp. 121–139). Mahwah, NJ: Lawrence Erlbaum Associates.

Johnson, D. W., & Johnson, R. (1994). Effects on conflict resolution training on elementary school students. *Journal of Social Psychology, 134,* 803–818.

Kasen, S., Berenson, K., Cohen, P., & Johnson, J. (2004). The effects of school climate on changes in aggressive and other behaviors related to bullying. In D. L. Espelage & S. M. Swearer (Eds.), *Bullying in American schools: A social-ecological perspective on prevention and intervention.* Mahwah, NJ: Lawrence Erlbaum Associates.

Latham, G. (1992). Interacting with at-risk children: The positive position. *Principal, 72,* 26–30.

Lewis, T. J., Powers, L. J., Kelk, M. J., & Newcomer, L. L. (2002). Reducing problem behaviors on the playground: An investigation of the application of schoolwide positive behavior supports. *Psychology in the Schools, 39,* 181–190.

Limber, S. P., & Small, M. A. (2000, August). *Self-reports of bully-victimization among primary school students.* Paper presented at the annual meeting of the American Psychological Association, Washington, DC.

Love, K. B., Swearer, S. M., Lieske, J., Siebecker, A. B., & Givens, J. (2005). *School climate, victimization, and anxiety in male high school students.* Poster presented at the annual meeting of the American Psychological Association, Washington, DC.

Lynch, M., & Cicchetti, D. (1998). An ecological-transactional analysis of children and contexts: The longitudinal interplay among child maltreatment, community violence, and children's symptomatology. *Development and Psychopathology, 10,* 235–257.

Lynch, M., & Cicchetti, D. (2002). Links between community violence and the family system: Evidence from children's feelings of relatedness and perceptions of parent behavior. *Family Process, 41,* 519–532.

Morrison, G. M., & Furlong, M. J. (1994). School violence to school safety: Reframing the issue for school psychologists. *School Psychology Review, 23,* 236–256.

Nansel, T. R., Overpeck, M., Pilla, R. S., Ruan, W. J., Simons-Morton, B. & Scheidt, P. (2001). Bullying behaviors among US youth. *Journal of the American Medical Association, 285,* 2094–2100.

Newman, D. A., Horne, A. M. & Bartolomucci, C. L. (2000). *Bully Busters: A teacher's manual for helping bullies, victims, and bystanders.* Champaign, IL: Research Press.

Oliver, R., Hoover, J. H., & Hazler, R. (1994). The perceived roles of bullying in small-town Midwestern schools. *Journal of Counseling & Development, 72,* 416–420.

Olweus, D. (1993). Bully/victim problems among schoolchildren: Long-term consequences and an effective intervention program. In S. Hodgins (Ed.), *Mental Disorder and Crime* (pp. 317–349). Thousand Oaks, CA: Sage Publications.

Olweus, D. (1994). Bullying at school: Long-term outcomes for the victims and an effective school-based intervention program. In L. R. Huesmann (Ed.), *Aggressive behavior: Current perspectives* (pp. 97–130). New York: Plenum.

Olweus, D., & Alsaker, F. D. (1991). Assessing change in a cohort longitudinal study with hierarchical data. In D. Magnusson, L. Bergman, G. Rudinger, & B. Torestad (Eds.), *Problems and methods in longitudinal research* (pp. 107–132). New York: Cambridge University.

Olweus, D., & Limber, S. (1999). *Blueprints for Violence Prevention: The Bullying Prevention Program.* Boulder, CO: Center for the Study and Prevention of Violence.

Orpinas, P., & Horne, A. M. (2006). *Bullying prevention: Creating a positive school climate and developing social competence.* Washington, DC: American Psychological Association.

Pellegrini, A. D. (2002). Affiliative and aggressive dimensions of dominance and possible functions during early adolescence. *Aggression & Violent Behavior, 7,* 21–31.

Pellegrini, A. D., & Long, J. D. (2002). A longitudinal study of bullying, dominance, and victimization during the transition from primary school through secondary school. *British Journal of Developmental Psychology, 20,* 259–280.

Peterson, R. L., Larson, J., & Skiba, R. (2001). School violence prevention: Current status and policy recommendations. *Law and Policy, 23,* 345–371.

Rodkin, P. C., & Hodges, E. V. E. (2003). Bullies and victims in the peer ecology: Four questions for psychologists and school professionals. *School Psychology Review, 32,* 384–400.

Salmivalli, C., Lagerspetz, K., Bjorkqvist, K., Osterman, K., & Kaukiainen, A. (1996). Bullying as a group process: Participant roles and their relations to social status within group. *Aggressive Behavior, 22,* 1–15.

School-Wide PBS. (n.d.). Retrieved May 2, 2006, from http://www.pbis.org/schoolwide.htm

Shumow, L., & Millert, J. D. (2001). Parents' at-home and at-school academic involvement with young adolescents. *Journal of Early Adolescence, 21,* 68–91.

Smith, J. D., Schneider, B. H., Smith, P. K., & Ananiadou, K. (2004). The effectiveness of whole-school antibullying programs: A synthesis of evaluation research. *School Psychology Review, 33,* 547–560.

Smith, P. K., Cowie, H., Olafsson, R. F., Liefooghe, A. P., Almeida, A., & Araki, H., et al. (2002). Definitions of bullying: A comparison of terms used, and age and gender differences in a fourteen-country international comparison. *Child Development, 73,* 1119–1133.

Smith, P. K., Morita, Y., Junger-Tas, J., Olweus, D., Catalano, R. F., & Slee, P. (1999). *The nature of school bullying: A cross-national perspective.* Florence, KY: Taylor & Frances/Routledge.

Smith, S. J. (1992). How to decrease bullying in our schools. *Principal, 72,* 31–32.

Solberg, M. E., & Olweus, D. (2003). Prevalence estimation of school bullying with the Olweus bully/victim questionnaire. *Aggressive Behavior, 29,* 239–268.

Sprague, J. R., & Horner, R. H. (2006). Schoolwide positive behavioral supports. In S. R. Jimerson & M. J. Furlong (Eds.), *Handbook of school violence and school safety: From research to practice* (pp. 413–427). Mahwah, NJ: Lawrence Erlbaum Associates.

Sprague, J. R., & Walker, H. M. (2005). *Safe and healthy schools: Practical prevention strategies.* New York: Guilford Press.

Sprague, J., Walker, H., Golly, A., White, K., Myers, D. R., & Shannon, T. (2001). Translating research into effective practice: The effects of a universal staff and student intervention on indicators of discipline and school safety. *Education and Treatment of Children, 24,* 495–511.

Steinberg, L. (1996). *Beyond the classroom.* New York: Touchstone.

Stop Bullying Now (n.d.). Retrieved May 2, 2006, from http://www.stopbullyingnow.hrsa.gov

Sugai, G., & Horner, R. (2002). The evolution of discipline practices: School-wide positive behavior supports. *Behavior Psychology in the Schools, 24,* 23–50.

Swearer, S. M., & Doll, B. (2001). Bullying in schools: An ecological framework. *Journal of Emotional Abuse, 2,* 7–23.

Swearer, S., & Espelage, D. (2004). A social-ecological framework of bullying among youth. In D. L. Espelage and S. M. Swearer (Eds.), *Bullying in American schools: A social-ecological perspective on prevention and intervention.* Mahwah, NJ: Lawrence Erlbaum Associates.

Twemlow, S. W., Fonagy, P., & Sacco, F. C. (2001a). An innovative psychodynamically influenced intervention to reduce school violence. *Journal of the American Academy of Child and Adolescent Psychiatry, 40,* 377–379.

Twemlow, S. W., Fonagy, P., & Sacco, F. C. (2001b). Creating a peaceful school learning environment: Report of a controlled study. *American Journal of Psychiatry, 158,* 808–810.

Twemlow, S. W., Fonagy, P., & Sacco, F. C. (2005). A developmental approach to mentalizing communities: II. The Peaceful Schools experiment. *Bulletin of the Menninger Clinic, 69,* 282–304.

Walker, H. M., Horner, R. H., Sugai, G., Bullis, M., Sprague, J., Bricker, D., et al. (1996). Integrated approaches to preventing antisocial behavior patterns among school-age children and youth. *Journal of Emotional and Behavioral Disorders, 4,* 194–209.

About the Authors

Susan M. Swearer is Associate Professor of School Psychology at the University of Nebraska–Lincoln. She examines the relationship between internalizing factors (depression, anxiety, and anger) and outward behavior (bullying/victimization, school failure, and conduct problems).

Dorothy L. Espelage is Associate Professor of Counseling Psychology and Educational Psychology at the University of Illinois at Urbana-Champaign. She investigates health-related behaviors, including bullying and youth aggression, disordered eating in adolescents and young adults, and psychosocial adjustment of families of children managing chronic illness.

Kelly Brey Love is a doctoral student in School Psychology at the University of Nebraska–Lincoln. She examines bullying and victimization in school-aged youth including the psychosocial correlates in bullying and victimization and the development of empirically based interventions.

Whitney Kingsbury is a graduate student in Counseling Psychology at the University of Illinois at Urbana-Champaign. She examines the attributions and coping strategies that are employed by students along the bully-victim continuum, and is also investigating the relation between victimization and obesity stigmatization.

9

School-Wide Approaches to Prevention of and Intervention for Depression and Suicidal Behaviors

James J. Mazza

William M. Reynolds

In the United States, one of the most evident trends in population-based prevention services for students has been the use of depression screening. The foundation and empirical development of school-based depression screening with children and adolescents was initially presented by Reynolds (1986a, 1986b, 1989a). More recently, programs such as the Columbia TeenScreen Program (Shaffer et al., 2004) and the Signs of Suicide (SOS) program (Aseltine & DeMartino,

2004) have used this approach to the prevention of depression and suicidal behaviors through early identification of youngsters with subclinical symptoms and directed intervention for students with more significant clinical levels of depression and suicidal behaviors.

Depression and suicidal behavior are significant mental health issues facing children and adolescents attending school, and they challenge school mental health professionals who are called on to intervene (Gould, Greenberg, Velting, & Shaffer, 2003; Mazza, 1997; 2006; Reynolds, 1989b, 1990a, 1994). For school-based youth, the prevalence of clinically relevant levels of depression is approximately 5% for children and 10% to 20% for adolescents (Reynolds & Johnston, 1994), with somewhat fewer students meeting the full criteria for a depression diagnosis. When working with school-based populations and prevention activities, there is substantial validity for examining depression using a clinical severity and subsyndromal depression orientation measure (Essau, Petermann, & Reynolds, 1999; Reynolds, 2006). This suggests that even though a student may not meet all criteria for a formal diagnosis of major depression, presenting significant levels of depressive symptoms is a meaningful indicator of psychological distress and a viable target for prevention activities. Likewise, it is important to consider the range of suicidal behaviors when considering students to be at risk. According to a report of the Centers for Disease Control and Prevention (CDC, 2006) 16.9% of high school students (approximately 1 out of 6) seriously thought about suicide in the past year, with 8.4% of students (approximately 1 out of 12) making an actual suicide attempt. These statistics highlight the importance of developing and implementing school-based depression and suicidal behavior prevention and intervention programs.

Depression

Within the scope of current systems of classification, depression in children and adolescents is an affective disorder similar in many respects to this disorder in adults. From another perspective, depression in children and adolescents may be considered as significant perturbation of mood. A depressed student may experience a range of symptoms, some of which are overt, such as irritability or distinctly sad appearance, and others that are covert, such as low self-worth, hopelessness, suicidal thoughts, and guilt. In children and adolescents, depression represents a negative psychological state that may be characterized as one of intense, subjective misery, despondency, and in some cases, irritability (Reynolds, 1998). Students who are depressed are often withdrawn from the world around them, finding little pleasure in positive events or settings, and showing significant disengagement from school and learning-related activities.

A number of characteristics unique to depression impact the use and format of depression assessment procedures that are integral to many prevention programs. Depression is an internalizing disorder (Reynolds, 1992; Reynolds & Johnston, 1994) that encompasses many symptoms not easily observed. For example, the cognitive symptoms of guilt, self-deprecation, suicidal ideation, hopelessness, and feelings of worthlessness, are among the symptoms of depression that are often overlooked or difficult for teachers and parents to notice unless a formal evaluation is conducted. Even somatic symptoms such as insomnia, appetite loss, and other problems may go undetected by parents and significant others. The clinical distress or severity level associated with many of these symptoms is also subjective. For example, suicidal ideation is an example of a covert symptom, the presence and severity of which can be ascertained only from the youngster.

Another aspect of children and adolescents with depression is their limited self-awareness of their psychological condition along with their lack of self-referral for mental health problems. The outcome of this is that many youngsters feel their lives are quite miserable, but are unaware that they may have a psychological problem or that they should let someone know of their condition so that treatment can be provided. We cannot expect children to know the symptoms of depression and to tell an adult if these symptoms occur. Because of this, as well as the general reticence of at-risk children and adolescents to seek help for emotional difficulties (Gould et al., 2004), there is a critical need for schools to institute screening and prevention activities for depression and suicidal behaviors.

A number of surveys have examined the prevalence of depression in children and adolescents, although differences in methodology, sample characteristics, and sampling procedures tend to produce differing estimates (Poznanski & Mokros, 1994). One consistent finding is the emergence of depression during the transition from childhood to adolescence (e.g., Hankin et al., 1998). The National Institute of Mental Health (NIMH, 2000) estimates that approximately 2.5% of children and 8.3% of adolescents in the United States experience depressive disorders. These estimates indicate that depression is one of the most prevalent mental health problems in students, especially adolescents, and support the need for empirically based procedures for the prevention and intervention of this disorder.

Since 1980, research has demonstrated the clinical efficacy of behavioral, cognitive, and interpersonal interventions for depression and depressive symptoms in clinic- and school-based samples of children and adolescents (e.g., Birmaher et al., 2000; Butler, Miezitis, Friedman, & Cole, 1980; Kahn, Kehle, Jenson, & Clark, 1990; Lewinsohn, Clarke, Hops, & Andrews, 1990; Mufson, Moreau, Weissman, & Klerman, 1993; Reynolds & Coats, 1986; Stark, Reynolds, & Kaslow, 1987; Vostanis, Feehan, Grattan, & Bickerton, 1996; Wood, Harrington, & Moore, 1996). These empirical studies have shown that psychological interventions are effective in the remediation of depressive symptomatology in children and adolescents. These and other studies have provided a basis for researchers to take the next step and investigate the potential of psychoeducational programs for preventing depression in students.

Suicidal Behavior

It is important to recognize that suicidal behavior is a continuum of behaviors from suicidal ideation on one end followed by suicidal intent, suicide attempt, and death due to suicide at the other end (Reynolds, 1988; Reynolds & Mazza, 1994). The behaviors along this continuum are not mutually exclusive, nor do all youth who are suicidal advance along the continuum. It should be noted, however, as one moves along the continuum, the frequency of each behavior decreases but its lethality increases. The four domains that comprise the suicidal continuum are discussed in the following sections.

Suicidal Ideation

Suicidal ideation, the first domain on the suicidal behavior continuum, is defined as the cognitions and thoughts about killing oneself and thoughts about suicide in general (Reynolds, 1988). Reynolds, who developed the Suicidal Ideation Questionnaire (SIQ; Reynolds, 1987) for adolescents, described these cognitions as ranging from general thoughts about never being born or wishes of being dead to more specific thoughts, such as a detailed suicide plan that includes how, when, and where the suicide would occur. Suicidal ideation is the precursor to other more lethal suicidal behaviors (Ladame & Jeanneret, 1982; Reynolds, 1988; Reynolds & Mazza, 1994; U.S. Department of Health and Human Services [DHHS], 2001).

Suicidal ideation among students is more prevalent than many think. According to the most recent Youth Risk Behavior Survey (YRBS), one out of six (16.9%) high school students seriously thought about attempting suicide in the past year (CDC, 2006). This number is higher for female students, with more than one out of five (21.8%) female students having these thoughts and one out of eight (12.0%) male students. In research using the SIQ to identify adolescents at or above a clinical cutoff score (90th percentile) for suicidal ideation, Mazza and Reynolds (2001) reported similar gender differences, with 16% of female students and 7% of male students endorsing clinically significant levels of suicidal ideation.

Suicidal Intent

Suicidal intent, the second behavior along the continuum, is defined as the students' objectives or intentions at the time of their suicidal attempt specific to their wish to die (Overholser & Spirito, 2003). Kingsbury (1993) described multiple components of suicidal intent: expressed intent, planning, communication, and concealment. As with suicidal ideation, the higher the degree of suicidal intent the more dangerous the suicidal behavior is. Behaviors that represent the components of suicidal intent include but are not limited to giving away prized or meaningful possessions, writing a will, engaging in minor self-destructive behaviors, and making subtle or overt threats (Reynolds, 1988). Several of these behaviors are overt and should be viewed by family members, friends, and significant others as a possible warning sign for suicide. When these occur, further follow-up assessment of the student's current mental health is needed. It should be noted that not all suicidal youth engage in these behaviors, and conversely, not all youth who display one or more of these behaviors are suicidal.

Suicide Attempt

A suicide attempt is defined as a self-injurious behavior with the intent of causing death (Reynolds & Mazza, 1994). The frequency of this behavior is alarming, with approximately 1 out of 12 (8.4%) high school adolescents attempting suicide within the past year (CDC, 2006), and roughly the same frequency for middle school youth (sixth, seventh, and eighth grades) at 7.7% (Reynolds & Mazza, 1999). Given the prevalence rate, approximately 11% to 14% of high school adolescents have attempted suicide by the time they have graduated (Mazza & Reynolds, 2001; Riggs & Cheng, 1988).

As with suicidal ideation, significant gender differences exist in the incidence and prevalence of adolescent suicide attempts. Female students attempt suicide approximately twice as frequently as male students (Gould et al., 1998; National Center for Health Statistics [NCHS], 2003). According to the most recent YRBS incidence data, 11.5% of adolescent female students attempted suicide within the past year and 5.4% of male students (CDC, 2006). Reynolds and Mazza (1995) reported a similar 2:1 ratio of female-to-male attempts in a nationwide sample of over 3,400 adolescents. In addition, they reported that 35% of female attempters had a history of multiple suicide attempts compared to 22% of males. Earlier work by Garfinkel and colleagues, who reviewed the medical records of 505 children and adolescents seen in an emergency room for attempting suicide, found that 78% of youth made low-lethality attempts, 21% made moderately lethal attempts, and only 1% made a highly lethal attempt (Garfinkel, Froese, & Hood, 1982). These results suggest that the vast majority of adolescents who are suicidal are ambivalent about taking their own lives, which is consistent with the findings that most youth who attempted suicide had a high likelihood of being rescued compared to the 3.4% who had low rescuability (Garfinkel et al., 1982).

Suicide

Suicide is the last and obviously the most lethal behavior along the suicidal behavior continuum. Suicide is defined as an intentional self-injurious behavior that results in death (Reynolds & Mazza, 1994). According to the most current information collected by the National Center for Injury and Prevention Control (NCIPC, 2006) for 2003, suicide was the third leading cause of death among adolescents 15 to 19 years old and youth 10 to 14 years old. Although suicide is the most lethal of the suicidal behaviors, it is also the rarest on the continuum of behaviors. The suicide rate for adolescents (ages 15–19) for 2003 was 7.3/100,000 while the rate for 10- to 14-year-olds was 1.2/100,000 (McIntosh, 2006). Suicide does occur among youth younger than 10 years but is a very rare event.

Gender differences in adolescents are found for deaths due to suicide, but are opposite to those for adolescent suicidal ideation and attempts, resulting in what has been termed the "gender paradox in suicide" (Canetto & Sakinofsky, 1998). Male adolescents die by suicide approximately five times more often than females, a ratio of 4.6:1 (CDC, 2006), even though females make more attempts and report more suicidal ideation. The ratio is a bit smaller among students aged 10 to 14 years old, with males dying by suicide over three times more frequently than same-age females, a ratio of 3.4:1 (CDC, 2006). Two explanations have frequently been proposed for the gender discrepancies. First, males tend to use more violent means to make their suicide attempts, which are more likely to result in death than the means used by females (Anderson, 2002; CDC, 2006). Second, males tend to have a higher rate of substance abuse, which research shows to be linked to suicide in adolescents (Shaffer et al., 1996).

The Need for School Interventions

Schools are logical places to implement assessment and intervention programs for depression and suicidal behavior for multiple reasons (Gould et al., 2005; Miller, DuPaul, & Lutz, 2002; Reynolds, 1986a, 1991, 2002). First, because students are expected to be at school during set hours Monday through Friday of each week, most children and adolescents spend much of their day in this setting and are readily available to participate in screening and intervention programs.

Second, depression represents a significant barrier to learning. Students who feel depressed and suicidal frequently do not have the energy or motivation to care about their academic performance. These students are often disengaged from the learning process. Programs that successfully address these needs also indirectly enhance academic performance (Eggert, Nicholas, & Owens, 1995).

A third reason for schools to engage in prevention and intervention for depression and suicide in students is more pragmatic. Given the social service systems in place in the United States, no institutions other than the school system directly oversee the mental health needs of individual children and adolescents. If we are to provide universal and selected preventive interventions for depression and suicidal behavior, then schools must take on this responsibility.

The significant prevalence and incidence of depression and suicidal behavior highlight the need for linking assessment information to intervention programs that address the mental health needs of students. Because schools are a common setting for most children and adolescents, they offer the opportunity to address social, emotional, and mental health needs, particularly for those problems that may interfere with learning. In this respect, schools are ideal places to implement prevention and intervention programs. Students with high levels of depression and/or suicidal behavior often require services that extend beyond the means of typical schools. This should not dissuade schools from engaging in prevention programs. Problem identification is a critical first step that may have life-saving outcomes for some students. When the problems are too severe for school intervention, schools should encourage and work with the students and/or their parents to seek the additional appropriate services.

School-Based Prevention and Intervention Programs

Schools offer an ideal setting for implementing depression and suicidal behavior prevention and intervention programs (Gould et al., 2005; Kalafat, 2003; Mazza, 2006; Reynolds, 1991). Although the majority of youth do not experience clinical levels of depression and are not at risk for suicidal behavior, providing programs that educate and raise the awareness of these issues is important (Brent, Perper, Kolko, & Goldstein, 1988; Eastgard, 2000; Kalafat & Elias, 1992). Determining the type of depression or suicidal behavior prevention program to implement is more complex than it may seem on the surface. Important factors to consider are the intended audience, who will implement the program, what curriculum or structure will be used, the amount of time necessary to implement the program, resources to carry out the implementation successfully, and program evaluation. "One-size-fits-all" approaches tend not to be effective (Kalafat, 2003; Mazza, 1997); what works for one school may not work for another.

Prevention activities directed toward reducing depression and suicidal behavior can be differentiated as *universal prevention, selected prevention,* and *indicated prevention* according to the Institute of Medicine (Muñoz, Mrazek, & Haggerty, 1996; see chapter 1, this volume, for more detail). These three forms of prevention specific to depression and suicidal behaviors are described in the following sections. Some prevention programs use procedures that cross over multiple categories. For example, when screening school populations for signs of depression and/or suicidal behavior, the initial group may be the entire school, with targeted subgroups identified for further evaluation, intervention, or referral. Depending on the program, the latter activities may be selected or indicated prevention procedures.

Universal Prevention Programs

Universal programs to prevent depression or suicidal behavior focus on increasing awareness of depression or suicide, providing warning signs and risk factors, dispelling myths, teaching appropriate responses to peers who may come into contact with someone who is feeling depressed or suicidal, and identifying youth who are experiencing depressive symptoms or have engaged in suicidal behavior (Kalafat, 2003). Most school-based suicide prevention programs target universal populations (Kalafat & Elias, 1994; Overholser, Hemstreet, Spirito, Vyse, 1989; Shaffer, Garland, Vieland, Underwood, & Busner, 1991).

Over the past decade, there have been a number of noteworthy empirically tested universal prevention programs for depression in school-based children and adolescents. Earlier work by Clarke and colleagues (Clarke, Hawkins, Murphy, & Sheeber, 1993) examined the efficacy of two of these and suggested that relatively time-limited programs (e.g., three- to five-session psychoeducational modules) did not result in significant reductions of depressive symptoms in students. Subsequently, more complex universal programs based on various theoretical models of depression (e.g., cognitive-behavioral, social skills, problem solving) were developed and tested by other researchers. These programs include the Resourceful Adolescent Program (RAP) by Shochet and colleagues (Shochet et al., 2001) which has been tested in a number of countries (e.g., Harnett & Dadds, 2004; Merry, McDowell, Wild, Bir, & Cunliffe, 2004), the Problem Solving for Life Program (PSFL; Spence, Sheffield, & Donovan, 2003, 2005), and the Desire for a Realistic View and Ease in Social Aspects of Everyday Life (LISA-T; Pössel, Horn, Hautzinger, & Groen, 2004). The RAP has also been used as an indicated prevention program (e.g., Muris, Bogie, & Hoogsteder, 2001).

These school-based prevention programs are typically administered school-wide to all students. In most cases, the programs are administered by trained personnel, either facilitators or teachers who receive training. For example, the PSFL program is administered by teachers who receive about six hours of training. This intervention relies heavily on the development of cognitive restructuring and problem-solving skills in students and is delivered in eight 45- to 50-minute classes, one per week.

Most programs have formal intervention manuals. The RAP is one of the most examined universal prevention programs (see http://www.hlth.qut.edu.au/psyc/rap/ for manuals and training material availability). It is a resilience-building program that focuses on the development of positive coping abilities, particularly when dealing with stressful and difficult circumstances. The RAP is administered by a trained facilitator (teacher, school psychologist, counselor, etc.) and given in 10 or 11 sessions of 50 to 60 minutes. It uses components of cognitive-behavior therapy and interpersonal therapy. Shochet and colleagues have developed a number of variants of the RAP, including a parent version (with parents as the target of intervention), adolescent and parent versions for indigenous populations, and a teacher version that focuses on enhancing teachers' ability to develop student connectedness with schools. Specific to the latter, Shochet, Dadds, Ham, and Montague (2006) have found school connectedness (how valued, accepted, respected, and included in the school milieu students feel) is predictive of lower levels of students' depression and better future mental health, and so is a viable target for school prevention activities.

Selected Prevention Programs

Selected programs focus on the subpopulation of children and adolescents that is at higher likelihood of experiencing depression or engaging in suicidal behavior. These include adolescents who have psychological difficulties, students who are making transitions from middle to high school and from high school to higher education, and those who have family members with an affective disorder or who have engaged in past suicidal behavior (DHHS, 2001). Components of a selected program may include developing and teaching decision-making skills and strategies, identifying resources in the community and school for help, coaching and practicing help-seeking behavior for those who work with adolescents, highlighting peer involvement and peers' role in responding to someone who may be depressed or suicidal, and developing strategies for identifying youth who are depressed, have already engaged in, or are currently engaging in suicidal behavior. Many selected programs use school-wide screening procedures to identify students who meet the criteria for at-risk status. Often these students manifest subclinical symptoms of depression or suicidal behavior. Researchers have found that simply asking questions about suicide and suicidal behavior as part of an assessment also produces intervention effects, with youth who completed the assessment showing lower levels of suicidal behavior compared to nonassessed peers (Gould et al., 2005; Thompson, Eggert, Randell, & Pike, 2001).

A school-based program that bridges selected and indicated prevention is the Reconnecting Youth (RY) program (Eggert, Nicholas, & Owens, 1995; Thompson et al., 2001). The RY program focuses on helping high school students at risk for school dropout stay in school and learn to make better decisions academically, emotionally, and with peers.

The RY curriculum includes four major components (Eggert, Nicholas, & Owens, 1995). The first component is self-esteem enhancement. This part of the curriculum helps youth restructure how they see themselves by identifying positive aspects of their behavior as well as learning how to receive and give constructive criticism and compliments. The second component is decision making; students learn a decision-making evaluation model and learn to set achievable goals and to manage their time. The third component is personal control. Students identify stress triggers and learn stress reduction strategies as well as how to ask for support. The last component is interpersonal communication. During this component, students learn how to send "I" messages, develop active listening skills, negotiate conflicts, and develop mood management strategies. These components are taught in a small classroom setting and use a standardized curriculum similar to a math or science type course.

Students who completed the one-semester RY program had lower dropout rates, higher grade point averages, reduced levels of depression, and significantly less suicidal behavior compared to control peers (Eggert, Thompson, Herting, & Nicholas, 1995). Subsequent work using shorter intervention programs have also been shown to be effective in reducing suicidal ideation and attitudes among high-risk adolescents (Randell, Eggert, & Pike, 2001; Thompson et al., 2001).

A number of selected depression prevention programs target adolescents who have characteristics that place them at risk for depression. For example, having a parent with an affective disorder is a known risk factor for childhood depression (Beardslee & Breedlove, 1994). Selected prevention programs by Beardslee and colleagues (Beardslee et al., 1997) have found relatively stable long-term reductions in depressive symptoms in children and adolescents of parents with depressive disorders. Other researchers have adapted the Penn Resiliency Program, which was originally developed as an indicated prevention program (Jaycox, Reivich, Gillham, & Seligman, 1994) to a selected prevention modality (e.g., Cardemil, Reivich, Beevers, Seligman, & James, 2007; Cardemil, Reivich, & Seligman, 2002; Quayle, Dzuirawiec, Roberts, Kane, & Ebsworthy, 2001). For example, Cardemil and colleagues (2002, 2007) targeted low-income Hispanic and African American children as at-risk groups for the prevention program, which draws heavily on the development of optimism and coping strategies. For the most part, specific prevention programs for depression have shown positive outcomes.

Indicated Prevention Programs

Indicated interventions target children or adolescents who have already engaged in suicidal behavior or are experiencing symptoms of depression at a clinical or subsyndromal level. Indicated populations are often identified by screening students for past or current behavior (Kalafat, 2003; Reynolds, 1986a, 1991).

The focus of indicated programs for suicide is to reduce the current crisis or conflict and to reduce the risk of further engagement in suicidal behavior. Components of these programs may include developing and teaching adaptive decision-making strategies that focus on times of stress or emotional dysregulation; accessing emergency help; providing ongoing support to a peer or friend during crisis; understanding psychological disorders and their relationship to depression and suicidal behavior; and identifying at least one caring adult in the home, school, and community from which to seek help (Kalafat, 2003).

Adolescents who have been hospitalized for suicidal behavior present as a subgroup for whom recidivism is a significant concern. In response, King et al. (2006) have developed the Youth-Nominated Support Team, an indicated prevention program that consists of a psychoeducational-social network intervention to increase social supports and treatment compliance, and lessen negative parental perceptions. Based on somewhat mixed although promising initial results, King and colleagues are continuing to develop and "fine tune" this program.

A number of indicated prevention programs have been developed for depression in children and adolescents. Most of these programs first use a school-based screening procedure to identify students who manifest symptoms of the disorder (but do not have a diagnosable affective disorder). Indicated prevention programs for depression include the Penn Resiliency Program (PRP; Chaplin et al., 2006; Gillham, Reivich, Jaycox, & Seligman, 1995; Gillham, Hamilton, Freres, Patton, & Gallop, 2006; Jaycox et al., 1994), the Penn Optimism Program (Gillham, Reivich, & Shatté, 2001; Yu & Seligman, 2002), and the Adolescent Coping with Emotions (Kowalenko et al., 2005). For example, Clarke and colleagues (1995) screened over 1,600 students to identify those with clinical levels of depressive symptoms but no diagnosed affect disorder. Students then either received a cognitive-behavioral prevention intervention (15 sessions) or were considered a "usual care" control. At a one-year follow-up, significantly fewer students in the prevention condition developed a depressive disorder compared to the "usual care" control condition.

Indicated prevention programs for depression and suicidal behaviors come closest to actual treatment in that they target those students who show meaningful signs of the respective psychological problems. Because these programs are designed to treat specific problems that students are experiencing, indicated prevention activities typically draw heavily from more individualized, empirically based interventions.

Summary

We are pleased to note that researchers have taken on the task of empirically testing prevention programs for depression and suicidal behaviors. Such research is critical for determining the efficacy of programs and what should and should not be used in school settings. For the most part, empirical research has not supported the use of universal prevention procedures for making enduring reductions in the development of depression and suicidal behaviors in students, although short-term reductions in depression have been reported. Fortunately, more lasting positive results have been found with the use of selected and indicated prevention procedures (Clarke, 1999; Horowitz & Garber, 2006) for depression. Thus, the most efficacious programs are those that first identify students who are either at risk as a function of a known etiological basis or comorbid condition (selected prevention programs), or manifesting a subsyndromal or clinically significant level of depressive symptoms (indicated prevention). Rapee et al. (2006) suggest that, in addition to indicated prevention programs being more effective in reducing depression, students who participate in them have greater consumer satisfaction than those who participated in universal prevention programs (Rapee et al., 2006).

Each type of prevention/intervention program has strengths and challenges. Each school district or individual school needs to decide what type of program fits best within their school system and with their school resources. What works well for one school may not work for another. Finally, it is important to recognize that these different types of programs are complementary, and each has different foci and intended outcomes.

Barriers and Challenges to the Implementation of Prevention Programs

A number of barriers prevent or challenge the implementation of empirically validated depression and suicide prevention/intervention programs. These barriers include, but are not limited to, lack of accurate information, parents' refusal, school administrative personnel and resources, and funding (Kalafat, 2003; Mazza, 2006; Reynolds & Mazza, 1994). Each of these barriers is discussed in more depth next.

Misinformation and Myths

Misinformation or perpetuation of myths is one of the most difficult barriers to overcome in a school system (Kalafat, 2003; Mazza, 2006). Several prominent myths must be dispelled, especially around the topic of suicidal behavior, in order for depression and suicide prevention programs to be implemented (Reynolds, 1988). The most pervasive myth is that "talking about suicide or suicidal behavior will only increase the likelihood of youth engaging in suicidal behavior." This myth has been mentioned by school administrators, parents, and community professionals. According to Potter and colleagues, numerous prevention and intervention programs have been implemented without causing harm (Potter, Powell, & Kachur, 1995). A randomized control study by Gould and colleagues (2005) further dispels this myth. The study randomly assigned classes to experimental and control groups within six high schools and conducted a two-day screening. The experimental group received questions about suicide during the first survey while those in the control condition did not. The second survey, two days later, was similar for both groups, including questions about suicidal behavior: outcomes of distress, depression, and suicidal ideation were examined. Results showed no differences between the two groups regarding distress scores after the first or second survey. In addition, adolescents identified as high risk (defined as those who have substance use problems, depressive symptoms, or had engaged in previous suicidal behavior) did not differ on distress or suicidal ideation scores between the two groups. Gould and colleagues concluded that there was no evidence that asking questions about suicidal behavior increased rate of suicidality. They confirmed that asking students about suicidal behavior, in the form of suicidal ideation screening, did not increase suicidal behavior. Kalafat and Elias (1992) reported that most adolescents had reasonable attitudes (that having suicidal thoughts is not normal and that help should be sought) and knowledge before a school-based awareness curriculum was implemented. Furthermore, because of the high incidence of suicidal behavior among adolescents, there is a high probability that many students already know of someone who has attempted or completed suicide.

A related myth surrounding suicidal behavior is that parents know if their child has engaged in suicidal behavior (Kashani, Goddard, & Reid, 1989). Unfortunately, children and adolescents do not frequently communicate their suicidal feelings to adults, including their parents. Kashani and colleagues reported that, in a sample of 210 community children and adolescents, 86% of parents were unaware of their child's suicidal thoughts and behaviors. Similar findings have been reported by other researchers (Velez & Cohen, 1988; Walker, Moreau, & Weissman, 1990; Zimmerman & Asnis, 1991). Fortunately, we know from the empirical examination of screening programs for depression and suicidal behavior that, when asked directly, children and adolescents will report their past and current suicidal behavior and depression (Reynolds, 1989b; Reynolds, 1990b; Reynolds & Mazza, 1994).

Parents' Refusal

Although parents often have the best interests of their children in mind, they are often reluctant to have their children and adolescents complete mental health screeners. In studies that required parental consent for their child to participate, the frequency of participation ranged from 33% to 66% (Gould et al., 2005; Levy, & Deykin, 1989; Mazza, 2000). Gould and colleagues (2005) had a 64% participation rate and reported that of the nonparticipants, 61% were due to parents' refusal of consent in comparison to 14% that were due to student refusal. Given the validity of the mental health screeners (Gould et al., 2005; Gutierrez, Watkins, & Collura, 2004; Reynolds, 1991; Reynolds & Mazza, 1999; Shaffer et al., 2004) and the Surgeon General's recommendation for mental health screening (DHHS, 2001), missing a significant proportion of potentially at-risk students because of parents' refusal to consent is a critical problem and one that needs to be addressed for the implementation of prevention programs. The authors' experience has been that once a school board approves a mental health screening for students (at any level from elementary to high school), informs parents of the program, and provides the opportunity for parents to have their child opt out of the screening, typically fewer than 5% of parents do so. The basic parameters of this screening approach for identifying children and adolescents at risk for depression has been described by Reynolds (1986a, 2002).

School Administrators and Personnel

School administrators and personnel can be friends or foes of depression and suicide prevention programs. In his 25-plus years of conducting research in schools, the second author of this chapter identifies school administrators as the single biggest barrier to conducting research that includes the identification of at-risk youth. Both authors acknowledge that school administrators and personnel can be powerful advocates and facilitate the implementation of prevention and intervention type programs, however, even mental health professionals such as school psychologists, social workers, and counselors, who often work closely with these high-risk children and adolescents, have been identified as potential barriers in identifying at-risk youth for depression and suicidal behavior (Eckert, Miller, DuPaul, & Riley-Tillman, 2003).

A study by Eckert and colleagues (Eckert et al., 2003) surveyed 211 school psychologists regarding the acceptability of three types of suicide prevention programs: (a) school-wide curriculum-based program administered to students, (b) faculty and staff in-service training, and (c) self-report screening program. They reported interesting findings. They found that the school-wide curriculum program and the in-service program were rated more acceptable than the screening program among school psychologists, yet it is the screening program that has the empirical evidence for identifying at-risk students. The school psychologists rated the screening program as more intrusive than the other two.

A similar study was conducted with school superintendents regarding suicide prevention programs who rated the in-service and school-wide curriculum as more acceptable compared to the screening program (Scherff, Eckert, & Miller, 2005). Furthermore, the superintendents also rated the screening program as more intrusive than the other two. Overcoming this barrier is directly related to dispelling misinformation about suicide screening: asking direct questions about suicide does not promote suicidal behavior.

School personnel need to be educated about the overwhelming evidence of the value of using such screening programs in proactively identifying at-risk youth (e.g., Gould et al., 2005; Gutierrez et al., 2004; Reynolds, 1991; Reynolds & Mazza, 1999; Shaffer et al., 2004), especially compared to the lack of empirical evidence supporting in-service and school-wide curriculum interventions (Mazza, 1997). Resources, in the form of trained school personnel or community agency personnel working with schools, are needed to follow up with students who have been self-identified as at risk (Kalafat, 2003; Reynolds, 1988, 1991). In some cases, school psychologists and administrators may be reluctant to implement school-wide screening programs if these follow-up resources are not available. Furthermore, the inability to follow up with at-risk students because of lack of resources may only increase the feelings of hopelessness, helplessness, frustration, and guilt (Dyck, 1991).

Funding

The barrier of funding is linked to several other barriers that have been discussed. First, if schools do not have the trained personnel to implement a depression and suicide prevention intervention or to follow up with identified at-risk youth, then money is needed to hire such personnel. Second, most depression and suicide prevention and intervention programs require funds to purchase materials or manuals and train teachers or other facilitators. Many school budgets are strapped for money, and using school dollars to implement a depression and suicide prevention program often means some other program may not be funded. Decisions such as these are difficult to make. However, if the cost-benefit factor is examined, one would be hard pressed to find a more important program that helps students who may be suffering emotional distress and are disengaged from the learning enterprise, and in some cases may saves lives.

Role of School Mental Health Professionals

The role of school mental health professionals in dealing with youth who are at risk for depression and suicidal behavior is twofold. First and foremost, it is important to educate and dispel any misinformation or myths that other school personnel, including administrators, have regarding the identification of at-risk students and implementation of depression and suicide prevention interventions. School mental health professionals are often viewed as the leaders in implementing such programs (Eckert et al., 2003; Mazza, 1997) and will need administrative support as well as additional resources (personnel and money) to increase the likelihood of an effective program.

The second role for school mental health professionals is overseeing and implementing the program itself, including components such as assessment, intervention, and follow-up (monitoring). Each component is discussed separately.

School mental health professionals need to understand that depression and suicidal behavior in children and adolescents are difficult to see externally (Reynolds, 1994; Reynolds & Mazza, 1994). As noted earlier, depression and components of suicidal behavior are internalizing problems. Further, it is important to understand that depression and suicidal behavior in youth are not synonymous, although they are strongly correlated. Reynolds and Mazza (1990), in conducting a school-wide screening for depression and suicidal behavior, found that one-third of the adolescents scoring above the clinical cutoff score on the Suicidal Ideation Questionnaire (Reynolds, 1987), were not above the cutoff score on the Reynolds Adolescent Depression Scale (Reynolds, 1986b).

With the understanding that depression and suicidal behavior are both internalizing disorders, school mental health professionals need to use proactive strategies for identifying youth who are at risk for these mental health problems. Such assessment is often a component of selective and indicated prevention programs. Unlike academic difficulties, for which teachers and/or parents often refer children to school psychologists, reliance on significant others to identify students with depression and suicidal behavior is highly problematic. As stated earlier, most parents do not know if their child is thinking about suicide or has engaged in suicidal behaviors. Instead, allowing students to identify themselves and what they are thinking through screening programs has been found to be an excellent proactive strategy with substantial empirical evidence of effectiveness (Gutierrez et al., 2004; Reynolds & Mazza, 1999; Shaffer et al., 2004) without any iatrogenic effects (Gould et al., 2005). In fact, the U.S. Surgeon General has recommended screening programs, in the *National Strategy for Suicide Prevention: Goals and Objectives for Action,* as an effective means for identifying those at risk for suicidal behavior and related mental health problems (DHHS, 2001).

It is important for school mental health professionals to provide follow-up and monitoring of youth who have been identified and are receiving services either at school or from an outside agency. The follow-up sends an important message to the children or adolescents that they have not been forgotten and that you still care about their mental well-being, even if the services are not being received at school. In addition, it is important that they have an adult contact in each of the major settings—home, school, and community—who is aware of the current situation and what services are being offered. Having helpful adults in each of these settings has been shown to be a protective factor against further adolescent mental health problems (Jessor, Van Den Bos, Vanderryn, Costa, & Turbin, 1995).

In those cases where an adolescent or child is hospitalized due to imminent risk of suicide, visiting the student in the hospital is an important and meaningful gesture. Again, this communicates they are not forgotten just because they are not at school, and that school personnel do care about their mental well-being. In these severe cases, it is also important to develop a school reentry plan that is gradual, with frequent monitoring from a designated school mental health professional. This reentry plan is to minimize the amount of pressure the youth feels in trying to catch up academically and slowly reacclimate the student to the school environment. This type of plan should increase the likelihood of a successful transition back to school.

There are no standardized procedures regarding the amount of monitoring that a depressed or suicidal youth requires. This should be predicated on the severity of the depression and suicidal behavior and the student's home situation. For example, if a student has been identified with mild depression or suicidal ideation, checking in once a week to see how he or she is doing would be appropriate. For those students in the moderate range of severity, a couple of times a week should be scheduled to monitor how they are doing as well as regular communication with parents or other caretakers. Severe cases, as mentioned earlier, require much more frequent monitoring, such as daily, until the students get settled back into the full routine of school, and then monitoring is resumed on a less frequent basis. A critical message is that school personnel notice and care about the mental health of their students.

Strategies for Implementing Depression or Suicidal Behavior Prevention Interventions

Implementing an effective depression and/or suicide prevention intervention requires organizations to provide the necessary foundation to ensure its success. There are several important strategies to be discussed before beginning the implementation stage. Listed in chronological order, these strategies are drawn from the authors' experiences in conducting their own research and in working with schools to implement programs.

The first strategy is to remove the stigma associated with youth depression and suicide. This can be accomplished using a standardized curriculum that helps educate students about the myths surrounding depression and suicidal behavior and also provides appropriate coping strategies to help a friend or classmate who may be dealing with one or both of these psychological problems. Examples of these curricula were mentioned earlier, such as Reconnecting Youth for suicidal behavior and for depression. We noted in the misinformation section that many people do not talk about suicide because they are worried that doing so gives students ideas they would not otherwise have. Second, many parents do not talk about the subject because of a misperception that if a child is suicidal, the parent is doing something wrong or it is their fault. This stigma often closes off avenues of communication and support from adults when a youth is severely depressed, seriously thinking of suicide, or has attempted suicide.

The second strategy is educating school and community stakeholders. This may be accomplished by providing workshops and educational forums to help school personnel and community advocacy networks understand the mental health needs of students and how depression and/or suicidal behavior prevention interventions would work in a particular school. These educational forums and workshops also provide an opportunity for stakeholders to ask questions about any misinformation they may have. Being open to questions and allowing for input lets stakeholders feel more a part of the team and be more likely to support the agreed-on program.

The third strategy is to acknowledge that not all students need a depression or suicidal behavior intervention. As discussed earlier, it is important that knowledge acquisition, identification procedures, and steps to take regarding a suicidal peer be taught universally (Kalafat, 2003; Kalafat & Elias, 1992). However, students who have already experienced depression and/suicidal behavior need indicated programs. Indicated programs are more resource demanding, and thus should be conducted with students in the moderate to severe categories based on the screening procedures.

It is critical to engage the school staff in the prevention program, whether the program is universal, selected, or indicated in its orientation. In some schools, faculty members who do not agree to implementation of the program may undermine the effort. If this happens, students may get the message that what they are doing is not important and that teachers view student academics as more important than their mental health needs. For example, this may occur when teachers are unwilling to use their third period of teaching for mental health screening even though that is the designated time for the entire school to administer the mental health screener. Conversely, faculty who do support the program are more likely to be perceived as caring about the students, and thus to be viewed as a trusted and caring adult by the child or adolescent.

The next component is the identification of community resources and support services. Once the organizational pieces have been established, the school administrators and staff are on board, and the steps to program implementation have been identified, then community service providers should be informed about the program timing and the potential need for their resources. For example, when screening programs for depression and/or suicide are implemented, schools often find students are at imminent risk and require hospitalization or immediate psychological treatment for the acute crisis. Preparing the community service centers and hospitals in advance allows them to plan accordingly and be able to handle such cases during the first few days of identification. Finally, it is important to ensure that students and parents, as well as other school professionals, know to whom in the community they can turn for help.

Summary

In this chapter we described and outlined a number of school-based strategies that have been developed to prevent depression and suicidal behaviors in children and adolescents. For some of these programs, particularly those considered indicated prevention programs, the activities that comprise the program may be considered directed interventions. We strongly urge schools and other professionals to adopt those programs that have demonstrated enduring effects. The effects of selected and indicated prevention programs have been shown to be more meaningful than those of universal programs (Horowitz & Garber, 2006). It is important to recognize that selected and indicated prevention programs typically rely on screening or other forms of risk identification to select program participants. We are pleased that an empirical base is emerging to show the benefits of individual programs as well as potential negative effects (e.g., Gould et al., 2005). Because of the significant impact that the burden of depression and suicidal behaviors has on many children and adolescents, as well as the potential for major life-threatening outcomes, school personnel need to become proactive in addressing these relatively pervasive psychological disturbances.

Discussion Questions

1. What barriers would your school need to overcome in order to implement an assessment and screening program for depression and suicidal behavior among students?

2. How might you integrate a selected or indicated prevention program for depression and suicide into the curricula offered in your district?

3. What community resources and partnerships could you draw on if your district decided to incorporate depression prevention programs into the middle and high schools?

4. If you were making a presentation on depression and suicidal behavior to community leaders and parents, how would you justify the implementation of a suicide prevention program in your district?

References

Anderson, R. N. (2002). Deaths: Leading causes for 2000. *National Vital Statistics Reports, 50*(16). Hyattsville, MD: National Center for Health Statistics.

Aseltine, R. H., & DeMartino, R. (2004). Outcome evaluation of the SOS Suicide Prevention Program. *American Journal of Public Health, 94,* 446–451.

Beardslee, W. R., & Breedlove, L. (1994). Children of parents with affective disorders: Empirical findings and clinical implications. In W. M. Reynolds & H. F. Johnston (Eds.), *Handbook of depression in children and adolescents* (pp. 463–479). New York: Plenum Press.

Beardslee, W. R., Wright, E., Salt, P., Gladstone, T. R. G., Versage, E., & Rothberg, P. C. (1997). Examination of children's responses to two preventive intervention strategies over time. *Journal of the American Academy of Child and Adolescent Psychiatry, 36,* 196–204.

Birmaher, B., Brent, D. A., Kolko, D., Baugher, M., Bridge, J., Holder, D., et al. (2000). Clinical outcome after short-term psychotherapy for adolescents with major depressive disorder. *Archives of General Psychiatry, 57,* 29–36.

Brent, D. A., Perper, J., Kolko, D. J., & Goldstein, C. E. (1988). Risk factors for adolescent suicide: A comparison of adolescent suicide victims with suicidal inpatients. *Archives of General Psychiatry, 45,* 581–588.

Butler, L., Miezitis, S., Friedman, R., & Cole, E. (1980). The effect of two school-based intervention programs on depressive symptoms in preadolescents. *American Educational Research Journal, 17,* 111–119.

Canetto, S. S., & Sakinofsky, I. (1998). The gender paradox in suicide. *Suicide and Life-Threatening Behavior, 28,* 1–23.

Cardemil, E. V., Reivich, K. J., & Seligman, M. E. P. (2002). The prevention of depressive symptoms in low-income minority middle school students. *Prevention & Treatment, 5.* Available at http://content.apa.org/journals/pre/5/1/8

Cardemil, E. V., Reivich, K. J., Beevers, C. G., Seligman, M. E. P., & James, J. (2007). The prevention of depressive symptoms in low-income minority children: Two year follow-up. *Behaviour Research and Therapy. 45,* 313–327.

Center for Disease Control and Prevention (CDC). (2006). Youth risk behavior surveillance—United States, 2005. *Mortality and Morbidity Weekly Review, CDC Surveillance Summaries, 55,* 1–107.

Chaplin, T. M., Gillham, J. E., Reivich, K., Elkon, A. G. L., Samuels, B., Freres, D. R., et al. (2006). Depression prevention for early adolescent girls: A pilot study of all girls versus co-ed groups. *Journal of Early Adolescence, 26,* 110–126.

Clarke, G. N. (1999). Prevention of depression in at-risk samples of adolescents. In C. A. Essau & F. Petermann (Eds.), *Depressive disorders in children and adolescents: Epidemiology, risk factors and treatment* (pp. 341–360). Northvale, NJ: Jason Aronson Inc.

Clarke, G. N., Hawkins, W., Murphy, M., & Sheeber, L. (1993). School-based primary prevention of depressive symptomatology in adolescents: Findings from two studies. *Journal of Adolescent Research, 8,* 183–204.

Clarke, G. N., Hawkins, W., Murphy, M., Sheeber, L. B., Lewinsohn, P. M., & Seeley, J. M. (1995). Targeted prevention of unipolar depressive disorder in an at-risk sample of high school adolescents: A randomized trial of group cognitive intervention. *Journal of the American Academy of Child and Adolescent Psychiatry, 34,* 312–321.

Dyck, R. J. (1991). System-entry issues in school suicide prevention education programs. In A. A. Leenaars & S. Wenckstern (Eds.), *Suicide prevention in schools* (pp. 41–49). New York: Hemisphere Publishing Corporation.

Eastgard, S. (2000). *Youth suicide prevention toolkit.* Seattle, WA: Youth Suicide Prevention Program.

Eckert, T. L., Miller, D. N., DuPaul, G. J., & Riley-Tillman, T. C. (2003). Adolescent suicide prevention: School psychologists' acceptability of school-based programs. *School Psychology Review, 32,* 57–76.

Eggert, L. L., Nicholas, L. J., & Owens, L. M. (1995). *Reconnecting Youth: A peer group approach to building life skills.* Bloomington, IN: National Educational Service.

Eggert, L. L., Thompson, E. A., Herting, J. R., & Nicholas, L. J. (1995). Reducing suicide potential among high-risk youth: Tests of a school-based prevention program. *Suicide and Life-Threatening Behavior, 25,* 276–296.

Essau, C. A., Petermann, F., & Reynolds, W. M. (1999). Classification of depressive disorders. In C. A. Essau & F. Petermann (Eds.), *Depressive disorders in children and adolescents: Epidemiology, risk factors and treatment* (pp. 3–25). Northvale, NJ: Jason Aronson Inc.

Garfinkel, B. D., Froese, A., & Hood, J. (1982). Suicide attempts in children and adolescents. *American Journal of Psychiatry, 139,* 1257–1261.

Gillham, J. E., Hamilton, J., Freres, D. R., Patton, K., & Gallop, R. (2006). Preventing depression among early adolescents in the primary care setting: A randomized controlled study of the Penn Resiliency Program. *Journal of Abnormal Child Psychology, 34,* 203–219.

Gillham, J. E., Reivich, K. J., Jaycox, L. J., & Seligman, M. E. P. (1995). Prevention of depressive symptoms in school children: Two-year follow-up. *Psychological Science, 6,* 343–351.

Gillham, J. E., Reivich, K. J., & Shatté, A. J. (2001). Building optimism and preventing depressive symptoms in children. In E. C. Chang (Ed.), *Optimism and pessimism: Implications for theory, research, and practice* (pp. 301–320). Washington, DC: American Psychological Association.

Gould, M. S., Greenberg, T., Velting, D. M., & Schaffer, D. (2003). Youth suicide risk and preventive interventions: A review of the past 10 years. *Journal of the American Academy of Child and Adolescent Psychiatry, 42,* 386–405.

Gould, M. S., King, R., Greenwald, S., Fisher, P., Schwab-Stone, M., Kramer, R., et al. (1998). Psychopathology associated with suicidal ideation and attempts among children and adolescents. *Journal of the American Academy of Child and Adolescent Psychiatry, 37,* 915–923.

Gould, M. S., Marrocco, F. A., Kleinman, M., Thomas, J. G., Mostkoff, K., Cote, J., et al. (2005). Evaluating iatrogenic risk of youth suicide screening programs: A randomized controlled trial. *Journal of the American Medical Association, 293*, 1635–1643.

Gould, M. S., Velting, D. M., Kleinman, M., Lucas, C., Thomas, J. G., & Chung, M. (2004). Teenagers' attitudes about coping strategies and help-seeking behavior for suicidality. *Journal of the American Academy of Child and Adolescent Psychiatry, 43*, 1124–1133.

Gutierrez, P. M., Watkins, R., & Collura, D. (2004). Suicide risk screening in an urban high school. *Suicide and Life-Threatening Behavior, 34*, 421–428.

Hankin, B. L., Abramson, L. Y., Moffitt, T. E., Silva, P. A., McGee, R., & Angell, K. E. (1998). Development of depression from preadolescence to young adulthood: Emerging gender differences in a 10-year longitudinal study. *Journal of Abnormal Psychology, 107*, 128–140.

Harnett, P. H., & Dadds, M. R. (2004). Training school personnel to implement a universal school-based prevention of depression program under real-world conditions. *Journal of School Psychology, 42*, 343–357.

Horowitz, J. L., & Garber, J. (2006). The prevention of depressive symptoms in children and adolescents: A meta-analytic review. *Journal of Consulting and Clinical Psychology, 74*, 401–415.

Jaycox, L. H., Reivich, K. J., Gillham, J. E., & Seligman, M. E. P. (1994). Prevention of depressive symptoms in school children. *Behaviour Research and Therapy, 32*, 801–816.

Jessor, R., Van Den Bos, J., Vanderryn, J., Costa, F. M., & Turbin, M. S. (1995). Protective factors adolescent problem behavior: Moderator effects and developmental change. *Developmental Psychology, 31*, 923–933.

Kahn, J. S., Kehle, T. J., Jenson, W. R., & Clark, E. (1990). Comparison of cognitive-behavioral, relaxation, and self-modeling interventions for depression among middle-school students. *School Psychology Review, 19*, 196–211.

Kalafat, J. (2003). Suicidal approaches to youth suicide prevention. *American Behavioral Scientist, 46*, 1211–1223.

Kalafat, J., & Elias, M. (1992). Adolescents' experiences with and response to suicidal peers. *Suicide and Life-Threatening Behavior, 22*, 315–321.

Kalafat, J., & Elias, M. (1994). An evaluation of adolescent suicide intervention classes. *Suicide and Life-Threatening Behavior, 24*, 224–233.

Kashani, J. H., Goddard, P., & Reid, J. C. (1989). Correlates of suicidal ideation in a community sample of children and adolescents. *Journal of the American Academy of Child and Adolescent Psychiatry, 28*, 912–917.

King, C. A., Kramer, A., Preuss, L., Kerr, D. C., Weisse, L., & Venkataraman, S. (2006). Youth-nominated support team for suicidal adolescents (Version 1): A randomized controlled trial. *Journal of Consulting and Clinical Psychology, 74*, 199–206.

Kingsbury, S. J. (1993). Clinical components of suicidal intent in adolescent overdoses. *Journal of the American Academy of Child and Adolescent Psychiatry, 32*, 518–520.

Kowalenko, N., Rapee, R. M., Simmons, J., Wignall, A., Hoge, R., Whitefield, K., et al. (2005). Short-term effectiveness of a school-based early intervention program for adolescent depression. *Clinical Child Psychology and Psychiatry, 10,* 493–507.

Ladame, F., & Jeanneret, O. (1982). Suicide in adolescence: Some comments on epidemiology and prevention. *Journal of Adolescence, 5,* 355–366.

Levy, J. C., & Deykin, E. Y. (1989). Suicidality, depression, and substance abuse in adolescence. *American Journal of Psychiatry, 146,* 1462–1467.

Lewinsohn, P. M., Clarke, G. N., Hops, H., & Andrews, J. (1990). Cognitive-behavioral treatment for depressed adolescents. *Behavior Therapy, 21,* 385–401.

Mazza, J. J. (1997). School-based suicide prevention programs: Are they effective? *School Psychology Review, 26,* 382–396.

Mazza, J. J. (2000). The relationship between posttraumatic stress symptomatology and suicidal behavior in school-based adolescents. *Suicide and Life-Threatening Behaviors, 30,* 91–103.

Mazza, J. J. (2006). Youth suicidal behavior: A crisis in need of attention. In F. A. Villarruel, & T. Luster (Eds.), *Adolescent mental health* (pp. 155–177). Westport, CT: Greenwood Publishing Group.

Mazza, J. J., & Reynolds, W. M. (2001). An investigation of psychopathology in nonreferred suicidal and nonsuicidal adolescents. *Suicide and Life-Threatening Behavior, 31,* 282–302.

McIntosh, J. L. (2006). Suicide statistics. Accessed on August 9, 2006, at http://www.suicidology.org/associations/1045/files/2003datapgb.pdf

Merry, S., McDowell, H., Wild, C. J., Bir, J., & Cunliffe, R. (2004). A randomized placebo-controlled trial of a school-based depression prevention program. *Journal of the American Academy of Child and Adolescent Psychiatry, 43,* 538–547.

Miller, D. N., DuPaul, G. J., & Lutz, J. G. (2002). School-based psychosocial interventions for childhood depression: Acceptability of treatments among school psychologists. *School Psychology Quarterly, 17,* 78–99.

Mufson, L., Moreau, D., Weissman, M. M., & Klerman, G. L. (1993). *Interpersonal psychotherapy for depressed adolescents.* New York: Guilford Press.

Muñoz, R. F., Mrazek, P. J., & Haggerty, R. J. (1996). Institute of Medicine report on prevention of mental disorders: Summary and commentary. *American Psychologist, 51,* 1116–1122.

Muris, P., Bogie, N., & Hoogsteder, A. (2001). Effects of an early intervention group program for anxious and depressed adolescents: A pilot study. *Psychological Reports, 88,* 481–482.

National Center for Health Statistics (NCHS). (2003). Historical tables for 1979–1998. Retrieved May 31, 2004, from http://www.cdc.gov/nchs/data/statab/gm290–98.pdf

National Center for Injury and Prevention Control (NCIPC). (2006). 10 leading causes of death, United States. Retrieved August 9, 2006, from http://webapp.cdc.gov/sasweb/ncipc/leadcaus10.html

National Institute of Mental Health (NIMH). (2000). *Depression in children and adolescents: A fact sheet for physicians.* (NIH Publication No. 00–4744). Rockville, MD: U.S. Department of Health and Human Services.

Overholser, J. C., Hemstreet, A. H., Spirito, A., & Vyse, S. (1989). Suicide awareness programs in the schools: Effects of gender and personal experience.

Journal of the American Academy of Child and Adolescent Psychiatry, 28, 925–930.

Overholser, J., & Spirito, A. (2003). Precursors to adolescent suicide attempts. In A. Spirito & J. Overholser (Eds.), *Evaluating and treating adolescent suicide attempters: From research to practice* (pp. 19–40). San Diego, CA: Academic Press.

Potter, L., Powell, K. E., & Kachur, P. S. (1995). Suicide prevention from a public health perspective. *Suicide and Life-Threatening Behaviors, 25,* 82–91.

Pössel, P., Horn, A. B., Hautzinger, M., & Groen, G. (2004). School-based universal primary prevention of depressive symptoms in adolescents: Results of a 6-month follow-up. *Journal of the American Academy of Child and Adolescent Psychiatry, 43,* 1003–1010.

Poznanski, E. O., & Mokros, H. B. (1994). Phenomenology and epidemiology of mood disorders in children and adolescents. In W. M. Reynolds & H. F. Johnston (Eds.), *Handbook of depression in children and adolescents* (pp. 19–39). New York: Plenum.

Quayle, D., Dzuirawiec, S., Roberts, C., Kane, R., & Ebsworthy, G. (2001). The effect of an optimism and life skills program on depressive symptoms in preadolescence. *Behaviour Change, 18,* 194–203.

Randell, B. P., Eggert, L. L., & Pike, K. C. (2001). Immediate post intervention effects of two brief youth suicide prevention interventions. *Suicide and Life-Threatening Behaviors, 31,* 41–61.

Rapee, R. M., Wignall, A., Sheffield, J., Kowalenko, N., Davis, A., McLoone, J., & Spence, S. (2006). Adolescents' reactions to universal and indicated prevention programs for depression: Perceived stigma and consumer satisfaction. *Prevention Science, 7,* 167–177.

Reynolds, W. M. (1986a). A model for the screening and identification of depressed children and adolescents in school settings. *Professional School Psychology, 1,* 117–129.

Reynolds, W. M. (1986b). *Reynolds Adolescent Depression Scale.* Odessa, FL: Psychological Assessment Resources.

Reynolds, W. M. (1987). *Suicidal Ideation Questionnaire.* Odessa, FL: Psychological Assessment Resources.

Reynolds, W. M. (1988). *Suicidal Ideation Questionnaire: Professional manual.* Odessa, FL: Psychological Assessment Resources.

Reynolds, W. M. (1989a). *Reynolds Child Depression Scale: Professional manual.* Odessa, FL: Psychological Assessment Resources.

Reynolds, W. M. (1989b). Suicidal ideation and depression in adolescents: Assessment and research. In P. F. Lovibond & P. Wilson (Eds.), *Clinical and abnormal psychology* (pp. 125–135). Amsterdam: Elsevier Science Publishers.

Reynolds, W. M. (1990a). Depression in children and adolescents: Nature, diagnosis, assessment, and treatment. *School Psychology Review, 19,* 158–173.

Reynolds, W. M. (1990b). Development of a semistructured clinical interview for suicidal behaviors in adolescents. *Psychological Assessment: A Journal of Consulting and Clinical Assessment, 2,* 382–390.

Reynolds, W. M. (1991). A school-based procedure for the identification of adolescents at-risk for suicidal behavior. *Family and Community Health, 14,* 64–75.

Reynolds, W. M. (1992). Depression in children and adolescents. In W. M. Reynolds (Ed.), *Internalizing disorders in children and adolescents* (pp. 149–254). New York: John Wiley.

Reynolds, W. M. (1994). Assessment of depression in children and adolescents by self-report questionnaires. In W. M. Reynolds & H. F. Johnston (Eds.), *Handbook of depression in children and adolescents* (pp. 209–234). New York: Plenum Press.

Reynolds, W. M. (1998). Depression in children and adolescents. In T. H. Ollendick (Ed.), *Comprehensive clinical psychology: Vol. 4. Children and adolescents: Clinical formulations and treatment* (pp. 419–461). New York: Pergamon Press.

Reynolds, W. M. (2002). *Reynolds Adolescent Depression Scale: Professional manual* (2nd ed.). Odessa, FL: Psychological Assessment Resources.

Reynolds, W. M. (2006). Depression. In M. Hersen (Ed.), *Clinical handbook of behavioral assessment, Vol. II: Child assessment* (pp. 291–311). New York: Academic Press.

Reynolds, W. M., & Coats, K.I. (1986). A comparison of cognitive-behavioral therapy and relaxation training for the treatment of depression in adolescents. *Journal of Consulting and Clinical Psychology, 54,* 653–660.

Reynolds, W. M., & Johnston, H. F. (1994). The nature and study of depression in children and adolescents. In W. M. Reynolds & H. F. Johnston (Eds.), *Handbook of depression in children and adolescents* (pp. 3–17). New York: Plenum Press.

Reynolds, W. M., & Mazza, J. J. (1990, April). *Suicidal behavior and depression in adolescents.* Paper presented at the annual conference of the American Psychological Association, Boston.

Reynolds, W. M., & Mazza, J. J. (1994). Suicide and suicidal behavior. In W. M. Reynolds & H. F. Johnston (Eds.), *Handbook of depression in children and adolescents* (pp. 520–580). New York: Plenum Publishers.

Reynolds, W. M., & Mazza, J. J. (1995, March). *Suicidal attempt behaviors in rural youth: Comparisons with urban and suburban school-based adolescents.* Invited paper presentation at the Child and Adolescent Rural Injury Control Conference, Madison, WI.

Reynolds, W. M., & Mazza, J. J. (1999). Assessment of suicidal ideation in young inner-city youth: Reliability and validity of the Suicidal Ideation Questionnaire–JR. *School Psychology Review, 28,* 17–30.

Riggs, S., & Cheng, T. (1988). Adolescents' willingness to use a school-based clinic in view of expressed health concerns. *Journal of Adolescent Health Care, 9,* 208–213.

Scherff, A. R., Eckert, T. L., & Miller, D. N. (2005). Youth suicide prevention: A survey of public school superintendents' acceptability of school-based programs. *Suicide and Life-Threatening Behaviors, 35,* 154–169.

Shaffer, D., Garland, A., Vieland, V., Underwood, M., & Busner, C. (1991). The impact of curriculum based suicide prevention programs for teenagers. *Journal of the American Academy of Child and Adolescent Psychiatry, 30,* 588–596.

Shaffer, D., Gould, M. S., Fisher, P., Trautman, P., Moreau, D., Kleinman, M., et al. (1996). Psychiatric diagnosis in child and adolescent suicide. *Archives of General Psychiatry, 53,* 339–348.

Shaffer, D., Scott, M., Wilcox, H., Maslow, C., Hicks, R., Lucas, C. P., et al. (2004). The Columbia Suicide Screen: Validity and reliability of a screen for youth suicide and depression. *Journal of the American Academy of Child & Adolescent Psychiatry, 43,* 71–79.

Shochet, I. M., Dadds, M. R., Ham, D., & Montague, R. (2006). School connectedness is an underemphasized parameter in adolescent mental health: Results of a community prediction study. *Journal of Clinical Child and Adolescent Psychology, 35,* 170–179.

Shochet, I. M., Dadds, M. R., Holland, D., Whitefield, K., Harnett, P. H., & Osgarby, S. (2001). The efficacy of a universal school-based program to prevent adolescent depression. *Journal of Clinical Child Psychology, 30,* 303–315.

Spence, S. H., Sheffield, J., & Donovan, C. L. (2003). Preventing adolescent depression: An evaluation of the Problem Solving for Life program. *Journal of Consulting and Clinical Psychology, 71,* 3–13.

Spence, S. H., Sheffield, J., & Donovan, C. L. (2005). Long-term outcome of a school-based, universal approach to prevention of depression in adolescents. *Journal of Consulting and Clinical Psychology, 73,* 160–167.

Stark, K. D., Reynolds, W. M., & Kaslow, N. J. (1987). A comparison of the relative efficacy of self-control therapy and behavioral problem-solving therapy for depression in children. *Journal of Abnormal Child Psychology, 15,* 91–113.

Thompson, E. A., Eggert, L. L., Randell, B. P., & Pike, K. C. (2001). Evaluation of indicated suicide risk prevention approaches for potential high school dropouts. *American Journal of Public Health, 91,* 742–752.

U.S. Department of Health and Human Services (DHHS). (2001). *National strategy for suicide prevention: Goals and objectives for action.* Rockville, MD: DHHS. Retrieved October 2, 2006, from http://mentalhealth.samhsa .gov/publications/allpubs/ SMA01-3517/

Velez, C. N., & Cohen, P. (1988). Suicidal behavior and ideation in a community sample of children: Maternal and youth reports. *Journal of the American Academy of Child and Adolescent Psychiatry, 27,* 349–356.

Vostanis, P., Feehan, C., Grattan, E., & Bickerton, W. L. (1996). A randomized controlled outpatient trial of cognitive-behavioural treatment for children and adolescents with depression: 9-month follow-up. *Journal of Affective Disorders, 40,* 105–116.

Walker, M., Moreau, D., & Weissman, M. M. (1990). Parents' awareness of children's suicide attempts. *American Journal of Psychiatry, 147,* 1364–1366.

Wood, A., Harrington, R., & Moore, A. (1996). Controlled trial of a brief cognitive-behavioural intervention in adolescent patients with depressive disorders. *Journal of Child Psychology and Psychiatry, 37,* 737–746.

Yu, D. L., & Seligman, M. E. P. (2002). Preventing depressive symptoms in Chinese children. *Prevention & Treatment, 5,* n.p. Available at http://journals .apa.org/prevention/volume5/pre0050009a.html

Zimmerman, J. K., & Asnis, G. M. (1991, August). *Parents' knowledge of children's suicide attempts: Findings and implications for treatment.* Paper presented at the Annual Conference, American Psychological Association, San Francisco.

About the Authors

James J. Mazza is Associate Professor of Educational Psychology at the University of Washington. His research focuses on adolescent mental health and the identification of youth who are at risk for depression or suicidal behavior.

William M. Reynolds is Professor of Psychology at Humboldt State University. His research interests include psychological test development (including published measures of depression and suicidal ideation, among others) and research investigating the nature and treatment of internalizing disorders in children and adolescents.

PART III

Policy and Evaluation

10

Evaluating Quality and Effectiveness of Population-Based Services

Bonnie K. Nastasi

John H. Hitchcock

The scope of population-based mental health services challenges traditional conceptions of service delivery and evaluation in contemporary schools. Doll and Cummings (chapter 1, this volume) define population-based school mental health services as follows.

> [Population-based mental health services are] designed to meet the mental health needs of all students enrolled in a school. They are predicated on the premise that students' psychological wellness is a precondition for their school success and that, in the same way that teachers are responsible for teaching all children to read, school mental health providers

are responsible for ensuring that all students have the psycho-logical competence needed for learning. . . . Ideally, population-based mental health services will have at least four goals: (a) to promote the psychological well-being of all students so that they can achieve developmental competence; (b) to pro-mote caretaking environments that nurture students and allow them to overcome minor risks and challenges; (c) to provide protective support to students at high risk for developmental failures; and (d) to remediate social, emotional or behavioral disturbances so that students can develop competence. (p. 3)

Doll and Cummings elaborate, noting that collaborative, community-based partnerships are needed to provide the systems of care that are hallmarks of population-based services, and that services can focus at levels ranging from a whole district to an individual student. Population-based services use data-based decision making to address the mental health needs of all students. This entails searching for trends to identify possible causes for concern and to develop services tailored to the context of a given school or district. This generally entails individual, classwide, school-wide, and/or district-wide inter-ventions, which in turn entail engaging stakeholders outside a school, such as families and community members.

From an evaluation perspective the preceding description speaks volumes, and it offers critical guidance on choosing an approach that can determine if application of population-based services in a given district or community is meritorious, and how these services might be altered to improve them. When it comes to evaluation, one must make a number of choices about purpose, scope, and methodology. This chapter is written to increase the reader's awareness of these choices and, subsequently, to describe a model that is equal to the task of adequately evaluating a population-based services program.

Moving From Traditional to Comprehensive Mixed-Methods Participatory Evaluation

A review of textbooks and journal articles on program evaluation spanning the last couple of decades suggests that evaluation remains as much an art as a science, and is anything but a unified field when it comes to fundamental issues of purpose, methodology, and the role of stakeholders (see, for example, Campbell, 1969; Cronbach, 1982; Fetterman, 1994; 2000; Rossi, Lipsey & Freeman, 2004; Weiss, 1998; Worthen & Saunders, 1987). Indeed, the field has been described as contentious (Rossi et al., 2004) and fragmented (Scriven, 1984);

there is even argument over basic terms in the field (see Worthen & Saunders, 1987). As Figure 10.1[1] on page 248 suggests, a byzantine set of decisions must be made about the status of scientific standards relative to the utility of the information, length of inquiry, methodological approaches, status of the evaluator relative to stakeholders, and focus of the questions to be asked. The goals of a given evaluation and the politics related to program goals influence a series of issues (e.g., utility of information vs. scientific standards) that lie on continua of decisions to be made, hence the bidirectional arrows.

Evaluation necessitates decision making about a number of issues, the first six of which are depicted as continua: (a) source of validity (practical utility ↔ scientific standards), (b) length of inquiry (short-term ↔ long-term), (c) methodology (qualitative ↔ mixed-method ↔ quantitative), (d) role of evaluator relative to participants (expert ↔ participatory), (e) complexity of target dimensions (multidimensional ↔ isolated), (f) propinquity of target outcomes (distal ↔ proximal), (g) evaluation goals, and (h) political issues. The multiplicity of issues underscores the complexity of decision making in evaluation. What further complicates the decision-making process is that these issues are neither mutually exclusive nor are they necessarily exhaustive.

Continua of Decisions

One issue is whether an evaluation will, first and foremost, generate scientifically rigorous information that can be used to inform a broader social problem, or findings should be tailored to the needs of specific stakeholders. As Rossi and colleagues (2004) note, it is ideal for both aims to be accomplished, but this is not always possible given the resources required to conduct scientifically rigorous evaluations. Thus, one needs to consider the context in which the work will be carried out and determine whether these two goals can be accomplished, whether they are at odds, and if so, whether some balance can be reached. An evaluator must also consider if a study is short or long term (which is often determined by finances), and if a design should isolate and measure specific outcomes or assess the multiplicity of variables tied to any given intervention. In the context of population-based services, the focus might be on a small number of outcomes measured by behavior checklists that are indicative of mental health, or perhaps on the complex interplay between school personnel, community members, and parents that occurs when these stakeholders attempt to implement a school-wide plan. Related to this question is whether an evaluator is interested in outcomes that, presumably, are closely tied to the intervention (i.e., proximal) or

Figure 10.1 Continua of Evaluation Decisions

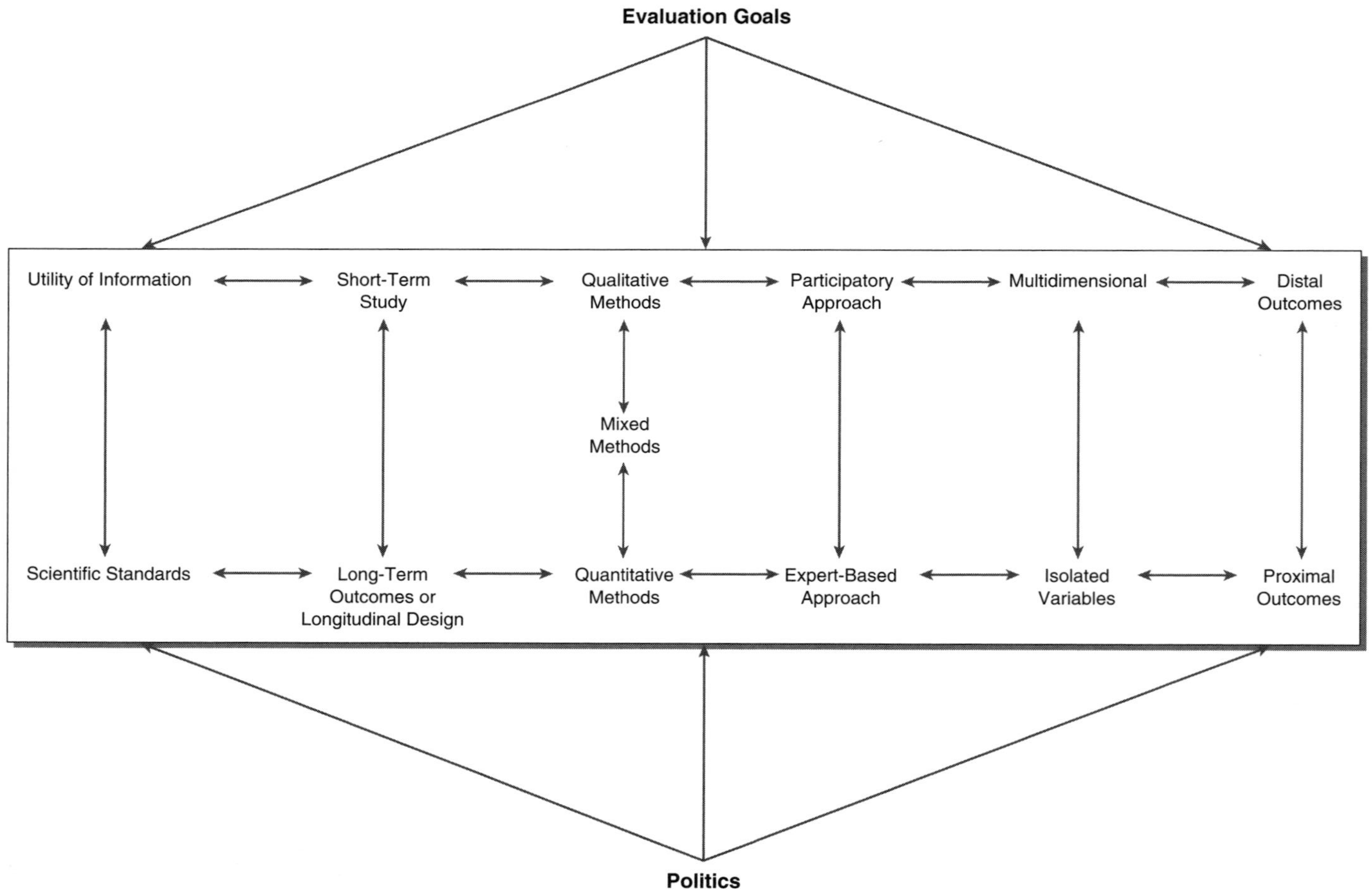

there is an interest in more distal outcomes. In population-based services, this might mean focusing only on indicators of, say, externalized and internalized behavioral concerns among students, versus gathering data on broader concerns such as whether mental health stigma might be reduced in the broader community.

The style or role of the evaluator in relationship to stakeholders can also be characterized along a continuum, ranging from an expert-based approach to a participatory one (Figure 10.1). The nature of the work will again inform what stance is most appropriate. In some cases stakeholders might be interested in having an external evaluator gather evidence on a program's effects and have little interest in how data are collected and analyzed as long as conclusions are defensible to a scientific community. Hence, an expert-based approach may be desirable. In other cases, stakeholders may be deeply vested in learning about the processes of the evaluation, have critical information to share, and wish to develop their own evaluation expertise in the hopes that they can better manage a long-term, sustainable program. This would likely require an evaluator who enters a context in an expert role and eventually transitions to a participatory approach, or perhaps adopts the participatory approach at the outset.

Figure 10.1 also depicts decisions to be made about methodologies to be adopted for the evaluation. Again, depending on context and the questions at hand, qualitative approaches may trump quantitative ones or vice versa. In many cases, a mixed-method approach that uses and mixes quantitative and qualitative traditions may be ideal. The term "mixing" suggests that quantitative and qualitative approaches are not used in a parallel fashion, but rather are combined to generate findings that each style might not uncover if used in isolation (Tashakkori & Teddlie, 2003). In a population-based services setting, one may endeavor to determine if the model yields better mental health outcomes among a group of students, after some given time period, relative to a counterfactual condition. An evaluator espousing a strict quantitative paradigm would likely prefer a place-based randomized controlled trial in which schools, districts, or perhaps communities are randomly assigned to a treatment and control condition.

Such social experiments are lauded as having the best internal validity among the available options (Boruch, 1997; Shadish, Cook, & Campbell, 2002) and are underutilized (Boruch, DeMoya, & Snyder, 2002). On the other hand, an evaluator may have questions that fall outside of whether population-based services were effective. A qualitative perspective might focus on unique interplays among stakeholders and the impacts that given entities have on the mental health needs of students in a specific community. If resources permit, it would be possible to mix these approaches and generate findings that might otherwise be hard to uncover. For example, attrition of research participants is always a concern in a randomized experiment, and qualitative methods might be used to study why it might have occurred and elucidate its impacts (Shadish, Cook, & Campbell, 2002). As another example, mixed methods might be used sequentially, using qualitative inquiry to identify hypotheses that can be further investigated with quantitative techniques (Chatterji, 2004–2005; Tashakkori & Teddlie, 2003). Consider the fact that communities are likely to vary on a number of socioeconomic and cultural factors, and that culture can have powerful influences over mental health services (American Psychological Association, 2003; U.S. Department of Health and Human Services, 1999, 2001). Decision makers would almost certainly take cultural issues into account when incorporating a population-based services model in their community, and this matter is better studied with descriptive methods, which are often qualitative. Once knowledge of best practices is developed and the population-based services program is tightened to deal with matters of culture and context, a longer-term experiment may be in order.

Goals and Politics

All of the issues depicted in Figure 10.1 are influenced by the goals of an evaluation and the politics surrounding it. Again, the evaluation literature is rife with debate about these matters, and a maze of decisions potentially awaits the program evaluator at the beginning of a project. Despite years of contention and changes surrounding matters of methodology, consultation models, and purpose of evaluations, careful considerations of goals, context, and politics will yield solid ideas regarding an evaluation plan. On this last point, the evaluation literature has long recognized that politics impacts an evaluation (Weiss, 1993). Consider an evaluation of a school that has recently implemented a response to intervention model (RTI), which is similar to population-based services if not a form of it. One would need to consider varying perspectives such as whether members of the school view RTI as a special education initiative being forced on so-called regular education staff. Perhaps psychologists in the school feel threatened by a diminished emphasis on more traditional IQ-achievement discrepancy approaches as a basis for placing students in special education. It would be worthwhile for the evaluator to have a sense of whether administrators are championing RTI as a fundamental shift in how business is done or view it as another fad being forced on them. Related questions might be what state-level policies say about implementing the approach and how community members react to seeing all elementary school students being screened for academic and even behavioral concerns. Indeed, the evaluator should consider what effect the act of evaluating the program might have on the perception of RTI. Would this yield confidence that the program is being systematically researched and outcomes will help steer implementation? Or could the presence of the evaluator lead school members to conclude that the jury is still out on an unproven approach? Careful examination of these political issues would certainly help determine how an evaluation should start and begin to separate out short- and long-term goals.

As far as goals are concerned, Rossi and colleagues (2004) suggest evaluations typically examine one or more of the following: "(a) the need for the program, (b), the program's design, (c) its implementation and service delivery, (d) its impact or outcomes, and (e) its efficiency" (p. 18). Clear delineation of evaluation goals will go a long way in identifying how to evaluate the quality and effectiveness of population-based services and will guide decisions such as whether a program should be formative or summative in nature (i.e., using evaluation to help develop a program or make an overall statement as to its worth),[2] what methodologies to use, and what variables should be identified. Of course, the need to identify goals as a way to address questions such as what methodologies to use appears at first glance to be elementary. But in practice, issues such as research paradigm wars can confuse even basic matters such as choosing methodologies that are suited to the task (Creswell, 2002; Onwuegbuzie, 2002; Rallis & Rossman, 2003).

Evaluating Population-Based Services: More Basic Considerations

So far we have discussed eight broad considerations when thinking through an evaluation plan (see Figure 10.1): (a) source of validity (practical utility versus scientific standards); (b) length of inquiry (short-term versus long-term); (c) methodology (qualitative versus mixed methods versus quantitative); (d) role of evaluator relative to participants (expert versus participatory); (e) complexity of target dimensions (multidimensional versus isolated); (f) propinquity of target outcomes (distal versus proximal); (g) evaluation goals; and (h) political issues. We also have noted that the opening description of population-based services speaks volumes about making related evaluation decisions. Now consider the elements that would go into a long-term, comprehensive program evaluation plan of these services. It would be capable of handling the views of multiple stakeholders, a balance of scientific rigor and providing data that are immediately useful to stakeholders. This in turn would require that the evaluation be able to handle cultural and/or contextual specificity, shifting evaluator roles ranging from expert-based to participatory approaches, and likely mixed methods. Ideally, the evaluation would be able to gather data on multiple outcome measures, whether they are distal and proximal. Finally, the approach should set the stage for asking causal questions (i.e., Does the use of population-based services lead to better student outcomes compared to the status quo?). Population-based services in schools are a relatively new concept, so it is safe to assume that there is little if any literature on how to proceed. The remainder of this chapter therefore endeavors to set the stage for this work. Because of the scope of varying evaluation goals in the context of population-based services, the major focus is on how to evaluate their implementation, impact, and efficiency.

Drawing from the preceding ideas, one can surmise that formative evaluations would focus on the need for a program and initial ideas on fitting population-based services to a particular school. This book provides much of the broader justification for such services through theory, clinical/practitioner, and policy-based arguments. Justifying the approach in a particular school might be a matter of analyzing archival school data (see Shadish, Cook, & Campbell, 2002, for some related caveats on data quality) and completing relatively simple descriptive work. More advanced formative evaluation approaches such as the use of focus groups and case study methodologies (see Yin, 1994) can also determine whether these services should be tried in a school and at what level. Finally, establishing a theory of how the population-based services might work (i.e., program theory; see Weiss, 1998) in a given school/district would help identify how best to implement program ideas and elucidate presumed causal mechanisms that explain their impacts. A program theory, in essence, posits an explanation of how program inputs and outputs are tied together, or put another way, an explanation of how a given program might cause change. For example, a data-based service plan is, by its very nature, context specific. Thus, articulating why a given service is expected to work in a given district will go a long way toward setting the stage for other evaluation goals, such as showing how these services are more effective than some comparison condition and how they can be improved and even sustained over a long period of time. As Weiss (1998) points out, the initial theory can be wrong, but establishing one is an important first step.

In that spirit, recall that population-based services involve mental health service plans for all students, whether referred or not, and involve school- to community-wide supports. Details will vary by context, but the implicit program theory is that a combination of universal, selected, and indicated services will yield superior planning compared to the status quo of focusing services on select students after they exhibit symptoms of distress. Furthermore, universal and selected services will be comprehensive, entail screening of students and data-based decision making, and capitalize on district-specific strengths that can generate a localized service plan. Hence, a population-based services evaluation approach would entail the aforementioned elements, where cultural-specificity and multiple stakeholder views are accounted for. Given the dual focus of these services on individual students and broader entities such as classrooms or schools, an evaluation approach should also have the flexibility needed to describe outcomes at multiple levels. This approach would almost certainly necessitate a mixed-method design. A quantitative design that yields causal data at various levels would entail a combination of place-based random assignment using a mixed-model (i.e., hierarchical linear modeling [HLM]) analysis framework, some application of growth curve modeling, or a combination of both approaches. Such an evaluation would be meritorious, but much preparation would be needed to set the stage for this work. Indeed, it is inadvisable to attempt such experiments without solid information about program implementation and theory of change (Shadish, Cook, & Campbell, 2002). It is hard to see how context-specificity surrounding localized service plans would be adequately addressed. A qualitative approach, meanwhile, would likely not be well suited for the large samples involved or be as effective in generating causal data.

Extended-Term Mixed-Methods (ETMM) Designs for Program Evaluation

In response to limitations of randomized controlled trials for evaluating educational programs implemented in real-life settings, Chatterji (2004–2005) proposed Extended-Term Mixed-Methods (ETMM) evaluation designs that capitalize on the methodological strengths of multiple designs and document the long-term (often, multiyear) efforts characteristic of field-based research and population-based mental health services. The general approach is sequenced, so that formative/descriptive evaluation plans and methodologies can be followed by more focused causal questions. Throughout the evaluation stages, mixed-method applications are used as needed and the approach is necessarily long term. Chatterji also recommends articulating program theory to set the stage for studying environmental, systemic, and site-specific factors. The net result of these long-term

efforts can yield detailed descriptive information about a program
that is informed by multiple stakeholder groups, causal data on its
effects, and capacity to inform the local needs of stakeholders (e.g.,
make program improvements and justify program sustainability).
In a population-based services context, this model can promote the
capacity to gather data on program effects at multiple units of analysis (e.g., student, classroom, district, and community) and generate a
unified picture of how services were implemented. This in turn can
inform program management efforts and set the stage for randomized controlled trials.

Chatterji's (2004–2005) framework provides broad ideas for how
to implement a useful population-based services evaluation plan
across a series of stages. What the reader still needs is an overview of
how to gather data in a manner that checks for idiosyncratic changes
across context that may arise because of aforementioned cultural
specificity, politics, and resources that differ across schools. In the
next section, we describe an evaluation model that is designed to be
comprehensive (multimethod, multisource, multipurpose), uses
mixed research methods, involves participation of key stakeholders,
addresses cultural specificity and political context, and focuses on
both needs and resources. The *Model for Comprehensive Mixed-Methods
Participatory Evaluation (CMMPE)* reflects the principles of ETMM
proposed by Chatterji (see Table 10.1) and encompasses criteria set
forth in the most recent revision of the *Procedural and Coding Manual
for Review of Evidence-Based Interventions* developed by the Task Force
on Evidence-Based Interventions in School Psychology.[3]

Table 10.1   Principles of Extended-Term Mixed-Methods (ETMM) Evaluation Designs

---

1. ETMM evaluation designs employ a long-term timeline that targets a significant part of the lifespan of a program at given site(s) for systematic study.

2. ETMM designs are guided by a program's theory and empirically based understandings of environmental, systemic, and site-specific factors that could potentially influence program outcomes.

3. ETMM designs deliberately incorporate formative and summative evaluation phases in the overall research plan, with at least one feedback loop for educating stakeholders and program personnel on improving "treatment fidelity" and program delivery.

4. ETMM designs incorporate sharply focused causal questions in appropriately timed field experiments, and incorporate well-defined treatment and interaction variables in the design.

5. ETMM designs effectively combine qualitative and quantitative research evidence to obtain understandings of how, why, and when a program works, and to inform causal interpretations.

Source: Chatterji (2004–2005, pp. 19–20).

Model for Comprehensive Mixed-Methods Participatory Evaluation (CMMPE)

In the next several sections we introduce a model for evaluating population-based school mental health services, Comprehensive Mixed-Methods Participatory Evaluation (CMMPE; see Figure 10.2 on page 256, reprinted from Nastasi, Moore, & Varjas, 2004) and describe its foundations, underlying assumptions, and ideas on how to implement this evaluation model. The CMMPE addresses all the key decisions involved in evaluation design, and can be applied along the continua of decisions relevant to source of validity, length of inquiry, methodology, role of evaluator, complexity of target dimensions, and propinquity of outcomes. Evaluation goals and political issues provide the backdrop for decision making as well. We will describe and illustrate the model using an example from a multiyear district-wide drug and sexual risk prevention program conducted in an urban school setting. We begin with a brief description of the foundations and assumptions of CMMPE. (More detailed discussion of CMMPE can be found in Nastasi, 2004; Nastasi, Moore, & Varjas, 2004.)

Foundations of CMMPE

CMMPE is founded on school psychology and applied anthropology concepts including participatory consultation, reflective (science-based) practice, participatory action research, and ethnography. These are the foundations of the Participatory Culture-Specific Intervention Model (PCSIM; see Nastasi, Moore, & Varjas, 2004), used to guide the design, implementation, and evaluation of school- and community-based interventions within a population-based framework. *Participatory consultation*, building on current models of collaborative consultation, involves stakeholders (those with vested interests or resources) as partners in the process of intervention development, with the goal of implementing change efforts (prevention, intervention, treatment) that are acceptable, socially valid, effective, sustainable, and institutionalized.

Reflective (science-based) practice (also referred to as *intervention-as-research*; Nastasi, 2004), consistent with current conceptions of data-based decision making, is characterized by the application of a research process (iterative data collection, analysis, and interpretation) to the design, implementation, and evaluation of interventions in field settings. Intervention-as-research also is consistent with action research models in applied anthropology (Partridge, 1985; S. L. Schensul, 1985), which uses an iterative theory-research-action process to facilitate social change.

Figure 10.2   Comprehensive Mixed-Methods Participatory Evaluation of
Population-Based School Mental Health Services. This model
addresses the multiplicity of evaluation decisions depicted in
Figure 10.1, and depicts the complexity of program
evaluation within a participatory culture-specific program
framework. Success is defined by the integration of multiple
components, based on perspectives of multiple stakeholders.
Determination of program success depends on the systematic
integration of qualitative and quantitative data, gathered via
mixed-methods design.

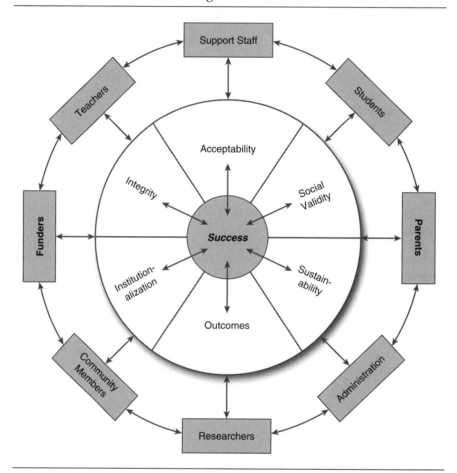

Source: Nastasi, B. K., Moore, R. B., & Varjas, K. M. (2004). *School-based mental health
services: Creating comprehensive and culturally specific programs.* Washington, DC: APA.
Copyright 2004 American Psychological Association. Reprinted with permission.

Conducted in partnership with key stakeholders, *participatory
action research* (PAR; e.g., J. J. Schensul, 1998; Schensul & Schensul,
1992) involves the following iterative process of program development (Nastasi, 1998): Theory and research → research questions →
formative research → culture-specific (local) theory → culture/specific

(local) intervention→ formative and summative evaluation → theory and research. The primary purpose of PAR is to generate social and cultural change that addresses culturally relevant issues and reflects the needs and resources within the local context. In the process of change, researchers/interventionists engage the local stakeholders in a participatory reflective process.

Culturally relevant change depends on a thorough understanding of the culture (shared beliefs, values, language, concepts, and norms) from the *emic* (insider's or participant's) perspective, typically acquired through ethnography (study of culture). Ethnographic research methods[4] (most commonly, participant observation; in-depth interviewing; and artifacts, permanent products, or documents) are consistent with tools of school mental health professionals such as school psychologists. Although typically placed within a qualitative framework, ethnographic methods reflect a mixed-method approach (see Schensul & LeCompte, 1999). Furthermore, the reliability and validity of ethnographic data depend on prolonged and long-term engagement in context and with participants; systematic multisource, multimethod data collection and analysis procedures; corroboration of data interpretation with participants; and detailed documentation of study procedures to facilitate judgments about transferability (see Lincoln & Guba, 1985).

Assumptions of CMMPE

Underlying CMMPE are several assumptions regarding program evaluation, which are applicable to population-based service models (Nastasi, 2004; Nastasi, Moore, & Varjas, 2004):

1. *Program success is dynamic and multidimensional.* As depicted in Figure 10.2, the dimensions of success include acceptability, social validity, integrity, outcomes, sustainability, and institutionalization. In addition, these dimensions are interactive, such that acceptability, social validity, and integrity influence outcomes; outcomes influence sustainability and institutionalization; and so on. Furthermore, perceptions of success can change through the life of a program as evaluations of different dimensions shift. For example, perceptions of acceptability and social validity may change throughout the course of an intervention, thus influencing perceptions of success as well as measurable outcomes.

2. *Definition and perspectives of program success are likely to vary among stakeholders.* Given the host of stakeholders in school- and community-based interventions (e.g., see Figure 10.2), one can expect

judgments regarding the different dimensions of success to vary. For example, behaviors that are considered to be socially valid are likely to be different within family, school, and community contexts. Similarly, adults and adolescents may have different expectations regarding outcomes of interventions.

3. *Program evaluation has multiple purposes.* During program implementation, evaluation helps program administrators monitor program implementation and immediate impact. Evaluation, particularly through the use of qualitative techniques, can facilitate identification of unintended effects (both positive and negative). In addition, ongoing evaluation guides decision making and program adaptation (e.g., addressing variations in implementation and impact across teachers and classrooms). In-depth program documentation facilitates examination of process-outcome relationships and provides detail necessary for decisions about transferability. Finally, evaluation can both assess and facilitate program institutionalization, especially when specific attention is given to questions regarding factors necessary for sustainability and capacity building.

4. *Comprehensive program evaluation requires mixed qualitative-quantitative methods.* The multiple purposes and perspectives inherent in comprehensive evaluation require both qualitative and quantitative data collection and analysis methods. For example, whereas quantitative instruments (e.g., behavior rating scales) can document pre-post changes in target behaviors, qualitative methods (e.g., observation and interviewing) can document program implementation and identify unintended outcomes. Furthermore, whereas quantitative rating scales may be available to examine perceptions of teachers or parents, qualitative measures (e.g., focus groups or semi-structured interviews) may be necessary to assess reactions of community members, students, or administrators.

5. *Comprehensive program evaluation requires participation of stakeholders.* Particularly if program planners are interested in sustainability and institutionalization, ownership and full participation of key stakeholders are necessary. Involving stakeholders (e.g., school administrators, parents, community members) from the early stages of rogram development can help to ensure more acceptable and socially valid programming. Providing opportunities for stakeholders to participate as partners and to develop program development and evaluation skills can facilitate capacity building necessary for sustainability and institutionalization.

6. *Comprehensive program evaluation requires advanced planning and is integral to service delivery.* The previous assumptions make it clear that proper implementation of CMMPE requires planning the evaluation before initiating population-based services. In practice, evaluation is often an afterthought or, at best, a marginal activity (Sanders, 2002), and this typically limits the conclusions one can make from the effort. In the case of CMMPE, a priori decision making and planning are required to properly utilize the model. Indeed, advanced planning is necessary if one intends to use data to inform program decisions over extended periods, as in Extended-Term Mixed Methods Evaluation Designs (see Chatterji, 2004–2005).

Implementing CMMPE

A comprehensive population-based mental health service delivery system ideally would involve the development of mental health programming targeted at system (school district or school community), provider (teacher, mental health professional), and individual (student) levels. Program plans would include mental health education for the general population through school-wide and classroom-based programming, training of teachers in mental health promotion strategies and screening, advance training of mental health professionals to address student needs related to specific mental health problems prevalent in the district/school, and delivery of mental health diagnosis and treatment by trained mental health professionals to referred students. Evaluation would involve examining outcomes at school/district, provider, and individual student/client levels and address acceptability, social validity, integrity, sustainability, and institutionalization from multiple perspectives. (See Nastasi, Moore, & Varjas, 2004, for full discussion of comprehensive mental health program development and evaluation.)

Table 10.2 (reprinted from Nastasi, Moore, & Varjas, 2004) outlines the key considerations for conducting program evaluation of population-based mental health services. The table provides a list of questions regarding purpose or goal (Why?), participants/stakeholders (Who?), tasks and activities (What?), and methods (How?) relevant to decision making about evaluation. In addition, the table provides considerations regarding the necessary skills for professional and paraprofessional evaluators (e.g., stakeholders), and potential challenges and opportunities relevant to CMMPE. These considerations overlap with the decision making related to evaluation depicted in Figure 10.1. In some instances, CMMPE necessitates decisions that

Table 10.2   Key Considerations for Evaluating Population-Based School Mental Health Services

Focus (key questions)—Why?

- Was the program successful or effective?
- What is the impact of the program?
- Were program goals met?
- What were unintended positive and negative (iatrogenic) consequences? (for individuals, groups, organizations)
- Were there any unintended negative (iatrogenic) effects?
- What factors influenced program effectiveness?
- Was the program acceptable?
- Was the program implemented with integrity?
- Does the program have ecological-social validity? Was culture specificity achieved?
- To what extent did program acceptability, integrity, and ecological-social validity (culture specificity) influence program effectiveness or success?
- How do the multiple and potentially diverse perspectives of partners (planners-interventionists-researchers; administrative, implementation, and evaluation staff; recipients, their caretakers, and community members) influence program success?
- How do we best use evaluation data for data-based decision making and monitoring to ensure program success?

Participants—Who?

- Program planner or planners (researcher, interventionist, consultant)
- Professionals with expertise in mixed-method program evaluation
- Program implementation staff
- Cultural brokers (who can facilitate access and interpret culture)
- Representatives of stakeholder groups

Tasks or Activities—What?

- Selecting or developing evaluation instruments or strategies
- Identifying and securing existing data
- Data collection
- Data management
- Data analysis
- Data interpretation
- Data dissemination
- Participatory data-based decision making
- Staff development in evaluation methods, including accountability and monitoring

Strategies or Methods—How?

- Data collection methods appropriate to specific program, using multimethod (combination of qualitative and quantitative methods), multisource (from various stakeholders) approach
- Recursive data collection, analysis, interpretation, and dissemination

- Systematic feedback process to facilitate program adaptation and staff development
- Participatory data-based decision making
- Facilitation of participatory process

Requisite Skills (potential focus for recruitment and training)

- Program evaluation skills relevant to engaging in a participatory process, examining process and outcome variables, use of mixed methods (qualitative and quantitative), and seamless intervention-evaluation process
- Instrument development
- Data collection, management, and analysis
- Data interpretation and dissemination to varied stakeholder groups
- Participatory data-based decision-making skills
- Participatory problem-solving skills—communication, negotiation, consensus building
- Group facilitation skills (e.g., engaging participants in idea generation, ensuring equitable participation, guiding group toward consensus)
- Professional and paraprofessional staff development and consultation skills

Challenges

- Identify or develop culture-specific instruments tied to program goals
- Ensure acceptability of evaluation by stakeholders
- Secure professional staff with expertise in evaluation
- Create seamless assessment-intervention process
- Access existing data within system or organization
- Address ethical and legal issues related to data collection activities
- Secure commitment to ongoing evaluation process
- Secure necessary resources
- Create a sustainable process and structure; build capacity within the system for sustainable program evaluation

Opportunities

- Ensure ecological validity and cultural specificity of mental health programs
- Develop sustainable and institutionalized evaluation system
- Educate stakeholders about value of evaluation
- Build organizational-community capacity for program evaluation
- Engage in systematic evaluation of program acceptability, social validity, integrity, effectiveness, sustainability, and institutionalization
- Contribute to the understanding of how to implement successful programs (how it works; what contributes to its success)—for participating system and larger professional community
- Contribute to knowledge base about intervention effectiveness and deployment of evidence-based programs in real-life settings
- Foster appreciation for the value and necessity of research, evaluation, and data-based decision making

reflect one end of the continuum, whereas in others, decisions are positioned along the continuum. First, addressing questions regarding purpose requires attention to the balance of practical utility and scientific standards, and consideration of program goals. The foundations and assumptions of CMMPE are such that both extremes (practical and scientific) are typically addressed. Second, answering questions about methods requires consideration of the balance of qualitative and quantitative methods within a mixed-methods design. Third, CMMPE involves a more participatory role in terms of the evaluator's relationship with participants, although the evaluator's role is likely to vary from expert to participatory across the life of a project. Fourth, the multiple dimensions of evaluation require consideration of both short-term (e.g., immediate impact) and long-term (sustainability) inquiry, as well as distal and proximal goals. Fifth, CMMPE by design requires focus on multiple rather than isolated dimensions, although different aspects of the program will likely require attention to isolated dimensions (e.g., changes in behavioral functioning related to individual treatment goals). Finally, the involvement of key stakeholders such as funders, administrators, and community members requires attention to political issues related to definitions of program success (e.g., social validity, acceptability, institutionalization).

Table 10.3 defines the evaluation dimensions depicted in Figure 10.2, and provides a set of questions relevant to each dimension to guide CMMPE of population-based school mental health services (see also Nastasi, 2004; Nastasi, Moore, & Varjas, 2004). In the next section, we provide an illustration of CMMPE applied to a district-wide (population-based) drug and sexual risk prevention program.

Illustration of CMMPE:
Population-Based School-District Intervention

To illustrate the application of CMMPE to population-based services, we draw from the first author's experiences in a four-and-a-half-year program conducted in a large urban school district in the northeastern region of the United States (Coe & Nastasi, 2006; Nastasi, Schensul, Balkcom, & Cintrón-Moscoso, 2004). The "Building Preventive Group Norms in Urban Middle Schools" (subsequently referred to as Building Group Norms) project[5] involved multiple levels of intervention directed at reducing risk for drug abuse and sexually transmitted diseases (STDs) among young adolescents.

Table 10.3   Evaluation Dimensions and Questions Relevant to CMMPE of Population-Based School Mental Health Services

Dimension	Definition	Evaluation Questions
Acceptability	Extent to which stakeholders view the program as feasible (given available resources), necessary (i.e., consistent with the needs of target population), and likely to be successful in attaining program goals; extent to which program philosophy is consistent with stakeholder worldviews	Do students, teachers, mental health professionals, school administrators, and community members view mental health services as necessary and desirable? Collectively, are the resources necessary to implement population-based services available or attainable across stakeholder groups and agencies? Do the stakeholder groups view mental health programming as likely to be successful? Is program philosophy and theoretical basis consistent with worldviews of various stakeholder groups? What is the level of stakeholder support for program goals and activities? In what ways are stakeholders involved in program development, implementation, and evaluation?
Social validity	Extent to which the program goals and intended outcomes are considered to be culturally relevant (i.e., reflect the values, norms, beliefs, concepts, and language of the respective stakeholder groups); extent to which program outcomes reflect socially valued competencies	How relevant are program goals and intended outcomes to the social-cultural demands across various contexts represented by stakeholders (e.g., school, family, peer group, community)? Are program goals and intended outcomes relevant to the daily lives of students, teachers, parents, community members? Are the program goals, target outcomes, and content and process of proposed interventions and evaluation measures relevant to the cultural experiences of the target group? Is the program culturally specific to the program recipients at multiple levels (system, provider, individual)?

(Continued)

Table 10.3 (Continued)

Dimension	Definition	Evaluation Questions
Integrity	Extent to which the core or critical elements of the program have been implemented, with documentation of adaptations of noncritical elements; extent to which program implementation is sufficiently documented to permit replication and decision making about transferability to other contexts and populations	Is program implementation consistent with program design? To what extent are the critical or core elements (i.e., those linked to program outcomes) implemented at each level? What adaptations are made to meet individual and contextual needs? Are these adaptations based on evaluation data? Do adaptations affect attainment of program objectives? Is program documentation detailed enough to permit examination of process-outcome relationships, identification of core and adaptable elements, replication of program procedures, and decision making about transferability?
Outcome	Extent to which program goals and objectives have been achieved at multiple levels—system, provider, individual; extent to which outcomes are maintained over time and generalized to other contexts; extent to which program is responsible for unintended positive or negative effects	Has the program achieved its objectives at individual, provider, and systems levels? What are short-term and long-term program outcomes at each level? Are these outcomes a result of the intervention; are rival explanations plausible? Do program outcomes generalize to other relevant contexts (e.g., from classroom to home, community)? How do the perceptions of outcomes vary across stakeholder groups? What are the unintended outcomes at each level (system, provider, individual)? During program implementation, is sufficient progress being made toward program goals and objectives? If not, what modifications are made and do those facilitate attainment of goals and objectives?

Dimension	Definition	Evaluation Questions
Sustainability	Extent to which program components continue after the formal program period concludes; for example, extent to which system and providers continue to implement and/or have the capacity to continue the program of population-based mental health services	Are program efforts maintained by organization and staff after completion of formal program? Are stakeholders (administrators, teachers, mental health staff, and community agencies) committed to program continuation? What are the facilitators and barriers to program continuation? How might program planners capitalize on facilitators and address barriers to sustainability? What actions are necessary at each level to promote sustainability?
Institutionalization	Capacity of the system to maintain long-term population-based mental health services and to adapt the current program to meet changing contextual, cultural and individual needs	What infrastructure is necessary to ensure institutionalization of school-based programming? What skills are necessary for stakeholders to maintain and modify mental health programming as needs and resources change over time? Is there sufficient capacity across the stakeholder groups to maintain a program of population-based mental health services? What policies, funding, staffing, expertise, administrative support, and other resources are necessary to facilitate institutionalization? What is the level of commitment to institutionalization across the key stakeholder groups (e.g., funders, lawmakers, school administrators, community members)?

The primary goal of the Building Group Norms project was to design, implement, and evaluate a district-wide group-norms approach to preventing drug and sexual risk among urban adolescents (Grades 6 and 7). More specifically, the project was designed to test the integration of the norms-based approach into existing grade-specific social development curricula, test the norms-based approach against the existing individually oriented approach (Weissberg, Caplan, Bennetto, & Stroup Jackson, 1999), and examine the acceptability, integrity, and sustainability of a system-wide intervention.

The district's existing social development curriculum had been developed in the 1980s in response to concerns about the social and emotional development of its students. The core of the program was focused on social problem solving (Weissberg et al., 1999), which also became the basis for addressing drug abuse and sexual risk (HIV) prevention. To monitor students' social and health status related to implementation of district-wide curricula, a standardized self-report instrument was developed by partners from Yale Child Study Center (Social and Health Assessment Survey, SAHA; Barone et al., 1995; Schwab-Stone et al., 1995) and administered district-wide on a regular basis (every two years).

The team of researchers and interventionists from the Institute for Community Research (ICR) developed a partnership with the district's social development department, which was responsible for sustainability of the existing program (e.g., through teacher training, support to schools and teachers, and ongoing monitoring), and the Yale Child Study Center, which was responsible for conducting the district-wide social and health assessment. The purpose of the partnership was to design and test an adaptation of the existing curriculum through a group-norm–based approach that involved the use of cooperative learning instructional techniques and opportunities for collaborative problem solving and consensus building by students working in small groups (Nastasi et al., 2000, 2001).

Although the primary focus of the program was the enhancement of knowledge, attitudes, and skills related to preventing drug abuse and sexual risks among middle school students, the Building Group Norms project involved intervention at multiple levels including district, school, teaching and support staff, classroom, the peer group (classmates), and individual students (Nastasi, Balkcom, & Schensul, 2002; Nastasi, Schensul, Balkcom, & Cintrón-Moscoso, 2004). Project activities over four and a half years included negotiating system entry and partnerships at district and school levels, curriculum development, training and consultation with teachers and district-level staff, program implementation, and evaluation.

Table 10.4 shows the evaluation techniques used to assess acceptability, social validity, integrity, outcomes, sustainability, and institutionalization at system (district and school), teacher, and

Table 10.4   Comprehensive Mixed-Methods Participatory Evaluation of Multiple Aspects and Multiple Levels of a Population-Based Drug and Sexual Risk Prevention Program

	Acceptability Social Validity	Integrity	Outcomes	Sustainability Institutionalization
System level	Key informant interviews and in-depth interviews (with district-level social development staff and school-level administrators and support staff) Participant observations (e.g., during weekly meetings with social development staff, and district-wide planning meetings)	Key informant interviews and in-depth interviews with social development staff and school-level administrators	District-wide SAHA Key informant interviews and in-depth interviews (with district-level social development staff and school-level administrators and support staff)	Key informant and in-depth interviews (with district-level social development staff and school-level administrators and support staff) Participant observation in meetings with social development staff and district-wide planning meetings
Teacher level	Participant observations (during program implementation in classrooms) In-depth interviews and informal dialogue with teachers (face-to-face, phone, e-mail) Session evaluations (completed by teachers)	Participant observations (during program implementation in classrooms) In-depth interviews and informal dialogue with teachers (face-to-face, phone, e-mail) Session evaluations (completed by teachers)	Participant observations (during program implementation in classrooms) Formal interviews and informal dialogue with teachers (face-to-face, phone, e-mail) Session evaluations (completed by teachers)	In-depth interviews with teachers Participant observations (during program implementation in classrooms)

(Continued)

Table 10.4 (Continued)

	Acceptability Social Validity	Integrity	Outcomes	Sustainability Institutionalization
Student level	Participant observation (during program implementation) Permanent products (student work generated during program implementation) Session evaluations (completed by individual students and groups of students)	Participant observation (during program implementation) Permanent products (student work generated during program implementation) Session evaluations (completed by individual students and groups of students)	District-wide SAHA In-depth interviews with students Permanent products (student work generated during program implementation) Participant observation (during program implementation) Key informant interviews (with teachers, administrators, support staff) Social network activity (using list of classmates, students indicate nature of relationship with each, e.g., "hang out," share personal problems, would choose as work partner) Curriculum-specific measures (social dilemmas)	In-depth interviews with students Participant observation (during program implementation) Social network analysis

Participant observations. Narrative or structured observations of intervention activities by intervention and evaluation staff during participation in project events (e.g., during implementation of curriculum in classrooms).

Key-informant interview. Unstructured interview with representatives of key stakeholder groups designed to gather information about the context or stakeholders in general.

In-depth interview. Semi-structured interview designed to gather detailed information about respondents' perceptions of evaluation dimensions (e.g., acceptability, impact); conducted in individual or focus-group format.

Session evaluation. Structured form designed to document implementation and evaluation of intervention/treatment (e. g., teachers record activities completed, modifications made to curriculum, and perceived effectiveness for meeting session objectives).

Permanent products. Tangible products, for example, school records or student products from curricular activities.

Social network activity. Activity used to generate a measure of interpersonal relationships or interactions. Social network analysis yields qualitative and quantitative indices based on data from interviews, structured activities (e.g., social network activity), and/or participant observation.

SAHA—Social and Health Assessment Survey. Self-report questionnaire designed to measure student knowledge, attitudes, and behaviors related to social and health status; developed specifically for participating district use (Barone et al., 1995; Schwab-Stone et al., 1995).

student levels, thus examining individual- to population-level impact. Evaluation methods included participant observation, key informant, and in-depth interviews; permanent products (from curriculum activities); session evaluations completed by students and teachers; social network analysis (to examine changes in peer groups within respective classrooms); curriculum-specific measures (standardized measure of student response to dilemmas involving risk and peer influence, designed by project staff to examine social problem solving related to drug and sexual risks) administered pre- and postintervention; and the SAHA administered on an annual basis (definitions of methods are presented in Table 10.4). The purpose of the evaluation at the systemic level was to examine the impact of the program on the district and participating schools, including assessment of outcomes at the district level with the SAHA. Evaluation at the teacher level was designed to examine the effectiveness of the program of teacher training and consultation on teachers' knowledge, attitudes, and behaviors related to the use of a group-norms approach to drug and sexual risk prevention. Evaluation at the student level was focused on the effectiveness of the new curriculum (compared to district's standard drug and sexual abuse curricula) on students' knowledge, attitudes, and behaviors related to drug abuse and sexual risk. The study design was a group randomized controlled trials design in which five pairs of schools were matched on a series of key demographic and drug and sexual risk indicators (risk indicators were obtained from the most recent district-wide administration of SAHA), and one school in each pair was randomly assigned to the intervention group (received the new curriculum) and one to the comparison group (maintained the existing curriculum). Within each school, teachers and students in sixth and seventh grade participated in the project.

As indicated in Table 10.4, multiple dimensions of program success were evaluated from multiple perspectives. Thus, data collection and analysis focused on acceptability, social validity, integrity, outcomes, sustainability, and institutionalization of intervention at each level (district/school, teacher, student). In addition, data were collected from direct program recipients (students), providers (teachers who delivered the curricula), school administrators and support staff, and district-level social development staff and administrators. Data collection and analysis involved the use of mixed qualitative-quantitative methods. Data were collected throughout program implementation and were used to monitor program success and make necessary adaptations to address context-specific (e.g., classroom) and individual (student) needs.

Decisions about program development, implementation, and adaptation; data collection, analysis, and interpretation; and sustainability and institutionalization involved participation of the various stakeholder groups. For example, data collected on an ongoing basis by the project evaluation team (e.g., classroom observations, informal interviews with teachers, session evaluations, and examination of student work) were used to facilitate regular (weekly, bimonthly, monthly) discussions with teachers, social development staff, and school- and district-level administrators about need for adaptations to the curriculum, follow-up teacher training, and involvement of support staff in program implementation. Data also provided the basis for yearly presentations to district-level staff and administrators and negotiation of changes in the overall project (e.g., moving from district-level to school-level decision making about program implementation).

Application of CMMPE to Population-Based School Mental Health Services: Implications for Role and Preparation of School Professionals

The successful transition from traditional to comprehensive mixed-method participatory evaluation of population-based services requires changes in the roles and professional identities of school mental health professionals. As indicated in Table 10.2, the requisite skills for engaging in CMMPE include participatory consultation; group facilitation; participatory problem solving; data-based decision making; staff development; mixed-methods data collection, analysis, and interpretation; and dissemination of findings to various audiences. Preparing school mental health professionals with expertise in evaluating population-based services using participatory mixed-methods designs will likely require expansion of current models of practice and training in school counseling, school psychology, and school social work. In particular, professional preparation needs to include training in qualitative and mixed-methods research and evaluation, and application of these methods at multiple levels (from individual to population); participatory models of evaluation, including strategies for identifying and engaging stakeholders, building evaluation capacity, and consensus building among diverse stakeholder groups; and data-based decision making for program modification/adaptation (i.e., using evaluation data to inform program change) to facilitate successful programming and meet cultural and contextual variations within systems and populations. Moreover, engaging in CMMPE of population-based services requires expertise in organizational consultation, systems change, and community psychology. Finally, successful engagement in evaluation of population-based services will necessitate broader conceptions of interdisciplinary practice that includes collaboration with professionals outside of schools (e.g., community agencies or universities) and from other disciplines such as anthropology, sociology, and public health.

Population-based mental health offers a unique opportunity for school counselors, school psychologists, and school social workers to expand their influence beyond individuals with identified problems to the general population of students and families. Successful participation in population-based services will depend in part on expertise in comprehensive participatory and mixed-methods evaluation.

Notes

1. The authors do not wish to suggest one end of a given continuum is superior to another; the appropriateness of such focus can only be driven by context.

2. This could be added as another issue in dimension one (Figure 10.1), but the topic fits better under a discussion of goals.

3. The *Procedural and Coding Manual for Review of Evidence-Based Interventions* was developed by a joint Division 16 of the American Psychological Association (Div 16-APA)-Society for the Study of School Psychology (SSSP) Task Force on Evidence-Based Interventions in School Psychology. The most recent revision of the Procedural and Coding Manual reflects a mixed-methods framework and includes criteria for ensuring sufficient attention to culture. Information regarding the development and criteria contained in the Manual can be found in Ingraham and Oka (2006), Kratochwill and Stoiber (2002a, 2002b), Nastasi and Schensul (2005), and Stoiber and Kratochwill (2000). For the most recent versions of the Procedural and Coding Manual, contact Thomas R. Kratochwill, PhD, School Psychology Program, University of Wisconsin–Madison, Madison, WI 53706-1796.

4. A full articulation of ethnographic, qualitative, and participatory action research is beyond the scope of this chapter. Readers are encouraged to consult the following sources: Bernard (1995); Camic, Rhodes, and Yardley (2003); Creswell (1997); Denzin and Lincoln (2000); Fetterman (1998); LeCompte, Millroy, and Preissle (1992); Lincoln and Guba (1985); Miles and Huberman (1994); Moustakas (1994); Nastasi (2006); Ryan and Bernard (2000); J. J. Schensul and LeCompte (1999); Spradley (1979, 1980); Stake (1995); Strauss and Corbin (1990); Wolcott (1990). For more detailed discussion

of the application of ethnographic methods to intervention research, see Nastasi & Berg (1999), and Nastasi and Schensul (2005).

5. The project was funded by a grant to The Institute for Community Research, Hartford, CT, from The National Institute on Drug Abuse, National Institutes of Health, "Building Preventive Group Norms in Urban Middle Schools," Grant # DA12015; Principal Investigator, Jean J. Schensul, PhD; Co-Principal Investigator and Project Director, Bonnie K. Nastasi, PhD. The project was conducted in partnership with the New Haven, CT, Public Schools, Yale University Department of Pediatrics and Child Study Center, and University of Massachusetts, Amherst.

Discussion Questions

1. What skills do you already have that could be used in evaluating your school's population-based services?

2. Imagine that you had created a Leadership Team to implement a program of population-based services in your school, and that you had secured an expert program evaluator to provide an evaluation of the services' success. What questions about your services would you want the expert to answer with the evaluation? How would your community define the services' success?

3. In the same situation, where you had implemented a program of population-based services in your school, who would be the important stakeholders who would need to have input into the evaluation and want to be informed of the results?

4. What could your school do to make an evaluative study of school mental health services highly acceptable to the people who would be asked to participate?

5. In what situations might it be more useful for your school to employ an expert-based evaluation of its population-based services? When might a participatory evaluation be more useful?

References

American Psychological Association. (2003). Guidelines on multicultural education, training, research, practice, and organizational change for psychologists. *American Psychologist, 58*, 377–402.

Barone, C., Weissberg, R. P., Kasprow, W. J., Voyce, C. K., Arthur, M. W., & Shriver, T. P. (1995). Involvement in multiple problem behaviors of young urban adolescents. *Journal of Primary Prevention, 15*, 261–283.

Bernard, H. R. (1995). *Research methods in anthropology: Qualitative and quantitative approaches*. Thousand Oaks, CA: Sage.

Boruch, R. F. (1997). *Randomized experiments for planning and evaluation: A practical guide*. Thousand Oaks, CA: Sage.

Boruch, R. F., De Moya, D., & Snyder, B. (2002). The importance of randomized field trials in education and related areas. In F. Mosteller & R. Boruch (Eds.), *Evidence matters: Randomized trials in education research* (pp. 50–79). Washington, DC: Brookings Institution.

Camic, P. M., Rhodes, J. E., & Yardley, L. (Eds.). (2003). *Qualitative research in psychology: Expanding perspectives in methodology and design.* Washington, DC: American Psychological Association.

Campbell, D. T. (1969). Reforms as experiments. *American Psychologist, 24,* 409–429.

Chatterji, M. (2004-2005). Evidence on "What Works": An argument for extended-term mixed-method (ETMM) evaluation designs. *Educational Researcher, 33(9),* 3–13. [Corrected version reprinted in 2005, *Educational Researcher, 34(5),* 14–24]

Coe, C., & Nastasi, B. (2006). Stories and selves: Managing the self through problem-solving in school. *Anthropology & Education Quarterly, 37,* 180–198.

Creswell, J. W. (1997). *Qualitative inquiry and research design.* Thousand Oaks, CA: Sage.

Creswell, J. W. (2002). *Educational research: Planning, conducting and evaluating quantitative and qualitative research.* Upper Saddle River, NJ: Prentice Hall.

Cronbach, L. J. (1982). *Designing evaluations of educational and social programs.* San Francisco: Jossey-Bass.

Denzin, N. K., & Lincoln, Y. S. (Eds.). (2005). *Handbook of qualitative research* (3rd ed.). Thousand Oaks, CA: Sage.

Fetterman, D. M. (1994). Steps of empowerment evaluation: From California to Cape Town. *Education and Program Planning, 17,* 305–313.

Fetterman, D. M. (1998). *Ethnography: Step by step* (2nd ed.). Thousand Oaks, CA: Sage.

Fetterman, D. M. (2000). *Foundations of empowerment evaluation.* Thousand Oaks, CA: Sage.

Ingraham, C. L., & Oka, E. R. (2006). Multicultural issues in evidence-based interventions. *Journal of Applied School Psychology, 22,* 127–150.

Kratochwill, T. R., & Stoiber, K. C. (2002a). Evidence-based interventions in school psychology: Conceptual foundations of the *Procedural and Coding Manual* of Division 16 and the Society for the Study of School Psychology Task Force. *School Psychology Quarterly, 17,* 341–389.

Kratochwill, T. R., & Stoiber, K. C. (2002b). *Procedural and coding manual for review of evidence-based interventions.* Madison: University of Wisconsin–Madison.

LeCompte, M. D., Millroy, W. L., & Preissle, J. (Eds.). (1992). *The handbook of qualitative research in education.* San Diego, CA: Academic Press.

Lincoln, Y. S., & Guba, E. G. (1985). *Naturalistic inquiry.* Thousand Oaks, CA: Sage.

Miles, M. B., & Huberman, A. M. (1994). *Qualitative data analysis* (2nd ed.). Thousand Oaks, CA: Sage.

Moustakas, C. (1994). *Phenomenological research methods.* Thousand Oaks, CA: Sage.

Nastasi, B. K. (1998). A model for mental health programming in schools and communities. *School Psychology Review, 27,* 165–174.

Nastasi, B. K. (2004). Mental health program evaluation: A multi-component, multi-perspective mixed-method approach. In K. E. Robinson (Ed.),

Advances in school-based mental health: Best practices and program models (chap. 9). Kingston, NJ: Civic Research Institute.

Nastasi, B. K. (2006). Advances qualitative research. In T. Gutkin & C. Reynolds (Eds.), *The handbook of school psychology* (4th ed.). New York: Wiley & Sons. Invited manuscript submitted for publication (under review).

Nastasi, B. K., Balkcom, C. T., & Schensul, J. J. (2002, August). *Promoting healthy decision making about drug use and sexual risks.* Paper presented in Symposium on "Building school-community partnerships to promote children's health" (Thomas J. Power, Chair), at the 110th annual convention of the American Psychological Association, Chicago.

Nastasi, B. K., & Berg, M. (1999). Using ethnography to strengthen and evaluate intervention programs. In J. J. Schensul & M. D. LeCompte (Eds.), *The ethnographer's toolkit. Book 7. Using ethnographic data: Interventions, public programming, and public policy* (pp. 1–56). Walnut Creek, CA: AltaMira Press.

Nastasi, B. K., Moore, R. B., & Varjas, K. M. (2004). *School-based mental health services: Creating comprehensive and culturally specific programs.* Washington, DC: American Psychological Association.

Nastasi, B. K., Schensul, J. J., Balkcom, C. T., & Cintrón-Moscoso, F. (2004). Integrating research and practice to facilitate implementation across multiple contexts: Illustration from an urban middle school drug and sexual risk prevention program. In K. E. Robinson (Ed.), *Advances in school-based mental health: Best practices and program models* (chap. 13). Kingston, NJ: Civic Research Institute.

Nastasi, B. K., Schensul, J. J., Tyler, C. L., Araujo, R., DeFalco, K., & Kavanaugh, M. (2000). *The New Haven Social Development Program: Social Problem Solving-Cooperative Education, Grade 6 Curriculum.* Hartford, CT: The Institute for Community Research.

Nastasi, B. K., Schensul, J. J., Tyler, C. L., Araujo, R., DeFalco, K., & Kavanaugh, M. (2001). *The New Haven Social Development Program: Social Problem Solving-Cooperative Education, Grade 7 Curriculum.* Hartford, CT: The Institute for Community Research.

Nastasi, B. K., & Schensul, S. L. (2005). Contributions of qualitative research to the validity of intervention research [Special issue]. *Journal of School Psychology, 43,* 177–195.

Onwuegbuzie, A. J. (2002). Why can't we all get along? Towards a framework for unifying research paradigms. *Education, 122*(3), 518–530.

Partridge, W. L. (1985). Toward a theory of practice. *American Behavioral Scientist, 29,* 139–163.

Rallis, S. G., & Rossman, G. B. (2003). Mixed methods in evaluation contexts: A pragmatic framework. In A. Tashakkori & C. Teddlie (Eds.), *Handbook of mixed methods in social and behavioral research* (pp. 491–512). Thousand Oaks, CA: Sage.

Rossi, P. H., Lipsey, M. W., & Freeman, H. E. (2004). *Evaluation: A systematic approach* (7th ed.). Thousand Oaks, CA: Sage.

Ryan, G. W., & Bernard, H. R. (2000). Data management and analysis methods. In N. K. Denzin & Y. S. Lincoln (Eds.), *Handbook of qualitative research* (2nd ed., pp. 259–309). Thousand Oaks, CA: Sage.

Sanders, J. R. (2002). Presidential address: On mainstreaming evaluation. *The American Journal of Evaluation, 23*, 253–259.

Schensul, J. J. (1998). Community-based risk prevention with urban youth. *School Psychology Review, 27*, 233–245.

Schensul, J. J., & LeCompte, M. D. (Eds.). (1999). *Ethnographer's toolkit* (Vols. 1–7). Walnut Creek, CA: AltaMira Press.

Schensul, J. J., & Schensul, S. L. (1992). Collaborative research: Methods of inquiry for social change. In M. LeCompte, W. L. Millroy, & J. Preissle (Eds.), *The handbook of qualitative research in education* (pp. 161–200). San Diego, CA: Academic Press.

Schensul, S. L. (1985). Science, theory, and application in anthropology. *American Behavioral Scientist, 29*, 164–185.

Schwab-Stone, M. E., Ayers, T. S., Kasprow, W., Voyce, C., Barone, C., Shriver, T., et al. (1995). No safe haven: a study of violence exposure in an urban community. *Journal of the American Academy of Child & Adolescent Psychiatry, 34*, 1343–1352.

Scriven, M. (1984). Evaluation ideologies. In R. F. Conner, D. G. Altman, & C. Jackson (Eds.), *Evaluation studies review annual* (Vol. 9). Beverly Hills, CA: Sage.

Shadish, W. R., Cook, T. D., & Campbell, D. T. (2002). *Experimental and quasi-experimental designs for generalized causal inference.* Boston: Houghton-Mifflin.

Spradley, J. P. (1979). *The ethnographic interview.* New York: Holt, Rhinehart, Winston.

Spradley, J. P. (1980). *Participant observation.* New York: Holt, Rhinehart, Winston.

Stake, R. (1995). *The art of case study research.* Thousand Oaks, CA: Sage.

Stoiber, K. C., & Kratochwill, T. R. (2000). Empirically supported interventions and school psychology: Rationale and methodological issues: Part I. *School Psychology Quarterly, 15*, 75–105.

Strauss, A., & Corbin, J. (1990). *Basics of qualitative research: Grounded theory procedures and techniques.* Newbury Park, CA: Sage.

Tashakkori, A., & Teddlie, C. (2003). *Handbook of mixed methods in social and behavioral research.* Thousand Oaks, CA: Sage.

U.S. Department of Health and Human Services. (1999). *Mental health: A report of the Surgeon General.* Rockville, MD: Department of Health and Human Services, Substance Abuse and Mental Health Services Administration, Center for Mental Health Services, National Institutes of Health, National Institutes of Mental Health.

U.S. Department of Health and Human Services. (2001). *Mental health: Culture, race and ethnicity—a supplement to mental health: A report of the Surgeon General.* Rockville, MD: Department of Health and Human Services, Substance Abuse and Mental Health Services Administration, Center for Mental Health Services, National Institutes of Health, National Institutes of Mental Health.

Weiss, C. H. (1993). Where politics and evaluation research meet. *Evaluation Practice, 14*, 93–106.

Weiss, C. H. (1998) *Evaluation: Methods for studying programs and policies* (2nd ed.). Upper Saddle River, NJ: Prentice Hall.

Weissberg, R., Caplan, M., Bennetto, L., & Stroup Jackson, A. (1999). *Sixth-grade social-problem solving module* (Rev. ed.). Chicago: University of Illinois at Chicago.

Wolcott, H. F. (1990). *Writing up qualitative research.* Newbury Park, CA: Sage.

Worthen, B. R., & Sanders, J. R. (1987). *Educational evaluation: Alternative approaches and practical guidelines.* New York: Longman.

Yin, R. K. (1994). *Case study research: Design and methods.* Thousand Oaks, CA: Sage.

About the Authors

Bonnie K. Nastasi is Director of the School Psychology program at Walden University.

John H. Hitchcock is Senior Associate with Caliber and ICF International.

11

School-Wide Approaches to Addressing Barriers to Learning and Teaching

Howard S. Adelman

Linda Taylor

Everyone wants higher test scores. Everyone wants to close the achievement gap. The call is for widespread school improvement, increased discipline, reduced school violence, and, of course, leaving no child behind.

None of it means much if such calls do not result in school-wide changes in the numerous schools where too many students lack an equitable opportunity to succeed. If the intent is to leave no child behind, essential improvements must be made in how schools address barriers to learning and teaching. To these ends, this chapter focuses on how student supports need to be reframed so they play a more significant role in addressing factors that result in so many students not doing well at school.

Addressing Barriers to Learning and Teaching

Over the years, awareness of the many external and internal factors that are barriers to learning and teaching has given rise to legal mandates and a variety of psychological, counseling, and social support programs, as well as to initiatives for school-community collaborations. Enactment of the No Child Left Behind Act and the 2004 reauthorization of the Individuals with Disabilities Education Act accelerated awareness of the need for schools to respond appropriately each day to a variety of barriers to learning and teaching.

Although reliable data do not exist, many policy makers would agree that at least 30% of the public school population in the United States are not doing well academically and could be described as having learning and related behavior problems. The percentage is higher in urban and rural schools serving students from low-income families (Center for Mental Health in Schools, 2005a).[1]

It has long been acknowledged that many factors negatively and profoundly affect learning (Dryfoos, 1990; Hawkins & Catalano, 1992; Huffman, Mehlinger, & Kerivan, 2000). Moreover, the resulting problems are exacerbated as youngsters internalize the debilitating effects of performing poorly at school and are punished for the misbehavior that is a common correlate of school failure. Schools that can't effectively address barriers to learning and teaching are ill-equipped to raise test scores to high levels (Adelman & Taylor, 2002, 2006a). Because of all this, school policy makers have a lengthy, albeit somewhat reluctant, history of trying to assist teachers in dealing with factors that interfere with schooling.

What Schools Do to Provide Student Supports

Currently, there are about 91,000 public schools in about 15,000 districts in the United States. Over the years, most (but obviously not all) schools have instituted programs designed with a range of learning, behavior, and emotional problems in mind. Some directly budget student support programs and personnel. Some programs are mandated for every school; others are carried out at or linked to targeted schools. In addition to those owned and operated by schools, services, programs, and personnel are brought to school sites by community agencies (U.S. Department of Education, 1996).

Student supports may be offered to all students in a school, to those in specified grades, or to those identified as at risk. The activities may be implemented in regular or special education classrooms or as "pullout" programs, and may be designed for an entire class, groups, or individuals. They encompass ecological, curricular, and clinically oriented activities designed to reduce barriers directly and create buffers against them (i.e., protective factors). Interventions to address barriers generally focus on response to crises, early intervention, and some forms of treatment. Focus may also be on prevention and enhancement of healthy development (e.g., promotion of positive physical, social, and emotional development) through use of health education, health services, guidance, and so forth—though relatively few resources are usually allocated for such activity.

While schools can use a wide range of persons to help students, most school owned and operated services are offered as part of what are called pupil personnel services or support services. Federal and state mandates tend to determine how many pupil services professionals are employed, and states regulate compliance with mandates. Governance of daily practice usually is centralized at the school district level. In large districts, psychologists, counselors, social workers, and other specialists may be organized into separate units. Such units overlap regular, special, and compensatory education.

It should be stressed that, while a variety of student support activity exists in any school district, it is common knowledge that few schools come close to having enough resources to respond when confronted with a large number of students experiencing a wide range of factors that interfer with learning and performance. Many schools offer only bare essentials. Too many schools cannot even meet basic needs. Primary prevention often is only a dream. Given all this, it is not surprising that teachers, students, and their families continually ask for help. And, given how student supports currently operate, it is not surprising that few feel they are receiving the help they need.

Fragmented, Marginalized, and Counterproductively Competitive Student Supports

At the school level, analyses of the current state of affairs consistently find that the majority of programs, services, and special projects designed to address barriers to student learning are viewed as supplementary (often referred to as auxiliary services), operate on an ad hoc basis, and are planned, implemented, and evaluated in a fragmented and piecemeal manner (Adelman & Taylor, 1997, 2006a; Dryfoos, 1994; Gardner, 2005). This results in a tendency for student support staff to function in relative isolation of each other and other stakeholders, with a great deal of the work oriented to discrete problems and an overreliance on specialized services for individuals and small groups. In some schools, a student identified as at risk for grade retention, dropout, and substance abuse may be assigned to three counseling programs operating independently of each other. Furthermore, an unproductive separation often is manifested in every facet of school operation between those focused on instruction and those concerned with addressing barriers to learning. Such fragmentation not only is costly in terms of redundancy and counterproductive competition, it works against developing comprehensive, multifaceted, and cohesive systems to serve the needs of most schools (Adelman, 1996; Adelman & Taylor, 1997, 1998).

Widespread recognition of the piecemeal nature of learning supports has produced some planning to enhance coordination. Better coordination is a good idea. But it doesn't address the fundamental systemic problem, which is that school-owned student supports are *marginalized* in policy and practice. Thus, while there is a good deal of observable activity in schools, the efforts are not a significant focus when it comes to planning school improvements. This is particularly ironic given the aura of dissatisfaction that surrounds current learning supports.

Most school improvement plans currently pay little attention to substantially enhancing the way schools provide student supports. At best, most reformers have offered the notions of establishing family resource centers and full-service schools to link community resources to schools and enhance coordination of services (Dryfoos, 1994). Connecting school and community resources is another good idea. But community involvement at schools is also marginalized, and when not done properly, it compounds the problems of fragmentation and counterproductive competition. These problems arise when the focus is primarily on coordinating *community* services and co-locating them at schools, rather than braiding resources and integrating the services with the ongoing efforts of school staff.

Leaving no child behind means addressing the problems of the many who are not benefiting from instructional reforms. Available evidence makes it clear that much more fundamental, systemic changes are needed. Because of the complexity of ensuring that all students have an equal opportunity to succeed at school, policy makers and practitioners need an operational framework to guide development of a comprehensive, multifaceted, and cohesive enabling/learning supports component (Adelman, 1995, 1996; Adelman & Taylor, 1994).

However, rather than address the problems surrounding school-owned support programs and services, policy makers seem to have become enamored with the concept of school-linked services, as if adding a few community health and social services to a few schools is a sufficient solution. The social marketing around "school-linked, integrated services" has led some policy makers to the mistaken impression that community resources alone can effectively meet the needs of schools in addressing barriers to learning. In turn, this has led some legislators to view linking community services to schools as a way to free dollars underwriting school-owned services. The reality is that even when one adds together community and school assets, the total set of services in impoverished locales is woefully inadequate. In situation after situation, it has become evident that as soon as the first few sites demonstrating school-community collaboration are in place, community agencies find their resources stretched to the limit.

As inadequate as school-owned student support services are at most schools, the resources invested in student support staff (e.g., school psychologists, counselors, social workers, nurses) usually exceeds to a considerable degree what local public agencies can afford to link to a school. Moreover, schools have other resources they can use to meet the challenge of ensuring all students have an equal opportunity to succeed at school. Besides traditional "pupil service personnel," student support is provided by compensatory education personnel (e.g., Title I staff), resource teachers who focus on prereferral interventions, and staff associated with a variety of school-wide programs (e.g., after school, safe and drug-free school programs).

Thus, while school-linked services might provide more referral resources for a few students in such locales, the number of students in need of support far outstrips what publicly supported community agencies can make available. Awareness is growing that there can never be enough school-based and linked support services to meet the demand in many public schools. Moreover, it is becoming more and more evident that efforts to address barriers to student learning will continue to be marginalized in policy and practice as long as the focus is narrowly on providing "services."

Another problem is that overemphasis on school-linked services exacerbates tensions between school district service personnel and their counterparts in community-based organizations. As *outside* professionals offer services at schools, school specialists often view the trend as discounting their skills and threatening their jobs. At the same time, the outsiders often feel unappreciated and may be rather naive about the culture of schools. Conflicts arise over turf, use of space, confidentiality, and liability. Thus, competition rather than a substantive commitment to collaboration remains the norm.

Reframing Student Supports

Reframing how all resources for student/learning supports are used can lead to

- more effective deployment of existing resources (by minimizing fragmentation, redundancy, counterproductive competition, and policy marginalization)
- reframing student supports as *learning supports* that address barriers to student learning and realigning support staff roles and functions to develop comprehensive, multifaceted, and cohesive approaches
- fully integrating learning support programs and staff into the school improvement agenda at every school
- revamping infrastructures to weave resources together and provide mechanisms for enhancing and evolving how schools address barriers to student learning

Toward Ending the Marginalization of Student Supports

Some policy makers have come to appreciate the relationship between the way student/learning supports are provided and limited intervention efficacy. (For the rest of this chapter, student supports will be referred to as learning supports.) For the most part, however, "reforms" have focused on the problem of fragmentation. This bypasses the underlying systemic issue, namely, that addressing barriers to learning and teaching remains a marginalized aspect of policy and practice. Fragmentation is likely a symptom, an inevitable by-product of the marginalization. So it is unlikely that the problem of fragmentation will be resolved appropriately without concerted attention in policy and practice to ending the marginalized status of learning supports.

Unfortunately, concern about marginalization is not even on the radar screen of most policy makers. This is reflected not only in school improvement planning, but in consolidated plans and certification reviews and the lack of efforts to map, analyze, and rethink how resource for learning supports are allocated (Center for Mental Health in Schools, 2005b). As long as educational decision makers ignore the need to end the marginalization and make fundamental systemic changes, the potential impact of learning supports for large numbers of children and adolescents cannot be demonstrated.

Analyses by our research group indicate that school reform is currently dominated by a two-component systemic model (Adelman,

1995, 1996; Adelman & Taylor, 1994, 1997, 1998). That is, the primary thrust is on improving instruction and school management. While these two facets obviously are essential, ending the marginalization of efforts to effectively address barriers to learning and teaching requires establishing a third component as primary, essential, complementary, and overlapping (Figure 11.1).

Figure 11.1 Moving from a Two- to a Three-Component Model for School Improvement

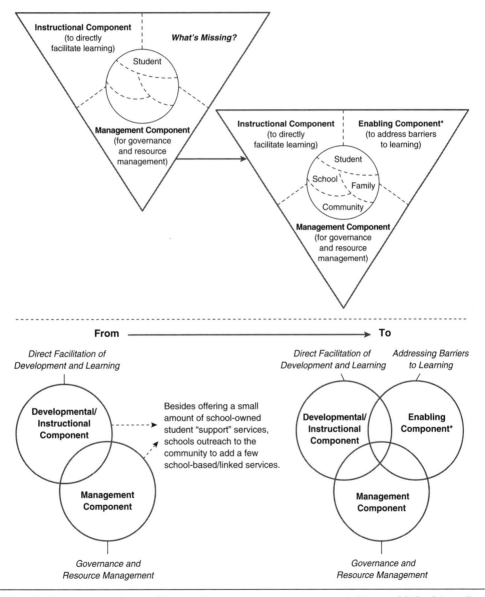

*The third component (an enabling or learning supports component) is established in policy and practice as primary and essential and is developed into a comprehensive approach by weaving together school and community resources.

As can be seen in Figure 11.1, we designate the component addressing barriers to learning as an Enabling Component; others who have adopted it use terms such as a Learning Supports Component (e.g., Iowa, 2004). The concept of an enabling or learning supports component is formulated around the proposition that a comprehensive, multifaceted, integrated continuum of enabling activity is essential in addressing the needs of youngsters who encounter barriers that interfere with their ability to benefit satisfactorily from instruction. The concept embraces healthy development, prevention, and addressing barriers. This third component not only provides a basis for combating marginalization, it establishes a focal point for developing a comprehensive learning supports framework to guide systemic changes. Its usefulness for these purposes is evidenced in its adoption by various states and localities. (Information about these trailblazing initiatives is online at http://smhp.psych.ucla.edu/summit2002/wheresithappening.htm.)

Toward a Comprehensive School-Wide System of Learning Supports

Problems experienced by students generally are complex in terms of cause and needed intervention. Therefore, in designing school-wide learning supports, school and community leaders must work together to develop a high-functioning, comprehensive, and multifaceted system.

How comprehensive and multifaceted? Table 11.1 outlines a proposed set of guidelines for a school-wide student support component.

In effect, the intention, over time, is for schools to play a major role in establishing a full range of interventions, including systems for

- promoting healthy development and preventing problems
- intervening early to address problems as soon after onset as is feasible
- assisting those with chronic and severe problems

As illustrated in Figure 11.2, the desired interventions can be conceived along a continuum. Such a continuum encompasses efforts to enable academic, social, emotional, and physical development and address learning, behavior, and emotional problems at every school. Most schools have some programs and services that fit along the entire continuum. However, the tendency to focus mostly on the most severe problems has skewed things so that too little is done to prevent

Table 11.1   Guidelines for a School-Wide Student Support Component

1. Major Areas of Concern Related to Barriers to Student Learning

   1.1 Addressing common educational and psychosocial problems (e.g., learning problems; language difficulties; attention problems; school adjustment and other life transition problems; attendance problems and dropouts; social, interpersonal, and familial problems; conduct and behavior problems; delinquency and gang-related problems; anxiety problems; affect and mood problems; sexual and/or physical abuse; neglect; substance abuse; psychological reactions to physical status and sexual activity; physical health problems)

   1.2 Countering external stressors (e.g., reactions to objective or perceived stress/demands/crises/deficits at home, school, and in the neighborhood; inadequate basic resources such as food, clothing, and a sense of security; inadequate support systems; hostile and violent conditions)

   1.3 Teaching, serving, and accommodating disorders/disabilities (e.g., learning disabilities; attention deficit hyperactivity disorder; school phobia; conduct disorder; depression; suicidal or homicidal ideation and behavior; posttraumatic stress disorder; anorexia and bulimia; special education designated disorders such as emotional disturbance and developmental disabilities)

2. Timing and Nature of Problem-Oriented Interventions

   2.1 Primary prevention
   2.2 Intervening early after the onset of problems
   2.3 Interventions for severe, pervasive, and/or chronic problems

3. General Domains for Intervention in Addressing Students' Needs and Problems

   3.1 Ensuring academic success and also promoting healthy cognitive, social, emotional, and physical development and resilience (including promoting opportunities to enhance school performance and protective factors; fostering development of assets and general wellness; enhancing responsibility and integrity, self-efficacy, social and working relationships, self-evaluation and self-direction, personal safety and safe behavior, health maintenance, effective physical functioning, careers and life roles, creativity)

   3.2 Addressing external and internal barriers to student learning and performance

   3.3 Providing social/emotional support for students, families, and staff

4. Specialized Student and Family Assistance (Individual and Group)

   4.1 Assessment for initial (first level) screening of problems, as well as for diagnosis and intervention planning (including a focus on needs and assets)

   4.2 Referral, triage, and monitoring/management of care

   4.3 Direct services and instruction (e.g., primary prevention programs, including enhancement of wellness through instruction, skills development, guidance counseling, advocacy, school-wide programs to foster safe and caring climates, and liaison connections between school

(Continued)

Table 11.1 (Continued)

and home; crisis intervention and assistance, including psychological and physical first-aid; prereferral interventions; accommodations to allow for differences and disabilities; transition and follow-up programs; short- and longer-term treatment, remediation, and rehabilitation)

4.4 Coordination, development, and leadership related to school-owned programs, services, resources, and systems—toward evolving a comprehensive, multifaceted, and integrated continuum of programs and services

4.5 Consultation, supervision, and in-service instruction with a transdisciplinary focus

4.6 Enhancing connections with and involvement of home and community resources (including but not limited to community agencies)

5. **Ensuring Quality of Intervention**

   5.1 Systems and interventions are monitored and improved as necessary

   5.2 Programs and services constitute a comprehensive, multifaceted continuum

   5.3 Interveners have appropriate knowledge and skills for their roles and functions and provide guidance for continuing professional development

   5.4 School-owned programs and services are coordinated and integrated

   5.5 School-owned programs and services are connected to home and community resources

   5.6 Programs and services are integrated with instructional and governance/management components at schools

   5.7 Program/services are available, accessible, and attractive

   5.8 Empirically supported interventions are used when applicable

   5.9 Differences among students/families are appropriately accounted for (e.g., diversity, disability, developmental levels, motivational levels, strengths, weaknesses)

   5.10 Legal considerations are appropriately accounted for (e.g., mandated services; mandated reporting, and its consequences)

   5.11 Ethical issues are appropriately accounted for (e.g., privacy and confidentiality; coercion)

   5.12 Contexts for intervention are appropriate (e.g., office, clinic, classroom, home)

6. **Outcome Evaluation and Accountability**

   6.1 Short-term outcome data

   6.2 Long-term outcome data

   6.3 Reporting to key stakeholders and using outcome data to enhance intervention quality

Source: Adapted from Mental Health in Schools: Guidelines, Models, Resources, and Policy Considerations, a document developed by the Policy Leadership Cadre for Mental Health in Schools. This document is available from the Center for Mental Health in Schools at UCLA; downloadable from the Center's website at http:// smhp.psych.ucla.edu/pdfdocs/policymakers/guidelinesexecsumm.pdf

A separate document providing the rationale and science-base for the version of the guidelines adapted for learning supports is available at http://smhp.psych.ucla .edu/summit2002/guidelinessupportdoc.pdf

Figure 11.2   Interconnected Systems for Meeting the Needs of All Students

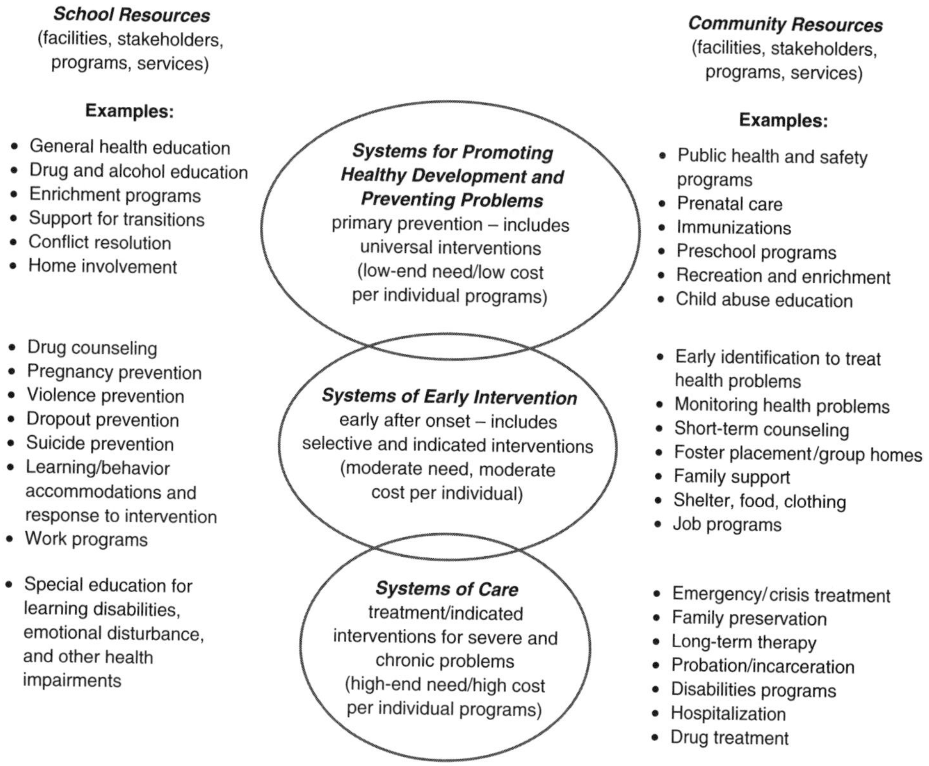

School Resources
(facilities, stakeholders,
programs, services)

Community Resources
(facilities, stakeholders,
programs, services)

Examples:

- General health education
- Drug and alcohol education
- Enrichment programs
- Support for transitions
- Conflict resolution
- Home involvement

Examples:

- Public health and safety programs
- Prenatal care
- Immunizations
- Preschool programs
- Recreation and enrichment
- Child abuse education

Systems for Promoting Healthy Development and Preventing Problems
primary prevention – includes universal interventions (low-end need/low cost per individual programs)

- Drug counseling
- Pregnancy prevention
- Violence prevention
- Dropout prevention
- Suicide prevention
- Learning/behavior accommodations and response to intervention
- Work programs

- Early identification to treat health problems
- Monitoring health problems
- Short-term counseling
- Foster placement/group homes
- Family support
- Shelter, food, clothing
- Job programs

Systems of Early Intervention
early after onset – includes selective and indicated interventions (moderate need, moderate cost per individual)

- Special education for learning disabilities, emotional disturbance, and other health impairments

- Emergency/crisis treatment
- Family preservation
- Long-term therapy
- Probation/incarceration
- Disabilities programs
- Hospitalization
- Drug treatment

Systems of Care
treatment/indicated interventions for severe and chronic problems (high-end need/high cost per individual programs)

Systemic collaboration* is essential to establish interprogram connections on a daily basis and over time to ensure seamless intervention within each system and among *systems of prevention of early intervention,* and *systems of care.*

---

*Such collaboration involves horizontal and vertical restructuring of programs and services
(a) within jurisdictions, school districts, and community agencies (e.g., among departments, divisions, units, school, clusters of schools)
(b) between jurisdictions, school and community agencies, public and private sectors; among schools; among community agencies

or intervene early after the onset of a problem. As a result, most approaches reflect a "waiting-for-failure" strategy.

Not only does the continuum span the concepts of primary, secondary, and tertiary prevention, it can incorporate a holistic and developmental emphasis that envelops individuals, families, and the contexts in which they live, work, and play. The continuum also provides a framework for adhering to the principle of using the least restrictive and nonintrusive forms of intervention required to appropriately respond to problems and accommodate diversity.

Moreover, given the likelihood that many problems are not discrete, the continuum can be designed to address root causes, thereby minimizing tendencies to develop separate programs for each observed problem. In turn, this enables increased coordination and integration of resources, which can increase impact and cost-effectiveness.

Operationalizing the Continuum: Reframing How Schools Address Barriers to Learning

An additional framework helps operationalize the concept of an enabling or learning supports component in ways that coalesce and enhance programs to ensure all students have an equal opportunity to succeed at school. A critical matter is defining what the entire school must do to enable *all* students to learn and *all* teachers to teach effectively. School-wide approaches to address barriers to learning are especially important at any school where large numbers of students are affected or that is not yet paying adequate attention to considerations related to equity and diversity. Leaving no child behind means addressing the problems of the many who are not benefiting from instructional reforms.

Various pioneering efforts have operationalized such a component into six programmatic arenas (see Table 11.2). In essence, these six arenas constitute the curriculum or content of an enabling or learning support component (Adelman, 1996; Adelman & Taylor, 1998, 2006b). This curriculum encompasses programs to

- *enhance regular classroom strategies to enable learning* (i.e., improving instruction for students who have become disengaged from learning at school and for those with mild to moderate learning and behavior problems)
- *support transitions* (i.e., assisting students and families as they negotiate school and grade changes and many other transitions)
- *increase home and school connections*
- *respond to, and where feasible, prevent crises*
- *increase community involvement and support* (outreach to develop greater community involvement and support, including enhanced use of volunteers)
- *facilitate student and family access to effective services and special assistance as needed*

Combining the six content arenas with the continuum of interventions illustrated in Figure 11.2 provides a full intervention picture to

Table 11.2   "Content" Areas for a Component to Address Barriers to
Learning

1. Classroom-based approaches encompass

   - Opening the classroom door to bring available supports in (e.g., peer tutors, volunteers, aids trained to work with students-in-need, resource teachers, and student support staff work in the classroom as part of the teaching team)
   - Redesigning classroom approaches to enhance teacher capability to prevent and handle problems and reduce need for out-of-class referrals (e.g., personalized instruction, special assistance as necessary, developing small-group and independent learning options, reducing negative interactions and overreliance on social control, expanding the range of curricular and instructional options and choices, systematic use of prereferral interventions)
   - Enhancing and personalizing professional development (e.g., creating a learning community for teachers; ensuring opportunities to learn through co-teaching, team teaching, and mentoring; teaching intrinsic motivation concepts and their application to schooling)
   - Curricular enrichment and adjunct programs (e.g., varied enrichment activities that are not tied to reinforcement schedules; visiting scholars from the community)
   - Classroom and school-wide approaches used to create and maintain a caring and supportive climate
   - Emphasis at all times is on enhancing feelings of competence, self-determination, and relatedness to others at school and reducing threats to such feelings.

2. Crisis assistance and prevention encompasses

   - Ensuring immediate assistance in emergencies so students can resume learning
   - Providing follow-up care as necessary (e.g., brief and longer-term monitoring)
   - Forming a school-focused crisis team to formulate a response plan and take leadership for developing prevention programs
   - Mobilizing staff, students, and families to anticipate response plans and recovery efforts
   - Creating a caring and safe learning environment (e.g., developing systems to promote healthy development and prevent problems; bullying and harassment abatement programs)
   - Working with neighborhood schools and community to integrate planning for response and prevention
   - Capacity building to enhance crisis response and prevention (e.g., staff and stakeholder development, enhancing a caring and safe learning environment)

3. Support for transitions encompasses

   - Welcoming and social support programs for newcomers (e.g., welcoming signs, materials, and initial receptions; peer buddy programs for students, families, staff, volunteers)

(Continued)

Table 11.2 (Continued)

- Daily transition programs (e.g., before school, breaks, lunch, after school)
- Articulation programs (e.g., grade-to-grade—new classrooms, new teachers; elementary to middle school; middle to high school; in and out of special education programs)
- Summer or intersession programs (e.g., catch-up, recreation, and enrichment programs)
- School-to-career/higher education (e.g., counseling, pathway, and mentor programs)
- Broad involvement of stakeholders in planning for transitions (e.g., students, staff, home, police, faith groups, recreation, business, higher education)
- Capacity building to enhance transition programs and activities

4. Home involvement in schooling encompasses
   - Addressing specific support and learning needs of family (e.g., support services for those in the home to assist in addressing basic survival needs and obligations to the children; adult education classes to enhance literacy, job skills, English as a second language, citizenship preparation)
   - Improving mechanisms for communication and connecting school and home (e.g., opportunities at school for family networking and mutual support, learning, recreation, enrichment, and for family members to receive special assistance and to volunteer to help; phone calls and/or e-mail from teacher and other staff with good news; frequent and balanced conferences—student-led when feasible; outreach to attract hard-to-reach families—including student dropouts)
   - Involving homes in student decision making (e.g., families prepared for involvement in program planning and problem solving)
   - Enhancing home support for learning and development (e.g., family literacy; family homework projects; family field trips)
   - Recruiting families to strengthen school and community (e.g., volunteers to welcome and support new families and help in various capacities; families prepared for involvement in school governance)
   - Capacity building to enhance home involvement

5. Community outreach for involvement and support encompasses
   - Planning and implementing outreach to recruit a wide range of community resources (e.g., public and private agencies; colleges and universities; local residents; artists and cultural institutions; businesses and professional organizations; service, volunteer, and faith-based organizations; community policy and decision makers)
   - Systems to recruit, screen, prepare, and maintain community resource involvement (e.g., mechanisms to orient and welcome, enhance the volunteer pool, maintain current involvements, enhance a sense of community)
   - Reaching out to students and families who don't come to school regularly—including truants and dropouts
   - Connecting school and community efforts to promote child and youth development and a sense of community

---

- Capacity building to enhance community involvement and support (e.g., policies and mechanisms to enhance and sustain school-community involvement, staff/stakeholder development on the value of community involvement, "social marketing")

6. Student and family assistance encompasses

  - Providing extra support as soon as a need is recognized and doing so in the least disruptive ways (e.g., prereferral interventions in classrooms; problem-solving conferences with parents; open access to school, district, and community support programs)
  - Timely referral interventions for students and families with problems based on response to extra support (e.g., identification/screening processes, assessment, referrals, and follow-up—school-based, school-linked)
  - Enhancing access to direct interventions for health, mental health, and economic assistance (e.g., school-based, school-linked, and community-based programs and services)
  - Care monitoring, management, information sharing, and follow-up assessment to coordinate individual interventions and check whether referrals and services are adequate and effective
  - Mechanisms for *resource* coordination and integration to avoid duplication, fill gaps, garner economies of scale, and enhance effectiveness (e.g., braiding resources from school-based and linked interveners, feeder pattern/family of schools, community-based programs; linking with community providers to fill gaps)
  - Enhancing stakeholder awareness of programs and services
  - Capacity building to enhance student and family assistance systems, programs, and services

---

guide school improvement planning in developing a system of learning supports (Adelman & Taylor, 2006a, 2006b; Center for Mental Health in Schools, 2005c). The resulting matrix is shown in Figure 11.3. This matrix creates a unifying umbrella framework to guide the reframing and restructuring of the daily, school-wide work of all staff who provide learning supports.

The focus for an enabling or learning support component begins in the classroom, with differentiated classroom practices as the base of support for each youngster. This includes

- addressing barriers through a broader view of basics and effective accommodation of learner differences
- enhancing the focus on motivational considerations, with a special emphasis on intrinsic motivation as it relates to learner readiness and ongoing involvement, with the intent of fostering intrinsic motivation as a basic outcome
- adding remediation as necessary, but only as necessary

Figure 11.3   Matrix for Reviewing Scope and Content of a Component to Address Barriers to Learning

Scope of Intervention

	Systems for Promoting Healthy Development and Preventing Problems	Systems for Early Intervention (Early after problem onset)	Systems of Care
Classroom-Focused Enabling			
Crisis/Emergency Assistance and Prevention			
Support for Transitions			
Home Involvement in Schooling			
Community Outreach/ Volunteers			
Student and Family Assistance			

Organizing Around the **Content/ "Curriculum"** (for address barriers to learning and promoting healthy development)

Accommodations for Differences and Disabilities

Specialized Assistance and Other Intensified Interventions (e.g., Special Education and School-Based Behavioral Health)

Note: Specific school-wide and classroom-based activities related to positive behavior support, the Centers for Disease Control and Prevention's "prereferral" interventions, and the eight components of Coordinated School Health Program are embedded into the six content ("curriculum") areas.

For individual youngsters, the intent of an enabling or learning supports component is to prevent and minimize as many problems as feasible and to do so in ways that maximize engagement in productive learning. For the school and community as a whole, the intent is to produce a safe, healthy, nurturing environment/culture characterized by respect for differences, trust, caring, support, and high expectations. In accomplishing all this, the focus is on restructuring support programs and melding school, community, and home resources. The process is designed from the school outward. That is, the initial emphasis is on what the classroom and school must do to reach and teach all students effectively. Then the focus expands to include planning how the feeder pattern of schools and the surrounding community can complement each other's efforts and achieve economies of scale. Central district and community agency staff then restructure in ways that best support these efforts. At each stage, the framework presented in Figure 11.3 facilitates mapping and analyzing the current scope and content of how a school, a family of schools, a school district, and the community address barriers to learning and teaching at each level.

What's the Data?

Research on comprehensive approaches is still in its infancy. There are, of course, many "natural" experiments underscoring the promise of ensuring all youngsters access to a comprehensive, multifaceted continuum of interventions. These natural experiments are playing out in every school and neighborhood where families are affluent enough to purchase the additional programs and services they feel will maximize their youngsters' well-being. It is obvious that those who can afford such interventions understand their value.

Most *formal* studies have focused on specific interventions. This literature reports positive outcomes (for school and society) associated with a wide range of interventions. Because of the fragmented nature of available research, the findings are best appreciated in terms of the whole being greater than the sum of the parts, and implications are best derived from the total theoretical and empirical picture. When such a broad perspective is adopted, schools have a large research base to draw on in addressing barriers to learning and enhancing healthy development. Examples of this research base have been organized into the preceding six arenas (Adelman & Taylor, 2006a; Center for Mental Health in Schools, 2004a).

Rethinking Infrastructure

A well-designed and supported *infrastructure* is needed to establish, maintain, and evolve the type of comprehensive approach to addressing barriers to student learning outlined earlier. Such an infrastructure includes mechanisms for coordinating among enabling activities, for enhancing resources by developing direct linkages between school and community programs, for increasing integration of school and community resources, and for integrating the instructional/developmental, enabling, and management components (Adelman & Taylor, 2006a; Center for Mental Health in Schools, 2005d).

As noted, *development* of comprehensive school-wide approaches require shifts in prevailing policy and new models for practice. In addition, for significant systemic change to occur, policy and program commitments must be demonstrated through effective allocation and redeployment of resources. That is, finances, personnel, time, space, equipment, and other essential resources must be made available, organized, and used in ways that adequately operationalize policy and promising practices. This includes ensuring sufficient resources to develop an effective structural foundation for system change, sustainability, and ongoing capacity building (Center for Mental Health in Schools, 2005e).

Key Mechanisms

To ensure sufficient resources, existing infrastructure mechanisms must be modified in ways that guarantee new policy directions are translated into appropriate daily practices (Center for Mental Health in Schools, 2005f). Well-designed infrastructure mechanisms ensure local ownership, a critical mass of committed stakeholders, processes that overcome barriers to stakeholders effectively working together, and strategies that mobilize and maintain proactive effort to allow implementing of changes and renewal over time. From this perspective, the importance of creating an atmosphere that encourages mutual support, caring, and a sense of community takes on another dimension.

Institutionalization of comprehensive, multifaceted approaches necessitates restructuring the mechanisms associated with at least six infrastructure concerns. These encompass processes for daily (a) governance, (b) leadership, (c) planning and implementation of specific organizational and program objectives, (d) coordination and integration for cohesion, (e) management of communication and information, and (f) capacity building. Properly redesigned infrastructure changes, for example, ensure integration, quality improvement, accountability, and self-renewal of an enabling or learning support component.

In redesigning mechanisms to address these matters, new collaborative arrangements must be established and authority (power) redistributed—easy to say, extremely hard to accomplish. Major systemic changes obviously require ensuring that those who operate essential mechanisms have adequate resources and support, initially and over time. Moreover, there must be appropriate incentives and safeguards for individuals as they become enmeshed in the complexities of systemic change.

Learning Supports Resource Team

In schools, the administrative leadership is obviously key to ending the marginalization of efforts to address learning, behavior, and emotional problems. Another key is establishing a mechanism that focuses specifically on how learning support resources are used at the school. In some schools as much as 25% of the budget may go to problem prevention and correction. Every school is expending resources to enable learning; few have a mechanism to ensure appropriate use of existing resources and enhance current efforts. Such a mechanism contributes to cost-efficacy of learner support activity by ensuring all such activity is planned, implemented, and evaluated in a coordinated and increasingly integrated manner. It also provides another means for reducing marginalization. Creation of such a mechanism is essential for braiding together existing school and community resources and encouraging services and programs to function in an increasingly cohesive way. When this mechanism is in the form of a "team," it is also a vehicle for building working relationships and can play an expanded role in solving turf and operational problems.

Resource-oriented mechanisms have been designated by a variety of names including *Resource Coordinating Team, Resource Management Team,* and *Learning Supports Resource Team.* For purposes of this discussion, we will use the last of these. We initially demonstrated the feasibility of such teams in the Los Angeles Unified School District, and now they are being introduced in many schools across the country (Lim & Adelman, 1997; Rosenblum, DiCecco, Taylor, & Adelman, 1995). Properly constituted, such a team provides on-site leadership for efforts to address barriers comprehensively and ensures the maintenance and improvement of a multifaceted and integrated approach (Adelman & Taylor, 2006a, in press).

One of the primary and essential tasks a learning supports resource-oriented mechanism undertakes is enumerating school and community programs and services that are in place to support students, families, and staff. A comprehensive "gap" assessment is generated as resource mapping is compared with surveys of the unmet needs of and desired outcomes for students, their families, and school staff. Analyses of what is available, effective, and needed provide a sound basis for formulating priorities and developing strategies to link with additional resources in other schools, district sites, and the community and enhance resource use. Such analyses also can guide efforts to improve cost-effectiveness.

In a similar fashion, a learning support resource-oriented team for a complex or family of schools (e.g., a high school and its feeder schools) and a team at the district level provide mechanisms for larger-scale analyses. This can lead to strategies for cross-school, community-wide, and district-wide cooperation and integration to enhance intervention effectiveness and garner economies of scale. For those concerned with school reform, such resource-oriented mechanisms are a key facet of efforts to transform and restructure school support programs and services.

When we suggest a learning supports resource team, some school staff quickly respond, "We already have one!" When we explore this with them, we usually find what they have is a *case-oriented team*—that is, a team that focuses on individual students who are having problems. Such a team may be called a student study team, student success team, student assistance team, teacher assistance team, and so forth.

To help clarify the difference between resource- and case-oriented teams, we contrast the functions of each (Table 11.3).

A resource-oriented team exemplifies the type of mechanism needed to pursue overall cohesion and ongoing development of school support programs and systems. As indicated, its focus is not on specific individuals, but on how resources are used. In pursuing its functions, the team provides what often is a missing link for managing and enhancing programs and systems in ways that integrate, strengthen, and stimulate new and improved interventions. For example, such a mechanism can be used to (a) map and analyze activity and resources to improve their use in preventing and ameliorating problems; (b) build effective referral, case management, and quality assurance systems; (c) enhance procedures for managing programs and information and communicating among school staff and with the home; and (d) explore ways to redeploy and enhance resources—such as clarifying which activities are nonproductive, suggesting better uses for resources, and establishing priorities for developing new interventions, as well as reaching out to connect with additional resources in the school district and community.

Minimally, a resource-oriented team can reduce fragmentation and enhance cost-efficacy by assisting in ways that encourage programs to function in a coordinated and increasingly integrated way. For example, the team can coordinate resources, enhance communication

Table 11.3   Contrasting Team Functions

A Case-Oriented Team	A Resource-Oriented Team
Focuses on specific *individuals* and discrete *services* to address barriers to learning	Focuses on *all* students and the *resources, programs, and systems* to address barriers to learning and promote healthy development
Sometimes called: • Child Study Team • Student Study Team • Student Success Team • Student Assistance Team • Teacher Assistance Team • IEP Team	Possibly called: • Resource Coordinating Team • Resource Coordinating Council • School Support Team • Learning Support Team
Examples of functions: • Triage • Referral • Case monitoring/management • Case progress review • Case reassessment	Examples of functions: • Aggregating data across students and from teachers to analyze school needs • Mapping resources • Analyzing resources • Enhancing resources • Program and system planning/development—including emphasis on establishing a full continuum of intervention • Redeploying resources • Coordinating and integrating resources • Social "marketing"

among school staff and with the home about available assistance and referral processes, and monitor programs to be certain they are functioning effectively and efficiently. More generally, this group can provide leadership in guiding school personnel and clientele in evolving the school's vision, priorities, and practices for learning support.

Although a resource-oriented mechanism might be created solely around psychosocial programs, it is meant to focus on resources related to all major learning support programs and services. Thus, it tries to bring together representatives of all these programs and services. This might include, for example, school counselors, psychologists, nurses, social workers, attendance and dropout counselors, health educators, special education staff, after-school program staff, bilingual and Title I program coordinators, safe and drug-free school staff, and union reps. It also should include representatives of any community agency that is significantly involved with schools. Beyond these service providers, such a team is well-advised to add the energies and expertise of administrators, regular classroom teachers, noncertificated staff, parents, and older students.

Where creating "another team" is seen as a burden, existing teams, such as student or teacher assistance teams and school crisis teams, have demonstrated the ability to perform resource-oriented functions. In adding these functions to another team's work, great care must be taken to structure the agenda so sufficient time is devoted to the additional tasks. For small schools, a large team often is not feasible, but a two-person team can still do the job.

Properly constituted, trained, and supported, a resource-oriented team complements the work of the site's governance body by providing on-site overview, leadership, and advocacy for all activity aimed at addressing barriers to learning and teaching.

Not an Isolated Mechanism, Part of an Integrated Infrastructure

Resource-oriented mechanisms at all levels cannot be isolated entities. The intention is to connect them to each other and be part of an integrated infrastructure. A learning supports resource team must be a formal unit of a school's infrastructure. And, it must be fully connected with the other infrastructure mechanisms at the school (e.g., those associated with instruction and management/governance). Figure 11.4 illustrates relationships of such a team to other major infrastructure units.

Having at least one representative from the resource team on the school's governing and planning bodies ensures the type of infrastructure connections that are essential if student and learning supports are to be maintained, improved, and increasingly integrated with classroom instruction. And, of course, having an administrator on the team provides the necessary link with the school's administrative decision making related to allocation of budget, space, staff development time, and other resources.

A Multisite Resource-Oriented Mechanism

Linking schools together is invaluable in maximizing use of limited resources. Schools in the same geographic or catchment area have

Figure 11.4   Learning Supports Resource Team as Part of an Integrated Infrastructure at a School Site

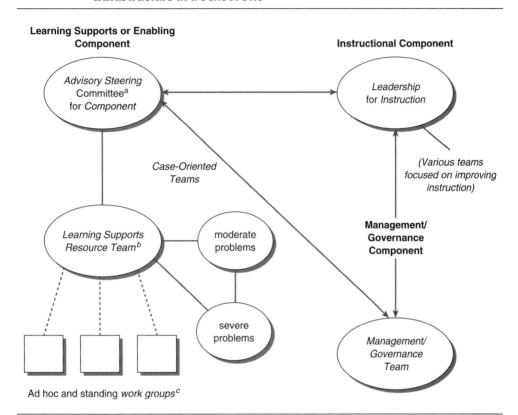

a. A learning supports or enabling component advisory/steering commitee at a school site consists of a leadership group whose responsibility is to ensure the vision for the components are not lost. It meets as needed to monitor and provide input to the learning supports resource team.

b. A learning supports resource team is the key to ensuring component cohension, integrated implementation, and ongoing development. It meets weekly to guide and monitor daily implementation and development of all programs, services, initiatives, and systems at a school that are concerned with providing learning supports and specialized assistance.

c. Adhoc and standing work groups are formed as needed by the learning supports resource team to address specific concerns. These groups are essential for accomplishing the many

a number of shared concerns, and schools in the feeder pattern often interact with the same family because each level has a youngster from that family who is having difficulties. Furthermore, some programs and personnel already are or can be shared by several neighboring schools, thereby minimizing redundancy and reducing costs.

A multisite team can provide a mechanism to help ensure cohesive and equitable deployment of resources and also can enhance the pooling of resources to reduce costs. Such a mechanism can be particularly useful for integrating the efforts of high schools and their feeder middle and elementary schools. This clearly is important in addressing barriers with those families who have youngsters attending more than one level of schooling in the same cluster. It is neither cost-effective nor good intervention for each school to contact a family separately in instances when several children from a family need special attention. With respect to linking with community resources, multischool teams are especially attractive to community agencies who often don't have the time or personnel to make independent arrangements with every school.

In general, a group of schools can benefit from a multisite resource mechanism designed to provide leadership, facilitate communication and connection, and ensure quality improvement across sites. For example, a multisite body, or what we call a *learning supports resource council,* might consist of a high school and its feeder middle and elementary schools. It brings together one or two representatives from each school's resource *team.*

The council meets about once a month to help (a) coordinate and integrate programs serving multiple schools, (b) identify and meet common needs with respect to guidelines and staff development, and (c) create linkages and collaborations among schools and with community agencies. In this last regard, it can play a special role in community outreach both to create formal working relationships and to ensure that all participating schools have access to such resources.

More generally, the council provides a useful mechanism for leadership, communication, maintenance, quality improvement, and ongoing development of a comprehensive continuum of programs and services. Natural starting points for councils are the sharing of needs assessments, resource maps, analyses, and recommendations for reform and restructuring. Specific areas of initial focus would be local, high-priority concerns, such as addressing violence and developing prevention programs and safe school and neighborhood plans.

Representatives from learning supports resource councils can be invaluable members of planning groups (e.g., service planning area councils, local management boards). They bring information about specific schools, clusters of schools, and local neighborhoods and do so in ways that reflect the importance of school-community partnerships.

When a family of schools in a geographic area collaborates to address barriers, the schools can share programs and personnel in many cost-effective ways. This includes streamlined processes to coordinate and integrate assistance to a family that has children at several of the schools. For example, the same family may have youngsters in the elementary and middle schools, and both students may need support during a family crisis. This might be accomplished by assigning one counselor and/or case manager to work with the family. Also, in connecting with community resources, a group of schools can maximize distribution of scarce resources in ways that are efficient, effective, and equitable.

Creation of resource-oriented mechanisms at schools, for families of schools, and at the district level is essential for weaving together existing school and community resources, enabling programs and services to function in an increasingly cohesive and cost-efficient way, and developing a full continuum of interventions over time. Such mechanisms are seen as vital in reducing marginalization and fragmentation of student and learner supports through transforming current approaches for addressing barriers to student learning and promoting healthy development.

Establishing and building the capacity of resource-oriented mechanisms, of course, are not simple tasks. As a result, it is essential to think in terms of a phase-in process (Center for Mental Health in Schools, 2005f). And, because establishing such a team involves significant organizational change, staff assigned to accomplish the tasks must have the skills of a systemic change agent. We designate this type of change agent as an *organization facilitator* (Adelman & Taylor 2006a; Lim & Adelman, 1997; Rosenblum, DiCecco, Taylor, & Adelman, 1995).

A Few Implications

Early in the 21st century, the following state of affairs is evident:

- Too many kids are not doing well in schools.
- To change this, schools must play a major role in addressing barriers to learning.
- However, support programs and services as they currently operate are *marginalized* in policy and practice and can't meet the needs of the majority of students experiencing learning, behavior, and emotional problems.
- Rather than address the problems surrounding school-owned support programs and services, policy makers seem to have become enamored with the concept of school-linked services, as if adding a few community health and social services to a few schools is a sufficient solution.

Given all this, it is not surprising that many in the field doubt that major breakthroughs can occur without a comprehensive, multifaceted, and integrated continuum of interventions. Such views add

impetus to major initiatives underway that are designed to restructure
how schools address learning, behavior, and emotional problems.

Everyone who wants to ensure that all students have an equal
opportunity to succeed at school needs to understand the full implications of all this. The bottom line is that limited efficacy seems
inevitable as long as the full continuum of necessary programs is
unavailable and staff development remains deficient; limited cost-
effectiveness seems inevitable as long as related interventions are carried out in isolation of each other; limited systemic change is likely as
long as the entire enterprise is marginalized in policy and practice.

A major shift in policy and practice is long overdue. We must
rethink how schools, families, and communities can meet the challenge
of addressing persistent barriers to student learning and, at the same
time, enhance how all stakeholders work together to promote healthy
development. We all need to press for policy establishing an enabling
or learning support component as a primary and essential facet of
school improvement that is fully integrated with the instructional component. In this respect, it will be useful to move boards of education
toward establishing a standing subcommittee focused specifically on
ensuring effective implementation of the policy for developing a component to address barriers to student learning at each school (Center
for Mental Health in Schools, 2004b).

We must, then, all play a role in guiding and facilitating the development of such a school-wide component in ways that effectively
address barriers to learning and teaching (and support the promotion
of healthy development) at every school. In doing so, we must think
in terms of

1. *phasing-in* development of the component's six programmatic
   facets at every school;

2. *expanding standards and accountability indicators* for schools to
   ensure this component is fully integrated with the instructional
   component and pursued with equal effort in policy and practice;

3. *restructuring* at every school and district-wide with respect to
   - redefining administrative roles and functions to ensure ded-
     icated administrative leadership that is authorized and has
     the capability to facilitate, guide, and support the systemic
     changes for ongoing development of such a component at
     every school
   - reframing the roles and functions of pupil services personnel
     and other student support staff to ensure development of the
     component

- redesigning the infrastructure to establish a team at every school and district level that plans, implements, and evaluates how resources are used to build the component's capacity; and

4. *weaving resources into a cohesive and integrated continuum of interventions over time.* Specifically, school staff responsible for the component must collaborate with families and community stakeholders to evolve systems for (a) promoting healthy development and preventing problems, (b) intervening early to address problems as soon after onset as feasible, and (c) assisting those with chronic and severe problems.

To these ends, it will be important to move pre- and in-service programs for school personnel toward including a substantial focus on the concept of an enabling or learning supports component and how to operationalize it in schools in ways that fully integrate with instruction.

All of the preceding requires substantive organizational and programmatic transformation. Thus, key stakeholders and their leadership must understand and commit to the changes. And the commitment must be reflected in policy statements and creation of an organizational structure at all levels that ensures effective leadership and resources. The process begins with activity designed to create readiness for the necessary changes by enhancing a climate/culture for change. Steps include:

1. building interest and consensus for establishing a comprehensive, multifaceted component to address barriers to learning and teaching;

2. introducing basic concepts to relevant groups of stakeholders;

3. establishing a policy framework that recognizes such a component is a primary and essential facet of the institution's activity; and

4. appointing leaders for the component who are of equivalent status to the leaders for the instructional and management facets, to ensure commitments are carried out.

The next decade must mark a turning point for how schools and communities address the problems of children and youth. In particular, the focus must be on initiatives to reform and restructure how schools work to prevent and ameliorate the many learning, behavior, and emotional problems experienced by students. This means reshaping the functions of all school personnel who have a role to play in addressing barriers to learning and promoting healthy development.

There is much work to be done as public schools across the country strive to leave no child behind.

Note

1. Many resources related to this chapter are accessible at the Center for Mental Health in Schools at UCLA website, http://smhp.psych.ucla.edu/.

Discussion Questions

1. Think carefully about all the programs, practices, and services that exist in your school for the purpose of strengthening students' behavioral, emotional, and social competence. What are these programs, which staff members contribute to them, and what proportion of the school's resources are engaged in these learning supports?

2. What is the difference between your school's student assistance team and the learning supports resource team that Adelman and Taylor describe?

3. What evidence do you see of service fragmentation in your school, and what steps might be taken to overcome it?

4. What advantages and disadvantages do you anticipate in collaborative school-community efforts to support children's learning and development?

5. In your own school, what evidence do you see of a climate for change suggesting that the school might be prepared to establish stronger learning supports? What evidence do you see that your school might resist change? What could you do to foster a stronger climate for change?

References

Adelman, H. S. (1995). Education reform: Broadening the focus. *Psychological Science, 6,* 61–62.

Adelman, H. S. (1996). Restructuring education support services and integrating community resources: Beyond the full service school model. *School Psychology Review, 25,* 431–445.

Adelman, H. S., & Taylor, L. (1994). *On understanding intervention in psychology and education.* Westport, CT: Praeger.

Adelman, H. S., & Taylor, L. (1997). Addressing barriers to learning: Beyond school-linked services and full service schools. *American Journal of Orthopsychiatry, 67,* 408–421.

Adelman, H. S., & Taylor, L. (1998). Reframing mental health in schools and expanding school reform. *Educational Psychologist, 33,* 135–152.

Adelman, H. S., & Taylor. L. (2002). So you want higher achievement scores? Its time to rethink learning supports. *The State Education Standard* (pp. 52–56), Alexandria, VA: National Association of State Boards of Education.

Adelman, H. S., & Taylor, L. (2006a). *The school leaders guide to student learning supports: New directions for addressing barriers to learning.* Thousand Oaks, CA: Corwin Press.

Adelman, H. S., & Taylor, L. (2006b).*The implementation guide to student learning supports: New directions for addressing barriers to learning.* Thousand Oaks, CA: Corwin Press.

Adelman, H. S., & Taylor, L. (in press). Best practices in the use of resource teams to enhance learning supports. In A. Thomas & J. Grimes (Eds.), *Best practices in school psychology–V.* Washington, DC: National Association of School Psychologists.

Center for Mental Health in Schools. (2004a). *Addressing barriers to student learning & promoting healthy development: A usable research-base.* Los Angeles: Center for Mental Health in Schools at UCLA. Retrieved April 4, 2007, from http://smhp.psych.ucla.edu/pdfdocs/briefs/BarriersBrief.pdf

Center for Mental Health in Schools. (2004b). *Restructuring boards of education to enhance schools effectiveness in addressing barriers to student learning.* Los Angeles: Center for Mental Health in Schools at UCLA.

Center for Mental Health in Schools. (2005a). *Youngsters' mental health and pyschosocial problems: What are the data?* Los Angeles: Center for Mental Health in Schools at UCLA. Retrieved April 4, 2007, from http://smhp.psych.ucla.edu/pdfdocs/prevalence/youthMH.pdf

Center for Mental Health in Schools. (2005b). *School improvement planning: What's missing?* Los Angeles: Center for Mental Health in Schools at UCLA. Retrieved April 4, 2007, from http://smhp.psych.ucla.edu/whatsmissing.htm

Center for Mental Health in Schools. (2005c). *Addressing what's missing in school improvement planning: expanding standards and accountability to encompass an enabling or learning supports component.* Los Angeles: Center for Mental Health in Schools at UCLA.

Center for Mental Health in Schools. (2005d). *About infrastructure mechanisms for a comprehensive learning support component.* Los Angeles: Center for Mental Health in Schools at UCLA. Retrieved April 4, 2007, from http://www.smhp.psych.ucla.edu/pdfdocs/infrastructure/infra_mechanisms.pdf

Center for Mental Health in Schools. (2005e). *Systemic change for school improvement: designing, implementing, and sustaining prototypes and going to scale.* Los Angeles: Center for Mental Health in Schools at UCLA. Retrieved April 4, 2007, from http://smhp.psych.ucla.edu/pdfdocs/systemic/systemicreport.pdf

Center for Mental Health in Schools. (2005f). *Developing resource-oriented mechanisms to enhance learning supports* (continuing education modules). Los Angeles: Center for Mental Health in Schools at UCLA. Retrieved April 4, 2007, from http://smhp.psych.ucla.edu/pdfdocs/contedu/developing_resource_oriented-mechanisms.pdf

Dryfoos, J. G. (1990). *Adolescents at risk: Prevalence and incidence.* New York: Oxford University Press.

Dryfoos, J. G. (1994). *Full-service schools.* San Francisco: Jossey-Bass.

Gardner, S. L. (2005). *Cities, counties, kids, and families: The essential role of local government.* Lanham, MD: University Press of America.

Hawkins, J. D., & Catalano, R. F. (1992). *Communities that care.* San Francisco: Jossey-Bass.

Huffman, L., Mehlinger, S., & Kerivan, A. (2000). *Research on the risk factors for early school problems and selected federal policies affecting children's social and emotional development and their readiness for school.* The Child and Mental Health Foundation and Agencies Network.

Iowa Department of Education. (2004). *Developing our youth: Fulfilling a promise, investing in Iowa's future—enhancing Iowa's systems of supports for learning and development.* Des Moines, IA: Author. Retrieved April 4, 2007, from http://smhp.psych.ucla.edu/pdfdocs/iowasystemofsupport.pdf

Lim, C., & Adelman, H. S. (1997). Establishing school-based collaborative teams to coordinate resources: A case study. *Social Work in Education, 19,* 266–277.

Rosenblum, L., DiCecco, M. B., Taylor, L., & Adelman, H. S. (1995). Upgrading school support programs through collaboration: Resource Coordinating Teams. *Social Work in Education, 17,* 117–124.

U.S. Department of Education. (1996). *Putting the pieces together: Comprehensive school-linked strategies for children and families.* Washington, DC: Author.

About the Authors

Howard S. Adelman is Professor of Psychology and Codirector of the School Mental Health Project and its federally supported national Center for Mental Health in Schools at UCLA. His research and teaching focuses on addressing barriers to students' learning (including educational, psychosocial, and mental health problems). In recent years, he has been involved in large-scale systemic reform initiatives to enhance school and community efforts to address barriers to learning and promote healthy development.

Linda Taylor is a clinical psychologist and Codirector of the School Mental Health Project and its federally supported national Center for Mental Health in Schools at UCLA. Throughout her career, she has been concerned with a wide range of psychosocial and educational problems experienced by children and adolescents through her work as Codirector of the Fernald Laboratory School and Clinic at UCLA and project director and provider of clinical services in the Los Angeles Unified School District. Her current work involves systemic reform initiatives designed to enhance school and community efforts to address barriers to learning and enhance healthy development.

12

Getting From Here to There

Jack A. Cummings

Beth Doll

At its core, the transformation from conventional to population-based services is a simple transition from focusing on the needs of a single child to focusing on the needs of all children. It is as if the mental health practitioners stepped away from a microscopic examination of one student and peered instead through a wide-angle lens at the collective mental health of all students. The transformation is simple in other respects as well. The tasks that comprise population-based services are familiar ones that many school mental health practitioners are already prepared to provide. Population-based practitioners will use the very familiar problem-solving steps to plan and deliver services, attend to community and policy makers' demands for accountability, and maintain their commitment to evidence-based practices.

Population-based models are compelling. It is clear from the 11 previous chapters that a shared vision for population-based services has emerged within the past decade—borrowing both from public health service delivery models and from the rich body of developmental research on children's psychological disturbance and wellness. Multiple examples of population-based practices have emerged, including developmental assets (described by Baker in chapter 3, this volume), response to intervention (described by Martínez & Nellis in chapter 6, this volume), social-emotional learning (described by Merrell, Gueldner, & Tran in chapter 7, this volume), and positive behavior supports (described by Bear in chapter 5, this volume). Population-based service models are especially compelling for school practice, since the principles underlying the models are highly compatible with schools' mission of educating all children. Indeed, school practitioners have never been able to focus on a "client" to the exclusion of all other students in a school.

Still, the actual transformation from traditional to population-based services is strikingly complex in its planning and implementation. Conventional service systems are firmly aligned with child-centered services, as evidenced by their reliance on referral as a mechanism for allocating services to students, the child-centered orientation of schools' student assistance teams, and the child- and family-centered rights and due process associated with education of students with disabilities, to name a few. Population-based services also require an inordinate degree of collaboration across disciplinary lines since counselors, social workers, and school psychologists working in isolation will not be able to accomplish what is possible through collective effort across disciplinary boundaries. Experiences with multidisciplinary practices have shown that this is exceptionally difficult to accomplish.

Perhaps most important, transformations to population-based models must occur within the context of insufficient resources for children's mental health, and with the expectation that substantial new resources will not be allocated to the effort. Consequently, transformations to population-based models must reallocate scarce existing resources, articulating overt decisions about which services are most worth providing, which needs must be met, and how children should be assigned to services. Rather than satisfying squeaky wheels (as is the case in referral-based systems), population-based services attempt to address the collective needs of the community's children— with the hope that, ultimately, these models can maximize the benefits that accrue from scarce resources. On the face of it, it seems there ought to be some benefits of scale that would make population-based services more cost-effective, but in actuality most communities identify substantial unaddressed needs that urgently require services.

As a result, population-based services often build tension and demand for new resources.

Throughout this volume, chapter authors have provided examples of how population-based services have been implemented and articulated visions of how they could be strengthened in the future. An additional but less visible contribution was made by chapter reviewers, particularly practitioner reviewers, who raised critical questions about how to transform school mental health services in useful ways. Across different chapters, a recurrent theme the reviewers raised was how to move from the current state of practice to the population-based models being advocated. Their questions were highly practical and took various forms: Where do you start when you want to recognize the needs of the population rather than just the needs of referred children? How do you sustain the effort to transform services? How do you know whether you are succeeding and moving in the right directions? How do you overcome the inertia that makes change from the status quo so challenging?

In this chapter, we synthesize the insights from the 11 preceding chapters into an integrated and practical step-by-step sequence for shifting from conventional services to the full continuum of population-based services. An important resource that we drew on was the practice rubric for school-wide implementation of social and emotional learning (Collaborative for Academic, Social and Emotional Learning; CASEL, 2006). While the CASEL rubric focuses on change within a single school, it generalizes well to other levels of change because it is strongly grounded in school reform research. Adelman and Taylor (chapter 11, this volume) provide another broad perspective on marshalling resources for change, and our explanation frequently refers back to their chapter. The criteria adapted from CASEL (2006) for assessing progress on the practical steps are described in Table 12.1, which is presented after the steps have been outlined.

Steps in the Transformation to Population-Based Services

Step One: Secure the approval of key administrators to form a population-based leadership team. Securing support from an administrator is a critical first step in implementing school-wide change. Because transformations to population-based services occur within districts and communities, there are likely to be multiple administrators with the potential to strengthen or weaken population-based efforts, and obtaining their support is an essential step toward change. For example, Mazza and Reynolds (chapter 9, this volume) note that school administrators can be either friend or foe to the implementation of school-wide interventions to address youth depression and suicide. Adelman and Taylor (chapter 11, this volume) explain that school administrators and policy makers do not readily recognize the critical role that mental health services play in students' school success. Without community data (as described by Baker, chapter 3, this volume), administrators may not realize the social and emotional challenges that are rampant in their student population. They may need to be educated about the patterns and trends in local data that link school success to demographic or behavioral risk (see Short & Strein, chapter 2, this volume). Alternatively, administrator interest might be prompted by state or federal statutes, such as those requiring schools to have effective anti-bullying programs (see Swearer, Espelage, Love, & Kingsbury, chapter 8, this volume.) Meaningful change will not happen without the full support of key administrators.

Step Two: Form the leadership team. Because population-based services are not the exclusive province of any one professional group, a leadership team to direct the transformation must be composed of key individuals from across the disciplines: counselors, school psychologists, social workers, teachers, and parents, to name a few. Ideally each of these team members will be respected by their peers and able to represent the views and perspective of their disciplinary colleagues. Collectively, they should represent a broad and deep understanding of children's social and emotional competence and the developmental factors that promote psychological wellness. Team members with multiple connections with the community will be invaluable, since broad community participation is needed to accomplish the planning, assessment, and intervention phases of the transformation. As a member of the leadership team, each professional needs to be aware that a substantial time commitment will be required. Transformation of mental health services is neither quick nor easy. Finally, in judging the adequacy of the leadership team, it is important that the opinions and perspectives of all major stakeholders are represented.

Issues of leadership teams are most directly addressed by Adelman and Taylor (chapter 11, this volume), as they describe the essential need for these teams to be integrated into schools' reform efforts. The importance of including families is emphasized by Christenson, Whitehouse, and VanGetson (chapter 4, this volume). Some chapters describe the important contributions of mental health professionals to the planning and provision of population-based services, including Mazza and Reynolds's description of services for depressed and suicidal adolescents (chapter 9, this volume) and Swearer, Espelage, Love, and Kingsbury's description of bullying prevention programs (chapter 8, this volume.) In contrast, other chapters describe interventions that rest heavily on the efforts of teachers and community members with little formal training in mental health, such as Bear's description of responses to behavior problems (chapter 5, this volume) and Merrell, Gueldner, and Tran's description of the Strong Kids curricula (chapter 7, this volume). Still other chapters emphasize the special contributions that can be made by team members with expertise in research and evaluation design, including epidemiological expertise (described by Short & Strein, chapter 2, this volume) and program evaluation expertise (described by Nastasi & Hitchcock, chapter 10, this volume).

Step Three: Create a vision of population-based mental health services for the community's children. Before team members can reflect on their potential contributions and contributions from their respective disciplinary colleagues, they will need to understand the principles of population-based services, discuss examples of such services as they might look in their community, and reach a consensus about the collective goal of the leadership team for the outcomes for children. This volume is designed to provide a useful orientation for a leadership team. In addition, we recommend close review of three prominent websites: the website of the Collaborative for Academic, Social, and Emotional Learning (CASEL; www.casel.org); the UCLA Center for Mental Health in the Schools website (http://smhp.psych.ucla.edu); and the Positive Behavior Interventions and Supports website (PBIS; www.pbis.org). Each of the sites is noncommercial and there is no charge for duplicating figures, graphs, charts, or other resources. For those who prefer the printed page to the electronic page, all three websites offer links to purchase books and articles.

The CASEL website (www.casel.org) emphasizes interventions and practices that promote children's self-awareness, social awareness, self-management, responsible decision making, and relationship skills (Zins, Weissberg, Wang, & Walberg, 2004). Links are provided for extensive information about current and completed projects; frequently asked questions about social-emotional learning; publications including technical reports, surveys, and newsletters; and dates of upcoming workshops. CASEL makes a compelling case for the leadership team to adopt goals of increasing the social competence and psychological wellness of children, as well as reducing the incidence of psychological disorders. Indeed, both kinds of goals are integral to population-based efforts. CASEL perspectives and the website are referenced by Merrell et al. (chapter 7, this volume) as they advocate for supporting children's mental health while building their prosocial skills. Moreover, as Bear argues (chapter 5, this volume), the promotion of competence can be essential for lasting efforts to reduce disturbances. (Again, it should be noted that the set of steps outlined in this chapter is based on the rubric developed by CASEL authors.)

A second very useful website is that of the UCLA Center for Mental Health in the Schools (http://smhp.psych.ucla.edu). It also has a rich set of resources for conceptualizing and implementing population-based services that elaborate the principles described by Adelman and Taylor in this volume (chapter 11). As their work reflects, a focus on removing the barriers to children's learning may be more palatable to some administrators and the public than efforts focused on mental health services.

Positive Behavior Interventions and Supports (PBIS) were highlighted by Swearer and colleagues in chapter 8 and by Bear in chapter 5 (this volume). The website (www.pbis.org) has valuable planning tools and an online library of resources with links to publications as well as proceedings from past conferences, implementation checklists, examples from schools where PBIS has been implemented, future workshops, and a host of other resources.

By assigning two or more team members to each website, a leadership team could quickly investigate multiple examples of interventions, planning tools, or assessment strategies that might be applied to their own community plan. For instance, part of the team could review www.casel.org, other members could review www.pbis.org, still others could examine http://smhp.psych.ucla .edu, while a last group might review chapters from this book or other print resources. Team members could share their perspectives, based on each one's experience and reading, on the most critical needs of, and the outcomes that would be important for, children in their own community. Adelman and Taylor (chapter 11, this volume) point out that this level of collaboration can be difficult and time-consuming for team members, particularly in communities where conventional services are fragmented and most professionals are working in isolation yet serving many of the same children. However, the potential benefits of population-based services depend on strong and effective leadership that cuts across school and community agencies, and leverages previously independent programs into an integrated, well-planned continuum of mental health services.

Step Four: Create a community resource map of children's mental health services. Resource mapping begins by determining the status of the human mental health resources that are currently serving the community's children (Adelman & Taylor, 2006). Its purpose is to determine how resources are currently being used as a prerequisite to effective management of resources. While initial focus should be on collecting information about school-based mental health personnel, community agencies and volunteer groups should also be recognized for the contributions they can bring to facilitating the transformation of services. Kretzman and McKnight (1993) describe the underlying philosophy of resource mapping as asset focused and contrast this with "deficiency-oriented" needs assessments that initiate planning by identifying and assessing the needs and problems of a community's children. Resource mapping describes the unique capacities in the school and community to promote children's mental health and the commitment of local individuals to change. Kretzman and McKnight note (1993, p. 4), "The hard truth is that development must start within the community and, in most of our urban neighborhoods, there is no other choice."

On its website, the UCLA Center for Mental Health in the Schools (CMHS, 2006) provides a technical manual that describes how to map resources in extensive detail. Several points from the manual bear repeating. First, mapping is a complex activity and will have to be staged over time. The initial focus should be on mapping what personnel do and the specific schools they serve. Both school and community personnel should be included in order to create a complete map. In the next phase of mapping, the focus shifts to existing programs. The purpose of this phase is to create a complete list of programs and the services each provides. Next, the financial resources devoted to services are mapped, including a list of facilities and equipment as well as personnel resources. The final information collected for resource mapping is the policies in place in each community agency that promote or restrict children's mental health services. Once the information is gathered, the leadership team needs to analyze the resources, drawing on the sample forms and spreadsheet templates provided in the CMHS technical manual. Three questions are particularly important to ask: How well are the various services coordinated or integrated? Which services or activities need to be improved or eliminated? What services or activities are missing—especially those that are as important as or more important than those currently provided?

In their discussion of infrastructures to support children's mental health, Adelman and Taylor (chapter 11, this volume) have operationalized six content areas for intervention: classroom instructional strategies that increase students' academic engagement; interventions to help families and students through important transitions; home-school partnerships that foster family involvement in children's education; crisis intervention and prevention strategies; interventions to mobilize community resources for children and families; and strategies to connect families and students to services they need in the community. A comprehensive resource map ought to include multiple interventions in each of these content areas. Additional discussions of resource mapping can be found in Doll and Cummings (chapter 1, this volume) and Adelman and Taylor (chapter 11, this volume), and reviews of academic interventions can be found in Martínez and Nellis (chapter 6, this volume).

Step Five: Plan and collect measures of the mental health of the community's children. Useful explanations of population-based assessments can be found in Baker (chapter 3, this volume) and Short and Strein (chapter 2, this volume). Additional discussions of population-based assessment can be found in Mazza and Reynolds's (chapter 9, this volume) example of a multi-gated screening for depression and suicidal behavior. Together, these chapters establish the utility of community portraits of students' mental health, and describe the decisions that can be made when population-based data are available. Just as important, the chapters make it clear that the collection and interpretation of population-based measures are already well within the competence of practicing school mental health professionals. Still, systematic monitoring of a school's mental health is a time-intensive activity representing one example of the heavy lifting required on the front end when shifting to a population-based model. Current demands do not evaporate while the shift is occurring. Susan Gray (1963) described the dilemma as one of balancing urgent versus important long-range demands on practitioners' time. One cannot ignore the urgent, but the urgent needs cannot continually postpone response to important long-range demands.

Baker (chapter 3, this volume) notes that only 2% of American high schools screen all of their students' mental health, and only 7% of the high schools screen some of their students. This low frequency of screening is not a function of the lack of instruments or the cost of screening instruments. Indeed, there is no need to develop local measures to assess the needs of a school's population since ample measures are available as downloads from websites, and other commercial measures are available for purchase. The following websites contain detailed information about assessment measures:

- http://www.who.int/school_youth_health/assessment/. This website of the World Health Organization includes information about the Psycho-Social Environment Profile (World Health Organization, 2003).
- http://www.casel.org/sel_resources/assessment2.php. The CASEL website also has a significant compilation of assessment tools to consider.
- http://www.annenberginstitute.org/tools/index.php. The website of the Annenberg Institute for School Reform has comprehensive lists of assessment tools, grouped according to the following domains: leadership, community connections, professional development, school organization, school climate, school supports, and comprehensive school improvement.

Step Six: Compare the assessment of the mental health of the community's children to mental health resources. Short and Strein (chapter 2, this volume) explain how to compile measures of children's mental health into a comprehensive understanding of the community's needs. The most useful compilation will include both descriptive information about the rates, proportions, and ratios of psychosocial health and disturbances in the community's children, and analytic descriptions of the host factors, agent factors, and environmental factors that are related to children's success or problems. Once the data have been compiled, they should be compared to the goals prioritized in Step Three's vision. Then personnel resources should be examined, with particular attention to the degree to which they are coordinated and/or integrated. Any redundancies of efforts should be considered and adjustments made. Next, the leadership team should specifically address the question of how to allocate available or redundant resources to satisfy the unmet priority needs. The team could recommend adjustments such as allocating personnel time to tasks, modifying policies and operational procedures, and forming new working relationships across disciplinary boundaries. When the needs of the community's children are juxtaposed against the competencies of the available personnel, gaps in training may be apparent. Such gaps might necessitate new partnerships or realignment of current partnerships and programs. Alternatively, Step Eight describes how continuing professional development should be pursued to fill such gaps through comprehensive training in applied skills.

Step Seven: Design a continuum of prevention and intervention strategies. The most important distinction between population-based mental health services and conventional service delivery systems lies in the organization and planning of the services, and not in the services themselves. Population-based services are planned around the needs identified in the community, with the intention of maximizing the benefits that accrue to the community's children from its scarce mental health resources. Particular attention has been paid to the organization of population-based services in Doll and Cummings (chapter 1, this volume) and Adelman and Taylor (chapter 11, this volume). A second, but less crucial, distinction is that population-based services are more likely to incorporate school-wide or district-wide interventions to address those needs that are especially prevalent in the community. Consequently, school-wide interventions have been emphasized in Bear (chapter 5, this volume), Merrell et al. (chapter 7, this volume), Swearer et al. (chapter 8, this volume), and Mazza and Reynolds (chapter 9, this volume).

Decisions about how to allocate resources to services bring important values to the forefront; these values were always present and operating within school mental health systems, but they were not clearly articulated. Decisions are clear when services have no costs or benefits. No dilemma exists when services hold a very high cost and benefit few, or when services cost very little and benefit many. Sticky dilemmas arise when services that cost a lot and hold high benefit for a few students compete for resources with services that have moderate costs and moderate benefits for many students. These kinds of dilemmas demand high-quality objective data about both costs and benefits, and they also demand that the leadership team be fully functional and able to discuss the difficult decisions knowledgeably and frankly. Incidentally, because the leadership team has data that elucidate the "cost" of service gaps, that information can ultimately become a tool for advocating for public responsibility in allocating more resources for children's mental health.

Throughout this volume, repeated reference has been made to multitiered arrays of services, including universal services that are delivered to all children in a school or district, selected services that will be delivered to children at demographic or functional risk of disturbances, and indicated services for children who already meet criteria for a disorder or a disturbance. Christenson, et al. (chapter 4, this volume) use a three-tiered model to describe services that promote, home-school partnerships, Martínez and Nellis (chapter 6, this volume) use a very similar three-tiered model to describe academic interventions, Bear (chapter 5, this volume) uses the model to describe services that foster self-discipline, and Merrell et al. (chapter 7, this volume) apply the model to social-emotional learning. It is tempting to think of these tiers as categories of students, very much like the categorical model that has dominated special education programs for the past four decades, but it would be inaccurate to do so. Rather than describing students, the tiers are describing kinds of services that are needed within most districts, and any single student might appropriately participate in services at multiple tiers, depending on individual needs. Tier models have also been proposed with two tiers or four tiers (and sometimes more), and leadership teams could select a tier structure that was most descriptive for their community. Still, there are alternatives to tier structures for planning and describing a continuum of services needed by a continuum. Services might also be described as preventive interventions, remedial interventions, or wellness-promoting interventions; or they might be identified as school-wide, classwide, small group, or individual interventions.

It is essential that local intervention services be built on a solid evidence base. Adelman and Taylor (2006) provide an annotated list of evidence-based interventions that address universal, selected, and indicated interventions. Alternatively, Osher, Dwyer, and Jackson (2004) catalog an array of interventions that have been identified as promising or evidence-based. Consulting published resources such as these permits the leadership team to build on the work of others. Three guiding questions should frame the team's evaluation of potential interventions (OSEP Center on Positive Behavioral Interventions and Support, 2004): Is the practice effective, and how likely is it that the team's desired outcomes will be achieved with the practice? Is the practice efficient, and what are the costs and benefits of adopting and sustaining the practice? Is the practice relevant, and does it fit the practice, the individuals who will use the practice, and the setting in which the practice will be used?

Leadership teams should also consult colleagues who have already made comparable intervention decisions so as to avoid unproductive and ineffective steps. There are several ways to communicate with those who have been down the path previously. For instance, the CASEL website has a listserv with information about ongoing projects and funding opportunities. Alternatively, the website of the UCLA Center for Mental Health in Schools has a link for networking and interacting with the center or with other practitioners. For example, in a recent communication, the Center helped a school employee plan the agenda for a community collaborative meeting between the heath department, mental health center, social services, and the county manager. In addition, the Center suggested a few online and print references that the team might consult. Online coaching can be invaluable for a leadership team that is just beginning its work.

Step Eight: Prepare personnel to implement the needed interventions.
A key aspect in fostering population-based services is to anticipate
the training needs of personnel who will implement the various interventions. Professional development takes time, and the leadership
team therefore must find the resources to ensure it is done well.
Professional development also takes multiple forms. This means professional development is more than the traditional workshop at the
beginning of the school year. Book groups, curriculum-focused or
grade-level meetings, and special event meetings are other vehicles for
continuous professional development. Clearly, a single-shot "bring in
the expert" workshop is the antithesis of continuous professional
development.

Intervention fidelity is a key part of evidence-based interventions,
and personnel training is a prerequisite to intervention fidelity. Fidelity
is enhanced when those who implement the interventions have
enough practice and feedback on their performance to become proficient in their roles. Since monitoring and evaluation take place
throughout the implementation of the various interventions, professional development is not a linear step but rather an ongoing effort of
training and monitoring. The OSEP Center on Positive Behavioral
Interventions and Support (2004) uses the phrase "train n' hope" to
capture the problem of implementation without systematic and ongoing staff training. The phrase captures the naivety of one-shot in-
service training.

In addition to teaching personnel to be proficient in interventions,
professional development is an opportunity to share the overall goals
and strategies of the project and provide each person with a sense of
their fit within the overall continuum of services. By this point in the
implementation, it is likely that new personnel have joined the effort
who are not fully versed in the conceptual framework, goals, and
anticipated outcomes of population-based services. Any resistance
to the underlying philosophy of the project has to be addressed
so that the leadership team and personnel share a common vision
(OSEP Center on Positive Behavioral Interventions and Support, 2004).
A common language is a third goal of personnel training. Understanding concepts and the words used to represent them contributes
to effective communication. Particularly when teams have been composed of members from multiple disciplines as well as those without
formal mental health training, personnel may use the same terms to
mean very different things, operate from competing explanations of
social and emotional phenomena, or be unfamiliar with the jargon of
each others' disciplines.

Step Nine: Implement population-based mental health services in a single school. Rather than launch population-based services system-wide, leadership teams will be most effective if they first focus on a single school. They will learn much from piloting the effort on a smaller scale, while communicating closely with the frontline implementers. The small-scale implementation will inform the leadership team of the need to adjust aspects of the effort, such as the program of professional development, cultural adaptation, and services to match the local context.

Ideally, this first school will be carefully selected as the one most eager to shift to a population-based model of school mental health. Key stakeholders in the building will have demonstrated interest in the transformation, and administrators and policy makers will be prepared to institute policies and shift resources to make the transformation possible. Adelman and Taylor (chapter 11, this volume) describe this as "creating a climate for change" and provide additional strategies for fostering support.

Further, evaluation of the quality and impact of the population-based services is an essential component of this small-scale implementation. Nastasi and Hitchcock (chapter 10, this volume) provide a detailed protocol for evaluation using the Comprehensive Mixed-Methods Participatory Evaluation model. This might require appointment of an outside evaluator who is respected by the school's community but independent from the effort, ensuring that the evaluation is perceived to be both technically sound and nonbiased. The evaluation will play a critical role in demonstrating the costs and benefits of the transformation to population-based services, and can provide essential insight into changes that might further strengthen the efficient and effective use of mental health resources in the school.

Step Ten: Scale up by systematically expanding population-based services to new schools. Using the lessons learned in the pilot, new schools may be brought on line. These new sites will require the same attention to climate building and service evaluation that was essential in the pilot school. In some respects, these subsequent schools will be easier transformations, because these can build on the insights achieved from the implementation of the pilot. In other respects, the subsequent schools can be more difficult, particularly if these schools were innately less amenable to the kinds of changes required to implement population-based services. In either case, the implementers from the pilot school will be a valuable resource. The first implementers will have "street credibility" and will be able to train and serve as a continuing support to those learning new roles. Ideally, the first implementers will become mentors.

Systematic assessment of the progress toward population-based mental health services will need to be embedded into the leadership team's efforts to extend population-based services to all schools in the community. This is a self-assessment of progress that is completed by the leadership team and a variety of stakeholders, using the rubric provided in Table 12.1. CASEL suggests assessing and reassessing the progress of a project at least twice a year, whereas the PBIS self-assessment tool is designed to be used quarterly. We advocate quarterly assessment at the front end of the population-based effort. Thus, for the first year quarterly assessment is appropriate. When the first year assessments document substantive progress and things are going well in the second year, it would possible to drop to assessments twice a year.

Following the model provided by the CASEL practice rubric, Table 12.1 also includes assessment of six sustainability factors: professional development, monitoring for continuous improvement, infrastructure, integration in school practices, partnerships with families and communities, and communication with the entire community. Professional development should be continuous and provide a vehicle for participating personnel to network and learn from others. "Continuous" means that there is a repeated focus over time, which allows for revisiting, reinforcing, and elaborating concepts and skills. Professional development should be both vertical and horizontal. It is an opportunity to impart new information (vertical) but must allow for implementers to learn from each other's experiences (horizontal). In the latter case, it should be conceptualized as collaboration among peers rather than training.

Continuous evaluation builds on the assessment and monitoring data that were collected in Step Six. These data serve as a baseline to judge the effects of the interventions. The assessment phase does not end with the initial assessment. On the contrary, assessment and monitoring are active components throughout the process. Assessment and monitoring data provide a basis for the leadership team to decide which aspects of the population-based service efforts are having the intended effects. The data also provide a means to judge elements of the efforts that are not working. The evaluative information is shared with key stakeholders including teachers, school mental health personnel, community agency personnel, parents, and others who participate in or are affected by the transformation. The bottom line is that systematic and repeated assessment is integral to continuous improvement.

In order for the transformation to be sustained over time, infrastructure must be in place to provide permanent resources for

(Text continues on page 330)

Table 12.1 Criteria for Assessing the Progress of the Transformation to Population-Based Services

Step One: Secure the approval of key administrators to form a population-based leadership team.

4 Fully Functional and Implemented	3 Mostly Functional and Implemented	2 Limited Functionality/Partial Implementation	1 Limited or No Functionality/Not Implemented
Administrators understand that the purpose of the leadership team is to implement population-based school mental health services and endorse the goal of reframing the district's mental health services around the identified needs of children. They recognize the relevance of this model to school success.	Administrators understand the purpose of the leadership team but have limited time to devote to the project, although they endorse the goal of reframing the district's mental health services around the identified needs of children.	Administrators have a cursory understanding of the goal but are concerned about the time the leadership team will take from team members' current duties.	Administrators are unaware of the goal; do not endorse the leadership team; and may not want to spend personnel resources on the effort.

Step Two: Form the leadership team.

4 Fully Functional and Implemented	3 Mostly Functional and Implemented	2 Limited Functionality/Partial Implementation	1 Limited or No Functionality/Not Implemented
Critical stakeholders are represented on the leadership team. Team members have multiple connections with the community. Team members are available for meetings.	One of the following is true: (a) most stakeholders are represented, but one or two critical stakeholders are missing; (b) some team members miss meetings due to conflicts; or (c) links to important community groups are missing.	Two or more of the following are true: (a) most stakeholders are represented, but one or two critical stakeholders are missing; (b) some team members miss meetings due to conflicts; or (c) links to important community groups are missing.	The team is not formed and has not met; or initial meetings have been cancelled.

(Continued)

Table 12.1 (Continued)

Step Three: Create a vision of population-based mental health services for the community's children.

4 Fully Functional and Implemented	3 Mostly Functional and Implemented	2 Limited Functionality/Partial Implementation	1 Limited or No Functionality/Not Implemented
Team members understand population-based services, and discuss examples of population-based services. They share their perspectives on the most critical mental health needs of children and the outcomes they hope to achieve. They reach a consensus on the project goals.	Team members understand population-based services, and discuss examples of population-based services. They also share their perspectives on the most critical mental health needs of children and the outcomes they hope to achieve. However, they do not reach consensus on the project goals.	Team members understand population-based services but do not share their perspectives on the most critical mental health needs of children or the hoped for outcomes. No consensus is reached on the project goals.	Team members do not understand population-based services. They do not share their perspectives on the most critical mental health needs of children or the hoped for outcomes, and they do not reach consensus on the project goals.

Step Four: Create a community resource map of children's mental health services.

4 Fully Functional and Implemented	3 Mostly Functional and Implemented	2 Limited Functionality/Partial Implementation	1 Limited or No Functionality/Not Implemented
An asset-focused resource map has been developed that includes human and facility resources. An analysis is conducted to examine the degree to which activities are coordinated or can be integrated. Missing services are noted, as are services that might be eliminated.	An asset-focused resource map has been developed that includes human and facility resources. However, the analysis of services that can be coordinated or integrated is incomplete, or there is disagreement on the team about missing services or those that might be eliminated.	An asset-focused resource map has been started but is not completed.	A resource map has been started but the focus is on service deficits rather than service assets.

Step Five: Plan and collect measures of the mental health of the community's children.

4 Fully Functional and Implemented	3 Mostly Functiona and Implemented	2 Limited Functionality/Partial Implementation	1 Limited or No Functionality/Not Implemented
The team has conducted a comprehensive review of screening measures that could be used to collect information about the mental health needs of children in the community. The team has selected measures to use and made careful plans for adapting these to the local context. Screening measures have been administered to the community's children.	The team has conducted a comprehensive review of screening measures that could be used to collect information about the mental health needs of children in the community. The team has selected measures to use and made careful plans for adapting these to the local context. The administration of screening measures to the community's children is not complete.	The team is developing their own screening measures to collect information about the mental health needs of children in the community, after consulting but not fully reviewing available screening measures in the research literature or on the Internet.	The team has not reviewed available screening measures but, instead, is developing their own measures without consulting the literature or extensive resources on the Internet.

Step Six: Compare the assessment of the mental health of the community's children to mental health resources.

4 Fully Functional and Implemented	3 Mostly Functiona and Implemented	2 Limited Functionality/Partial Implementation	1 Limited or No Functionality/Not Implemented
Analysis of the population's data has provided a comprehensive view of the children's mental health needs. These needs have been compared to the assets listed on the community's mental health resource map.	Analysis of the population's data has provided a comprehensive view of the children's mental health needs but these results have not been compared to the community's mental health assets listed on the resource map.	Data are available for only some children in the community. Missing data make it impossible to achieve a comprehensive view of the mental needs of the community's children.	Measures of the children's mental health needs have not been compiled or analyzed.

(Continued)

Table 12.1 (Continued)

Step Seven: Design a continuum of prevention and intervention strategies.

4 Fully Functional and Implemented	3 Mostly Functional and Implemented	2 Limited Functionality/Partial Implementation	1 Limited or No Functionality/Not Implemented
The leadership team has selected a continuum of evidence-based interventions based on the needs of the community's children and the resources available for mental health services. The team selections were made after a comprehensive review of existing interventions and the work completed in other communities. The interventions selected have been shared with other stakeholders.	The leadership team has selected a continuum of evidence-based interventions based on the needs of the community's children and the resources available for mental health services. The team selections were made after a comprehensive review of existing interventions and the work completed in other communities. The interventions have not yet been shared with other stakeholders.	The leadership team has begun a comprehensive review of existing interventions but has not yet compared these against the needs of the community, and has not selected a continuum of interventions for the community.	Some members of the leadership team have begun to collect information about various interventions, but these have not been shared with the broader team, and no effort has been made to link these to data describing the community's needs.

Step Eight: Prepare personnel to implement the needed interventions.

4 Fully Functional and Implemented	3 Mostly Functional and Implemented	2 Limited Functionality/Partial Implementation	1 Limited or No Functionality/Not Implemented
The community's mental health professionals understand how they fit within the overall scheme of population-based services and show little or no resistance to the project. Professionals from different agencies share a common understanding of	Most of the community's mental health professionals understand how they fit within the overall scheme of population-based services and show little or no resistance to the project. There is evidence that the mental health professionals are proficient in	A majority of the community's mental health professionals understand how they fit within the overall scheme of population-based services. Still, there is moderate resistance to the project's underlying philosophy or implementation. Professionals	Most of the community's mental health professionals do NOT understand how they fit within the overall scheme of population-based services. There is moderate to heavy resistance to the project's underlying philosophy or the

4 Fully Functional and Implemented	3 Mostly Functional and Implemented	2	1
concepts and language. There is evidence that the mental health professionals are proficient in their respective roles.	their respective roles. The mental health professionals are working toward but do not yet fully share a common understanding of concepts and language.	have not reached a common understanding of language and concepts, and need more training before carrying out their roles with fidelity.	implementation. Professionals have not been trained in their respective roles.

Step Nine: Implement population-based mental health services in a single school.

4 Fully Functional and Implemented	3 Mostly Functional and Implemented	2 Limited Functionality/Partial Implementation	1 Limited or No Functionality/Not Implemented
A pilot transformation to population-based services has been conducted in a single school. Implementation has been carefully monitored. Modifications have been made as needed to adapt the services to the local school context.	A pilot transformation to population-based services has been planned for a single school. It has been partially implemented or implemented without adapting the model to the local school context.	A pilot transformation to population-based services has been planned, but implementation has not yet begun.	A pilot transformation to population-based services has not been planned or implemented.

(Continued)

Table 12.1 (Continued)

Step Ten: Scale up by systematically expanding population based services to additional schools.

4 Fully Functional and Implemented	3 Mostly Functional and Implemented	2 Limited Functionality/Partial Implementation	1 Limited or No Functionality/Not Implemented
The leadership team has analyzed the evaluative feedback from the pilot implementation of population-based services in a single school. Modifications and adjustments were made to address local school circumstances. Those involved in the population-based services have been fully trained. Ongoing assessment systems have been implemented to monitor progress over time.	The leadership team has analyzed the evaluative feedback from the pilot implementation of population-based services in a single school. However, modifications and adjustments have been planned but not yet implemented. Most but not all of those involved in the services have been trained. Ongoing assessment systems to monitor children's mental health have been planned but are not yet in place.	The leadership team has partially analyzed the evaluative feedback from the pilot implementation of population-based services in a single school. No modifications and adjustments have been planned and most of those involved in the services have not been trained. Ongoing assessment systems to monitor children's mental health have been planned but are not yet in place.	The leadership team has no evaluative data from pilot implementation of population-based services in a single school. Those involved in the future population-based services have not yet been trained. The team has not planned any ongoing assessment systems to monitor children's mental health.

Sustainability Factor A: Continuous professional development

4 Fully Functional and Implemented	3 Mostly Functional and Implemented	2 Limited Functionality/Partial Implementation	1 Limited or No Functionality/Not Implemented
Administrators allocate time and resources for staff to engage in professional development in population-based services. A comprehensive program of professional development	Administrators allocate time and resources for staff to engage in professional development in population-based services. A program of professional development engages most but	Professional development focuses on exposure to concepts, rather than skill proficiency, and is characterized by single session workshops. There is only limited time for professional	Professional development has not been planned or conducted.

4 Fully Functional and Implemented	3 Mostly Functional and Implemented	2 Limited Functionality/Partial Implementation	1 Limited or No Functionality/Not Implemented
engages staff in regular professional development; prepares them to be proficient in key services; and allows for collaboration across disciplines and agencies. New staff are quickly oriented to the population-based approach.	not all staff in regular professional development; prepares them to be proficient in key services; and allows for collaboration across disciplines and agencies. Most but not all new staff are oriented to the population-based approach.	development and collaboration. New staff are included in professional development only when it is convenient. However, there are plans to improve the professional development program, and to prepare staff to be proficient in key services.	

Sustainability Factor B: Evaluation for continuous improvement

4 Fully Functional and Implemented	3 Mostly Functional and Implemented	2 Limited Functionality/Partial Implementation	1 Limited or No Functionality/Not Implemented
In the first year of implementation, evaluations of the population-based services are conducted quarterly and, thereafter, twice a year. The leadership team reviews evaluation data on a regular basis and decides which aspects of the services are having the intended effects. Evaluation data are shared with others.	Evaluations of the population-based services are conducted annually. Leadership team reviews evaluation data on a regular basis and decides which aspects of the services are having the intended effects. Evaluation data are only occasionally shared with others.	Evaluations of the population-based services are planned, but not yet implemented, or are only partially implemented.	There are no plans for evaluations of the population-based services.

(Continued)

Table 12.1 (Continued)

Sustainability Factor C: Infrastructure development

4 Fully Functional and Implemented	3 Mostly Functional and Implemented	2 Limited Functionality/Partial Implementation	1 Limited or No Functionality/Not Implemented
A leadership structure has emerged with reporting lines consistent with accomplishing the goals of the leadership team. Personnel lines have been budgeted to support population-based monitoring and interventions. Policies have been revised and new policies developed where gaps exist.	A leadership structure has emerged with reporting lines consistent with accomplishing the goals of the leadership team. Personnel lines have not yet been budgeted to support population-based monitoring and interventions. Policies are in the process of being revised.	Leadership structure exists, but reporting lines are fuzzy. Personnel lines have not yet been budgeted to support population-based monitoring and interventions. Policies still need to be discussed.	Leadership team has not addressed infrastructure considerations.

Sustainability Factor D: Integration of population-based principles and practices

4 Fully Functional andImplemented	3 Mostly Functional and Implemented	2 Limited Functionality/Partial Implementation	1 Limited or No Functionality/Not Implemented
The discourse of administrators, school mental health practitioners, and teachers reflects awareness and use of population-based approaches as part of a continuum of services for students and their families.	The discourse of most administrators, school mental health practitioners, and teachers reflects awareness and use of population-based approaches as part of a continuum of services for students and their families.	The discourse of some administrators, school mental health practitioners, and teachers reflects awareness and use of population-based approaches as part of a continuum of services for students and their families.	Awareness and use of population-based approaches is limited to the discourse of the leadership team.

Sustainability Factor E: Partnerships with parents and community agencies

4 Fully Functional and Implemented	3 Mostly Functional and Implemented	2 Limited Functionality/Partial Implementation	1 Limited or No Functionality/Not Implemented
Community agencies and parents have had input into the planning and implementation of services. The mutual benefits of the partnership are clear to all partners. The expectations of each partner are written and understood.	Community agencies and parents have had some input into the planning and implementation of services. The mutual benefits of the partnership are clear to most partners. The expectations of each partner are partially formulated.	Community agencies and parents have not had input into the planning and implementation of services. Preliminary discussions of partnerships have occurred but the expectations of each partner are not formulated.	Partnerships with parents and community agencies have not been formed or are inactive.

Sustainability Factor F: Communication

4 Fully Functional and Implemented	3 Mostly Functional and Implemented	2 Limited Functionality/Partial Implementation	1 Limited or No Functionality/Not Implemented
Communication is multifaceted and updates have been provided at key points. Face-to-face meetings/presentations, print materials, e-mail, and web pages have been used to update project accomplishments. Communication has been implemented to solicit input as well as to inform.	Updates have been provided regularly. Communication has been limited to one or two channels (e-mail and web only, or only face-to-face meetings). Limited communication has been implemented that was designed to solicit input.	Infrequent dates have been provided. Communication has been limited to one channel (e-mail only, web only, or only face-to-face meetings). Communication has been designed without opportunity for others to provide input.	The members of the leadership team have communicated only with each other.

Source: Adapted with permission from E. Devaney, M. U. O'Brien, H. Resnik, S. Keister, & R. P. Weissberg. (2006). *Sustainable schoolwide social and emotional learning: Implementation guide and toolkit.* Chicago: Collaborative for Academic, Social, and Emotional Learning. An online version of the CASEL Practice Rubric for Schoolwide SEL Implementation is available at: http://www.casel.org/downloads/Rubric.pdf (retrieved April 4, 2007).

(Text continued from page 320)

population-based services. Budget lines need to be allocated to the effort, and a permanent leadership structure should emerge with reporting lines to accomplish the goals that were established based on the population-based assessment data. In addition to leadership and budgeting, existing school policies have to be considered and reformulated. New policies may need to be drafted when there are gaps in the existing policies.

As evidence of the sustainability of the effort, population-based principles and evidence-based practices will be integrated into the discourse of the school. In particular, the discourse of administrators, school mental health practitioners, and teachers should reflect an awareness of population-based approaches and the value of the interventions that have been implemented.

Christenson et al. (chapter 4, this volume) amply document the value of meaningful relationships between home and school. They emphasize "families and schools as partners" with two-way dialogue about educational programming and children's academic and behavioral performance at school. The presence of vital and productive partnerships with families and community agencies will be essential to the transformation.

Integral to these partnerships, and to other activities of the population-based leadership team, effective communication with the entire community is essential. Even during the readiness phase, communication of the needs and opportunities will increase the likelihood of acceptance when it comes time to implement the population-based services. As one example, Grimes, Kurns and Tilly (2006) used multiple communication systems when implementing a problem-solving service delivery system in the Heartland Area Education Agency. They sent representatives to disciplinary meetings of counselors, social workers, and school psychologists. Similar messages were conveyed in meetings of superintendents, curriculum directors, and special educators; and the Internet was used to post a description of the problem-solving process for parents, the complete program manual, a staff development plan, and a guide for teachers and parents. (Examples of these materials can be found at the Heartland Area Education Agency's website at www.aea11.k12.ia.us/spr.)

Implications for Preparation of School Mental Health Practitioners

Graduating mental health professionals with adequate skills in population-based approaches will require more than passing coverage in program curriculum. Sugai and Horner (2006) address both in-service and preservice training when they state that "exposure level presentations" are inadequate. Even training to the level of skill fluency will not be sufficient if administrators do not support a continuum of population-based services. Consequently, programs that prepare critical decision makers, school principals, and superintendents will need to be shifted toward population-based models in addition to those of school mental health practitioners. Moreover, cross-disciplinary interaction while administrators, counselors, school psychologists, and social workers are in their graduate studies would facilitate such interaction when they eventually take positions in the schools. Dismantling the silos that exist in the schools could begin with dismantling training silos.

Still, it is unrealistic to expect newly minted graduates will change traditions that have developed over an extended period of time and are difficult to modify (Shapiro, 2006). As an alternative to preservice training of administrators, Shapiro suggests that leadership at the local level can be created through collaboration with faculty at institutions of higher education. Martínez and Nellis (chapter 6, this volume) provide one example of a school-university partnership that shifted academic screening and decision making in a local district and also benefited graduate students in the school psychology program. Local school personnel bring contextual knowledge to these collaborative efforts as well as past experiences within the system, while university faculty contribute expertise in population-based approaches and systems change.

Unfortunately, population-based approaches were not part of the graduate preparation of most current university faculty in school mental health. Hence, the first challenge will be to train the trainers. Workshops at conferences provide one vehicle for training the faculty, but this would continue the practice of training in silos. For instance, counselors attend meetings of the American Counseling Association (ACA), while school psychologists attend meetings of the National Association of School Psychologists (NASP) and school social workers attend meetings of the School Social Work Association of America (SSWAA).

Webcasting offers an inexpensive alternative for disseminating information across disciplinary boundaries. Webcasting can be either audio only or audio and video, and are easily accessed worldwide. A series of webcasts may be viewed by remote groups, as was the case with the Multisite Futures Conference (Cummings, Harrison, Dawson, Short, Gorin, & Palomares, 2004). During the two-and-a-half-day conference, multiple presentations were webcast. Remote groups of faculty, students, and practitioners had simultaneous discussions and problem-solving sessions, the results of which were communicated via

Web-based discussion forums. Even though participants were in distant locations (e.g., Alaska, Hawaii, California, Florida, Connecticut), they were able to see each other's work in the web discussion forum. An important benefit of webcasts is that they can be archived for later retrieval. Even more flexibility might be found with podcasting, in which the user downloads an audio or video file and can then play it on a personal audio/video player (iPod).

Webcasts are normally thought to be linear presentations. A potential challenge would be moving beyond what Sugai and Horner (2006) termed "exposure level training." Skill fluency could be achieved by a series of presentations that would be iterative. Participants at remote sites would engage in activities at their local site with data from their activities being fed back to those with expertise. Subsequent webcasts would be adjusted based on the experiences of those at the remote sites. Webcasts that proved effective with university faculty could also be used by local leadership teams, including school personnel in the webcast as well as university faculty from counseling, school psychology, and social work.

Summary

Transformations from conventional to population-based services are a logical next step in the evolution of schools' mental health service systems. Population-based services operationalize the substantial understanding of children's mental health and developmental competence that has emerged in the past few decades to create a model of practice in the schools. The transition is logical, also, in that these services build on skills that already exist among school mental health providers, and the population-based principles merge naturally with schools' historical responsibilities for educating all children. Still, transformations from conventional to population-based systems are mighty tasks that alter current practice in very distinctive and important ways. These kinds of school change cannot occur swiftly or easily. Instead, they will require thoughtful and careful planning on behalf of a full leadership team to realign school mental health resources with the most pressing needs of children.

Discussion Questions

1. In your own school district, who should be included on a leadership team to lead the district into population-based services? Why are these team members important to include?

2. What data does your school and community already collect that might be used in Step Five, the assessment of children's current mental health?

3. What assistance would your school district need to seek from outside the district in order to compile data on children's mental health into a community portrait of needs?

4. If children's mental health needs were compared to your district's current mental health resources, what gaps would you expect to be identified?

5. How might your own role and responsibilities change if your district were to adopt a population-based model of school mental health services?

References

Adelman, H. S., & Taylor, L. (2006). *The school leader's guide to student learning supports: New directions for addressing barriers to learning.* Thousand Oaks, CA: Corwin Press.

Center for Mental Health in the Schools at UCLA (CMHS). (2006). *A technical aid package on resource mapping and management to address barriers to learning: An intervention for systemic change.* Retrieved October 10, 2006, from http://smhp.psych.ucla.edu/pdfdocs/resourcemapping/resourcemappingandmanagement.pdf

Collaborative for Academic, Social and Emotional Learning (CASEL). (2006). *CASEL practice rubric for schoolwide SEL implementation.* Retrieved October 4, 2006, from http://www.casel.org/downloads/Rubric.pdf

Cummings, J. A., Harrison, P. L., Dawson, M., Short, R. J., Gorin, S., & Palomares, R. (2004). The 2002 Conference on the Future of School Psychology: Implications for Consultation, Intervention, and Prevention Services. *Journal of Educational and Psychological Consultation, 15,* 239–256.

Gray, S. W. (1963). *The psychologist in the schools.* New York: Holt, Rinehart and Winston.

Grimes, J., Kurns, S., & Tilly, W. W. (2006). Sustainability: An enduring commitment to success. *School Psychology Review, 35,* 224–244.

Kretzman, J. P., & McKnight, J. L. (1993). *Building communities from the inside out: A path toward finding and mobilizing a community's assets.* Evanston, IL: The Asset-Based Community Development Institute, Northwestern University. Retrieved October 11, 2006, from http://gearup.ous.edu/gusaccess/documents/pdf/BuildingCommunitiesInsideOut.pdf

OSEP Center on Positive Behavioral Interventions and Support. (2004). School-wide Positive Behavior Support: Implementers' Blueprint and Self-Assessment. Retrieved April 4, 2007, from http://www.pbis.org/files/Blueprint%20draft%20v3%209-13-04.doc

Osher, D., Dwyer, K., & Jackson, S. (2004). *Safe, supportive, and successful schools: Step by step.* Longmont, CO: Sopris Press.

Shapiro, E. S. (2006). Commentary: Are we solving big problems? *School Psychology Review, 35,* 260–265.

Sugai, G., & Horner, R. R. (2006). A promising approach for expanding and sustaining school-wide positive behavior supports. *School Psychology Review, 35,* 245–259.

World Health Organization. (2003). *Creating an environment for emotional and social well-being: An important responsibility of a health-promoting and child friendly school.* Retrieved on January 31, 2006, from http://www.who.int/school_youth_health/assessment/en/sch_childfriendly_03_v2.pdf

Zins, J. E., Weissberg, R. P., Wang, M. C., & Walberg, H. J. (Eds.). (2004). *Building academic success on social and emotional learning: What does the research say?* New York: Teachers College Press.

Index

**CORWIN
PRESS**

The Corwin Press logo—a raven striding across an open book—represents the union of courage and learning. Corwin Press is committed to improving education for all learners by publishing books and other professional development resources for those serving the field of PreK–12 education. By providing practical, hands-on materials, Corwin Press continues to carry out the promise of its motto: **"Helping Educators Do Their Work Better."**

**NATIONAL
ASSOCIATION OF
SCHOOL
PSYCHOLOGISTS**

The National Association of School Psychologists represents and supports school psychology through leadership to enhance the mental health and educational competence of all children.